Asia's Debt Capital Markets

Prospects and Strategies for Development

The Milken Institute Series on Financial Innovation and Economic Growth

Series Editors:

James R. Barth
Lowder Eminent Scholar in Finance at Auburn University
and Senior Research Fellow at the Milken Institute

Glenn Yago
Director of Capital Studies at the
Milken Institute

Other Books in the Series:

Barth, James R., Brumbaugh Jr., R. Dan and Yago, Glenn (eds.),
Restructuring Regulation and Financial Institutions

Evans, David S. (ed.),
Microsoft, Antitrust and the New Economy: Selected Essays

Trimbath, Susanne
Mergers and Efficiency: Changes Across Time

Mead, Walter Russell and Schwenninger, Sherle (eds.),
The Bridge to a Global Middle Class: Development, Trade and International Finance

Barth, James R., Trimbath, Susanne, Yago, Glenn (eds.),
The Savings and Loan Crisis

Asia's Debt Capital Markets

Prospects and Strategies for Development

edited by

Douglas Arner
Asian Institute of International Financial Law
Faculty of Law, University of Hong Kong
Hong Kong

Jae-Ha Park
Korea Institute of Finance
South Korea

Paul Lejot
Asian Institute of International Financial Law
Faculty of Law, University of Hong Kong
Hong Kong

Qiao Liu
Faculty of Business and Economics
University of Hong Kong
Hong Kong

Springer

ISBN-13: 978-1-4419-2041-6
e-ISBN-10: 0-387-25090-5
e-ISBN-13: 978-0-387-25090-8

Printed on acid-free paper.

9 8 7 6 5 4 3 2 1

springeronline.com

Table of Contents

Note from the Editors

James Barth, and Glenn Yago, Series Editors

Milken Institute Series on Financial Innovation and Economic Growth

This volume focuses on the importance of bond markets for economic growth and development. It provides a comprehensive and detailed analysis of the importance of these markets to all countries, regardless of geographic location. The financial turmoil that occurred in East Asia in mid-1997 disrupted spectacular rates of economic growth and taught policymakers, academics and practitioners that excessive reliance on financial institutions as the primary vehicle through which savings are channeled to investment projects significantly exacerbates economic downturns when the banking sector suffers a crisis. Diversification through bond markets enables firms to tap capital markets directly during difficult times when banks curtail the extension of credit to improve their balance sheets. Through the diversification of risk throughout the financial system, less systemic risk and vulnerability are observed and credit crunches can be overcome.

Asian countries experienced rapid and impressive economic growth until the 1997 crisis. Monetary and fiscal stability, along with rapid financial sector development, mainly through an expansion of bank loans, were important factors contributing to the "Asian Miracle". In the years following the crisis, however, it became readily apparent that bank concentration and dependency propagated financial shocks (both internal and external). The lack of a diversified financial infrastructure posed recurring threats to economic stablilty. A consensus emerged that Asia needed strong local-currency bond markets that could act as financial insulators to various disruptions to maintain its current open and growing trading relationships. While the book focuses on Asian bond markets and economic trends in the region, it does not advance the notion that any single approach to development is appropriate for all nations in the region.

There has actually been considerable progress in the development of bond markets in Asia in recent years. At the end of 2003, the volume of domestic bonds outstanding in eight Asian countries was equivalent to 47 percent of their combined GDP, more than double the 20 percent figure at year-end 1995. Over that time, the contribution of bonds to total financing rose to 19 from 11 percent. Despite this impressive growth, Asian bond markets collectively still lag behind those of developed economies in terms of breadth and depth. At less than 50 percent of GDP, many Asian domestic bond markets are still small relative to those in the United

States and Japan, where domestic bond markets are over 100 percent of GDP. Furthermore, bond markets in Asia still lack liquidity and remain largely fragmented.

The costs of underdeveloped Asian capital markets and greater diversification in financial services has taken its toll on Asian growth prospects. Among the countries hit by the Asian crisis, only Korea has approached its pre-crisis growth rate. National savings exceeds national investment in most Asian markets as is reflected in their current-account surpluses. With the exception of China, the decline of capital goods imports, the combination of continued lower rates of foreign direct investment and higher relative unemployment rates since 1998, and overall declining rate of capacity utilization all point to lower rates of job creation and capital formation. In short, the timeliness of this volume in addressing a key structural change necessary for democratizing Asian capital markets remains more urgent than ever.

The Milken Institute and the University of Hong Kong jointly hosted the first Asian Bond Market Forum in 2003 in Hong Kong. The four-day event included several round tables, in which a collaborative network of practitioners, academics and regulators discussed various ways to promote the development of local-currency bond markets in Asia. The ultimate goal of this activity was to suggest reforms that could be taken to enhance financial infrastructure throughout Asia in order to better facilitate strong, stable and sustainable growth. As a result of these roundtables and other interactions among attendees, it was apparent that a book that thoroughly reviews and analyzes the current bond market situation and address impediments to further development was needed. Since 2003, the participants have worked diligently to further detail their empirical analyses and sharpen their recommendations that appear here. This book thus adds to the still relatively few volumes that are dedicated to developing broader bond markets worldwide.

An up-to-date analysis of the underlying financial infrastructure contributing to the Asian crisis and an assessment of current economic condition today are provided. Most importantly, the role of bond markets in promoting growth and stability in Asia are emphasized. Comprehensive information is utilized throughout the book to provide a blueprint for bond market development. The book is the result of a unique collaboration of experts with experience and perspectives gained from backgrounds in the academic, legal, governmental and practical investment fields.

Preface

The Development of Effective Securities Markets

Gary Schinasi

International Monetary Fund

One of the more important lessons of the crisis of the 1990s—not just the Asian Crisis—is that the performance and structure of a country's financial system is an important fundamental factor for assessing that country's overall economic performance and prospects, and as a destination for investment and asset returns. Market participants that are presently managing international portfolios now understand this very well. And as we all know, many countries are making strong efforts to reform their financial infrastructures, and move their financial systems more in the direction of a market-intermediated financial system and away from an exclusively bank-intermediated system.

These reform efforts are putting in place some of the important infrastructure elements that are *necessary* for developing effective securities markets. However, emphasis should be placed on the word necessary: as many of these measures, and all of them taken together, are *only* necessary and not sufficient for establishing effective security markets.

By all accounts, the measures taken so far by many countries in Asia are certainly in the right direction. But they are only a beginning, and they do not necessarily establish well-functioning effective markets per se, at least not yet. And there are risks. One concern that may be on the minds of market participants is that countries will view their efforts to date as very substantial and become overly comfortable with them to the point of becoming complacent in the judgment that they have done enough. It has taken many decades for effective bond markets to develop in the United States and Europe, so it would be reasonable to expect that it would take some time for them develop in Asia, though probably not as long because of the advances in information and computer technology in the past two decades.

Why might reforms to date *not* be sufficient to ensure the establishment of effective bond markets in countries in Asia? Broadly speaking, finance—both bank oriented and market oriented finance–is primarily about **pricing** and **allocating capital** and **financial risk.** Countries can import and implant the most highly sophisticated trading platforms, clearance and settlement systems, and even supervisory and regulatory infrastructures. However, this does not necessarily establish effective financial markets and an effective and well-functioning financial system.

Markets are comprised of market participants, and the pricing and trading activities surrounding the financial products they supply and demand. These financial activities can be allowed and encouraged to evolve more or less naturally and appropriately within the context of the particular economy, economic and financial history, and culture, otherwise the imported sophistication will count for very little… except perhaps to attract foreign capital, and then only temporarily.

So how can the development of a "**finance culture**" be encouraged and fostered? There are no clear uniform answers or blueprints appropriate for all countries. But in all countries the accurate **pricing** of risk is key.

In this last respect—the pricing and allocating of risk—the role of securities markets in Asia is no different from in other countries. And Asia would seem to be in a position to benefit from effective securities markets. From a broad perspective, Asia has

- high domestic savings rates
- great investment needs
- large **gross** capital inflows and outflows
- and primarily, bank-dominated financial systems

In Asia, as elsewhere, reliance on securities markets can

- improve opportunities and returns for savers,
- reduce costs for borrowers
- improve opportunities for financial risk taking,
- and improve the ability to manage financial risk

Moreover, from a national perspective they can

- reduce concentration of risk in the banking and payments system
- improve ability to prevent systemic problems, by dispersing the ownership of risk
- facilitate the repricing and reallocation of risk as economic and financial circumstances change.

There would be at least two important benefits associated with developing effective securities markets. First, they provide a more transparent and in some ways more effective way of pricing and distributing risk. Effective securities markets are a way of diversifying the financial system.

Second, in order to attract and sustain capital flows from abroad, and to more effectively allocate domestic savings at home, investors prefer well designed and appropriately regulated markets that are deep, liquid, and transparent, to those that are not. Given the choice, investors will gravitate to the safer markets that are more likely to ensure liquidity, even during turbulent period.

Looking at the experience of countries that have the most highly developed securities markets, one can point to important elements of their development that may account for the roles they are playing in their respective economies. An important, and often overlooked element, and one that I shall only state, is the level of sophistication and maturity of their economic system. Financial systems work best when they are appropriate for the economic system. By looking at the United States and Europe one cannot help but conclude that well developed government securities markets played an important role.[1] More recent work on the U.S. Treasury Securities markets suggests that government paper seems to provide some financial characteristics that are important, but which U.S. market participants are capable of learning to do without by finding private substitutes.[2]

What are some of the more important elements of effective **private** securities markets, and in particular for **pricing** and **allocating** funds? A list would certainly include the following:

- *Well-functioning money markets* appear to be a critical first step in developing corporate fixed-income markets.
- *Development of an investment-banking culture* for effectively matching demanders of funds with suppliers of funds within markets, rather than across bank balance sheets. Along with this is the need to establish well-functioning primary and secondary securities markets.
- *The emergence of a domestic investor base* is important for developing domestic securities markets, and particularly markets for corporate fixed income securities.
- *Elimination of impediments to market development, which can emanate from within the financial industry* itself, most often from market power in the financial industry that stifles access to securities markets or impedes the functioning of securities markets.
- *Appropriate and effective regulation.* Ineffective regulation in primary or secondary markets is one of the most important reasons historically for the lack of development of corporate debt securities markets in many economies. Of course, weak regulation and supervision of securities markets has also stunted the development and growth of securities markets. Finding the right balance of regulation and market discipline is an important practical issue.

These factors do not constitute an exhaustive list of influences on the development, or lack thereof, of debt securities markets, and there are other more fundamental determinants such as legal structures (including commercial codes), cultures, and histories. Accordingly, there is no simple recipe for "how to" foster the development of securities markets. These factors can be seen as necessary but not sufficient characteristics of effective securities markets, or at a minimum as useful

---

[1] See the reference cited in footnote 1.

[2] See "Financial Implications of the Shrinking Supply of U.S. Treasury Securities", with C. Kramer and R. T. Smith, IMF *Working Paper*, 01/61 (May 2001).

for avoiding some historical obstacles to the development of debt securities markets. They also offer some guidance on valuable market practices.

There are characteristics of markets that I have not discussed that are key determinants of the development of effective securities markets. Market liquidity, for example, is a key characteristic of highly developed securities markets. Investors must feel confident that they can buy and sell securities of relatively large quantities without significantly affecting prices and that they can liquidate their holdings in a reasonable period of time, if not immediately. As such, market liquidity can neither be legislated nor dictated by regulations; it must be promoted and nurtured by instilling investor confidence, in part by fostering market integrity, investor protection, and an effective market infrastructure. Each of these factors underlying liquidity can take a considerable time to develop.

Similarly, an essential element of a debt securities market is a finance culture and an investor base with an appetite for evaluating and trading in credit risk. It is relatively straightforward to describe the characteristics of an active and sophisticated investor base, but again it cannot be decreed, and in practice investor bases have developed only gradually as the above characteristics of markets have evolved. The advantage of developing securities markets in the current global financial environment is that there is a ready made international investor base eager to invest in countries with sound fundamentals, reasonable returns, and relatively efficient markets and financial infrastructures. There are a host of additional factors that I have not discussed.

There are also somewhat more fundamental, deeper characteristics of financial architecture and economic structure that influence how the art of finance develops in a particular nation. Historically, U.S. corporate debt securities markets flourished for periods of time in environments characterized by extreme segmentation in the financial system, financial crises and panics, often confusing and overlapping systems of financial supervision and regulation, and a lengthy list of distortion-prone financial sector policies. The strict separation of commercial banking and securities markets, for example, may have encouraged the development of a competitive and efficient set of investment banks and securities firms. Moreover, the more fundamental legal structure of the commercial code and bankruptcy laws, and the systems and patterns of corporate governance that emerged through time also played an important role. Thus, taken together all of these factors might have worked together to encourage finance in the United States to focus to a larger extent than in other countries on tradable and marketable securities rather than closely held, non-traded loan agreements between two counterparts.

By contrast, the underlying legal infrastructures, commercial codes, and governance mechanisms through time encouraged the development of the universal banking concept in European countries, which by encouraging bilateral loan agreements might have discouraged, or at least not encouraged, the more active use and development of tradable and marketable securities and the market structures to price and allocate them. These more fundamental influences are in some ways more important than the factors I have identified because they heavily influence the evolution of economic and financial relationships over long periods of time. As such, they may be difficult to change quickly even if there is the desire to do so.

Introduction

Douglas Arner[1], Jae-Ha Park[2], Paul Lejot[1] and Qiao Liu[3]

[1]Asian Institute of International Financial Law, Faculty of Law, University of Hong Kong; [2]Korea Institute of Finance; [3]Faculty of Business and Economics, University of Hong Kong

The essays in this book share two features. All describe financial sector reform, and all concern the possible. Some describe recent national or regionally sponsored changes, and others make proposals to introduce new concepts or scale to those changes. Some describe why the possible has yet to transpire, showing why eight years of post-crisis discussion has been insufficient to induce reliable change. The role and value of markets for traded debt has excited extreme views at intervals since the seventeenth century, but the contents of these essays exclude any discussion of optimal solutions. Instead, they are intended to inform the region's ongoing financial considerations with practical proposals, and give examples of the means by which active markets can assist resource allocation, risk management and investment decisions.

Aims of the Book

Recent history has seen large parts of East Asia enjoy economic growth at rates and for periods admired by all other regions. When the causes of that material success are debated, as if an Asian elixir might then be offered to poorly performing countries, an observer might fairly ask what can be seriously wrong with the region? This paradox is exaggerated by a recent heightening of political and developmental attention towards Africa's economic future, with startling examples: per capita national income was similar in Ghana and Korea in the late-1950s, but now differs by a multiple of over thirty times.[1]

---

[1] Gross domestic product per capita at current prices (2004 projection), Ghana, US$423.73, Korea US$ 13446.08 (source IMF World Economic Outlook 2004). Easterly and Levine (1997) note that in the early-1960s sub-Saharan Africa was widely thought to face better

None of the chapters presented in this book advocates market reform for ideological reasons, nor to promote the 'export' of any single system from an advanced economy. The risks and errors associated with such an approach were seen in the fate of the 'law and development' movement in the 1970s, which began with widespread academic and official support but ended discredited and unlamented, with few positive results in the nations to which a transplant of unwanted systems had been promoted.[2] Instead, the authors argue for a greater element of choice for domestic and foreign participants in Asia's financial sectors. Together, these essays suggest that certain of Asia's financial markets serve poorly both the region's users and its constituent economies, notwithstanding a commendable growth performance over two generations, and that welfare, resource allocation and macroeconomic risk management could all be enhanced by market-orientated reform.

At a national level of analysis, it has recently become common to ask whether China, in particular, with a startling post-1970s economic and private sector performance, represents an exception to the increasingly accepted view that measured prosperity is in a variety of ways predicated upon institutional factors, notably the quality, integrity and transparency of law, regulation, enforcement and way that those factors impact upon national financial systems?

Empirical analysis has only begun to consider this question, but it can be considered plausible that the value of institutions is not confounded by China's experience, despite its financial sector being weak and dysfunctional. Instead, China may have created a different, informal set of rules that serve as a framework for saving and financing, but that with the adoption of more conventional institutions its national and sectoral performance could be still better, less wasteful and more productive. It could then provide a model for the next wave of growth and reform among the region's emerging economies.[3]

The book's approach is intended to be practical, and while it generally favors the value of well-functioning price mechanisms, it carries no superfluous ideology, whether political or financial. Although that value is taken to include the risk management qualities of such markets to lessen the chance of financial contagion, none of the authors suggests that the reforms they advocate would produce a comfortable Marshallian equilibrium in or among Asia's markets.

The book considers:

---

income prospects than developing East Asia, but instead experienced widespread shrinkage in per capita growth in the period 1960-95.

[2] A decline notably recorded by Trubek and Galanter (1974) and Merryman (1977).

[3] Boyreau and Wei (2005). Allen *et al* (2002, 2005) argue that informal institutions may substitute for those commonly seen elsewhere.

- All existing domestic currency markets for debt securities in East Asia (excluding Japan); and the most important cross-border public debt markets for Asian credit risk.[4]
- The role of governments as borrowers and participants in the financial sector; and the main roles of the commercial banking sector in each economy, including intermediation and its contribution to domestic credit expansion.

The Value of Reform

The nature of Asia's 1997-98 crisis suggests that the region may become less prone to financial contagion by reducing reliance on its banking sectors for credit and intermediation, and improving efficiency in deploying savings. Asia is generally free from non-cyclical aggregate shortages of capital but its capability to apportion financial resources is pervasively suspect. Liquid debt securities markets exist comprehensively in no economy other than Japan, even though notes or bonds are issued in most and Asian international borrowers are well-regarded, though only a handful are prolific. The book argues that active debt markets will improve national and regional resource allocation by providing an unbiased, visible price mechanism and widen the choice available to investors. In so doing, such markets will also diminish potential instability and contagion.

A further supportive argument often made since 2000 is that Asia suffers a loss of economic welfare by failing fully to muster savings for investment within the region. The most visible sign of post-crisis adjustment is asset accumulation, which has propelled national holdings of foreign reserves to levels far greater than prior to 1997, whether measured in cash terms or in relation to national income, trade volumes or domestic monetary bases. This is seen by some as a buttress to western consumption, especially in the United States, but by others as representing a deficiency that needs correcting as Asia continues its socio-economic emancipation.

Is Asia different?

Five questions are implicit in an appraisal of Asia's financial infrastructure:

1. Does Asia's financial culture make mature bond markets infeasible?
2. Are weak markets indicative merely of evolutionary underdevelopment?
3. Can bond markets expand without continuous risk-free benchmark yield curves?
4. Could new regional structures assist trading, fundraising and impaired asset resolution?

---

[4] The book considers the People's Republic of China ('China'), Hong Kong SAR, China ('Hong Kong'), India, Indonesia, Korea, Malaysia, the Philippines, Singapore, Taiwan, China ('Taiwan') and Thailand. Its proposals have implications elsewhere in East and South Asia.

5. Do potential gains in welfare justify policy engagement to strengthen Asia's bond markets?

Official interest in these issues signals a desire for financial stability. Most commentators favor active markets, although pronounced reform is unwarranted for those believing organic development sufficient for the purpose,[5] a view historically popular in official circles or factions that especially value bank-borrower relationships. The book describes Asia's bond markets, their roots in funding patterns, and the concerns of policymakers examining their future. It traces the origins of advanced markets, their legacy for developing economies, and suggests prescriptive lessons using research into the interplay between legal systems and financial institutions.

Markets for debt securities exist in a comprehensive way in few Asian economies, even though short or medium-term bonds have been issued in almost all, and Asian borrowers are established (though not prolific) international issuers. This book is concerned with markets for debt issues by governments, government proxies (for example, specialist national agencies), and tradable non-government debt securities; and secondly, with the value and appropriateness of structured finance techniques to expand general usage of Asia's debt markets. The book examines the condition of the domestic and offshore[6] debt capital markets for Asia-Pacific risk. It traces common patterns of development among the established and nascent public debt securities markets in the region, and looks at the dynamics that will affect these markets in the medium term. It seeks to identify whether Asia's financial systems and institutions (that have for some time admitted 'single' transactions executed by negotiation) can be made to accommodate continuous issuing and trading activity typical of advanced markets, and to consider the associated advantages and considerations.

The core of the book seeks to identify:

1. Whether well-established market-based initiatives can combine symbiotically with recent proposals and reforms in public policy to result in the permanent expansion of existing markets and the successful opening of new developing markets in the region.
2. Obstacles to growth in Asian debt securities market activity, notably in issuance volumes and liquidity. In particular, the book analyses factors common to the sectors under review, notably, financial and system structure, regulatory guidelines facing financial intermediaries and investors, national

---

[5] For example, Yoshitomi & Shirai (2001).

[6] Offshore markets and instruments include all cross-border debt securities or issuance programmes in any currency, including the currency of the domicile of the issuer of risk. Unless stated a 'major' currency is a 'core' or 'G-3' currency (euro, yen or US dollar) or one used as a continual cross-border currency of issue, currently Australian or Canadian dollars, Swiss francs or Sterling.

legal impediments and differences in national laws that influence investor behavior, questions of corporate culture, and political and special interest factors, including national fiscal objectives.
3. Whether Asia is 'different' from advanced economies frequently identified as financial market models, either intrinsically or in terms of its stage of financial development, needs or other features.

Reasons for reform

Policy interest in these issues signals a general desire for financial stability. Most commentators favor active markets, although pronounced reform is unwarranted for those believing organic development sufficient for the purpose[7] or factions that especially value bank-borrower relationships. Paradoxically, proposals arising from earlier analysis have typically lacked sufficient scale to command official attention and achieve policy traction. Before and since the 1997-98 Asian regional crisis, many commentators have sought overriding reasons for the relative lack of depth or activity in the region's debt securities markets. It has become clear that there is no plausible shared or singular explanation save the coincidence of history. What most constrains Malaysia's market differs from limiting factors in China or Thailand.

The book takes account of discussions and initiatives of several policy working groups that are reviewing proposals for changes in financial architecture in the region. These groups are assisted by international financial organizations and private sector representatives, and the book is informed by certain of this work, especially in its depiction of contemporary concerns. Historically, private sector lobbying has often driven financial sector reform. For example, the Singapore domestic debt market's expansion in 1998-2000 sprang from prolonged pressure for liberalization by foreign banks and investors, whereas in Korea and Thailand the need for legislation to improve upon the perfection of title was a prerequisite for post-crisis securitized transactions using impaired financial assets.

Yet throughout East Asia, reforms have produced disappointing new issue volumes and trading activity has characteristically failed to expand such as to give full confidence to permitted new investors, whether domestic or offshore. The book suggests how governments can create a culture conducive to debt market growth with measured structural initiatives and detailed reforms introduced domestically in a cooperative regional way. Such a coordinated approach would boost the confidence of private sector participants to invest further in market-driven activity.

Outline

The book has three parts. Part I addresses the characteristics and roots of the markets under review. Part II examines the origins of contemporary bond markets to discover

---

[7] For example, Yoshitomi and Shirai (*op cit*), and in some official circles.

whether and how they contribute to general welfare; looks at the relationship between the banking and governmental sectors in Asia's money markets; and takes a detailed view of prospects for reform in China's government and corporate debt markets. Part III explains the micro-level impediments and obstacles that must be the first targets of any reforms, gives an appraisal of attempts to date at regional cooperation to stimulate structural reform, and finally contributes two major proposals to accelerate the growth and usefulness of bond markets in Asia, which are:

1. A collaborative regional public debt market for domestic and major currency issues, monitored by confederal regional regulation in an established Asian financial centre.
2. A regional body as part of an institutional mechanism for credit enhancement to support credit risk transfer and facilitate and encourage the securitization of a wide range of assets and risks, and the creation of a new source of well-rated risk.

Acknowledgements

In producing a book of this nature, we have been supported by many others. In particular, we would like to thank the following:

- The Milken Institute, in particular Jim Barth, Glenn Yago, Ed Phumiwasana, and Jeff Schatz for their support and professionalism, as well as for their efforts and those of their colleagues at the Milken Insitute in co-organizing the Asian Bond Market Forum held at the University of Hong Kong in November 2003;
- All the participants and sponsors of the Asian Bond Market Forum, for their comments and support;
- the Asian Institute of Financial Law (AIIFL) of the University of Hong Kong, especially Charles Booth and Flora Leung: This work was partially supported by a grant from the University Research Committee (URC) of the University of Hong Kong to AIIFL to the support the URC Strategic Research Area of corporate and financial law and policy;
- the Hong Kong Institute of Economics and Business Strategy (HIEBS) of the University of Hong Kong, for financial support: This work was partially supported by a grant from the University Grants Committee (UGC) of the Hong Kong Special Administrative Region, China (Project No. AoE/H-05/99) to the HIEBS;
- the Research Grants Committee (RGC) of the UGC: This work was partially supported by a grant from the RGC of the HKSAR, China (Project No. HKU 7401/05H); and
- the Hong Kong Institute of Monetary Research (HKIMR): This work was partially supported by a research project commissioned by the HKIMR.

Without their support and those of our partners and families, the production of this volume would not have been possible.

References

Allen, F., Qian Jun and Qian Meijun (2002). Law, finance and economic growth in China, Wharton Financial Institutions Center working paper 02-44; 2005 *Journal of Financial Economics*, 77: 57 116.

Boyreau-Debray, G. & Wei Shang-jin (2005). Pitfalls of a state-dominated financial system: the case of China, Washington: National Bureau of Economic Research working paper 11214.

Easterly, W., & R. Levine (1997). 'Africa's growth tragedy: policies and ethnic divisions', 112 Quarterly Journal of Economics 4: 1203.

Merryman, J.H. (1977). Comparative law and social change: on the origins, style, decline and revival of the law and development movement, 25 Am. J. Comp. L. 457.

Trubek, D. & M. Galanter (1974). Scholars in self-estrangement: some reflections on the crisis in law and development studies in the United States, Wis. L. Rev 1062.

Yoshitomi, M. & S. Shirai (2001) Designing a financial market structure in post-crisis Asia; how to develop corporate bond markets, Asian Development Bank Institute working paper 15.

Part I

Asia's Debt Capital Markets: Opportunities and Prospects

Chapter 1

Opportunities and Challenges in Asian Bond Markets

James R. Barth, Donald McCarthy, Triphon Phumiwasana, and Glenn Yago

Milken Institute

1. Overview

The remarkable growth of East Asian economies that has often been termed the "Asian Miracle"—an Asian analogue of the post-World War II "German Miracle"—rested to a large extent on the ability of firms to gain access to capital on easy terms, overwhelmingly in the form of bank loans. The Asian Crisis, however, demonstrated that too great a reliance on banks may lead economies on a slower and more volatile path to prosperity. In the wake of the crisis, Asian banks, burdened by bad debts and depleted of capital, cut their lending drastically leading to what some call a "credit crunch." Asian policy makers took this lesson to heart and, among the many changes and reforms made during the recovery years of 1998-2003, a common policy was to strengthen domestic financial structures by seeking to develop efficient domestic bond markets. To some extent these efforts have been effective. Indeed, bond markets in Asia have become an increasingly important way for entrepreneurs to access capital; which in turn promotes economic growth and stability.

The relationship between finance and growth is now better understood and appreciated. Economic development requires a safe and sound financial system to serve as a transmission mechanism that transfers funds from savers to entrepreneurs seeking capital for productive investments. Considerable recent research underscores the importance of financial markets for economic development.

The size of a nation's financial market (the sum of bank assets, equity market capitalization and value of outstanding bonds) is positively and significantly correlated with its level of economic development (see Barth, Nolle, Root and Yago, 2001). Levine (1997) provides a thorough and comprehensive review of evidence demonstrating the importance of financial markets for economic growth. A more general and recent treatment of this linkage is provided in a World Bank publication (World Bank, 2001).

All three of the individual components of a nation's total financial market are positively and significantly correlated with its level of economic development. Levine and Zervos (1998), Rajan and Zingales (1998) and Beck and Levine (2004), among others, demonstrate the importance of both banks and equity markets for economic growth. Similar studies are not available for bond markets due to the lack of readily available data for a large number of countries, which prevents a rigorous assessment of their importance for growth. Nonetheless, Herring and Chatusripitak (2001) note "that the absence of a bond market may render an economy less efficient and significantly more vulnerable to financial crisis." Domowitz, Glen and Madhavan (2001), moreover, find that macroeconomic stability is highly and positively correlated with the development of bond markets.

Based upon available data for a limited number of countries, one finds that the governmental share of a nation's bonds outstanding is negatively and significantly correlated with its level of economic development (see Barth, Nolle, Root and Yago, 2001). This suggests that even though the ability of firms to raise funds externally through the issuance of bonds is important for economic development, government borrowing may "crowd out" private borrowers.

The composition (i.e., bank assets relative to equity market capitalization plus bonds outstanding) of a nation's financial market, more generally, is *not* significantly correlated with its level of economic development. This is consistent with the view that banks and capital markets should be viewed as net complements, not substitutes. Policy should therefore not overly favor the development of banks at the expense of capital markets or vise versa. Demirgüç-Kunt and Levine (2001) provide analyses that document the complementary nature of banks and capital markets. More generally, as Miller (1998) points out, "[h]aving a wide spectrum of financial markets available keeps a country from having to put all its development eggs in one basket … in particular, from relying too heavily on commercial banking … [which] is a disaster-prone strategy requiring enormous amount of direct government supervision to reduce the frequency of explosion and subsequent implosion." This suggests that some degree of substitutability exists among the different components of a financial system.

Although having both banks and securities markets can be thought of as providing a more diversified financial system, Davis and Ioannidis (2002), for example, argue that increased securities issuance in times of crisis may not be effective in fully offsetting a decline in bank lending. Yet, the general view is that while having a securities market cannot fully substitute for a healthy banking sector, it *can* reduce the pressure on a weakened banking system in time of crisis by providing an alternative source of credit when banks' curtail lending.

Table 1 shows that high-income countries have overwhelmingly more financial assets than the middle- or low-income countries. While high-income countries comprise just 15 percent of world population, they comprise 97 percent of world bank assets, 93 percent of world equity market capitalization and 96 percent of world debt securities.

Table 1: Differences in Size and Composition of Financial Markets Around the World, 2003[1]

		Percent of total accounted for by:			
	World Totals	High Income Countries	Middle Income Countries	Low Income Countries	*Asia**
Population	6.3 billion	15.5	47.7	36.8	*44.9*
GDP	$36.4 trillion	80.5	16.4	3.0	*10.2*
Bank Assets	$50.6 trillion	87.2	11.6	1.2	*11.8*
Equity Market Capitalization	$31.9 trillion	91.1	7.9	1.0	*9.1*
International Debt Securities	$11.7 trillion	95.6	3.9	0.5	*3.9*
Domestic Debt Securities	$39.6 trillion	90.9	4.7	0.1	*2.1*

Note: *Asia refers to the ten selected Asian economies—China, Hong Kong, India, Indonesia, Malaysia, Philippines, Singapore, South Korea, Taiwan and Thailand.

Source: Statistical Abstract of the United States, U.S. Census Bureau; *World Development Indicators*, World Bank; *World Economic Outlook and International Financial Statistics*, International Monetary Fund; *Size of World Bond Market Capitalization*, Merrill Lynch; *Quarterly Review: International Banking and Financial Market Developments*, Bank for International Settlements; *Mutual Fund Fact Book*, Investment Company Institute; *Financial Statistics,* Central Bank of China (Taiwan).

Table 1 also shows that banks are significantly more important than capital markets as a source of finance in middle- and low-income countries. This is to be expected insofar as bank loans typically precede equity and bond financing as the most important source of external funds for firms as countries evolve from being more agriculture based to more industrial and service oriented. However, to promote sustainable and stable economic growth, financial markets and the institutions that support them must develop and evolve to serve more diverse and complex economies.

The financial systems of most Asian countries, and in fact, of most emerging market economies, have always been bank-based. Bank lending is more readily available to firms for external financing relative to market financing through the issuance of stocks and bonds. However, as mentioned above, countries have learned from the Asian Crisis that a heavy reliance on banks for financing can result in a too narrowly focused financial system, which in turn increases the systemic vulnerability

[1] Economies are divided among income groups according to 2003 GNI per capita, calculated using the World Bank Atlas Method. The groups are: low income, $765 or less; middle income, $766-$9,385; and high income, $9,386 or more.

to a financial crisis.[2] Figures 1 and 2 compare the financial structures in Asian countries in 1997 and then again in 2004. Between 1997 and 2004, the share of banking sector financing has decreased for every economy with the decline varying between 47 percent (Taiwan) and 2 percent (India). Conversely, the share of bonds in these economies increased substantially. Indeed, in the Philippines, Taiwan and Indonesia the share of total financial sector assets accounted for by bonds increased more than 18 percentage points and in Singapore it increased by more than 12 percentage points.

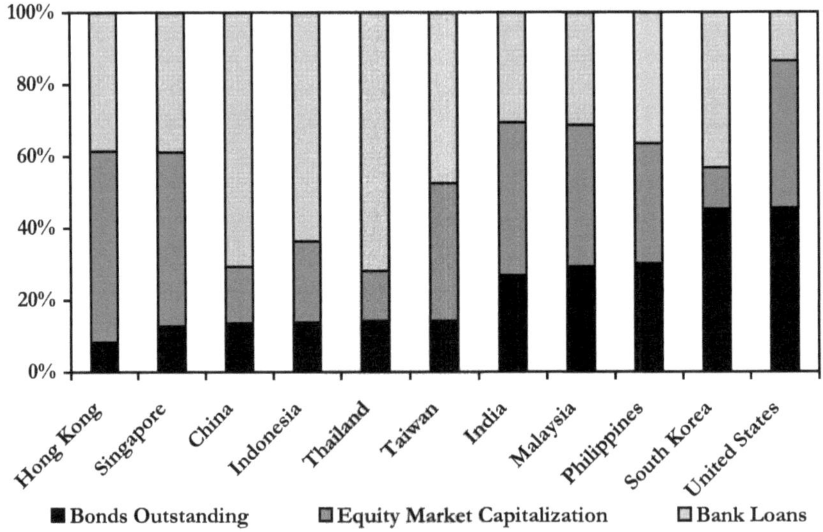

Figure 1-1. **Composition of Asian financial markets, 1997**

Note: "Bank loans" refers to claims on the private sector, IFS line 22d; "bonds outstanding" is the sum of international bonds and domestic bonds outstanding.

Source: Emerging Stock Markets Factbook, Standard & Poor's; *BIS Quarterly Review*, Bank for International Settlements; *International Financial Statistics* (IFS), International Monetary Fund.

2. The Importance of Bond Markets

From a macroeconomic perspective, bond market development is not only positively associated with real GDP per capita, but also enhances the stability of an economy.[3]

---

[2] For further discussions on the relationship between financial systems and growth, see Barth, Nolle, Root and Yago (2001).

[3] Phumiwasana (2003) found that among high-income countries, market-based financial systems have a negative and significant relationship to the standard deviation of growth when

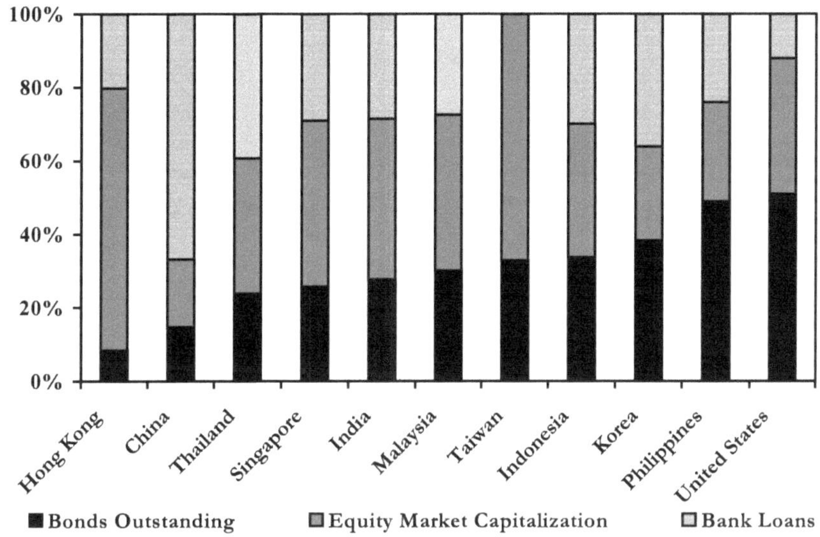

Figure 1-2. **Composition of Asian financial markets, 2004**

Note: "Bank loans" refers to claims on the private sector, IFS line 22d; "bonds outstanding" is the sum of international bonds and domestic bonds outstanding.

Source: Emerging Stock Markets Factbook, Standard & Poor's; *BIS Quarterly Review*, Bank for International Settlements; *International Financial Statistics* (IFS), International Monetary Fund.

Figure 3 shows that countries with more domestic bonds outstanding relative to GDP have higher levels of real GDP per capita. Moreover, this relationship is highly significant (with a t-statistic of 5.287 and a p-value of 0.000004).[4] Figure 4 shows that countries with more domestic bonds outstanding relative to GDP have lower volatility in real GDP per capita growth. This relationship is also highly significant (with a t-statistic of –3.672 and a p-value of 0.000675). These strong relationships are consistent with intuition as the availability of bond financing provides firms with an alternative to banks as a source of borrowing. In the colorful terminology of Alan Greenspan (1999), Chairman of the Federal Reserve System, this form of financing serves as a financial "spare tire," so that an economy can better withstand an economic downturn.

---

controlling for factors affecting growth volatility. This means that greater reliance on markets relative to banks can lead to lower volatility of growth for developed countries.

[4] We also find positive and significant relationship between international bonds outstanding to GDP and real GDP per capita, relationship between international bond outstanding to GDP and the standard deviation of real GDP per capita growth is also negative and significant.

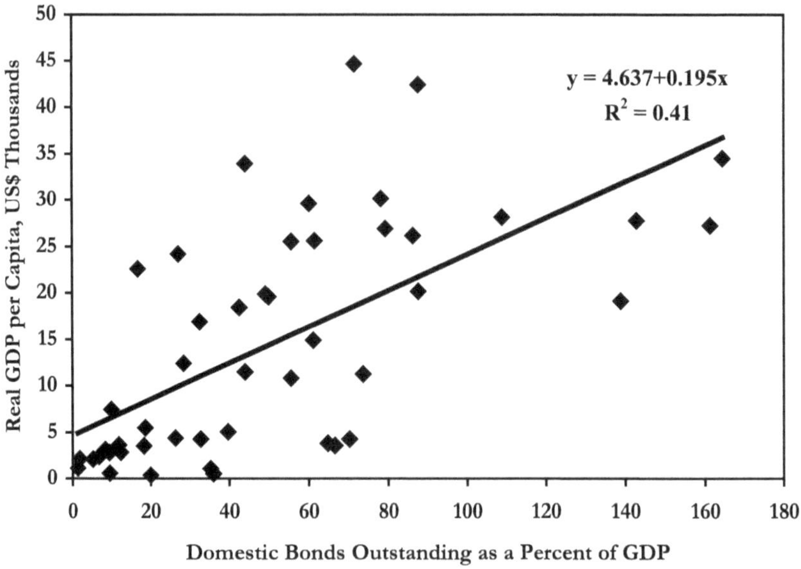

Figure 1-3. **Domestic bonds outstanding and GDP per capita are positively correlated, 1995-2004**

Local currency-denominated bond markets are crucially important. Local currency bond market development is important for government financing, which was much needed after the Asian Crisis due to the resulting budget deficits in countries that had hitherto tended to run surpluses. A large portion of the deficits after the crisis were due to the costs of recapitalizing the banking system and setting up asset management corporations to deal with the large amounts of non-performing loans. Local currency bond markets are also important to non-government borrowers. They allow borrowers to match the currency risks of their assets and liabilities without hedging (no small matter in countries where cross-currency swap markets are undeveloped) as well as reducing a country's dependence on foreign funds. In 1997-1998, many Asian countries learned the painful lesson that dependence on foreign lenders can increase a country's exposure to international financial shocks and to the curtailment, if not reversal, of capital inflows. An additional benefit of these types of bonds is that having nationals rather than foreigners as holders of government debt may subject government officials to an additional source of political discipline. A default may be politically far more costly if the bond holders are one's constituents rather than faceless (and voteless) foreign investors. Furthermore, with broader, deeper and more liquid markets, and in the absence of interest rate controls, secondary bond markets yield spreads might signal the public's view of the sustainability of government spending, thus pressuring the government to pay more attention to public opinion with regard to its policies.

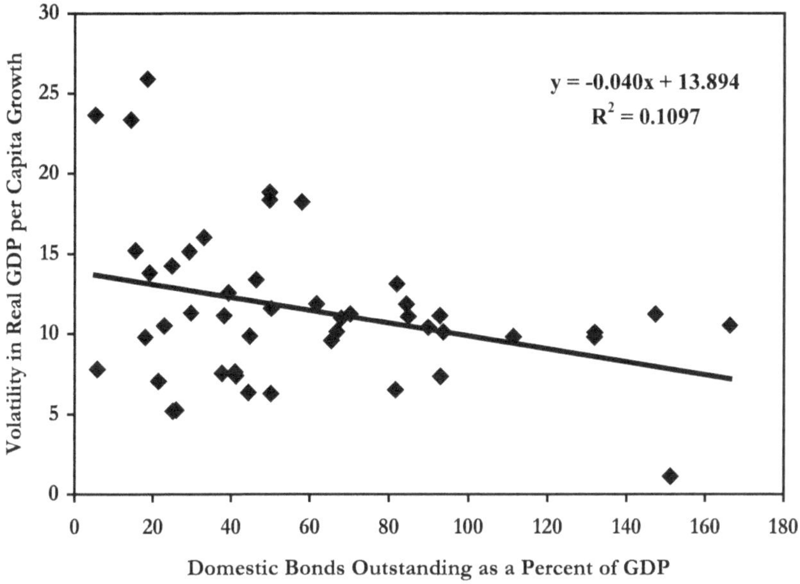

Figure 1-4. **Domestic bonds outstanding and the volatility of real GDP per capita growth are negatively correlated, 1995-2004**

At the firm level, the development of a bond market allows corporate financiers to choose from a broader range of financial instruments to fund their operations. As business conditions change, the financial needs of firms similarly changes. Financing flexibility is important for this reason and becomes especially crucial during a crisis for solvent but illiquid firms that need financing to allow them to continue operations. Without additional lending by banks or alternative financing options such as bonds, otherwise viable firms may close, further exacerbating a downturn.

The development of bond markets creates opportunities for Asian economies to develop a wider range of financial instruments that can support growth and prosperity. It sets the stage for the development of securitization that, among other things, will allow banks to better deal with their nonperforming loans during bad times. In addition, as is evident in the United States, the bond market can strengthen the housing market through the process of securitization. The securitization and sale of mortgages permits loan originators to avoid holding onto loans and instead transfers risk to investors who are best able to manage it.

3. Issues in Developing Asian Bond Markets

3.1. Size Trap

Asian bond markets, like those of most emerging markets (see Table 1), are less well-developed than those of the U.S. and the rest of the developed world. There are a number of potential reasons why bond markets in Asia are small and poorly developed and Asian economies have typically relied on bank finance. Asian countries may find themselves in a "trap"—a low level bond market development equilibrium, where a small market size leads to illiquidity and illiquidity discourages issuances and reinforces the small size of the market (Eichengreen, 2004).

Eichengreen and Luengnaruemitchai (2004) note that "liquid securities markets have a certain minimum efficient scale" and thus the small economies of Asia face difficulties in developing bond markets. They further argue that many Asian countries lack market-supporting institutions, such as creditor rights and adequate contract enforcement.

3.2. Legal System and Asymmetric Information

Inadequate legal institutions can impede bond market development while allowing bank finance to flourish. A legal system that allows high degrees of information asymmetry may be quite adequate so long as banks are the primary source of finance. When banks are the main lenders, they intermediate between borrowers and lenders and thus—along with the government if there is deposit insurance—help shield depositors against the risk of default. Additionally, bank loans allow lenders to control the behavior of borrowers (through the use of protective covenants) to a far greater extent than bonds. Bondholders, moreover, are exposed to default risk, have less access to protective covenants and also face a collective action problem with respect to borrower monitoring. If there are a large number of bondholders, the dominant strategy of bondholders may be to attempt to free-ride on the monitoring of other lenders, thus leading to below optimal levels of borrower monitoring and thus higher default rates.

One of the basic challenges for developing a bond market given an existing bank-based financial system is how to decrease information asymmetry, thereby decreasing the complexity of insolvency and bankruptcy procedures, which increase exponentially with the number of lenders. Transparent and standardized bankruptcy procedures—such as rules for the establishment of a standing committee of representatives from various classes of creditors—would allow the relevant parties to open multilateral lines of communication, reduce information asymmetry among stakeholders, and act quickly and efficiently in a case of default.

There are theoretical reasons, therefore, to support the view that institutions matter and that the development of a domestic corporate debt market depends in part on the existence and efficiency of the bankruptcy process. Using simple cross-country correlations we found that these theoretical reasons enjoy empirical support insofar as the ratio of total domestic corporate debt relative to GDP is negatively and significantly correlated with the cost of bankruptcy proceedings and positively and significantly correlated with the recovery rate.[5] Furthermore, although the

[5] Cross-country data were obtained from BIS and the World Bank Doing Business: Closing Business websites. Corporate sector debt is an average over 1993 to 2003. Time or length of bankruptcy is average time (years) to complete a procedure. Cost of bankruptcy includes court

relationship between time to complete a bankruptcy procedure and corporate debt relative to GDP are negative but not significant, the lengthiness of the bankruptcy procedure is negatively and significantly correlated with the recovery rate.

3.3. Irregular Benchmark Bond Issuances

The lack of high-quality, large and regular bond issuances is another major impediment to the development of this market. Though excessive issuance of government securities can lead to "crowding out" of private borrowing, insufficient government securities issuance can lead to the lack of a benchmark yield curve. The existence of a government securities yield curve and based upon risk-free interest rates is essential to the efficient pricing of riskier bonds, including corporate debt. Schinasi and Smith (1998) note the importance of a liquid yield curve for price discovery in the bond market and thus to the development of efficient bond markets in emerging markets. Evidence from developed countries suggests that a deep and liquid government bond market is a catalyst for development of a strong corporate debt market (IMF, 2002).

This argument is echoed by Brandt and Kavajecz (2004) who stress that "the use of riskless interest rates permeates almost ever facet of economics and finance." Additionally, they find that changes in the yield curve due to large sell and buy orders are much greater in periods of low liquidity—conditions that consistently describe the recent situation in Asian bond markets.

The current state of selected Asian countries' yield curves is illustrated in Table 2, which also offers comparable data on the U.S. Treasury securities reflected in yield curves for benchmark purposes. There is a large degree of commonality in one respect—the participation of foreigners. The major Asian markets—with three exceptions—allow non-residents to trade government debt. Just three markets—China, India and Malaysia—impede the usefulness or informativeness of their yield curves by either denying (China and India) or limiting (Malaysia) the ability of foreign traders to buy and sell government bonds. There is a greater amount of variance, however, when one considers the liquidity of these markets. The turnover of the markets—a simple measure of liquidity—varies from 44 in Hong Kong to 0.5 in the Philippines. While the most liquid market has about the same annual turnover as the U.S. Treasury market at 48, the second most liquid Asian market, Singapore, has a turnover that is just 10 percent of the U.S. market, while the least liquid market has a turnover that is just 1 percent of the U.S. figure.

---

costs, fees of insolvency practitioners, independent assessors, lawyers, accountants, but not bribery. The recovery rate measures the efficiency of foreclosure or bankruptcy procedures. It indicates how many cents on the dollar claimants—creditors, tax authorities, and employees—recover from an insolvent firm.

Table 2: Characteristics of Asian Sovereign Yield Curves, 2003

Country	Number of Maturities	Range of Maturities	Annual Turnover Ratio[6]	Non Resident Participation
China	12	3m – 15y	3.1	No
Hong Kong	11	3m – 10y	44.1	Yes
India	15	3m – 30y	0.4	No
Indonesia	10	3m – 10y	2.5	Yes
South Korea	7	3m – 10y	2.9	Yes
Malaysia	12	3m – 15y	2.3	Limited
Philippines	11	3m – 20y	0.5	Yes
Singapore	7	3m – 15y	5.5	Yes
Taiwan	6	2y – 30y	2.1	Yes
Thailand	14	3m – 15 y	2.2	Yes
Memorandum:				
United States	15	3m – 30y	47.7	Yes

Source: Asian Development Banks, Bloomberg, Deutsche Bank, National Central Banks, Federal Reserve Bank of New York and Milken Institute.

Noteworthy is the fact that the two least liquid markets, India (0.2) and Malaysia (0.5), either prohibit or limit the ability of foreigners to participate in the market. The two most liquid markets, Taiwan and Hong Kong, are outliers in the group. The next most liquid Asian market, Singapore, has a liquidity ratio of 4.4, less than 10 percent of Hong Kong.

In terms of a range of maturities embodied in the yield curve, only one of the economies, India, has a curve as extensive in terms of different maturities as the U.S, which has 15 different maturities ranging from 3 months to 30 years. Despite this situation, all Asian economies except Taiwan have very short term bonds and all countries' yield curves extend at least to 10 year maturities. Both India and Taiwan have yield curves that extend to the 30 year "bucket" and China, Malaysia, Philippines, and Thailand all have 15 year bonds. The average number of different maturity issues is 10.5, with India having the most at 15 and Taiwan the least at 6. One can note, however, that Taiwan, with the fewest "buckets" on its yield curve, nevertheless is the most liquid market. Conversely, India with the most is the least liquid. Also, Hong Kong—the second most liquid market—has one of the shortest curves, while India, the most illiquid, has the longest.

[6] Taiwan figure is as of October 2004, based on GreTai Securities Market website.

Additionally, macroeconomic policies may have a negative effect on bond market development (Eichengreen and Luengnaruemitchai, 2004). Domestic interest rate volatility—a feature of several Asian economies—lessens the attractiveness of long-term fixed-income securities to investors (particularly given the lack of efficient hedging opportunities).

Other issues slowing the development of Asian bond markets are the lack of issuer variety (an issue explained more fully below), a buy and hold investment strategy on the part of bond buyers that leads to a lack of liquidity and thereby slows development of secondary bond markets, and local financial institutions' tendency to view bond markets as a substitute and thus a threat, rather than a complement, to bank loans.

4. Emerging Asian Bond Markets

4.1. Size of Domestic Bond Financing

As mentioned above, Asian bond markets are less well-developed than those of the U.S. Domestic bonds outstanding in Asia range between $25 and $568 billion, whereas there are some $19 trillion of domestic bonds outstanding in the U.S. Similarly, domestic debt as a share of GDP ranges between 30 percent and 91 percent in Asia, whereas domestic bonds outstanding are more than 160 percent of US GDP (Table 3).

However, Asian markets are not homogenous in terms of size and composition, as seen in Table 3. The size in terms of dollar value of outstanding issues of the domestic bond markets of these economies varies considerably. As of September of 2004, South Korea has the largest market at $568 billion, followed quite closely by China's market at $483 billion. These two markets are more than twice the size of the next two markets, which comprise the second tier of Asian bond markets: India at $239 billion and Taiwan at $192 billion, respectively. Four of the five remaining markets do not exceed $100 billion in size, with the only exception being Malaysia at $107 billion. After Malaysia, there are three markets of roughly similar size: Singapore ($66 billion), Thailand ($65 billion) and Indonesia ($59 billion). The smallest Asian bond market is that of the Philippines and is roughly half the size of the other markets at $25 billion.

While this may provide a relatively accurate view of the importance of the various Asian bond markets as components of the world financial system, it does not assess their relative importance as a source of finance. One should therefore consider the size of the different domestic bond markets relative to GDP (Table 3). Doing so, one finds that the two economies with the largest bond markets are Malaysia (91 percent) and South Korea (83 percent). The next largest is Taiwan (63 percent) following closely by Singapore (62 percent), with the remaining five markets all ranging in size between 22 percent and 40 percent of GDP. Of the smaller markets, the largest is Thailand's at 40 percent, India's (36 percent), the Philippines' (30 percent), China's (29 percent), and Hong Kong's (28 percent). China's market, while the largest in absolute dollar terms, ranks just 9th when compared to its GDP. Conversely,

Malaysia is ranked 5th in dollar terms yet 1st in terms of bonds outstanding relative to GDP.

***Table 3:* Domestic Bond Markets, 2004**

Country	Domestic Debt (US$ Billions)	Total Outstanding as Share of GDP (%)
Hong Kong	46.50	28.26
India	239.20	36.19
Philippines	25.20	29.60
Indonesia	57.80	22.41
South Korea	568.40	83.41
Malaysia	106.60	90.51
Taiwan	191.80	62.84
China	483.30	29.30
Thailand	64.90	39.70
Singapore	66.30	62.07
Memorandum:		
United States	19186.60	163.52

Notes: "Financial assets" is defined as the sum of domestic bonds outstanding, equity market capitalization and bank claims on the private sector.

Source: Emerging Stock Markets Review, Standard & Poor's; *BIS Quarterly Review Q4 2004*, Bank for International Settlements; *International Financial Statistics* (IFS), International Monetary Fund, *World Economic Outlook.*

4.2. Bond Markets Are Growing

The dollar value of outstanding domestic debt in these 10 Asian markets has grown by 77 percent—an annualized average growth rate of 6 percent (Table 4). The fastest growing bond market of the 10 economies during this period is Indonesia's which grew by a stunning 1760 percent or 34 percent per year. The next fastest growing was the bond market of China, which increased more than 6 times since 1995, an increase equal to an average annual increase of 22 percent. Thailand's bond market increased by 309 percent or 15 percent on average per year, making it the 3rd most rapidly expanding market. Another two markets grew at an average rate of at least 10 percent per year, with India by 13 percent (239 percent) and Singapore by 11 percent (191 percent). Other markets grew more slowly and the Philippines' market contracted over the period.

Table 4: **Domestic Bond Markets Are Growing**

Country	Ten Year Increase 1995-2004 (%)	Annual Growth 1995-2004 (%)
China	623.50	21.88
Hong Kong	95.38	6.93
India	238.81	12.98
Malaysia	70.83	5.50
Philippines	-3.82	-0.39
Singapore	190.79	11.26
South Korea	150.18	9.60
Taiwan	153.37	9.74
Thailand	308.18	15.10
Indonesia	1764.52	33.99
All Countries	77.65	5.91
Memorandum:		
United States	81.60	6.15

Source: Bank for International Settlements.

4.3. Suppliers and Holders of Bonds

Government issues comprise a greater share of Asian bond markets than is usual in more developed and market-based financial systems. Whereas central government bonds comprise 29 percent of total U.S. domestic debt, 54 percent of outstanding bonds in the Asian economies are government bonds (Table 5). It is highest in the Philippines and India where 99 percent and 98 percent of the market, respectively, are comprised of government issues. Only in Hong Kong, Malaysia and Taiwan are the government shares of the total market less than 50 percent. In some economies, like Singapore, this is not due to deficit spending, but rather to an effort to develop the domestic bond market through the issuance of local currency debt and the maintenance of a yield curve.

Next most important in terms of shares is the debt issued by financial institutions, which comprises 29 percent of total debt in these economies. This is lower than in the U.S., in which case 58 percent of total debt is issued by financial institutions. Again, as with government debt, there is considerable variation in the importance of financial institutions. The share is highest in Hong Kong, with 54 percent of the market, and lowest in the Philippines and India, both with a little less than 1 percent.

China and South Korea have similar shares at 38 percent and 42 percent, respectively. Singapore has a considerably smaller proportion than either country, with 25 percent of the market made up of the bonds of financial institutions. Malaysia, Taiwan and Thailand's, have relatively low shares of financial institution issuance at between 13 and 18 percent of the total and just 5 percent of Indonesia's issuance is comprised by financial institution offerings.

Asian corporate bond issuance accounts for just 17 percent of the total with the share of corporate debt in Malaysia being the highest at 42 percent. Between 20 and 33 percent of total debt in Thailand, Taiwan and South Korea is issued by corporations and in Hong Kong the corporate share of debt issuance is about 13 percent. All remaining markets have corporate debt less than 10 percent of total debt.

***Table 5:* Composition of Suppliers of Outstanding Domestic Bonds, 2004**

Country	Public Sector (%)	Financial Institutions (%)	Corporate Sector (%)
China	59.47	38.01	2.52
Hong Kong	33.98	53.55	12.47
India	98.24	0.59	1.17
Malaysia	42.40	15.38	42.21
Philippines	98.81	0.79	0.40
Singapore	66.67	25.04	8.30
South Korea	30.19	41.78	28.01
Taiwan	49.01	18.25	32.69
Thailand	55.78	13.56	30.66
Indonesia	88.24	5.02	6.57
All Countries	54.35	28.51	17.14
Memorandum:			
United States	28.80	57.74	13.45

Source: Bank for International Settlements

In addition to comprising a relatively small portion of the Asian bond markets, the corporate bond sector of most Asian markets in highly concentrated. Table 6 shows the share of total corporate bond issuance accounted for by the three largest issues. Concentration in Asian corporate bond markets ranges from 9.4 percent in the Philippines to 27.7 percent in Thailand. Interestingly, with the exception of Taiwan (for which no data are available), the largest corporate bond markets (as a share of total market size) are among the most concentrated. Thailand, South Korea and Malaysia all have corporate bond markets that account for more than 30 percent of their total bond markets and all have more than 20 percent concentration of corporate issuance.

***Table 6:* Concentration of Corporate Bond Issuance**

Country	Corporate Bond Concentration (Share of the 3 Largest issuance)
China	19.8
Hong Kong	10.1
India	15.2
Malaysia	23.7
Philippines	9.4
Singapore	25.3
South Korea	26.2
Thailand	27.7

Note: Data for Indonesia and Taiwan are not available. The data is as of second half of 2004.

Source: Asian Development Bank.

Although complete data for the holders of Asian debt issued by all economies is unavailable, Table 7 provides information for six of the 10 selected markets. In these markets, banks are the dominant holders of debt, comprising 57 percent of all holdings. Bank dominance is common in five of the six economies, and is most striking in Indonesia, where 96 percent of debt is held by banks. Institutional investors are important holders of debt in four of the economies for which data exists: Hong Kong (34 percent), India (19 percent), South Korea (20 percent) and Thailand (26 percent). Other financial institutions are important in Malaysia (24 percent) and Thailand (24 percent).

There are additional, largely untapped sources of individual and institutional demand (Table 8). Time and saving deposits remain very high in the Asian economies, especially Hong Kong and Taiwan. Total time and saving deposits for China is equal to GDP for a year. Mutual fund assets are large in Hong Kong ($183 billion) and South Korea ($212 billion). Indeed, these assets are close to 50 percent of the total value of the domestic bond market in South Korea and 325 percent in Hong Kong. In Singapore, Korea and Malaysia, pension funds and insurance companies are important sources of capital. Singapore's pension fund and insurance company assets are more than $83 billion (nearly 150 percent of the domestic bond market), nearly $80 billion in South Korea and about $50 billion in Malaysia.

***Table 7:* Composition of Holders of Outstanding Domestic Bonds, 2002**

Country	Banks (%)	Institutional Investors (%)	Other Financial Institutions (%)	Other (%)
Hong Kong	66	34	0	0
India	68	19	0	13
Indonesia	96	0	4	0
Malaysia	7	0	24	69
South Korea	65	20	14	1
Thailand	50	26	24	0
Memorandum:				
United States	18	23	35	24

Note: Data for China, the Philippine, Singapore and Taiwan are not available.

Source: Mihaljek, Scatigna and Villar (2002) and *Flow of Funds Accounts of the United States*, Board of Governors of the Federal Reserve System.

4.4. Secondary Bond Markets

Secondary debt markets in the Asian economies consist of an exchange-based portion and an over-the-counter portion. Bonds in China are traded on the two main stock exchanges—the Shanghai Stock Exchange and the Shenzhen Stock Exchange. However, two thirds of trading in the government bond market—which comprises two-thirds of the total bond market—is over-the-counter. Hong Kong bonds are traded on the Stock Exchange of Hong Kong but, as in China, most trading is not exchange based. The Hong Kong Monetary Authority (HKMA) has established a market-making system in Exchange Fund Bills and Notes (EFBNs)—obligations issued by the HKMA in an effort to develop the bond market through the supply of highly rated Hong Kong dollar denominated debt (Dalla, 2003). Indian bonds are traded on the Bombay Stock Exchange and the Wholesale Debt Market of the National Stock Exchange and are also traded over-the-counter (Patil, 2001). As in other Asian economies, India is seeking to develop bond market liquidity. Thus, in 2002, the Reserve Bank of India launched the Negotiated Dealing System, an electronic trading platform for market makers in government bonds. Indonesian bonds, including corporate bonds, are traded on the Surabaya Stock Exchange. However, as with other Asian economies, over-the-counter trading is more important. South Korean bond trading is also dominated by over-the-counter activity, with 95 percent of trades executed on the Korean Securities Dealers Association's over-the-counter market, although 90 percent of bonds are listed on the Korean Stock Exchange (Dalla, 2003).

Table 8: **Potential Holders of Domestic Bonds, 2003**

Country	Time and Savings Deposits/GDP (%)	Mutual Fund Assets (US$ Billions)	Pension Fund Assets (US$ Billions)**	Insurance Industry Premiums (US$ Billions)
China	99	n.a	n.a	46.9
Hong Kong	236	255.8	2.0	12.4
India	46	29.8	n.a	17.3
Indonesia	41	n.a.	4.0	3.1
Korea	68	121.5	43.4	59.7
Malaysia	74	n.a	46.9	5.6
Philippines	44	0.8	7.2	1.2
Singapore	98	n.a	51.5	8.9
Taiwan	129	76.2	n.a	32.4
Thailand	82	n.a	8.3	4.9
Memorandum:				
United States	27	6,669*	6,951*	1,056

Note: * Mutual fund assets for the United States include money market funds, mutual funds and closed-end funds. Pension fund assets include private pension funds, state and local government retirement funds and federal government retirement funds. **pension fund assets are 2002 figures for both private and public funds.

Source: Asian Development Bank. *Flow of Funds Accounts of the United States*, Board of Governors of the Federal Reserve System, and *World Development Indictors*, Word Bank, *Mutual Fund Fact Book*, Investment Company Institute.

Neither Malaysia nor the Philippines has an active secondary market, although bonds are listed on both the Kuala Lumpur Stock Exchange and the Philippines Stock Exchange. Singapore, like Hong Kong, has sought to stimulate growth in its domestic bond markets through the issuance of government bonds. Unlike many other Asian economies, government bonds are not listed on the main stock exchange. Instead, there is a network of 11 market-makers or primary dealers in Singapore Government Securities. The Taiwanese secondary bond market is focused on the GreTai Securities Market (GTSM), Taiwan's second largest securities exchange that is largely over-the-counter. Unlike the Taipei Stock Exchange, the GTSM allows over-the-counter trading. The Thai Bond Dealing Center was established in 1998 as that country's bond exchange and information dissemination center. However, as with most economies in Asia and indeed worldwide, the over-the-counter market is more important in terms of volume traded. A recent secondary market development is the establishment of the Bond Market Exchange, an exchange aimed at retail investors and corporate issuers.

In terms of volume traded, China has the largest domestic government bond market with an annual trading volume of $773 billion, followed closely by Hong Kong and South Korea, with a volume of $675 and $546 billion, respectively (Table 9). These three are followed by two smaller markets, Singapore and Taiwan, with annual trading values of $194 and $179 billion. Malaysia and Thailand are among the third-tier with annual trading volume of $91 and $58 billion, respectively. The smallest government bond traded value is that of India ($19 billion). Traded value for domestic corporate debt, however, is largest in Korea with an annual value of $490 billion. Taiwan's and Malaysia's annual trading value are about one tenth of that of Korea's ($52 billion and $42 billion, respectively).

***Table 9:* Domestic Bond Markets Are Illiquid, 2003**

Country	Government Bond Annual Traded Value (US$ Billions)	Corporate Bond Annual Traded Value (US$ Billions)	Annual Turnover Ratio
China	773.0	4.4	2.0
Hong Kong	674.8	n/a	44.1
India	18.7	0.8	0.4
Malaysia	91.4	51.7	2.0
Singapore	194.1	n/a	1.6
South Korea	546.8	490.4	5.4
Taiwan	178.8	42.4	2.0
Thailand	57.8	8.0	1.5

Note: Data for Indonesia and Philippines are not available.

Source: Asian Development Bank.

While trading volume is greatest in South Korea, turnover as a share of outstanding debt is highest in Hong Kong, where annual trading is 44.1 times the value outstanding (Table 9). South Korea has the next most liquid secondary market with a multiple of 5.4. China, Malaysia and Taiwan liquidity is lower at multiples of 2.0. They are followed by Singapore at 1.6 and Thailand at 1.5. India has the smallest trading in terms of government bonds, corporate bonds and annual turnover ratio.

4.5. New Developments in Asian Bond Markets

Securitization, the issuance of bonds backed by cash flows from an underlying asset, is a relatively new phenomenon in Asia. Hong Kong was the location of one of the first non-Japanese Asian securitizations when the first residential mortgage securitization was completed in 1994. In 1997, the Hong Kong Mortgage

Corporation (HKMC) was formed to purchase mortgage loans and issue securities based on their cash flows in a manner similar to Freddie Mac and Fannie Mae in the U.S. The HKMC began developing its mortgage-backed securities in 1999 and then in 2001 launched $3 billion of mortgage backed securities. The first noteworthy securitization in South Korea was the $270 million receivables securitization carried out by the Korean Export-Import Bank in 1998. Since then South Korea has passed the Mortgage Backed Securitization Law in an effort to stimulate the mortgage-backed securities market, with significant activity in the securitization of banks' nonperforming loans (Giddy, 2001).

Malaysia has a relatively well developed asset-backed securities market based, largely based on the activities of Cagamas Berhad (National Mortgage Corporation), which was established in 1986 to promote a secondary mortgage market in Malaysia. Cagamas, as it is usually known, acts much like Freddie Mac and Fannie Mae in buying mortgages and issuing bonds backed by their cash flows. At present Cagamas issues four types of mortgage-backed securities: fixed rate bonds, floating rate bonds, notes and Islamic bonds (known as Sanadat Mudharabah Cagamas). Singapore is also developing an asset-backed securities market. The first securitization in Singapore was the 1998 sale of the headquarters of the Neptune Orient Lines to a special purpose vehicle with the sale funded by the issuance of fixed-rate mortgage-backed bonds. A number of successful commercial real estate securitizations have followed this initial transaction and have comprised the majority of asset-backed issuances in Singapore. A recent and unusual divergence from this trend is the Small and Medium Enterprise loan securitization planned for 2004 under the auspices of the Singapore government.

Additional innovations have come in the area of derivatives with the development of products used to hedge bond positions. These products fall into two categories: interest rate derivatives used to hedge interest rate risk and bond derivatives used to hedge the market and credit risk associated with bond investing. Interest rate swaps—products that allow a trader to swap fixed-rate for floating-rate cash flows—are available in all of the markets for which data exist, partly no doubt, due to their over-the-counter nature. However, interest rate options—calls or puts on benchmark interest rates—are not available in either India or the Philippines and have only limited availability in Indonesia (Table 10). Bond futures and options are less commonly available in Asia. Bond futures—exchange traded products that are contracts to buy or sell a given bond at a certain future price—are not available in China, India, Indonesia, the Philippines or Taiwan. Also, bond options—calls or puts on given bonds—are not available in China, India, Indonesia, the Philippines, Singapore and Thailand.

5. Challenges and Opportunities

Broadening and deepening the Asian bond markets requires active participation from both investors and issuers. Currently, the agenda for expanding the bond markets in Asia has focused on the development of institutional investors. The growth of investors, however, is slow and is impeded by many regulations limiting asset allocation. An important and perhaps neglected part of developing this market is financial education for retail investors. Traditionally, Asian investors deposited their savings into banks, in part because most banks were either owned by or implicitly guaranteed by governments, and saving deposit rates prior to and during the Asian crisis were relatively high. In recent years this situation has been changing. A combination of relatively low interest rates and privatization of government-owned banks has increased the demand for alternative financial instruments to bank deposits. Financial education enables the public to better understand how bond markets work, including what risks are involved and how they help achieve personal financial goals. Greater retail demand for bonds would, in turn, supplement the development of institutional investors.

Table 10: **Availability of Fixed-Income Derivatives, 2003**

Country	Interest Rate Options	Interest Rate Swaps	Bond Futures	Bond Options
China	No	No	No	No
Hong Kong	Yes	Yes	Yes	Yes
India	No	Yes	No	No
Indonesia	Limited	Yes	No	No
South Korea	Yes	Yes	Yes	Yes
Malaysia	Yes	Yes	Yes	Yes
Philippines	No	Yes	No	No
Singapore	Yes	Yes	Yes	No
Taiwan	Yes	Yes	No	Yes
Thailand	Yes	Yes	Yes	No
Memorandum:				
United States	Yes	Yes	Yes	Yes

Source: Deutsche Bank and Milken Institute.

To attract retail investors and increase their financial awareness, it is necessary initially to promote high-quality issuance, including both government and corporate bonds. In addition, developing a money market, which has similar characteristics to bank deposits, could speed up learning and facilitate greater acceptability of alternative financial instruments. In fact, Haüsler, Mathieson and Roldos (2003) argue that a well-functioning money market is a critical step for developing corporate bond markets because it provides an anchor to the short end of the yield curve and is thus critical for the pricing of bonds.

Though developing broad, deep and liquid bond markets is a key step to strengthening Asian financial systems, bond markets are only one alternative source of capital. Governments must still promote safe and sound banking systems insofar as banks remain important sources of capital and still dominate the financial systems of Asian countries. Bankers should view the development of bond markets as an opportunity for new sources of businesses and not as a threat to their survival. Banks are complements to bond markets and provide the necessary infrastructure for the development of bond markets. With their networks of branches throughout Asian cities and towns, banks are in a unique position to not only help educate the public, but also to become holders, underwriters, brokers, and guarantors of bonds.

An important challenge for policy makers is to create a comprehensive financial structure, prudential regulations and supervisory practices that will not only enhance economic and financial stability, but also protect consumers and promote competition. If successful, countries can better assure that all firms of all sizes have access to capital, which is so essential for prosperity.

References

Barth, James R., Daniel E. Nolle, Hilton L. Root and Glenn Yago. 2001. "Choosing the Right Financial System for Growth," *Journal of Applied Corporate Finance*, 13(4), 116-123.

Beck, Thorsten and Ross Levine. 2004. "Stock Markets, Banks, and Growth: Panel Evidence," *Journal of Banking and Finance*, 28(3), 423-442.

Brandt, Michael and Kenneth Kavajecz. *Price Discovery in the U.S. Treasury Market: The Impact of Orderflow and Liquidity on the Yield Curve*. Wharton School working paper.

Brandt, Michael W. and Kenneth A. Kavajecz. 2004. "Price Discovery in the U.S. Treasury Market: The Impact of Order flow and Liquidity on the Yield Curve" *Journal of Finance*, 59, 2623-2654.

Dalla, Ismail. 2003. *Harmonization of Bond Market Rules and Regulations in Selected APEC Economies*, Mandaluyong City, Philippines: Asian Development Bank

Davis, E. Philip and Christos Ioannidis. 2002. "Does the Availability of Bank Borrowing and Bond Issuance Smooth Overall Corporate Financing," *Brunel University Working Paper*.

Demirgüç-Kunt, Asli and Ross Levine, editors. 2001. *Financial Structure and Economic Growth: A Cross Country Comparison of Banks, Markets, and Development*, Cambridge, MA: MIT Press.

Domowitz, Ian, Jack Glen and Ananth Madhavan. 2001 "International Evidence on Aggregate Corporate Financing Decisions," in Asli Demirgüç-Kunt and Ross Levine, editors, *Financial Structure and Economic Growth: A Cross Country Comparison of Banks, Markets, and Development*, Cambridge, MA: MIT Press, 263-295.

Eichengreen, Barry and Pipat Luengnaruemitchai. 2004. "Why Doesn't Asia Have Bigger Bond Markets?," NBER Working Papers 10576, National Bureau of Economic Research, June.

Eichengreen, Barry. 2004. "The Unintended Consequences of the Asian Bond Fund," unpublished manuscript, University of California, Berkeley, February.

Giddy, H. Ian. 2001. "Financial Institution Risk Management: The Impact of Securitization," presented at the seminar on *Risk Management in Financial Institutions*, Sogang University, Seoul, October 2001

Greenspan, Alen. (1999) "Lessons from the global crises," Speech before the World bank group and the IMF, Program of Seminars, Washington, D.C. September 27th.

Haüsler, Gerd, Donald J. Mathieson and Jorge Roldos. 2003. "Trends in Developing-Country Capital Markets around the World," in Robert Litan, Michael Pomerleano and V. Sundararajan editors, *The Future of Domestic Capital Markets in Developing Countries*, Washington D.C. Brooking Institution Press, 21-44.

Herring, Richard J., and Nathporn Chatusripitak. 2001. "The Case of the Missing Market: The Bond Market and Why it Matters for Financial Development," The Wharton School Financial Institutions Center, Working Paper 01-08, August.

International Monetary Fund (IMF). 2002. "Global Financial Stability Report. In *Emerging Local Bond Markets*. Washington, D. C.

Levine, Ross and Sara Zervos. 1998. "Stock Market, Bank, and Economic Growth," *American Economic Review*, 88(3), 537-558.

Levine, Ross. 1997. "Financial Development and Economic Growth: Views and Agenda," *Journal of Economic Literature*, 35(2), 688-726.

Mihaljek, Dubravko, Michaela Scatigna and AgustinVillar. 2002. "Recent Trends in Bond Markets," *The Development of Bond Markets in Emerging Economies*, BIS Papers No. 11. Basel, Switzerland: Bank for International Settlements, 13-41.

Milken, Michael. 2002. "The Corporate Financing Cube: Matching Capital Structure to Business Risk," *Milken Institute Review*, 4th Quarter, 78-85.

Miller, Merton. 1998. "Financial Markets and Economic Growth," *Journal of Applied Corporate Finance*, 11(3), Fall, 8-15.

Patil, R. H. 2001. "Broadbasing & Deepening the Bond Market in India," The Wharton Financial Institutions Center, Working Paper 01-32.

Phumiwasana, Triphon. 2003. *Financial Structure, Economic Growth and Stability*, Claremont Graduate University, Department of Economics, Ph.D. Dissertation.

Rajan, Raghuram G. and Luigi Zingales. 1998. "Financial Dependence and Growth," *American Economic Review*, 88(3), 559-86.

Schnasi, Garry and R. Todd Smith. 1998. *Fixed Income Markets in the United States, Europe and Japan: Some Lessons for Emerging Markets*. International Monetary Fund working paper.

World Bank. 2001. *Finance for Growth: Policy Choices in a Volatile World*, A World Bank Policy Research Report, Oxford University Press.

Chapter 2

Developing Asian Bond Markets Using Securitization and Credit Guarantees

Jae-Ha Park[1] and Gyutaeg Oh[2]

[1]*Korea Institute of Finance;* [2]*Korea Fixed Income Research Institute*

1. Introduction

The development of bond markets is one of the most important policy goals in the region in that they would be instrumental towards preventing another financial crisis by redressing the double mismatch problem, i.e. maturity mismatch and currency mismatch problems. In retrospect, it is now widely accepted that one of the essential causes of the financial crises in 1997-98 was heavy dependence on inefficient banking systems to finance domestic investment. Asia's distinctly bank-dominated financial systems had actually proved effective in promoting rapid economic growth in that they could efficiently mobilize and allocate financial resources to the corporate sector. Unfortunately, these systems caused the corporate sector to become over-reliant on short-term bank borrowing, making it very vulnerable to external shock.

Maturity mismatch is generally inherent in the banking sector as commercial banks accept short-term deposits and lend the proceeds out long-term. Nevertheless, the massive volume of unhedged short-term capital inflows before the financial crisis, largely in the form of inter-bank loans, served to shorten the maturities of bank liabilities, thereby exacerbating the maturity mismatch. The currency mismatch also became more serious as massive capital inflows of foreign currency were converted into domestic currency in order to finance the boom in domestic investment in the 1990s. This double mismatch of maturities and currency led to a rapid deterioration in the balance sheets of domestic financial institutions, eventually leading to collapse.

In addition, interest in the development of bond markets has been on the rise throughout Asia after the crisis, as the need to recycle the vast amounts of accumulated capital directly back into the region has increased. Since the financial crisis, Asian countries have accumulated substantial foreign exchange reserves, reflecting a surge in exports and high personal savings. However, the bulk of these reserves have been invested in the developed markets, including the U.S. and Europe, and only later recycled back to the region in the form of risky assets, such as equities and foreign direct investment. The two most significant structural impediments to funneling Asian savings back into the region are the currency risks inherent in cross-border flows of capital and the quality gap between the low credit ratings of issuers and the minimum credit requirements of investors.

Recognizing the need to develop sound and liquid bond markets to prevent another capital account crisis, countries in the region have stepped up their efforts to develop and strengthen bond markets. However, no significant progress has been made; the bond markets are not yet able to intermediate between the high savings and huge investment demands of Asian countries.

Many useful tasks and initiatives have already been proposed to develop the bond markets in the region. Among others, in November 2002, Korea proposed the Initiative on Capital Market Development at the third Meeting of the ASEAN+3 Study Group. In response to this proposal, member countries agreed to undertake joint research. One interesting feature of the proposals is the active use of securitization and credit guarantees. This reflects the fact that one of the most serious hindrances to the development of the bond markets in the region is the credit quality gap between the generally low credit ratings of issuers and the minimum credit quality requirements of investors.

It has strongly been suggested by numerous experts that the credit quality gap could be narrowed very effectively by means of securitization coupled with credit guarantees. Securitization enables borrowers to issue asset-backed securities with a higher credit rating than would apply otherwise. When combined with credit enhancement and guarantee arrangements, these securities can become investment grade quality according to the international credit rating agencies, thereby becoming acceptable to investment managers. Securitization would also enable smaller, unknown corporate entities to access the bond markets and to reduce their reliance on short-term commercial bank finance. Utilizing Korea's own experience in bond market development, we propose an initiative to promote the development of Asian bond markets using securitization and credit guarantee, and to establish a regional credit guarantee facility.

2. The Need and Rationale for the Development of Asian Bond Markets

2.1. Causes of the Asian Financial Crisis: The Double Mismatch Problem

There has been intensive and extensive discussion on the nature and causes of the 1997 Asian financial crisis. Two models have been primarily employed to explain it: the first generation model and the second generation model.[1] The first generation model attributes the main cause of the speculative attacks to the inconsistency between maintaining a fixed exchange rate regime and improving internal economic fundamentals. This model essentially explains the current account problem. The second generation model suggests that the crisis was self-fulfilling. According to this model, the economy can collapse due to a sudden shift in market expectations and investor confidence.

In the aftermath of the Asian crisis, the widely accepted view was that it was an example envisioned in the second-generation model. However, it was later pointed out that neither of the two models sufficiently analyzed the Asian financial crisis. Yoshitomi and Ohno (1999), for example, pointed to the problems of the financial sector with its balance sheet effects, the sharp reversal in capital flows, sharp decline in absorption, and the free fall of the exchange rate in the framework of two crises. Kaminsky and Reinhart (1999) assert that the first and second generation models do not sufficiently address the correlation of the banking and currency problems despite the fact that many countries experienced both difficulties in the past.

Of the many factors cited as causes of the economic breakdown, some were common to most of the crisis-hit countries, whereas others were country-specific. However, the most notable characteristic of the Asian economic meltdown was the fact that it was a capital account crisis, distinct from a conventional current account crisis that is often caused by weak macroeconomic fundamentals. What preceded the financial crisis was a massive volume of short-term capital inflows attracted by large interest rate differentials between local currency and dollar rates under good macroeconomic performances. This was followed by the sudden reversal of these flows triggered by a cyclical domestic downturn and change in market perceptions. Such large swings in capital accounts amounting to 15-20 per cent of GDP among the crisis-hit economies in the space of less than one year led to an international liquidity crisis and a domestic banking crisis as the balance sheets of financial institutions and corporations rapidly deteriorated. This, in turn, was caused by the serious maturity and currency mismatches, the so-called double mismatch problem, more or less inherent in the banking sector, which constitutes the backbone of the financial markets of emerging economies.

Many experts claimed that the heavy-dependence on poorly functioning banking systems was the root cause of the economic crisis and that the affected countries should develop deep and liquid capital markets, especially bond markets, to prevent the recurrence of another economic failure in the region. In addition, a well-developed and sound bond market can efficiently mobilize and allocate savings, manage risks, improve corporate behavior, and facilitate government policies, all of which is conducive to sustained economic growth and maintaining financial soundness in an increasingly open and risky economic environment.

2.2. The Need for the Development of Bond Markets in Asia

In recent years, there has actually been considerable progress in the development of the bond markets. At the end of 2003, the volume of domestic bonds outstanding in eight Asian economies[1] was equivalent to 47 percent of their combined GDP, more than double the 20 percent at the end of 1995. Over that eight-year period, the bond

---

[1] Hong Kong, Indonesia, Korea, Malaysia, Philippines, Singapore, Taiwan and Thailand.

market's share in total financing rose from 11 percent to 19 percent. Despite this impressive growth, the Asian bond markets collectively still lag behind those of the developed economies in terms of breadth and depth. At less than 50 percent of GDP, the many Asian domestic bond markets are still small relative to those of the U.S. and Japan, where the domestic bond markets are 100 percent of GDP. Furthermore, the bond markets in Asia still lack liquidity and remain largely fragmented.

The disadvantages of not having a developed bond market were brought home to us during the Asian financial crisis of 1997-1998. An efficient and mature bond market can play an important role during times when the other channels of financial intermediation—the banks and the equity markets—falter or fail. Most importantly, the development of an alternative source of funding would reduce the corporate sector's over-reliance on short-term foreign currency loans. A sound and healthy corporate sector contributes directly to macroeconomic and financial stability, and improved financial intermediation brings such microeconomic benefits as efficiency gains and diversification of tools for both borrowers and savers. The absence of a developed bond market in the region was one of the main factors behind the extreme volatility that precipitated the Asian financial crisis. The crisis itself spurred governments in the region to focus on bond market development.

Since the crisis, other important reasons for a stronger, deeper, and broader debt market in the region have also come to the fore. The huge current account surpluses of economies in the region have led to very sizeable accumulations of reserves by the public sector. The total foreign exchange reserves of the major Asian economies outside of Japan[2] nearly doubled between 2000 and 2003, from about $ 700 billion in 2000 to over $ 1,200 billion in 2003. This has increased the demand for investment in financial instruments, especially bonds. However, the absence of deep bond markets in the emerging Asian economies means that a vast amount of this higher demand has been satisfied by investments in bonds denominated in major foreign currencies.

According to the statistics published by the U.S. Treasury, Asian investors are significant buyers of U.S. securities. Table 4 shows that the net purchase of U.S. Treasuries and agency paper by Asian economies amounted to $ 270 billion in 2003, more than 60 percent of the world total. Indeed the net foreign portfolio investment by the emerging Asian economies has increased sharply over the past five years—from $ 50 billion in 1998 to $ 225 billion in 2003. Emerging Asia as a whole is now a large net exporter of portfolio capital.

However, a closer examination of the patterns of portfolio investment flows into and out of the Asian region reveals an inherent instability. The fund flows of Asia have been characterized by large bond investment fund outflows to the industrialized economies due to the higher credit ratings and the greater depth of the G3 bond markets. Some of these funds are recycled back into the region in institutional form, managed by foreign financial intermediaries. They are mostly in equities and their derivatives, a more volatile form than in bank lending or debt financing. While the flows of foreign funds into Asia certainly help diversify the financial intermediation

---

[2] China, Hong Kong, India, Indonesia, Korea, Malaysia, the Philippines, Singapore, Taiwan, Thailand.

Table 1. **Volume of Different Types of Financing in Asian Economies and Selected Countries in 2003**

Country or Economy	GDP	Bank Loans		Stock Market Capitalization		Bond Market		Of which: Public Sector Bonds		Of which: Private Sector Bonds	
	$ bn	$ bn	%	$ bn	%	$ bn	%	$ bn	%	$ bn	%
Hong Kong	159.1	239.3	150.4	714.6	449.3	71.8	45.2	22.8	31.7	49.1	68.3
Indonesia	212.2	45.7	21.5	54.7	25.8	6.2	2.9	4.6	74.0	1.6	26.0
Korea	605.1	571.3	94.4	298.2	49.3	380.0	62.8	201.8	53.1	178.2	46.9
Malaysia	103.2	104.6	101.4	168.4	163.2	78.9	76.5	36.4	46.1	42.5	53.9
Philippines	78.5	23.5	29.9	23.2	29.5	2.3	3.0	1.5	64.6	0.8	35.4
Singapore	93.6	101.6	103.5	148.5	158.6	62.6	66.9	39.3	62.7	23.4	37.3
Taiwan	290.0	374.5	129.2	379.0	130.7	126.8	43.7	76.2	60.1	50.6	39.9
Thailand	149.9	113.5	75.7	119.0	79.4	63.6	42.4	48.2	75.9	15.3	24.1
Average	211.4	196.8	93.1	238.2	112.7	99.0	46.8	53.8	54.4	45.2	45.6
United States	11,262.0	8,321.4	73.9	14,173.1	125.8	20,137.1	178.8	12,003.6	59.6	8,133.5	40.4
United Kingdom	1,965.2	2,792.0	142.1	2,425.8	123.4	1,030.9	52.5	582.6	56.5	448.3	43.5
Japan	4,650.4	4,533.2	97.5	2,953.1	63.5	5,981.2	128.6	4,988.8	83.4	992.4	16.6
Average	5,959.2	5,215.5	87.5	6,517.4	109.4	9,049.7	151.9	5,858.3	64.7	3,191.4	35.3

Sources: International Financial Statistics, International Federation of Stock Exchanges, Japan Securities Dealers Association, IFC Bond Database, Thai Bond Dealing Centre, Thomson Financial, CEIC, and various central banks.

Notes:

Bank loans are domestic credit extended to the private sector. All bank loan data, except Taiwan, are reported on line 32d in the International Financial Statistics (September 2003).

All outstanding bond data are as of end-2003, except for Japan and Singapore (end-2002), Indonesia (end-2000) and the Philippines (end-1999). Figures are local-currency denominated debt.

Bond figures for Hong Kong, Korea, Malaysia, Taiwan, the United States, the United Kingdom, and Japan are from central banks. Figures for Indonesia and the Philippines are from IFC Emerging Markets Information Centre Bond Database. Figures for Thailand are from the Thai Bond Dealing Centre. Figures for Singapore are estimates based on data from MAS and Thomson Financial.

Public sector refers to government bodies and quasi-government entities.

Private sector refers to non-public sector and includes financial institutions, corporations, and overseas institutions.

***Table 2.* Financing Structure of Asian Economies and Selected Countries in 1995 and 2003**

Country/ Economy	Bank Loans	Stock Market	Bond Market	Bank Loans	Stock Market	Bond Market
	As % of total financing					
Hong Kong	39.6	55.6	4.8	23.3	69.7	7.0
Indonesia	60.2	38.0	1.7	42.9	51.3	5.8
Korea	44.6	29.4	26.1	45.7	23.9	30.4
Malaysia	22.4	65.3	12.4	29.7	47.9	22.4
Philippines	30.1	64.9	4.9	47.9	47.3	4.7
Singapore	31.5	60.0	8.4	32.5	47.5	20.0
Taiwan	62.9	31.2	5.9	42.5	43.1	14.4
Thailand	50.8	43.9	5.3	38.3	40.2	21.5
Total	45.0	44.5	10.6	36.8	44.6	18.5
United States	21.1	30.4	48.5	19.5	33.2	47.2
United Kingdom	42.5	44.5	13.1	44.7	38.8	16.5
Japan	43.4	27.8	28.8	33.7	21.9	44.4
Total	30.2	30.7	39.1	25.1	31.4	43.5

Sources: Same as Tables 1

Notes:

Total financing is defined as total outstanding amount of bank loans, stocks and bonds.

Bank loans are domestic credit extended to the private sector. All bank loan data, except Taiwan, are reported in line 32d in the International Financial Statistics.

For 2003, all outstanding bond data are as of end-2003, except for Japan and Singapore (end-2002), Indonesia (end-2000) and the Philippines (end-1999). For 1995, all outstanding bond data are as of end-1995, except for the United Kingdom (end-March 1995). Figures are local-currency denominated debt.

Bond figures for Hong Kong, Korea, Malaysia, Taiwan, the United States, the United Kingdom and Japan are from central banks. Figures for Indonesia and the Philippines are from IFC Emerging Markets Information Centre Bond Database. Figures for Thailand are from Thai Bond Dealing Centre. Figures for Singapore are estimates based on data from MAS and Thomson Financial.

Percentage shares may not add up to 100% due to rounding.

***Table 3.* Net Purchases of U.S. Bonds and Notes by Asian Economies from U.S. Residents**

	Treasuries (A)		Agencies (B)		Sub-Total (A + B)		Corporates (C)		All Bonds (A + B + C)	
USD billions	**2002**	**2003**	**2002**	**2003**	**2002**	**2003**	**2002**	**2003**	**2002**	**2003**
China	24.1	30.5	29.3	30.0	53.4	60.5	6.0	4.6	59.4	65.1
Hong Kong	-9.1	6.0	12.6	12.0	3.5	18.0	3.7	4.3	7.2	22.3
Indonesia	0.8	0.6	0.5	0.5	1.3	1.1	0.1	0.0	1.4	1.1
Japan	30.5	148.3	37.6	24.4	68.1	172.6	10.9	12.5	79.0	185.1
Korea	12.9	5.2	0.7	8.5	13.6	13.7	1.5	0.8	15.1	14.5
Malaysia	0.9	-0.3	1.3	-1.2	2.2	-1.5	0.1	0.0	2.3	-1.5
Philippines	0.2	0.5	0.3	0.0	0.5	0.5	0.1	0.1	0.6	0.6
Singapore	-2.6	-8.3	2.2	0.7	-0.4	-7.6	1.3	3.3	0.9	-4.3
Thailand	-1.9	-6.0	0.1	0.2	-1.8	-5.8	0.2	0.4	-1.6	-5.4
Taiwan	-0.6	9.0	10.8	9.5	10.2	18.5	1.4	1.6	11.6	20.1
Total:	55.2	185.5	95.4	84.6	150.6	270	25.3	27.6	175.9	297.6
Memo items:										
% of World Total	66.3	68.1	49.8	51.7	54.8	61.9	13.9	10.1	38.5	42.0
Total World	83.2	272.4	191.6	163.5	274.8	435.9	182.3	272.3	457.1	708.2

Source: US Treasury

channels, these flows are more susceptible to changes in market sentiment. Also, the foreign financial intermediaries are usually large international financial institutions with considerable market power and influence, in terms of the volumes they can mobilize, relative to the size of the domestic financial markets of the emerging economies. In a situation when the market is under duress, they can "push" prices in a particular direction. The implications for the emerging markets are greater market volatility, greater tendency for overshooting, and consequently, greater challenges in maintaining monetary and financial stability.

2.3. Factors Hindering Recycling of Asian Capital through Bond Markets

Before we can discuss specific measures for circulating Asian capital directly into the region, we must first ask why the bond markets have remained underdeveloped in Asia. We may cite factors on both the demand side and supply side, and also problems with the infrastructures in East Asia.

First, one of the most important factors hindering bond market development in the region is the limited supply of quality bonds. Most bond-issuing firms in East Asia have poor credit ratings, and there is only a limited number of large, reputable firms. As is well known, the credit ratings of many East Asian economies have been below investment grade, which on the whole is discouraging to international investors. Japan's overseas capital investment is mostly concentrated in bonds. Because of the low credit ratings of major East Asian economies, Japan's options for portfolio investment in East Asia are necessarily limited. With East Asia's underdeveloped bond markets and low liquidity, it is difficult to expect foreign investment in East Asian bonds. This is, not surprisingly, discouraging capital movements in the region.

One of the reasons for the low credit ratings is the high political risk of East Asian countries such as Indonesia. This makes the corporate bonds of companies located in such countries risky assets. Political risk suggests risk of returns on investment brought on by sovereign acts. For example, there is no limit on the repatriation of investment proceeds by foreign investors, but a change in government, war, shortage of foreign exchange, and embargo are possibilities that can pose limits in the future.

Second, in most of the East Asian economies, the demand base for bonds is limited. Most East Asian institutional investors are small-sized and underdeveloped, and they are not diversified, reflecting low per capita incomes and low levels of asset accumulation. Pension, mutual fund, and insurance companies' assets constitute a small portion of the overall financial market in Asian countries. Although the number of institutional investors in emerging economies, such as Korea and Thailand, is increasing, most East Asian countries, particularly China, are still far from financial institutionalization. There are several reasons for this. First, financial intermediation in most East Asian economies is handled almost entirely by banks. The extensive branch networks of banks is tapping the high domestic savings and hindering the development of institutional investors. Second, the corporate governance structures in East Asia are not conducive to the development of institutional investors. With the family-controlled conglomerates dominating corporate governance, corporations generally seek to increase capital by retaining profits or taking out bank loans rather than go to the capital market. Third, diversification of assets under management by institutional investors is precluded by the absence of a long-term capital market and lack of long-term investment products. Fourth, government regulation or restrictions on pension funds or investment criteria of insurance companies are hampering the development of the institutional investor base.

Third, many economies are controlling and regulating capital flows in diverse ways. For the most part, governments cannot completely restrain the entire flow of cross-border capital by means of capital controls, but controls can raise the cost of capital flows to such a degree that specific types of capital flows are suppressed. Of the numerous types of controls that may be employed, it is not unusual for a government to impose restrictions on the entry of foreign financial institutions into the domestic financial market or to cap foreign equity ownership in domestic financial institutions. These restrictions can reduce the level of competition in the domestic financial market and guarantee profits to domestic financial institutions.

Although such restrictions have been eliminated in advanced economies, many East Asian economies still impose limits on foreign financial institutions. Capital flows in East Asia before the 1990s were mainly only financial financing and bank loans, largely because of capital controls and regulation.

Japan, Korea, Hong Kong and Singapore do not impose restrictions on capital flows, whereas China, Malaysia, Indonesia, the Philippines and Thailand still do in many ways. There are some notable features of the capital flow controls that these economies impose. First, there are more restrictions on capital outflows than on capital inflows. This is a reflection of the concerns on the part of some countries in light of their experience during the 1997-98 East Asian currency crisis. Second, some economies impose heavier controls on foreign investments in bonds than on stocks. In China, foreign investment in stocks is allowed only in B-type stocks, while foreign investment in bonds is prohibited. In Korea, the restrictions on foreign investment in the stock market are less severe than in the bond market.

In addition to capital controls, many economies in East Asia impose other kinds of regulations that effectively hinder the development of the bond markets. For example, some economies regulate interest rates on government and corporate bonds and require institutional investors to hold large volumes of bonds for prudential reasons. They may also impose stamp duties or taxes on bond transactions, or require time consuming and complicated processes for bond issuance.

Finally, many economies in East Asia have inadequate infrastructures and expertise for information gathering, credit rating, clearing and settlements, trading, accounting, auditing, disclosure, etc. For this reason, investors cannot readily obtain information and manage the risks of bonds and market conditions, thereby impeding the development of the bond markets. Perhaps not surprisingly, the risk-averse behavior of East Asian investors, a result of the 1997-98 Asian crisis, is also discouraging capital movements within the East Asian region.

3. Efforts to Develop Asian Bond Markets

3.2. APEC: Development of Securitization and Credit Guarantee Markets

The Initiative on Development of Securitization and Credit Guarantee Markets, co-chaired by Hong Kong, Korea, and Thailand was endorsed at the 9th APEC Finance Ministers' Meeting in Los Cabos in September 2002. The Initiative aims to promote understanding and awareness of the importance securitization and credit guarantees to bond market development in the region, and to assist APEC economies to identify and take concrete steps to remove impediments to the development of securitization and credit guarantees to bond markets.

This action-oriented initiative comprises two core parts. The first part is policy dialogues involving both public and private sectors to promote the understanding of and exchange views on securitization and credit guarantee markets. The second part of the Initiative involves the provision of expert advice through expert panel visits, to the APEC economies interested and committed to develop their domestic securitization and credit guarantees to bond markets.

Four member economies including China, Thailand, Mexico and the Philippines have volunteered to receive expert advice. Seven economies, including China, Japan, Australia, the U.S.A., Thailand, Korea and Hong Kong have provided experts. The World Bank has also provided experts. Panels of experts for the interested economies were formed and have already visited twice. After the first and second visits to Thailand, China and Mexico, the panels drafted and delivered action plans and policy recommendations to remove impediments to the development of securitization and credit guarantee markets in each economy. The inter-departmental taskforce of those countries reviewed the plans and recommendations and discussed on them at the second panel visits. In addition, the first and second high-level policy dialogues were held in Seoul in April 2003, and in Hong Kong in March 2004, respectively.

3.2. ASEAN+3: Asian Bond Market Initiative (ABMI)

Although the Asean+3 Asian Bond Markets Initiative (ABMI) was officially endorsed at the ASEAN+3 Finance Ministers Meeting in Manila, Philippines on August 7, 2003, a couple of informal meetings and seminars had already been held since early 2003. On February 28, 2003, an informal session on "Fostering Bond Markets in Asia" was held by AFDM+3 in Tokyo, Japan. Various proposals were presented by the member countries to contribute to the development of the bond markets in the region. The delegates agreed that the proposals and ideas need to be studied further and in-depth to achieve tangible results as soon as possible. Incorporating diverse views, suggestions, and proposals of the delegates, six working groups of volunteers were established to conduct detailed studies on various aspects of bond market development. The six working groups and chairing countries are: Creating New Securitized Debt Instruments (Thailand), Credit Guarantee and Investment Mechanisms (Korea and China), Foreign Exchange Transactions and Settlement Issues (Malaysia), Issuance of Bonds Denominated in Local Currencies by MDBs, Foreign Government Agencies and Asian Multinational Corporations (China), Rating Systems and Information Dissemination (Singapore and Japan), and Technical Assistance Coordination (Indonesia, Malaysia and the Philippines).

The working groups analyze two areas: (i) facilitating market access through a wide variety of issues and (ii) improving the market infrastructure to foster the bond markets in Asia. The issues related to market access include: (i) sovereign bond issuance by Asian governments to establish benchmarks, (ii) bond issuance by Asian governments' financial institutions (governments) to finance domestic private enterprises, (iii) creation of asset-backed securities markets, including collateralized debt obligations (CDOs), (iv) bond issuance in the region by multilateral financial institutions and government agencies, (v) bond issuance for funding foreign direct investment in Asian countries, and (vi) issuance of bonds in a wider range of currencies and introduction of currency-basket bonds. The issues concerning the creation of market infrastructure to foster bond markets in Asia are: (i) provision of credit guarantees through the active use of existing guarantors, and the possible establishment of the Asian Regional Guarantee Facility, (ii) strengthening of the rating system by enhancing the role of domestic rating agencies, as well as considering the possible establishment the Asian Credit Rating Board, (iii) establishment of a mechanism for disseminating information on issuers and credit rating agencies, (iv) facilitating foreign exchange transactions and addressing settlement issues on cross-border transactions, (v) enhancing capacity building by conducting market research and technical assistance programs to promote policy dialogue and human resources development among member countries, and (vi) examining components of the legal and institutional infrastructure, such as company/corporate laws, securities transaction laws, and tax laws.

***Table 4.* Six Working Groups of Volunteers for the ABMI**

Working Group	Chair Country
1. Creating new securitized debt instruments	Thailand
2. Credit guarantee and investment mechanisms	Korea, PRC
3. Foreign exchange transactions and settlement issues	Malaysia
4. Issuance of bonds denominated in local currencies by multilateral development banks (MDBs), foreign government agencies, and Asian multinational corporations	PRC
5. Local and regional rating agencies; dissemination of information on Asian bond markets	Singapore and Japan
6. Technical Assistance Coordination	Indonesia, the Philippines and Malaysia

Since the creation of the six working groups, many seminars and symposiums have been organized by each working group to facilitate the exchange of views among academics, think tanks, and the private sector. In addition, ASEAN+3 officials are having regular dialogues and discussions among themselves. In the course of the activities of the six working groups, however, government officials of the ASEAN+3 countries realized that there were difficulties in efficient coordination. Therefore, at the informal ASEAN+3 Finance and Central Bank Deputies (AFDM+3) meeting in November 2003 in Seoul, the ASEAN+3 countries agreed to establish a Focal Group (FG) to coordinate the work of the six working groups. The main role of the FG is to monitor the progress of the six AMBI working groups and to coordinate their future action plans, including, (i) drafting of a summary progress report of the ABMI to be submitted to the ASEAN+3 Finance Ministers' or Deputies' meeting, (ii) providing a progress update for each working group, (iii) coordinating meeting schedules of the six working groups, and (iv) sharing future plans of the working groups. Focal Group meetings will be held twice a year, prior to the AFDM+3 meetings.

After almost two years since inauguration of ABMI in December 2002, many concrete achievements have been realized such as (i) issuance of Ringgit denominated bonds by ADB in Malaysia and permission given to multilateral development banks to issue local currency denominated bonds in Thailand, (ii) creation of a new scheme of cross-country primary CBOs by Korea and Japan, (iii) provision of credit guarantee by JBIC and NEXI for bond issued by Asian multilateral companies, and (iv) launch of the Asian Bonds Online Website.

3.3. EMEAP: ABF 1 and ABF 2

The ABF is the first fund of its kind in the region. The first phase of the initiative, the ABF (ABF1), was launched in June 2003 and is fully invested in US dollar-denominated bonds in the EMEAP economies. Since then, EMEAP has been working on the second phase of the project—broadening the ABF to cover bonds denominated in local currency, or ABF2. ABF 2 was launched in December 2004. Both phases of the initiative are aimed at promoting the development of the bond market by improving the domestic and regional bond market infrastructures.

3.3.1. ABF 1: The Critical First Step

The establishment of ABF1 was announced in June 2003. All eleven EMEAP central banks invested in ABF1 at its launch, which had a capitalization of about $ 1 billion. The fund is now fully invested in US dollar-denominated bonds issued by sovereign and quasi-sovereign issuers in eight EMEAP economies (China, Hong Kong, Indonesia, Korea, the Philippines, Malaysia, Singapore and Thailand). The developmental benefit of ABF1 is more than the first-round demand effect of $ 1 billion invested by the central banks. Indeed the seed money invested by EMEAP central banks serves to attract additional money from the private sector, thereby deepening and broadening the demand in the markets. The promotional effect of ABF1 would generate second-round investor and issuer interest in the Asian bond markets, broadening the investor base and increasing market liquidity over time.

Furthermore, the ABF1 initiative is a milestone in regional central bank cooperation. As noted, ABF1 is the first of its kind in Asia, and its success is as symbolic as it is material. The successful launching of ABF1 not only sent a strong message to the financial markets that the regional authorities are committed to stepping up their cooperative efforts in promoting bond market development, it also paved the way for the development of ABF2. The remarkable one-year timeframe from the initial discussions to the actual commitment of funds and the subsequent launching of ABF1 testifies to the rapport and sense of ownership among EMEAP members, which will prove valuable towards the development of ABF2. ABF2 is going to involve many more complex and technical issues than ABF1, and the precedent of ABF1 should be very helpful in efforts to garner political support and commitment in the challenges to the development of ABF2.

3.3.2. ABF 2: The Bold New Second Phase

Building on the momentum of developing ABF1, EMEAP has proceeded to study the feasibility and design of ABF2. Owing to the complexity of the project and the likelihood of opening up the funds for private sector investment in the future, the EMEAP Group has appointed financial advisers from the private sector to advise on the design and structure as well as the construction of benchmark indices for ABF2.

In April 2004, the EMEAP Group issued a press release setting out the basic design and latest thinking behind ABF2. It was proposed that ABF2 would consist of two components: a Pan-Asian Bond Index Fund (PAIF) and a Fund of Bond Funds (FoBF) (Figure 2). Finally in December 2004, it was officially announced that the

ABF 2, which have an initial fund size of US$ 2 billion, will invest in domestic currency bonds issued by sovereign and quasi-sovereign issuers in all EMEAP economies except Australia, Japan and New Zealand. All the 11 EMEAP members will invest in ABF 2.

The PAIF is a single bond index fund investing in local-currency denominated bonds in EMEAP economies. It will act as a convenient and cost effective investment fund and new asset class for regional and international investors who wish to have a well-diversified exposure to bond markets in Asia.

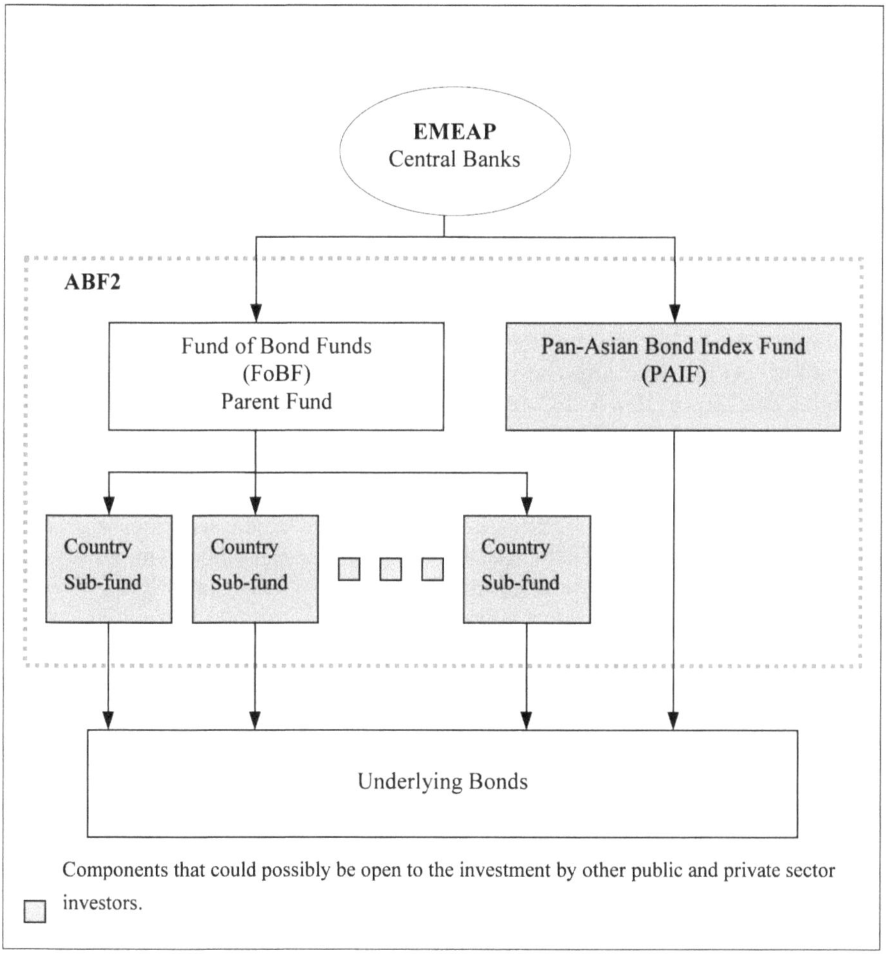

Figure 1. ABF 2 Framework

The FoBF is a two-tier structure with a parent fund investing in a number of country sub-funds comprising local currency denominated bonds issued in the respective EMEAP economies. While the parent fund is confined to EMEAP investment, the country sub-funds are intended to provide local investors with low-cost and index-driven investment vehicles and at the same time give regional and international investors the flexibility to invest in the Asian bond markets of their choice.

The ABF2 funds are intended to be passively managed against a set of transparent and pre-determined benchmark indices, covering local-currency bonds issued by sovereign and quasi-sovereign issuers in EMEAP economies. ABF2 is being designed in such a way that it will facilitate investment by other public and private sector investors. In addition to attracting additional money into the bond market as in the case of ABF1, ABF2 seeks to achieve a larger and longer-lasting positive impact on regional bond market development. Several features of the design of ABF2 are conducive thereto.

4. Proposed Instruments to Develop Asian Bond Markets

4.1. Use of Securitization as an Efficient Tool to Resolve Credit Quality Gaps and Maturity Mismatch Problems

Securitization combined with credit guarantees are advocated as efficient solutions to resolve the credit quality gap, which is regarded as one of the most critical impediments hindering the development of the regional bond markets. With this recognition, APEC has also been trying to develop securitization and credit guarantee markets in the APEC region since September 2002, when the finance ministers endorsed these issues. In reality, securitization is adopted as a main tool by several proposals that have been presented for creating and developing Asian bond markets, such as Chaipravat et al (2003), Ito (2003) and Oh and Park (2003).

Securitization is a form of structured financing in which securities are issued through repackaging a series of assets that generate cash flows in a way that separates these assets from the credit profile of the company that originally owned them. Securitization can take on a broad variety of attributes depending on the structure, the underlying assets, the way underlying assets are managed and the types of asset backed securities (ABS) issued.

Potential benefits of securitization include cost efficient funding, credit risk mitigation, diversification of funding sources, tenor and currency management. In the majority of cases, the real motivation for securitization is more likely to be risk mitigation and de-leveraging of the balance sheet at the cheapest cost rather than just access to cheap funding.

Securitization is useful in resolving the maturity mismatch problem in several ways. First of all, the true sale nature of the securitization deal allows the creditworthiness of the ABS to be independent of the creditworthiness of the company that originally owned the underlying assets. The credit assessment of ABS is made solely on the basis of the cash flows created by the underlying assets. In addition, securitization schemes such as collateralized bond obligations (CBOs) and collateralized loan obligations (CLOs) can reduce the overall credit risk of the asset pool by diversifying the idiosyncratic credit risk of each borrower.

Despite the benefits from credit risk diversification, securitization by itself cannot remove the credit risk. Instead, it enables the issuers to sell the credit risk at a lower cost. It reduces the overall cost of raising funds by creating securities whose credit risk profile is tailored to the risk preference of investors. In particular, bonds with a higher credit rating than the underlying assets can be issued by using the senior/subordinate tranches. Generally, senior bonds receive higher credit ratings than the collateralized assets, and hence can be absorbed more easily by the market. In addition to senior/subordinate tranching, other credit enhancement methods such as over-collateralization, spread accounts, cash collateral accounts, credit swaps and credit guarantees can be used to enhance the creditworthiness of the asset-backed securities and make them attractive to even a greater range of investors.

There are, however, a few stumbling blocks in making use of the securitization schemes to develop Asian bond markets. First, there is a wide difference in the legal frameworks for securitization among East Asian economies, as recognized by a relatively recent World Bank report (2002). For example, while the common practice of Hong Kong, Singapore and Malaysia that acknowledges trusts already provides the institutional foundation required for securitization, civil law countries need to enact the securitization law to recognize the true sale nature of the transactions between asset originators and special purpose companies and grant pass-through status to special purpose companies. Other stumbling blocks can be found in different accounting standards and tax treatments for special purpose companies in different jurisdictions. With the exception of Japan, Korea, Hong Kong and Singapore, issuers and investors are not familiar with securitization schemes. Scarcity of records or historical performance data are also problems in securitization deals in the region.

4.2. Fostering SME Financing by Using Two-Tier Securitization: The "Oh and Park Proposal"

One example of the use of securitization to promote Asian bond markets is the two-tier securitization scheme for small and medium enterprise (SME) financing proposed by Oh and Park (2003). As is shown in Figure 2, this securitization scheme consists of two steps of the securitization process: the first step in each of the capital importing countries and the second in the capital exporting country. A two-tier process is necessary because of the differences in the financial and legal systems among the participating economies in the region.

In the first step, a local special purpose company (SPC) is set up in each of the capital importing countries to securitize SME loans or bonds. The loans and bonds to be collateralized may be denominated in the local currency in order to eliminate the currency mismatch problem. In order to minimize the moral hazard problem, the junior tranche bonds will be assumed by local institutions that are in charge of selecting the firms to be included in the CLO or CBO pool. The senior tranche bonds are sold in the local bond markets and the remainder will be transferred to the second SPC established in the capital exporting country. The senior tranche bonds may be guaranteed by the local credit guarantee agency to increase their marketability.

In the second step of the securitization, the SPC established in the capital exporting country issues CBOs using the senior bonds it acquired from the SPCs located in capital importing countries as collaterals. Once again, different tranches of bonds will be issued to better satisfy the diverse preferences of investors. In order to further enhance creditworthiness and marketability, the senior tranche bonds may acquire credit guarantees.

It should be noted that cooperation among participating institutions is critical for the smooth functioning of this system. The coupon rates of both underlying assets and asset backed securities, fees for underwriting and credit guarantee, and the portion of senior tranches compared to respective junior tranches are notable examples of many areas where cooperation among participating institutions is critical. Furthermore, because this proposal allows for the adoption of securitization with proper risk sharing, moral hazard is expected to be minimal.

A slight modification of the first proposal is illustrated by Figure 3. This modified proposal is nearly the same as Figure 2. The only difference is that it calls for providing currency swaps to investors who are not willing to assume currency risk. A government agency (GA) or other proper institution in country "A" would provide the SPC with currency swaps and then hedge the currency risk using back-to-back swaps with swap dealers. This would be done through the currency swap market if it exists in the developing country, or with the help of the central bank in the developing country if there is no swap market.

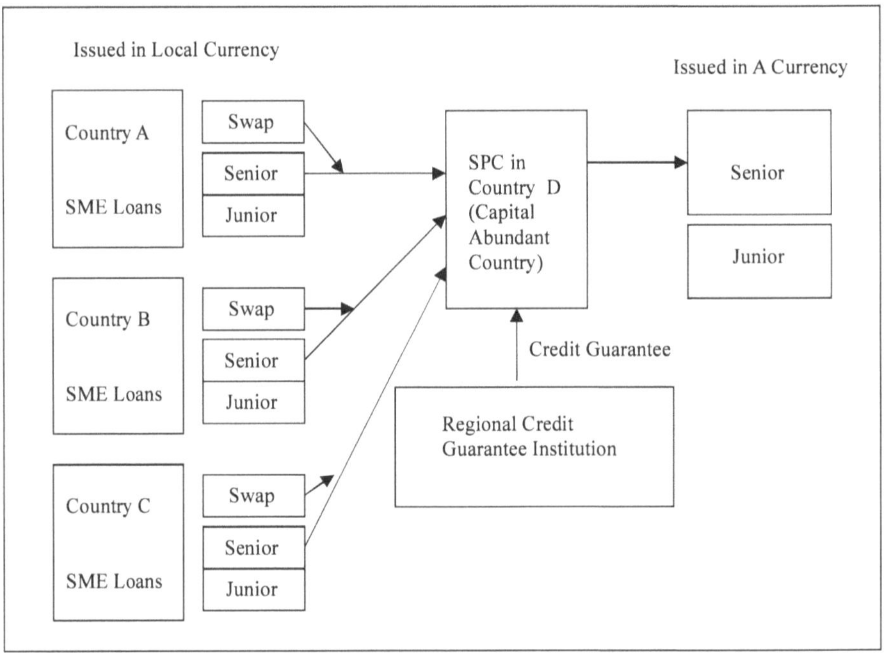

Figure 2. SME Financing without Currency Swaps

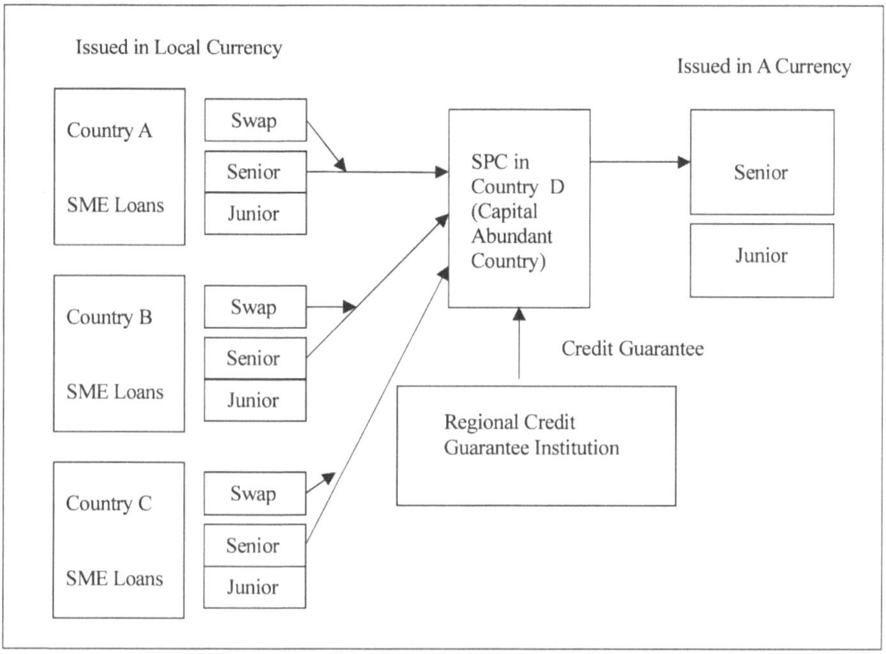

Figure 3. SME Financing with Currency Swaps

4.3. Cross-border Yen Denominated Korean CBO completed by Korea and Japan

Based on the idea presented in the above scheme, in December 2004, the Korean and Japanese governments announced completion of a proposed cross-border Yen denominated Korean collateralized bond obligation transaction ("Korean CBO") that will provide much needed financing to SMEs in Korea as shown in the figure 4. The Korean CBO was a further advancement as it was structured as an international issue for placement outside of Korea. By incorporating an innovative dual guarantee structure, the Korean CBO was able to tap into the Asian investor base and provide much needed liquidity to the Korean SME sector at an extremely competitive rate.

The issue size is 10 billion Yen and the underlying portfolio comprises a pool of 46 SME bonds. In line with other domestic Korean CBOs, the contemplated issuance was in the form of senior and subordinated bonds with the Small Business Corporation of Korea (SBC) subscribing to the subordinated bonds thereby providing the first loss protection to the capital market issuance. In order to appeal to a broad spectrum of investors in Asia, however, the Industrial Bank of Korea (IBK) extended a fully covered credit facility to support the timely payment of senior obligations under the senior bonds.

In order to pave the way for the initiatives in developing the regional bond markets, Ministry of Finance of Japan decided to amend the Ministerial Notification governing the Japan Bank for International Cooperation (JBIC) guarantee policy.

This legitimized JBIC taking a more proactive role in its guarantee operation for appropriately structured and credit enhanced debt instruments within the region. With this amendment, JBIC started its deliberation to issue the guarantee to the inaugural launch of the Korean CBO.

The joint effort by the both sides in this pioneering endeavor is a reflection of the increasing economic collaboration and harmonization between the two countries. With the provision of credit enhancement measures by quasi-sovereign institutions to appropriately structured transactions within Asia, it is hoped that the perceived risk-return imbalance in the regional markets can be curtailed and at the same time the endeavor serves as the catalyst to foster the growth of the regional bond markets.

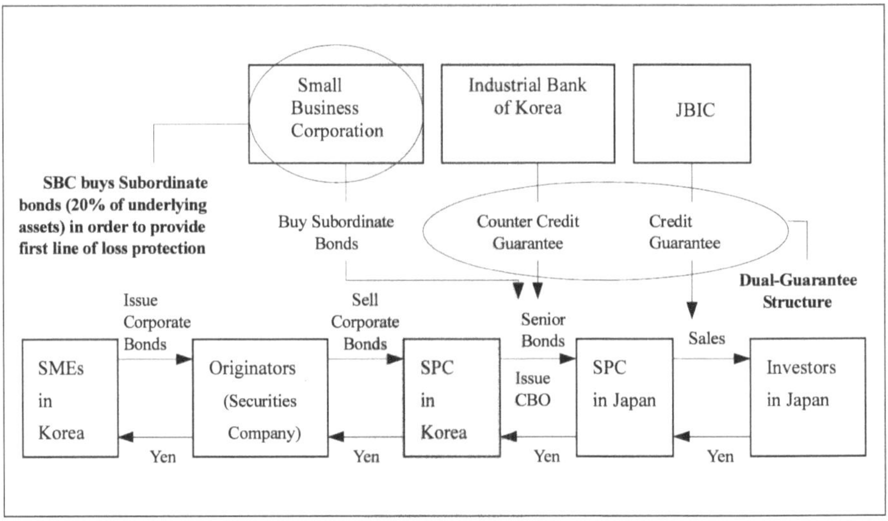

Figure 4. Yen-Denominated CBO Scheme made by Korea and Japan

4.4. Need to Establish Regional Credit Guarantee Facility

Our final proposal explores ways to establish a multilateral agency that can enhance the efficiency of securitization in the Asian bond markets by providing credit guarantees. This agency would serve multi-functional purposes, such as providing guarantees and swap arrangements, structuring securitization deals, and acting as a market maker in the region.

Notwithstanding the need to clarify the specifications of a regional credit guarantee facility, there should be sufficient paid-in capital that the facility could qualify for a high rating of AAA, or AA at the minimum. The facility would play a critical role in fostering the development of regional bond markets. Governments, government agencies of member countries and international financial institutions may voluntarily subscribe to a share of the facility. The business should cover both the developed and developing countries in the region, and the facility should be managed professionally by staff with experience in the credit guarantee business.

There is one good example of a multilateral agency that had been established for the purposes of facilitating development of the bond markets in the region. Asian Securitization & Infrastructure Assurance (Pte) Ltd. (ASIA Ltd.) was the first and only regional credit guarantee agency established in Asia (Singapore) with more than a commercial objective; to facilitate the development of fixed income markets in Asia. ASIA Ltd. was established in 1995, and its shareholders included CapMAC Asia Ltd., Apmac Investment Pte Ltd., the Asian Development Bank (ADB), Employees Provident Fund of Malaysia, American International Assurance Co. Ltd., Kookmin Bank, Netherlands Development Finance Co. and DEG Deutsche Investitions und Entwicklungsgesellschaft mbH. ASIA Ltd. began with total paid-in capital of $ 150 million. It intended to set up local agencies in the second phase of development to cater to local currency-denominated bonds, while the Singapore main office would handle non-local currency (notably US dollar) denominated bonds. However, the Asian financial crisis led to a downgrading of its claim-paying ability rating in 1998, and currently it is in a run-off mode.

In retrospect, the business mode of the company had many structural problems which made it vulnerable to outside shocks. First, at the time ASIA Ltd was building its book of business in 1996-97, its risk management practices seemed prudent based on the assumption that the country risk among Asian countries was not highly correlated. However, the reality turned out to be completely different, i.e. the crisis swept through most East Asian countries to varying degrees. Second, the company prohibited the provision of any direct guarantee policies to non-Asian economies and certain developed Asian economies (Japan and Australia). The Asian Development Bank (an equity owner of the venture) had insisted on this restriction, but it not only significantly reduced the potential business available to the company, it also exacerbated the correlation risk and concentration problem among the Asian countries. Third, in relation to the second problem, there were too few business deals for the company since it could only serve developing countries. This, coupled with the fact that the company could not closely monitor the local market conditions in each developing country, meant that the company was forced to become involved in overly risky businesses. There should have been closer collaboration with local financial institutions and guarantee agencies. Fourth, the initial capital was inadequate to absorb the great risks inherent in the provision of guarantees to developing Asian countries. Making the situation worse, additional callable capital was not injected by participating shareholders during the periods of high stress, contrary to the original agreement. Fifth, the company was exposed to big currency risks because it dealt with only US dollar-denominated bonds. Finally, the company's initial credit rating, single A, was too low to support its business.

By the end of 1999, the company's $ 934 million credit insurance portfolio consisted mostly of sovereign, asset-backed, infrastructure and financial institution debt obligations throughout Asia. In terms of geographical distribution, as of the end of 1999, 24 percent of ASIA Ltd.'s guarantees and assumed reinsurance were outstanding to South Korea, 11.4 percent to Malaysia, 10.3 percent to Indonesia, 9.1 percent to Hong Kong, and 20.9 percent to OECD countries (except South Korea). As of the end of March 2000, ASIA Ltd. had outstanding guarantees totaling $924 million.

ASIA Ltd. applied zero-loss underwriting standards for its operations with a concentration of business in the credit rating range of BBB+ to BBB-. Rating requirements for ASIA Ltd. were such that a maximum of 25 percent of a guaranteed portfolio in non-investment grade bonds still kept an A rating. After the onset of the financial crisis and particularly the credit downgrades of Indonesia and Korea, the claims paying ability of ASIA Ltd. was downgraded by Standard and Poor's from A to BB in January of 1998. At this time, the agency had to stop writing new business.

Following the downgrade of its claims paying ability, ASIA Ltd. sought to raise additional claims paying resources to restore its investment grade rating to A. The shareholders were, however, unable to agree on the terms of a recapitalization plan due to dissension over broadening the geographical coverage of ASIA Ltd. In April 1999, ASIA Ltd. contracted out its day-to-day operations, including surveillance of its credit insurance portfolios, to an affiliate of MBIA, and it is now effectively under the management of MBIA Singapore Pte Ltd. Inclusive of the Reinsurance Treaty with ERC Frankona Ruckversicherungs Aktiengesellschaft of \$ 100 million, ASIA Ltd. now has total claims paying resources of approximately \$ 250 million.

With the mandate to facilitate the development of fixed income markets in the less developed parts of Asia, Asia Ltd has shown in retrospective examination that its concentration of business in the non-developed parts of Asia was one of the main causes of its difficulties. Underpricing of the emerging risk in Asia, coupled with the pressure from shareholders to solicit large volumes of business to boost return on capital (RoC), were the other reasons that led to underestimation of the risks the company had taken on before the financial crisis. Although the downgrade of its own claim paying ability in the beginning of 1998 has since prevented Asia Ltd. from undertaking new business, some consider the fact that the company has only recently recorded one claim payment (\$ 0.5 million out of \$ 2.5 billion gross par outstanding of bonds guaranteed initially) as proof that the model was in fact a success. Some analysts believe that the company could still serve a useful purpose in Asia if it had survived the financial crisis by capital enhancement.

In light of the experiences of ASIA Ltd., our proposal for credit guarantee facilities is to establish them initially as "public" but "commercially viable" entities. First, as pointed out earlier, securitization permits the issuance of senior bonds with credit ratings acceptable to investors by using the senior/subordinate tranches. However, the success of securitization depends on how subordinate bonds are disposed. The volume or price of subordinate bonds has the most important effect on the volume and cost of funds created through securitization. East Asian economies have an average credit rating of BBB. Because a substantial portion of East Asia's overseas assets are held as foreign exchange reserves, senior bonds with ratings of AAA are necessary to support regional savings being invested in the region. Clearly, an effective means of narrowing the credit quality gap must be found.

Credit guarantees are beneficial to issuers in that they offer an alternative form of access to funds at higher investment grades. Credit guarantees and their providers provide structuring expertise, along with ease and certainty of execution and confidentiality during periods of stress. Due to reduced borrowing costs and increased marketability that they would bring, the investor base could be expanded. Credit guarantees also offer price protection, increase secondary market liquidity through disciplined risk management, and ensure rigorous surveillance and remedial management. Credit guarantees eliminate credit losses, downgrade risks and "headline" risk while enhancing secondary market liquidity. We recommend that the regional credit guarantee facility target its credit rating in the range of AA to AAA. We also recommend that the credit guarantee facilities have \$ 500 million to \$ 5 billion in paid-in-capital, a part of which could be in local currencies, with a leverage ratio range of 20:1 ~ 40:1. The facilities would be established both in the developed and developing economies of the region, offering multiple services including credit guarantees, swap transactions, ABS arrangement, market making, etc. The facilities would be professionally managed by experienced staff, alongside the institution of proper risk management.

Our proposal for the development of a regional credit guarantee facility would involve a stronger commitment in the form of capital injections from participating countries during stress periods. Moral hazard problems should be mitigated by instituting a proper ownership structure, and each economy's exposure to such problems should be limited through structuring and reinsurance. Cross-border risks should also be limited through an emphasis on local currency business.

We believe the credit guarantors' role in the capital markets is to first make timely payments of interest and principal in an unconditional, irrevocable and immediate manner. They have the right but not the obligation to accelerate payment to the beneficiary. Guaranteed transactions carry the ratings of the financial guarantors; in effect, the guarantors "rent" their high ratings to the transactions. The guarantors also sell their strong credit and structuring, surveillance, and remediation skills.

Finally, in summary, the major considerations in setting up a credit guarantee company are: the business purpose, rating and investor acceptance, rating and investor acceptance, capital and shareholders, management and staff skills, target market and market attractiveness, product definition, regulations and licensing, and risk management.

5. Conclusion

Development of the bond markets has been one of the most important policy goals in the region since the financial crisis. This reflects a clear recognition that the Asian crisis was partly a result of the unbalanced financial structures of Asian countries, which are dominated by the banking sector. Corporate over-reliance on short-term bank borrowing for long-term investment coupled with huge unhedged short-term capital inflows led to a serious double mismatch problem, namely maturity and currency mismatches. In addition, the completely changed pattern of capital flows in the East Asian region after the crisis provided momentum to develop the Asian bond markets.

Based on this recognition, many efforts have been made to develop the Asian bond markets throughout various fora such as APEC, ASEAN+3 and EMEAP. Although these fora have endeavored towards the common goal of the development Asian bond markets, they can be differentiated in the approaches, participating economies and institutions, etc. Most notably, APEC took a country-specific approach in trying to develop domestic bond markets of selected countries focusing on securitization and credit guarantees. EMEAP is basically a demand-side approach, forming funds to invest in bonds issued by Asian entities. Finally, ASEAN+3 took a comprehensive approach including supply of quality bonds in Asia and establishment of infrastructure. In this respect, these initiatives are complementary among themselves, rather than overlapping or competitive.

In this chapter, we first examined the background and rationale for creating regional bond markets in Asian in an environment of bank-dominated financial structures, a strong need to recycle Asian savings back into industrialized markets in the region, and volatile foreign capital inflows. In addition, we presented several different, viable schemes to facilitate the recycling of the huge savings in East Asia directly back into the region. We suggest utilizing securitization and credit guarantees to narrow the credit quality gap between the low credit ratings of issuers and the minimum credit quality requirements of investors. Korea's experience proved that securitization and credit guarantees could be an effective method to narrow the credit quality gap and significantly further the development of the bond markets. In order to apply these schemes in the real financial markets, however, they need to be mapped out in greater detail and require close collaboration among economies, agencies and companies.

Establishment of a new and more fitting guarantee institution that can meet the Asian bond markets' current needs is also necessary. It is true that there are many existing guarantee institutions, including multilateral institutions and private guarantee companies, but none of these are in a position to satisfy the already high demand for guarantees in Asia, which is expected to grow over time. Considering the lessons from the previous experience of ASIA Ltd., the new institution should be heavily capitalized, and the expected return on capital should be lower. The development of a regional credit guarantee institution would also entail a stronger commitment of capital injection from participating countries during stress periods. Thus, the institution should initially be a public but commercially viable entity.

References

Bank of Japan (2002), "Japan's International Investment Position at Year-End 2001," Quarterly Bulletin.

Chen, Zhaohui, and Mohsin S. Khan (1997), "Patterns of Capital Flows to Emerging Markets: A Theoretical Perspective", IMF Working Paper WP/97/13.

Crocket, Andrew D. (2002), "Capital Flows in East Asia since the Crisis", ASEAN + 3 High Level Seminar on Management of Short-term Capital Flow and Capital Account Liberalization, Beijing China.

Eichengreen, Barry (2002), "Whither Monetary and Financial Cooperation in Asia?" paper presented at the 2002 APFA/PACAP/FMA Finance Conference.

Goldstein, Morris, Donald J. Mathieson, and Timothy Lane (1991), "Determinants and Systemic Consequences of International Capital Flows" IMF Occasional Paper.

Hill, Claire A. (1997), "Securitization: A Low Cost Sweetener for Lemons," Journal of Applied Corporate Finance, Vol. 10, pp. 64-71.

----------------- (1998), "Securitization: A Financing Strategy for Emerging Markets Firms," Journal of Applied Corporate Finance, Vol. 11, pp. 55-65.

IMF (2001), International Capital Markets: Developments, Prospects, and Key Policy Issues, World Economic and Financial Surveys.

Institutional Investor (2002), "How quickly they forget," October, pp 76-82.

Kaminsky, Graciela L. and Carmen M. Reinhart (1999), "The Twin Crises: The Causes of Banking and Balance-of Payments Problems," American Economic Review, Vol. 89, No. 3, pp473-500

Lopez-Mejia, Alejandro (1999), "Large Capital Flows: A Survey of the Causes, Consequences, and Policy Responses," IMF Working Paper WP/99/17.

Oh, Gyutaeg, and Jae-Ha Park (2003), "Fostering Asian Bond Markets using Securitization and Credit Guarantee," Korea Institute of Finance, Financial Economic Series No. 2003-04

Scobie, H. M., and G. Caliesi (2000), Reserve Management, European Economic and Financial Centre.

Yoshitomi, Masaru and Kenichi Ohno (1999), "Capital Account Crisis and Credit Contraction," ADB Institute Working Paper, No. 2

Standard and Poor's (2002), Bond Insurance Book, New York.

The World Bank (2002), Asset-Backed Securities Market in Selected East Asian Countries, mimeograph.

U.S. Department of Treasury (2002), "Report on Foreign Holdings of U.S. Long-term Securities."

Chapter 3

Contemporary Markets for Asian Debt Capital Market Instruments

Paul Lejot[1], Douglas Arner[1] and Qiao Liu[2]

[1]*Asian Institute of International Financial Law, Faculty of Law, University of Hong Kong;* [2]*Faculty of Business and Economics, University of Hong Kong*

1. Introduction

This chapter traces the effects on certain of Asia's financial institutions and market practices of economic trends and commercial customs associated with the region. Its analysis extends over two phases, the extended period of rapid expansion that spread from Japan to Korea and then to southeast Asia and China between the 1950s and 1990s, and the aftermath of the financial crisis of 1997-98, the most profound systemic shock experienced by the modern East Asian economy. These events moulded Asia's banking and capital markets, first by expansion to fuel growth in trade and output; then by making policymakers and practitioners question the need for reforms that might accord with new expectations for prosperity and financial stability.

The chapter begins by examining the recurring features of the principal East Asian economies in order to give a contextual setting to capital market development, past and future. It then considers the results of the main market-driven initiatives seen since 1990, describes the current state of Asia's domestic debt markets and the international markets for Asian risk, and sets out how market reforms might best be applied in making those markets perform effectively.

2. Market Characteristics

The Asian bond has been an 'emerging market' creation since well before 1985, when the term may first have been used.[1] At various times fêted, scorned, reformed,

---

[1] By the International Finance Corporation (IFC).

reinvented, discarded and prized, the Asian bond is a victim of inconsistency and indecision, whose tragedy has been never to know its true role. Yet there is evidence that this irregular life is changing, which may—with constructive responses from policymakers—bring benefits for the region's spectrum of financial markets and for economic stability.

Asian governments and central banks have for many years issued modest amounts of domestic debt securities for fundraising or regulatory purposes, respectively to capture individual savings or as money market tools to influence banking liquidity.[2] Tangible interest has existed for some time in building 'true' markets for the issuance and trading of debt securities in East Asia's developing and newly-industrialized economies. One cause has been East Asia's generally high savings ratios, which private sector bank originators regard as highly exploitable. From the mid-1980s, Asian financial market participants—issuers and banks—sought to replicate certain transactions and trading behavior observed in most advanced economies. Prior to the full wave of the 1997-98 Asian crisis, risk-preferring overseas investors helped underpin this effort with sporadic buying support, especially in periods of falling nominal interest rates, although Asian-domiciled investors (other than banks) failed then to contribute funds on any material or consistent scale. National policymakers and regulatory agencies responded in the mid-1990s to these initiatives with a variety of legal and administrative reforms. None has been fully successful.

The result today is a family of disparate domestic markets commonly identified as either under-utilized or deficient, and therefore weak in stabilisation qualities as a policy tool,[3] and a cross-border market for Asian risk that is largely transactional, illiquid, and limited as to true investor participation.[4] Until the 1997-98 crisis public policy failed whole-heartedly to respond to private sector initiatives; indeed, commercial banks often lobbied successfully against changes promoting debt capital market activity.[5] By 1997, funding transactions were feasible in almost all East Asian currencies but no market offered the reliability of continual dealing that characterizes modern major markets and gives confidence to new borrowers or investors.

---

[2] The Philippines and Thailand were first to issue in the 1930s (Emery, 1997); Hong Kong and Singapore only in the 1970s. Asian foreign bonds were known in western centers in the late 19th century.

[3] Bond market literature concentrates on new financial architecture more than considering a lack of willing usage by potential participants. Harwood (introduction, 2000) is a rare exception.

[4] Except for private banking sources, market convention sees commercial bank end-investment in medium-term bonds, other than for regulatory or treasury purposes, as an ephemeral lending substitute and generally indicative of sector weaknesses.

[5] As recently as 1992-93 many large Hong Kong investors refrained from buying local currency bonds due to lobbying by major commercial banks, all reluctant to lose access to cheap deposits.

The supply of bonds into domestic and cross-border markets has since risen but remains comparatively low. By contrast, Asia has devoted massing external surpluses to acquire highly-rated, mainly non-Asian assets, representing a significant post-crisis portfolio adjustment.[6] Although non-Asian investors have helped balance this flight of capital with risk-preferring direct investment, the trend now seems extreme and represents a loss of welfare justifiable only in the absence of appropriate institutions for crisis mitigation.

A contemporary Tolstoy might suggest that Asia's markets differ in their own fashion. Some are well-developed but poorly used: Hong Kong and Singapore have well-integrated systems but like the unused spare wheel, their stress performance is unknown.[7] Liquidity is shallow, with only ephemeral exceptions. The quality of information offered to participants is fractured as to yields or market risks.[8] Low-risk money market instruments are available only transiently to institutional fund managers, which decreases portfolio flexibility, deters investors and encourages contagion by denying defensive assets to those liquidating long-term investments. The markets offer no cushion against Knightian uncertainty; are poor in primary resource allocation; and only in Korea and Malaysia have recycled impaired financial assets to final investors. Bond markets are important but inessential: this encapsulates the failures of policy to achieve traction and private initiatives to become generic.

3. The Underlying Economies

3.1. Savings and growth

Alone of emerging markets groupings, the Asia-Pacific region of the late twentieth century has frequently been characterized by consistently high personal and government sector savings, recurring central government fiscal surpluses or low deficits, strong and steady growth in exports, investment and fixed capital formation, generally low external borrowing, and intermittently favorable external balances. The result has been habitually high rates of growth. Since 1997 East Asia has realized sizeable current account surpluses and remarkable levels of international reserves relative to output. There have been periodic exceptions, typically after exogenous shocks or policy corrections, and certain countries have frequently followed distinct macroeconomic policies with consequences for government and

[6] Crockett (2002); Oh, Park, Park & Yang (2003).

[7] Greenspan (2000) famously saw the US bond market as its economy's spare tyre, supplanting a stricken banking sector during crises. This article uses the appraisals of non-Japan Asia's ten largest economies in Lejot, Arner & Liu (2004).

[8] Distinct from asymmetric information that is favourably available to banks.

external financing,[9] but the region's modern financial characteristics are long-standing. More recently, East Asia's growth recovered unexpectedly soon after the 1997-98 crisis, though not before considerable permanent losses in national income, especially in Southeast Asia and Korea.[10] In examining the region's flows of capital as a basis for financial market policy proposals, it is important to distinguish between observations made before and since the crisis. Despite a consensus among market users and most policymakers over the need for structural financial reform it may be wise not to build on temporary foundations.

The region's more developed economies display considerable differences in per capita national income: a range nearly matched by variations in financial market sophistication. This is a group of nations at varying stages of a regional shift from command or centrally-directed economies to forms of managed capitalism,[11] facilitated by a generation of exceptionally high rates of economic growth.[12] The secret of the region's rapid growth may have been in productivity gains,[13] the mobilisation of increasingly voluminous factors of production,[14] or some multifarious combination, but aspects of the contemporary performance of the review economies are unparalleled, and since the mid-1980s regarded as common to all. Thus although the markets and offshore borrowers of East Asia have been classed 'emerging' since the term was first spoken, there are historically more macroeconomic dissimilarities than shared features between East Asia and emerging Eastern Europe, Latin America or the former Soviet republics. Asia's 'difference' can be distilled to a single truth that its core currency bonds (and occasionally its domestic issues) have habitually been the costliest of all emerging sectors for the investor to acquire, that is, with relatively low prevailing yields or margins. Asia's reliance on bank credit creation and its modest debt market activity have roots not only in the region's relative stage of development,[15] but also in the cultural pattern of flows of funds within and between its constituent economies. Similar characteristics were observed of Japan in its post-1940s phase of export-led growth.[16] These patterns will inform all future market development, both in terms of its character and success.

---

[9] Malaysia's central government has traditionally been active in direct spending on infrastructural investment; while the Philippines has a comparatively weak national tax base. Both have maintained fiscal deficits over extended periods.

[10] Cerra & Saxena (2003).

[11] With the exception of Hong Kong, for many years after 1945 a haven of laisser-faire capitalism.

[12] Except for Japan, Asia's period of extraordinary growth is uniform from 1978, interrupted only by the post 1997 crisis, though beginning earlier in Korea, Singapore and Taiwan.

[13] For example, Bhagwati (1996).

[14] For example, Krugman (1994); Young (1995).

[15] Yoshitomi & Shirai (2001).

[16] Goldsmith (1983) pp160-187.

3.2. Flows of funds

The region's 'base' funds flow pattern varies with cycles in confidence but it can be taken that for contemporary East Asia, it is the offshore investor that has emerged rather than the borrower as elsewhere. The immediate reasons for Asia's 'difference appeal' to investors have been the variables cited in the preceding sections, regardless of whether the investor's interest becomes manifest as loan, bond, share or direct interest, and often without close regard for sovereign credit rating ceilings. Such conditions arise from underlying internal and external flows of funds at enterprise and national levels. They affect the financing choices of governments and of all companies. To the extent that the region's flows reflect cultural factors[17] rather than one stage in a universal path of development, the financial reformer may ask whether it is inevitable for Asia to anticipate flourishing debt capital markets that operate independently from the banking sector. Would such securities markets otherwise form naturally? Asia's half-built, half-used bond markets suggest that these roots are not so entrenched that effective markets would be infeasible or of little use. However, it is equally probable that the customary way that Asia's companies and governments have been financed requires care in using a generic model to promote reform. Chapter 4 reinforces this view by showing the non-continuous ways in which the world's major debt markets have 'evolved'. Asia's enterprises may be too small or financially well-provided to support a corporate debt market taken from an Australian or U.S. template, for example, yet both system and participants are in need of a different or adapted guide. Applied to regulatory and risk issues, for which Asia's prevailing corporate organisation, ownership and disclosure are often troublesome, this implies adopting standards, rigorous in all respects but appropriate to the region's raw material, in order to stimulate interest and usage.

Table 3-1 summarizes the salient characteristics of Asia's contemporary economies, highlighting common aspects of the region's performance since the early 1980s and in the post-crisis recovery.

3.3. Structural results and concerns

The World Bank's 2003 *Global Development Finance* report expresses concern at Asia's susceptibility to external shocks, its high corporate leverage, fiscal imprudence and the region's risk preferences in investment. Such unease rehearses arguments voiced widely in 1998, that 'structural and policy distortions' were chiefly to blame for the onset of the crisis.[18]

---

[17] This is not to endorse the contention that Asia's economic success reflects an adherence to 'Confucian' capitalism, a popular 'Orientalist' view.

[18] Corsetti, Pesenti & Roubini (1998 Part I p1). The authors were far from alone, writing in September 1998, 'There are many reasons to believe that the East Asian cycle will not take the V-shaped form of Mexico [in 1994], and that the contraction in economic activity in the region

***Table 3-1.* Common features of East Asian national economies**

External trade, current account, international reserves	Historically very strong export growth. Rapid expansion of current account surpluses since 1999, partly leading to substantial increases in international reserves.
Output growth	Consistently high rates of growth, except in isolated cases and immediately after 1997-98.
Government fiscal balance	Frequently conservatively managed. No consistent pattern; neither is there a systematic tendency to contracyclical deficit financing. Limited post-crisis reflation measures.
External financing	Consistent public and private direct investment from overseas and within the region; portfolio investment cyclical and strongly correlated to domestic US trends. Debt finance more reliant on loans than public issues of securities. Relatively narrow direct tax bases.
External debt	Comparatively low, relative to other regions, to national output and since 1999 relative to international reserves.
Savings	Private and public sector savings have been consistently and appreciably higher than all other regions. Recent establishment of provident funds and growth of institutionalized consumer savings.
Investment	Consistently far higher than other regions; relatively large proportion of private sector contribution compared to other emerging markets.
Financial intermediation	Relatively concentrated or cartelized banking sectors; non-bank credit institutions important in domestic lending prior to 1998. Modest non-bank financial intermediation of private savings. Low liquidity in money market instruments other than in the banking sector and for monetary policy use. High levels of impaired assets (except in Hong Kong and Singapore), often poorly reported.
Company finance	Internal finance is more important than for companies elsewhere. Bond issues used far less than bank loans and equity new issues.

3.3.1. Systemic vulnerability

First as to Asia's proneness to volatility, the 'extreme openness of the region leaves it vulnerable to global shocks.'[19] Historically, the World Bank is an unlikely

will last for much longer.' (*ibid* Part II p26). Growth became positive throughout East Asia in 1999, although in some cases 1997-98 output losses were not made good until more recently.

[19] World Bank (2003, ch2 p29).

proponent of capital controls[20] but the remark shelters a critical paradox. The great expansion in investment in Asia has largely been privately funded, whether from domestic or foreign sources. Yet since the crisis, private markets are known to contribute heavily to the risk of destabilizing shocks.[21] What was once beneficial for Asia's development[22] became a cause of suffering. Market innovation must be responsive to this problem, especially in relation to risk appraisal in capital investment and bank risk management.[23] Product innovation needs to make low risk instruments freely available outside the banking sector.

3.3.2. Financing risks

Second, on corporate leverage and fiscal policy, '[t]here has been a remarkable recovery in the health of much of the region's corporate sector since the dark days of 1998. But levels of corporate leverage remain high.'[24] Yet leverage was apparent in Asia well before the crisis and is identified as a threat regardless of duration and currency composition. The Bank's data may mask differences between leverage in individual economies,[25] revealing no systematic disparity between corporate Asia and corporate G-7. Instead, the importance of changes in leverage was identified soon after the crisis: the 1992-96 rate of increase in corporate leverage was highest in countries most affected by the crisis (Indonesia, Korea, Malaysia and Thailand).[26] Inter-regional comparisons of leverage may also neglect a proliferation in advanced economies of contingent financing and funding designed to be lightly weighted for balance sheet purposes (although major Asian companies are equally attracted to these tactics).

The World Bank continues, 'Fiscal deficits have risen sharply since 1997 and averaged 3.4 per cent of GDP in 2002.'[27] Asia's fiscal balances are a recurring issue only in India, Malaysia and the Philippines. The Bank's comment implies that some or all current fiscal deficits are part cyclical, part structural: to the extent that the

---

[20] World Bank opinion on capital controls has grown catholic since 1998, influenced by its then chief economist's hostility to the possible effects of 'short-term' flows (Stiglitz et al, 1999).

[21] For example, Eichengreen, Hausmann & Panizza (2002), whose remedy is basket currency financing.

[22] Taking the Japan of the 1950s and 1960s as a model, see Bhagwati (*op cit*).

[23] The primacy of the region's export orientation is changing, with domestic consumption more important than previously, which itself will demand reliable local currency financing. China and Thailand are examples.

[24] *ibid.*

[25] Practitioners may doubt the reliability and consistency of the source data on leverage in Asia.

[26] Pomerleano (1998).

[27] *ibid.*

cause arises from difficulties in raising revenue (narrow direct tax bases that force a reliance on sales and property taxes or duties) the suggestion is that 'true' Asian debt capital markets will facilitate effective central government funding and debt management. A pre-1997 funding analogy is that contemporary high current account deficits would have caused less concern as part of coherent exchange rate policy.[28] Today's fiscal deficits need appropriate debt management policies for which cash bond markets of some sophistication are valuable.

3.3.3. Savings dilemma

Third, on the region's post-crisis portfolio management and risk preferences, the Bank suggests that 'the breadth and amount of central bank reserve accumulation over the past couple of years is striking'.[29] Certainly, precautionary motives have been at play since 1999 with governments hoping to avoid the pain of crisis by building reserves for currency support, a traditional risk averse strategy. A preference for low-risk assets is widely observed throughout high-savings Asia, although such ratios partly reflect a lack of forced or contractual savings schemes compared to most advanced economies.[30] It may also echo an alarming scarcity of appropriate investment opportunities. Even in basic form, enhanced debt markets will provide an alternative to extra-regional investment.

4. Financing patterns

East Asia's flows of funds are shaped by historic and cultural dynamics, some of which are highly relevant to its contemporary financial markets. Those raw conditions translate into constraints and options for local and cross-border funding by corporate and government borrowers. Such limiting conditions (self-imposed or otherwise) result in inefficient domestic markets. Except in times of crisis, governments fund their current spending needs with local currency bond issues bought (by choice or otherwise) largely by commercial banks.[31] Often irregular, such supply cannot simultaneously sustain monetary policy needs, bank liquidity requirements and meet demand from institutional investors. Companies rely on internal funding sources or bank credit; most are unwilling or unable to meet new issue requirements for business scale or transparency; some are crowded out by the

---

[28] Especially for Malaysia, Philippines and Thailand (Corsetti, Pesenti & Roubini, *op cit*).

[29] *ibid* p37.

[30] Non-bank investor data on portfolio composition are meagre. Even prominent international organisations rely on weak material: an OECD (Akhtar 2001) study of investor behavior uses as source the results of a limited survey published twelve months earlier in *Institutional Investor*, a respectable but non-authoritative magazine.

[31] Foreign holdings of Asian government bonds are insignificant, except for Japanese government and state agency issues. Major currency sovereign debt issues account for a small share of government borrowing.

public sector or by discriminatory regulation. Asian companies are no less rational than their western counterparts; internal finance is relatively inexpensive when the costs associated with asymmetric information are high.[32]

Dependence on bank credit has roots not only in the region's relative development but in cultural flows of funds similar to those seen in Japan from the 1950s.[33] If financial markets reflect the characteristics of underlying capital flows then Asia's bond markets may have evolved to a limited state to meet limited purposes. Conversely, it is important to consider how flows may respond to reform. Despite structural change (a general shift to managed capitalism) and great differences in *per capita* incomes, Asia is characterized by consistently high personal savings, recurring central fiscal surpluses or small deficits, strong recurring growth in exports and capital investment, generally low external borrowing, and intermittently favorable external balances. Since 1997 the region has collected sizeable current surpluses and international reserves, albeit non-uniformly. There have been periodic exceptions after shocks and several countries have followed distinct fiscal policies, but the region's economic characteristics are long-standing.

For twenty-five years, Asia's orientation has been to export promotion with fast growth in capital asset formation. The greater part of that investment has been privately sourced and deployed, with a reliance on internal funding and bank borrowing. Governments have generally avoided heavy military spending as a share of national output, and comprehensive state welfare or pension schemes are largely absent. The effect of that want in encouraging precautionary savings cannot be gauged but Asian savings rates appear to remain above global averages in the few cases where directed provident schemes are broadly established, such as in Singapore. Home ownership is generally prized but is significantly lower than in advanced economies and the markets supporting private home purchase are sophisticated only in Hong Kong, Malaysia and Taiwan.[34] High savings ratios are often thought to indicate more than risk aversion and generally show no inverse correlation with *per capita* income. They may also be a function of a lack of entrenched welfare systems and underdeveloped institutional savings industries, and although there is some evidence that savings ratios decline marginally when these institutional factors are established, Japan suggests this is not a sufficient explanation.[35] These conditions mould borrowing by companies and governments, and contribute to inefficient markets. Governments fund current spending with notes and bonds bought (willingly or otherwise) largely by banks.[36] Often irregular, such

---

[32] These 'agency costs' arise from the varying interests of management and ownership and will make external finance prohibitive for less transparent companies; Takagi (2000).

[33] Goldsmith (1983 *op cit*) pp160-187.

[34] Although there is intense competition in residential mortgage lending throughout the region.

[35] Post-2000 data are confused by deflationary conditions that might encourage saving, *ceteris paribus*.

[36] Foreign holdings of domestic government issues are insignificant.

supply cannot both fill liquidity requirements and institutional demand. Most companies are unwilling or unable to submit to new issue disclosure requirements; some are crowded out by the public sector or discriminatory regulation. Asian companies are no less rational than their foreign counterparts: internal finance is cheap when the costs associated with asymmetric information are high. The results are:

4.1. Structural features

The results of the conditions described in the preceding sections fare manifested in eight main qualities.

4.1.1. Corporate ownership

Corporate ownership is generally more concentrated than in advanced countries.[37] This promotes a primary reliance on internal funding. Secondary debt financing is sourced mainly from banks, from which arises an emphasis on relationship financing, which in turn militates against disclosure and transparency.[38] Investment decision making and capital allocation are heavily influenced by the innate preferences of the relationship bank: immediately before the crisis Asian lenders were more content to finance speculative property development by advancing against collateral (which was familiar) than credible projects for which whole business cash flow analysis was essential and they are historically ill-prepared. Bank preferences heavily influence investment decisions.

4.1.2. Funding

Bank funding depends upon retail and inter-bank deposits, a narrower base than for banks operating in major markets. Tradable certificates of deposit and regulatory capital debt issues are either trivial or unavailable, in spite of the wishes of all institutional investors. Asia's money markets are dominated by short-term government debt issues, even though they lack much of the liquidity that established markets offer to non-bank participants. The absence of markets in short-term corporate debt[39] cramps corporate investing and borrowing culture and limits the options available to all company treasurers.

---

[37] Conglomerate organisations that internalise much external funding have historically been widespread in Asia. The structure has become less entrenched since the Asian crisis.

[38] These remarks should not be taken as referring to a 'pecking order' finance theory.

[39] Similar to the US or euro commercial paper markets or the Dutch inter-corporate note market. These markets often depend upon intense rating agency coverage, which is still limited in Asia, and a willingness by banks to provide standby credit facilities, which is untested. In several cases including Hong Kong, promising markets for short-term corporate

4.1.3. Monopoly practices

Reform must address regulations or cartels that in some countries require corporate issues to be guaranteed by a financial institution, usually a commercial bank, regardless of the credit standing of the issuer. The practice may spring from investor protection motives that a robust rating culture would diminish but is usually induced by monopolistic banks.[40] It is clearly not conducive to capital market development.[41] Such anomalies question whether the region's young domestic debt capital markets have provided corporate borrowers with any real alternative to bank credit. Some views are optimistic, holding that this was the case in Hong Kong after the crisis when new bond issues 'partially filled the gap' in financing that opened in 1998-99 when total bank lending fell.[42] Yet the amount raised was modest (representing in 1999 only 13.7 per cent of that year's fall in domestic lending) and the buyers of new bonds were mainly banks. A large share of the corporate debt issued in this period comprised securitized floating rate notes issued by asset-rich companies, structured solely to overcome prevailing bank credit policies.

4.1.4. Informal funding

In its process of reform since the late 1970s China has developed a positive association between growth and financial development, but the non-state corporate sector has not used domestic institutions for finance in a material way.[43] Most spending by non-state enterprises relies on internal funding, while external financing sources divide crudely between bank lending for state-owned enterprises and foreign direct investment for the non-state sector. However, an unknown but significant share of foreign direct investment for non-state enterprises may be more loan than capital in character, disguised to avoid capital controls on cross-border lending. This

---

notes have been extinguished by the weight of government money market issuance and regulatory incentives.

[40] Nowhere does the practice encourage lending to SMEs. Such credit substitution is seen frequently in Southeast Asia and Taiwan. Guaranteed bonds were a standard tool of Korean companies prior to 1998. The adoption of Basel II capital adequacy guidelines may make the practice prohibitively costly for all except poorly-rated companies.

[41] These remarks do not apply to measures adopted in Korea during the post-1998 recovery by which external credit enhancement has been extended to borrowing companies by public agencies such as the Korea Credit Guarantee Fund.

[42] Jiang, Tang & Law (2001: p14). The fall in lending was partly credit driven; partly involuntary, due to capital shortages among Japanese banks, hitherto substantial lenders in Hong Kong.

[43] Aziz & Duenwald (2002). Allen, Qian & Qian (2002 pp4-5) postulate 'effective, non-standard financing channels' funding private companies (suggesting equivalents elsewhere), including 'privately placed bonds and loans' (*ibid* p32). Recent research indicates that revenue and income profit disguising is widespread and an effective external source of funds (Cai *et al*, 2004; Liu & Lu, 2004; Liu and Xiao, 2004; Xiao, 2004).

is observed with mainland China enterprises controlled and funded from Hong Kong.[44]

4.1.5. Bank lending

Certain aspects of corporate funding behavior impact both domestic and cross-border debt markets. In the three years before the Asian crisis sources of credit broadened in several economies, with secondary banks and finance companies lending heavily to companies and consumers.[45] These lenders were typically more lightly regulated than banks and operated to poor risk management standards. Directly and indirectly, this quasi-bank sector was funded substantially with foreign currency loans: the phenomenon is central to the evolution of the crisis. The critical long-term lesson is that the growth of corporate lending by finance and leasing companies suggests that the banking sector provides poorly for the needs of medium-scale businesses (SMEs). Chapter 10 points to a solution using capital markets techniques to improve bank funding and asset refinancing.

Such structural weaknesses have become clear in the period since the Asian crisis. Some very large companies with established foreign currency revenues were immune to the regional withdrawal of credit in 1998-99 but all others suffered in funding or refinancing due to a scarcity of bank capital and improvements in regulatory accounting that forced banks better to recognize substandard assets. Alternative sources of corporate funding would not only lessen this problem but encourage bankers to raise their corporate client product skills beyond the secured lending and trade finance to which they are trained and accustomed. The net amount raised from offshore major currency debt markets has been consistently dominated by the volume of direct investment, shown in Table 3-2. A comparison of recent aggregate bank lending and bond issues shows the severe extent of funds withdrawn or repaid after 1997.

Table 3-3 shows that except in 1996-97, Asian organisations issued only modest volumes of international debt. Only a handful of Asian borrowers have ever enjoyed a core currency liquidity premium: investor expectations of low supply make this impossible even if a scarcity of acceptable Asian credit risk can make new issues comparatively expensive for the investor.[46] Encouragingly, local market liquidity premiums have prevailed for sustained periods in Hong Kong, Korea and Malaysia, but in each case for no more than one or two issuers, without exception public sector organisations. Premiums are likely to arise for creditworthy borrowers in the event

---

[44] Fernald & Babson (1999).

[45] Particularly in Korea and Thailand, but also in Indonesia, Malaysia and the Philippines.

[46] Investors may allow frequent issuers new issue terms that are marginally more favourable than occasional borrowers of the same credit quality. Such liquidity premiums are never constant. At intervals, major currency liquidity premiums have been associated with Korea Development Bank, Hutchison Whampoa Ltd and Petroliam Nasional Bhd. Others existed in myth before the crisis, or have since collapsed under the irredeemable weight of their frequent issues.

that a true separation opens between the banking and debt capital markets. Domestic liquidity premiums explain why occasional borrowing companies have not supported the capital markets but sought 'cheaper' funding from banks.

Table 3-2. **Summary of external financing (East & South Asia)**

US$ bn	1995	1996	1997	1998	1999	2000	2001	2002
Net FDI inflow	54.2	62.1	67.1	61.1	52.0	47.1	53.0	62.0
Net equity inflow	10.7	14.2	2.9	(3.3)	7.0	21.0	4.5	6.2
Total equity inflow	64.9	76.3	70.0	57.8	59.0	68.1	57.5	68.2
Official creditors	7.9	4.6	17.6	17.0	15.0	7.5	6.0	(0.4)
ST private debt inflow	29.4	20.7	2.3	(45.2)	(13.3)	(11.2)	(1.3)	1.2
Bonds	na	na	15.6	4.9	(0.3)	3.8	(0.4)	6.1
Bank loans	na	na	5.2	(4.2)	(12.0)	(13.8)	(14.6)	(13.1)
Others	na	na	4.4	(0.3)	(0.6)	(0.8)	(1.9)	(1.2)
LT private debt inflow	19.3	29.3	25.2	0.4	(12.9)	(10.8)	(16.9)	(8.2)
Net private debt flow	48.7	50.0	27.5	-44.8	-26.2	-22.0	-18.2	-7.0
Total external financing	121.5	130.9	115.1	30.0	47.8	53.6	45.3	60.8
Gross LT bank lending	52.3	53.3	54.2	23.8	16.6	25.4	12.8	23.6
Gross international bond issuance	10.7	22.2	22.9	4.6	8.7	5.1	7.2	12.5
Gross international equity issuance	4.4	6.5	11.8	4.1	7.1	23.0	4.0	7.5
Gross market-based capital flows	67.4	82.0	88.9	32.5	32.4	53.5	24.0	43.6
Gross LT bank lending	52.3	53.3	54.2	23.8	16.6	25.4	12.8	23.6

Source: World Bank Global Development Finance 2003; IMF International Financial Statistics. For consistency data are for all East and South Asia. The amounts relating to non-review economies are insignificant.

Table 3-3. **Volume trends in new international debt issues, net of repayments**

Net international debt issues (US$ bn)	**1994**	**1995**	**1996**	**1997**	**1998**	**1999**	**2000**	**2001**	**2002**	**2003**
China	3.8	0.3	1.8	4.2	(0.5)	(0.1)	0.3	0.8	(1.1)	2.4
Hong Kong	6.0	0.7	2.4	7.8	(1.1)	4.0	5.1	7.5	3.1	9.0
India	0.2	0.3	1.0	1.8	(0.3)	(1.0)	(0.4)	(0.5)	(0.7)	0.0
Indonesia	1.8	0.1	6.7	7.1	(0.4)	(4.3)	(1.9)	(1.9)	0.5	0.0
Korea	3.9	8.2	17.6	9.2	0.6	(3.7)	1.1	(0.1)	5.4	7.8
Malaysia	0.1	1.7	2.6	3.6	(0.7)	2.4	1.5	1.7	5.5	(0.6)
Philippines	1.1	0.8	3.7	3.1	0.6	3.8	1.3	0.5	4.0	4.0
Singapore	0.3	(0.2)	2.1	1.3	0.9	1.6	4.4	6.9	(1.7)	5.0
Taiwan	1.7	0.3	1.2	2.7	1.4	(0.1)	(0.2)	0.6	4.3	7.0
Thailand	2.5	1.4	5.3	2.3	(0.3)	0.3	(0.7)	(2.5)	(0.3)	(1.3)
East Asia	21.2	13.3	43.4	41.3	0.5	3.9	10.9	13.5	19.7	33.3
Total	21.4	13.6	44.4	43.1	0.2	2.9	10.5	13.0	19.0	33.3

Source: Bank for International Settlements (BIS) securities statistics

The share of developing country borrowers in net new international debt issues has fallen over the period 1994-2002 (a complete US dollar interest rate cycle). Table 3-4 shows how Asia's post-crisis contribution became almost insignificant, albeit at a time when frequent issues from developed countries grew prolifically. Bank lending shows a similar picture: Table 3-5 provides a contribution analysis for international syndicated loans, which represent an alternative feasible source of funding for borrowers able to access the bond markets. The difference in Asia's share of new loans probably results from the lending market being marginally more tolerant of lesser credits compared to the debt securities market.

4.1.6. Bank long-term funding

Commercial and public sector banks from all review economies except Taiwan have been accustomed to issuing foreign currency debt; most commonly unsubordinated floating rate notes, almost always denominated in US dollars and little traded.[47] The significant new features of the post-crisis transaction market have been a handful of large issues to raise regulatory capital, especially by Hong Kong, Korean and

[47] Capital controls have traditionally restrained Taiwanese foreign debt issues except equity-linked transactions.

Singapore banks, and sizeable, infrequent issues of asset-backed securities as part of the recycling of impaired financial assets, chiefly from newly-formed state-sponsored asset management organisations in Korea, Malaysia and Thailand.[48]

Table 3-4. **Sectoral contributions to net new issues (by volume)**

Share of annual net new debt issues (%)	**1994**	**1995**	**1996**	**1997**	**1998**	**2000**	**2001**	**2002**	**2003**	**1994**
All advanced economies	80.1	85.9	77.8	77.4	84.7	93.5	93.5	93.5	93.0	80.1
Hong Kong	2.4	0.3	0.5	1.4	-0.2	0.4	0.6	0.3	0.6	2.4
Singapore	0.1	-0.1	0.4	0.2	0.1	0.4	0.5	-0.2	0.3	0.1
Other Asia-Pacific	6.2	5.1	7.7	6.1	0.1	0.0	-0.1	1.9	1.4	6.2
Other developing economies	8.0	4.6	9.2	11.1	7.2	3.9	4.3	2.4	3.2	8.0
International institutions	3.2	4.1	4.4	3.9	8.1	1.9	1.2	2.1	1.5	3.2
Total	100	100	100	100	100	100	100	100	100	100

Source: BIS securities statistics

4.1.7. Syndicated lending

Since 1999-2000 Asia's private sector banks have contributed a high level of participation in new international bond issues and loans. This has been identified favorably as a sign of financial integration that could militate against contagion in the event of new crises.[49] While an alternative explanation is suggested in section 4.4 (*infra*) both suggest that the banking market's risk of contagion has not diminished since the crisis.

4.1.8. Credit ratings

International credit ratings for Asian bonds begun to be widespread only after 1997-98 and are still far from numerous. For example, as at 31 July 2003 Standard and Poor's maintained 502 ratings relating to entities in the ten review countries,

---

[48] Similar bodies now exist in China, Indonesia and Taiwan, all using the US Resolution Trust model.

[49] McCauley, Fung & Gadanecz (2002).

compared to 398 in Japan, 421 in Australia and New Zealand and 480 in Latin America.[50] Asia's rated issues include a proportion from financial institutions that at 72.7 per cent is comparable to economies with sophisticated markets (Australia and New Zealand, Europe, the U.S.), and higher than in areas where the banking sector is concentrated (Japan, 48.2%; Latin America, 40.4%; Canada, 38.3%), suggesting that the international rating agencies have defined the ratable universe of Asian companies of sufficient scale for the foreseeable future. Local rating agencies were created from the early or mid-1990s in India, Indonesia, Korea, Malaysia and Thailand.[51] Their reputations are unalike, despite most having alliances with one of three international rating organisations. Domestic rating agencies have often suffered from weak revenues but India's leading agency undertakes related non-rating work that may be a model for other firms. Inadequate rating cultures constrain active markets only indirectly; given the wide gap between the highest and least well-rated issuers, the investor's need for adequate credit ratings will be met when new issue supply materially increases.

***Table 3-5.* Contributions to new international syndicated loans (by volume)**

Share of new international syndicated loans (%)	1994	1995	1996	1997	1998	1999	2000	2001	2002	2003
All advanced economies	88.2	86.8	87.2	83.6	90.5	93.6	90.7	91.9	92.4	91.2
Hong Kong	2.0	1.6	1.9	2.4	0.6	0.6	2.2	2.0	1.4	1.2
Singapore	0.4	0.3	0.3	0.5	0.1	0.2	0.3	0.4	0.3	0.3
Other Asia-Pacific	7.0	6.7	6.1	5.9	2.5	1.6	2.2	1.5	2.2	2.6
Other developing economies	2.4	4.7	4.4	7.5	6.3	4.0	4.5	4.1	3.7	4.6
International institutions	0.1	0.0	0.0	0.0	0.0	0.0	0.0	0.1	0.0	0.0
Total	100	100	100	100	100	100	100	100	100	100

Source: BIS international banking statistics

[50] As at 31 July 2003, including a large number of financial stability ratings for insurers.

[51] Taiwan's new securitization legislation in 2001-02 required that new issues be rated by domestic agencies. Three global rating agencies have accordingly opened Taiwan offices with local partners.

4.2. Post-crisis credit squeeze

Asia's banks' most marked post-crisis action was a herd withdrawal of credit. The squeeze affected all but a limited number of corporate borrowers and took hold everywhere, including those economies least affected by capital flight or losses in confidence. It encouraged loan delinquency by healthy medium and large scale enterprises that might otherwise have anticipated the customary renewal of credit. The fall in credit creation had no single cause but it is clear that many banks quickly became unable to support 'good' lending due to real loan losses, increasingly rigorous risk management and regulatory enforcement of capital standards, in some cases as part of national bargains for IMF funds. Corporate demand for loans duly slackened. With few low risk assets available from traditional sources, Asia's commercial banks began to acquire non-Asian risks, adopting the portfolio choice of their sponsor central banks, and after 1999-2000 a growing number of G3 currency new issues, the object of the 'Asian bid' that so efficiently saps market liquidity.[52]

Asia's post-crisis lenders have shown increasing interest in synthetic structured finance transactions,[53] and as both buyers and sellers of credit protection in free-standing credit derivatives such as core currency credit default swaps (CDS) and total return swaps,[54] the latter encouraging commercial banks to seek enhanced returns through techniques based upon traditional portfolio theory.[55] The parochial regional argument remains, that the bulk of these transactions are arranged by non-Asian banks and traded with to passive counterparties. Almost a decade's exposure to synthetic transactions and credit derivatives has not materially increased sophistication among Asian banks, nor has it provided a means for non-standard risks to raise funds, notably small-scale businesses or infrastructural borrowers. Credit limitations continue in some markets despite over five years of bank balance sheet repair.

If active bond markets assist efficiency and welfare,[56] is output growth impeded when they are deficient?[57] The Asian crisis resulted partly from high external debt acquisition under fixed exchange rates. Yet outside China there were few pre-1997 restrictions on domestic credit availability: in view of the region's general long-term growth performance, this was not always inefficient. Would Asia's crisis have been

---

[52] This is also a central criticism of the notional effects of the first EMEAP Asian bond fund. See also Chapter 8.

[53] Particularly collateralized bond and loan obligations (CBOs and CLOs).

[54] Total return swaps are arguably not credit derivatives but financing transactions involving a basis swap but dealing and documentation conventions support their inclusion.

[55] Asia may account for some 10 per cent of global turnover in credit derivatives; see British Bankers' Association Credit Derivatives Report 2003-04, available at www.bba.org.uk/.

[56] Herring & Chatusripitak (2000).

[57] Gerschenkron (1962) argued that bank-based systems particularly assist formative industrialization.

milder had it been less reliant on bank intermediation? International credit lines are finite, so banks funding local lending with unhedged foreign liabilities would always have met limits. Was economic collapse inevitable after a cessation of lending? Functioning local capital markets might have encouraged more benign an outcome, providing they were sufficiently uncorrelated with bank credit activity. Exogenous and other shocks are inevitable but the seizure that characterizes contagion is preventable.[58]

4.3. Market activity today

Asia lacks efficient financial systems, not funding. While sectoral sources of funds within each economy are non-uniform, the contribution of debt securities is far smaller and bank lending more prominent than elsewhere. Have inadequate domestic markets led to a compensating strengthening of offshore markets for Asian risk in terms of liquidity or the certainty of supply of funds? This might account for Asian risk usually commanding narrower credit spreads than suggested by relative sovereign ratings.[59] Some Asian borrowers are internationally well-established but very few maintain continuous markets in issued debt. Irregular supply and the conservative stance of most investors able to hold Asian risk have caused comparatively tight secondary conditions for much of the last decade. Disclosed Asian issues of G3 currency bonds grew to $ 34.0 bn in 2003, equivalent to the Euromarket's new issue volume in 1982.[60]

The use of offshore sources for want of domestic liquidity has policy consequences, revealing a lack of built-in stabilizers against unforeseen volatility. It has been suggested that integration has increased within Asia's national financial sectors since the crisis, shown in Asian bank participation in international bond (and loan) transactions, and that this might prevent stress turning contagious. Yet transaction involvement may also indicate bank passivity or a lack of harvestable self-originated opportunities of sufficient return, and is mainly confined to deals for highly-rated borrowers. Any such integration provides no alternative intermediation and cannot lessen contagion risk without liberal last resort lending. A further hostile view is that access enjoyed by Asian issuers to offshore markets reduces incentives for local development. If a well-rated borrower's needs are fed by investment banks competing for limited transaction supply, would it encourage growth of its home bond market and compromize local bank funding?[61] Except in Korea and Singapore,

---

[58] Borio (2003) believes the crisis literature neglects the contagion effects of counterparty risk.

[59] Its modern default history makes the Philippines an exception.

[60] *Euromoney* June 1989, Dealogic.

[61] Local banks today dominate purchases of domestic currency public debt issues. Such buying might crowd out the same banks' corporate lending, *ceteris paribus*.

top-tier companies have promoted domestic market expansion only at the conference lectern. Similarly, banks make little use of local markets to raise regulatory capital.[62]

Before the Asian crisis, the most important drivers of regional debt market innovation were non-Asian banks, all hoping to apply home product management skills to fresh markets. Their returns were mixed: hampered by weak domestic distribution and with few natural local investors, the greater share of bank income from Asian currency new issues in 1990-97 came from accruals on unsold bond inventory. Such market-driven innovation brought some success in Hong Kong, Korea and Malaysia, latterly with official sympathy. The amounts raised were modest and secondary trading was inevitably constrained. Some markets (including Indonesia and Thailand) were trivial in scale and impact, while others (Singapore and Taiwan) were effectively closed to new issues, with official opinion fearful that free capital movements might conflict with monetary or currency management policy. Table 3-6 shows the evolution of domestic bond issuance since 1990, including government, corporate and financial sector new issues. If Korea is excluded the total net amount of new long-term debt of all kinds made available in 2002 was $ 39.0 bn, less than two-thirds the comparable net amount issued by Fannie Mae in the same period.[63]

***Table 3-6.* Net annual issuance of domestic bonds**

All long-term securities (> 1 year remaining life)									
US$ bn	**1994**	**1995**	**1996**	**1997**	**1998**	**1999**	**2000**	**2001**	**2002**
China	20.2	25.8	26.0	41.8	66.8	64.4	61.9	63.7	61.8
Hong Kong	9.1	7.1	9.8	7.6	(1.3)	2.8	0.2	0.8	1.7
India	8.0	15.3	12.4	0.9	16.6	18.5	19.2	20.3	24.9
Indonesia	0.1	0.2	0.3	0.6	(0.1)	0.2	0.7	(0.2)	0.1
Korea	24.9	39.0	32.3	19.2	49.7	11.1	34.1	34.3	53.5
Malaysia	8.7	8.6	10.5	12.7	3.6	4.2	8.5	8.1	0.4
Philippines	(1.4)	2.1	1.6	(0.1)	2.3	2.0	2.5	2.0	0.9
Singapore	1.4	2.2	1.4	3.5	5.3	6.9	8.3	11.2	0.6
Taiwan	7.9	9.9	25.2	18.2	20.2	(1.6)	3.9	8.1	15.7
Thailand	1.0	1.7	2.1	0.1	10.7	8.4	4.1	5.7	10.5
East Asia	71.9	96.6	109.2	103.6	157.2	98.4	124.2	133.7	145.2
Total	79.9	111.9	121.6	104.5	173.8	116.9	143.4	154.0	170.1

Source: BIS, Bank Indonesia[64]

[62] Only Korean and Singaporean banks have so far raised local currency regulatory capital in non-trivial amounts.

[63] Federal National Mortgage Corporation annual report 2002. Korea itself raised less than Fannie Mae.

[64] In some cases BIS data effectively measure credit creation, not tradable issuance. China is the most notable example.

The total amounts of long-term debt issues reported as outstanding to the Bank for International Settlements gives more a picture of the volume of debt issued and held for regulatory purposes by financial institutions, or (in the case of China) low denomination bonds placed with individual investors, rather than traded aggregates. This is shown in Table 3-7, the central feature of which is the generally slow rates of growth in year-end amounts of debt outstanding in the same markets.

***Table 3-7.* Outstanding volumes of domestic bonds**

All long-term securities (> 1 year remaining life)									
US$ bn	**1994**	**1995**	**1996**	**1997**	**1998**	**1999**	**2000**	**2001**	**2002**
China	66.1	93.1	119.4	161.6	228.4	292.9	354.8	418.7	480.4
Hong Kong	16.7	23.8	33.6	41.1	39.9	42.6	42.7	43.6	45.3
India	63.5	70.6	81.2	75.2	85.7	102.1	113.6	130.2	155.8
Indonesia	0.5	0.8	1.1	1.7	1.6	1.8	2.5	2.3	2.4
Korea	185.2	227.2	239.0	130.3	240.1	265.5	269.0	292.7	380.9
Malaysia	53.6	62.4	73.1	57.0	61.9	66.1	74.7	82.8	83.2
Philippines	25.9	26.2	27.9	18.4	21.0	22.4	20.3	21.6	21.9
Singapore	20.0	22.9	24.6	23.8	29.4	36.2	43.2	51.3	55.2
Taiwan	68.4	75.7	100.2	101.2	124.3	125.9	122.8	124.3	141.2
Thailand	13.9	15.5	17.4	9.5	23.6	31.5	31.1	36.2	47.3
East Asia	450.3	547.6	636.3	544.6	770.2	884.9	961.1	1,073.5	1,257.8
Total	513.8	618.2	717.5	619.8	855.9	987.0	1,074.7	1,203.7	1,413.6

Source: BIS, Bank Indonesia

In nine of the review East Asian economies[65] at the end of 2002, government issues accounted for 46.5 per cent of the total volume outstanding, weighted by the total amounts in issuance in each category, compared to 24.5 per cent and 37.0 per cent for financial institutions and corporate borrowers, respectively. In the 13 year period shown, government issues accounted for a relatively stable share of debt outstanding, falling from 52.1 per cent in 1990. In contrast, amounts due from financial institutions and corporates were volatile, clearly affected by the crisis and its aftermath. Issues by banks and other financial sector borrowers ranged over the period between weighted averages of 24.5 per cent and 65.5 per cent of the total. The highest share was seen in December 1997, reflecting a pre-crisis peak of domestic debt issuance by Asian banks (much of which would have been sold to offshore speculative investors). Conversely, outstanding corporate issues peaked in 1998 at a weighted average of 44.2 per cent, more reflective of a collapse in sales of bank debt

[65] The remarks in this paragraph exclude India.

than any confidence in the corporate sector. Outstanding corporate issues otherwise remained generally steady over the period at between 29.0 per cent and 39.8 per cent. Corporate issues were most prolific in Korea and Malaysia and latterly in Taiwan; finance sector issues were more important elsewhere, with the exception of the Philippines where extant non-government issues are trivial.[66]

The 1997-98 crisis exposed faults in Asia's use of available debt markets that remain largely unsealed. Most commentators believe that structural flaws helped provoke and intensify the crisis, partly by making the region over-dependent on its domestic banking sectors, partly by encouraging undisciplined foreign currency borrowings. Later, the same fragilities slowed a post-crisis recovery: the debt capital markets have contributed patchily in helping repair the balance sheets of Asia's commercial banks. Asia now sustains domestic currency bond markets of varying depths and value. Yet these markets are still under-utilized and fail to occupy the core status of most advanced economy bond markets in promoting an efficient flow of savings and investment and providing governments with effective tools of policy.

Since the crisis, the supply of new debt into Asian domestic and cross-border markets has gradually risen but remains generally low.[67] In each case it is unclear to what extent this reflects structural factors or a cyclical lack of demand for funds. From a practical perspective, weak supply stems partly from credit risk concerns: the international markets were closed in 1998-99 to most East Asian borrowers following a precipitate down-grading of sovereign and issuer credit ratings. By contrast, in normal conditions the refinancing of maturing obligations represents a highly significant share of new issues in all major capital markets: the post-crisis period has shown substantial and continuing capital outflows from all review economies. This has been described as a form of post-crisis balance sheet repair: Asia has devoted rising current account surpluses to acquire highly-rated non-Asian assets, representing a significant portfolio adjustment from pre-crisis to recovery.[68] Although non-Asian investors have partly balanced this outflow of Asian 'capital to quality' with inflows of risk-preferring direct investment, there is now a consensus that the trend has become extreme and represents a loss of welfare to Asia's economies.[69]

[66] The division between financial and corporate issuers is unreliable: several local currency debt markets require corporate issues to carry bank guarantees. See section 4.1, bulleted paragraph 3 (*supra*).

[67] Korea is the sole exception. Although post-1997 issuance has been inconsistent and subject to shocks, all markets have provided substantial amounts for Korean corporate funding and refinancing.

[68] Crockett (*op cit*); Oh, Park, Park & Yang (*op cit*); and many others.

[69] Reflecting both a diversion of available funds from possible investment in Asia, and a restrictive monetary stance in conditions of low price inflation (other than if the exchange rate is undervalued).

The attention given to the debate by policymakers since 2001-02[70] suggests that structural reforms, where necessary to remove or circumvent transaction or trading impediments or to promote usage, can shortly be made feasible. That attitudes to market development and risk appraisal are changing is evident from caricature: prior to the crisis, supportive bankers would claim that the Asian bond market would be a 'good idea', while officials might voice support but worry as to the consequences of losing control to the market. All views today seem more pliable and constructive, not least because the US dollar's 2002-03 decline suggested to the Asian investor that capital preservation may not be compatible with a passive accumulation of U.S. government bonds.

The features and dynamics of the debt securities markets under review economies are encapsulated in Table 3-8, a market's sketch of the relative maturity of each domestic currency sector, accounting for transparency, liquidity, depth, the role of government, and the number of active participants.

***Table 3-8.* Relative maturity of Asian domestic debt markets**

Effective but underused	Hong Kong Singapore
Effective but not efficient	Korea Malaysia
Semi-effective	India Taiwan Thailand
Underdeveloped	China Indonesia Philippines

A similar table prepared in 1996 would have shown a more tolerant view in one or two cases due to private sector transaction promotion. In the period approaching the crisis, Southeast Asian markets[71] attracted buying or arbitrage interest from overseas banks and foreign high-yield investors, encouraging participants to anticipate a permanent rise in liquidity. Domestic financial, corporate and public agency borrowers were persuaded to respond with a significant number of modest new issues. Such versions of low coupon 'carry trades'[72] disappeared in the spring

[70] Including the announcement in May 2003 by the EMEAP central banks group of a first Asian bond fund. EMEAP, the Executives' Meeting of East Asia-Pacific Central Banks, comprises Australia, China, Hong Kong, Indonesia, Japan, Korea, Malaysia, New Zealand, the Philippines, Singapore and Thailand.

[71] Other than Singapore.

[72] Unhedged purchases of high-yielding assets using low interest rate foreign currency resources.

and summer of 1997 with the currency crisis, making an orphan of this market-based initiative for five years. It has recently resumed with Korean and Thai risk. Thus domestic debt markets subsist in principle in all established Asian economies, with varying degrees of sophistication indicated by architecture and participants, issue volume and trading activity. National differences in financial development may be explained by a range of factors, including the origins of governing law, exemplified in the treatment of investor or property rights, or how legal systems adapt to commercial circumstances.[73] True markets are less apparent: in some cases they exist in a latent sense, as suggested in Table 3-6, more as forums for specific transactions than continuously functioning financial sectors.[74]

One direct consequence is that the quality of information offered to investing or borrowing participants is fractured or substandard, for example, as to prevailing yields or the credit risks associated with certain issuers, except in some cases in very short maturities.[75] A purist could argue that the operation of financial markets reflects the characteristics of underlying flows of capital and thus Asia's bond markets have evolved to their limited state to serve a limited purpose. Before the crisis only modest domestic capital markets could be supported or were strictly necessary; post-crisis, and with time assisting a recovery in the region's balance sheet, the structural reforms resulting from contemporary policy forums are likely to change this simple state. In the long-term, the most intriguing issue is the extent to which the ensuing pattern of funds flows responds to those reforms.

The dynamics of the review economies and a sample of advanced economy comparisons are shown quantitatively in Table 3-9, which re-works data shown in a number of studies[76] using the illustrative pre- and post-crisis data points of end-1996 and 2002.

While the contributions of the main sources of funds within each economy are non-uniform, the role of debt securities in East Asia is consistently less prominent than elsewhere, both before and after the 1997-98 crisis.[77] The overall conclusion

---

[73] Beck, Demirgüç-Kunt & Levine (2002). The specification of explanatory variables in similar analyses reflects a common law perspective that some consider tendentious.

[74] Furthermore, low-risk local currency money market instruments are available only transiently to non-bank institutional investors (and never to money market funds). This typically increases portfolio management costs, deters foreign and domestic investors and may encourage a post-shock contagion.

[75] Distinct from information available asymmetrically, or given preferentially to banks.

[76] For example, Jiang, Tang & Law (*op cit*); Rhee (2000); Rajan (2002).

[77] It is unsafe to draw too detailed conclusions from these comparisons. For example, the modern German economy has been financed by far higher levels of privately-held non-traded equity investment and on private, tradable debt securities, relative to other advanced industrial economies. Parochial customs infect data: the statistical treatment of refinanced residential mortgage loans differs between Germany and the US to a greater extent than their respective financial systems (the *pfandbrief* and federal agency debt markets).

***Table 3-9.* Simplified internal sources of finance**

Year ending	**1996**			**2002**		
Outstanding share of GDP (%)	**Debt securities**	**Bank loans**	**Equity cap-italisation**	**Debt securities**	**Bank loans**	**Equity cap-italisation**
China	14.6	95.2	3.9	33.3	139.9	13.3
Hong Kong	21.5	158.4	241.1	27.4	148.7	246.8
India	21.5	29.8	18.0	33.4	16.8	17.1
Indonesia	n.a.	14.6	8.0	18.1	23.2	13.9
Korea	45.9	41.2	10.7	82.5	115.5	43.0
Malaysia	72.4	63.3	122.3	86.9	105.9	98.3
Philippines	33.7	24.2	35.5	28.4	31.8	20.6
Singapore	26.9	80.4	113.8	63.9	108.1	102.4
Taiwan	35.8	120.9	50.2	50.2	149.7	67.3
Thailand	9.6	59.6	20.1	37.4	80.5	25.9
Australia	48.9	54.1	43.8	52.0	n.a.	90.6
Germany	79.2	87.7	10.7	87.6	n.a.	16.3
Japan	100.1	103.2	60.9	169.0	107.9	52.1
United Kingdom	56.1	74.1	131.2	65.3	90.3	110.1
United States	144.3	64.3	75.9	155.8	78.1	87.8

Sources: BIS, IMF International Financial Statistics, World Bank Economic Outloook, Datastream, national data. Equity capitalization data exclude non-traded shares of quoted public sector companies.

from these sample data is that the debt capital markets in non-Japan East Asia, with the sporadic exception of Korea, fail to provide the resource potential for national economies in the way commonly expected among established market economies. Bank lending generally supports external financing activity within the economy to a greater and more consistent extent than outside the region. This observation held true through the 1997-98 crisis and in the immediate recovery. One similar study illustrated the difference in scale using data from the early-1990s to show that in advanced economies, the level of outstanding debt issues averaged 110 per cent of aggregate output measured by GDP, with the corresponding proportions for aggregate outstanding equity and bank debt being 80 per cent and 150 per cent, respectively. For East Asia, domestic debt totaled 10.0 per cent and external debt 3.0 per cent, respectively of GDP.[78]

4.4. *Offshore markets*

Has a lack of flourishing domestic debt capital markets led to the corresponding strengthening of offshore foreign currency markets for Asian risk, either in terms of liquidity or the certainty of supply of funds? This would show Asia using the international capital markets as a proxy for domestic market development and be consistent in risk terms with many pre-1997 overt foreign exchange regimes in Asia. It might also account for the clear and consistent difference between the generally prevailing terms of Asian medium-term bonds compared to other emerging market sources: by comparison with East European or Latin American foreign currency debt, Asian risk has always traded at narrower credit spreads to the respective benchmark yield curve than would be implied by differences in sovereign credit ratings.[79] The answer is partly affirmative, though measured by insubstantial amounts. Some Asian borrowers and professional intermediaries are well-established in the international credit markets, either as issuers or (relatively passive) investors. A small number of Asian borrowers are prolific and very few[80] have maintained a continuous market in issued debt securities. Irregular supply and the generally conservative stance of those investors able to hold Asian risk has meant that tight secondary conditions have been prevalent for much of the last decade. Asian issues of G3 currency public medium-term debt instruments totaled around US$34.0bn in 2003, an amount first (nominally) exceeded by the euromarkets in 1982.[81]

If offshore markets have provided a partial substitute for illiquid domestic debt capital markets, are there identifiable results (other than in funds raised) for public policy? For example, fractured national markets may suggest that contagion remains a worry, in that any deleterious external shock could be prolonged or more widespread, as if the markets collectively lacked built-in stabilizers to unforeseen or

---

[78] Pettis (2000). This stark comparison remains applicable, and survives cyclical changes in mark-to-market valuations of bonds or equity.

[79] Anecdotal reasons cite supply failing to meet investor demand and Asia's general lack of a modern default-to-rescheduling history prior to 1997. The Philippines is the sole exception: its borrowers have at all times won less favourable terms for international issues, closer to prevailing East European or Latin American levels than for others in East Asia.

[80] Fewer than 10 Asian organisations have been regarded as frequent borrowers in market parlance. CDSs currently trade on only 30 single name risks from non-Japan Asia (according to index provider iTraxx, part of Deutsche Börse affiliate International Index Company, see http://www.indexco.com.

[81] This inexact comparison is intended only to suggest scale. The 'euromarket' is in no sense synonymous with European risk. Sources: *Basis Point* 551, 3 October 2003; *Euromoney* Supplement, June 1989; *Euroweek Asian Review of the Year*, January 2004.

unwarranted volatility.[82] Some writers suggest that integration among East Asia's national financial sectors is relatively advanced and has risen in the post-crisis recovery, shown in two aspects of major currency cross-border markets: the level of participation by Asia-domiciled banks as lenders or syndicate members in international bond (and loan) transactions.[83] Furthermore, the validity of this observation implies that Asian commercial bank behavior has become a potential dampening force against severe conditions turning contagious. Yet the extent of Asian bank involvement in public bond issues as underwriters and investors and in syndicated credits may indicate passivity on the part of those banks or a lack of harvestable self-originated opportunities of sufficient return, and in any event is confined to transactions for large highly-rated borrowers. Similar evidence could suggest that potential contagion has not been lessened, for 'integration' in this form is a sign that Asian banks are less resourceful in arranging and distributing risk transactions than their foreign competitors.

A further (hostile) market-orientated view is that, given the generally favorable prevailing conditions enjoyed by Asian issuers relative to those from other emerging regions, access to the international debt markets has historically tended to lessen any incentive for local capital market development. If a well-rated borrower has free access to the major markets where its needs are fed by investment banks competing for limited debt supply, would it willingly lend resources to encourage growth in its home currency bond market, when such support might limit its access to domestic funding?[84] Except in Korea and Singapore, there is little evidence of top-tier companies encouraging domestic debt market expansion other than by conference lectern exhortation. Similarly, Asian banks have made surprisingly scant use of domestic currency markets to raise hybrid or regulatory capital, which would represent the application of established techniques to stimulate local market growth.[85]

---

[82] It has been argued that the 1997-98 crisis was 'triggered' by the withdrawal of foreign currency credit from Southeast Asia by Japanese commercial banks, partly in response to deteriorating risk but mostly their impending 1998 submission to Basel I rules requiring adequate risk capital to support impaired domestic assets (King, *op cit*). In a true crisis, the investor will sell the asset for which it obtains a price.

[83] McCauley, Fung & Gadanecz (*op cit*). This pro-integration case may overstate the role of underwriting syndicates for distribution purposes, rather than publicity. Furthermore, syndicate size has fallen steadily since 1994. Borio (op cit) notes that not all shocks are exogenous and may be kindled by herd behavior. King (2001) believes imminent new capital requirements forced Japanese banks to trigger the Asian crisis, withdrawing Southeast Asian lending to avoid writing-off impaired domestic assets.

[84] Because local banks dominate nascent bond market investment.

[85] Korea and Singapore are again exceptions: several banks have issued local currency subordinated debt to raise Tier II capital, although the aggregate amounts are modest.

5. Policy Reform and Considerations

Converting expectation into practice is to confound the region's complex patterns of internal and external financing, and tends to assume that the adoption of bond market models from elsewhere is feasible and desirable. This view is hazardous, and risks neglecting the costs associated with bond market development.[86] More realistic (but no less demanding on a regional basis) may be the design of specialist structures that allow the pooling of risk or enhancement of credit quality and which are tailored for East Asia in its present stage of financial evolution. A second route would require challenging levels of collaboration and legal harmonization but little in new systems or structure: this is the promotion of a regional hub for offshore Asian currency debt issues.

5.1. Market inefficiencies

Under-utilized markets are inefficient in two particular respects: from the resources absorbed by both public and private sectors in administration and the high marginal costs of transaction execution for participants. Asia's semi-liquid domestic markets bring all the costs yet only some of the true benefits associated with debt capital markets. For the markets to flourish and deliver their full value (if this becomes an agreed goal of policy), governments in the region must inculcate usage, not only with specific reforms, fiscal, regulatory or legal, but with suasion and innovation. Mechanical changes to improve the functioning of domestic markets may alone be inadequate, creating a vehicle that is sleek but stationary. The nature of funds flows in East Asia suggests that by itself, time will fail to be the cause of a signal rise in trading volume, issuance, or draw new participants to any domestic market. The contemporary cross-border bond market, competitive for a handful of borrowers, unreliable for long-term investors, will indirectly sustain the quasi-monopoly of the region's banking system by discouraging financial innovation, especially in identifying new ways to finance second tier enterprises. Hong Kong and Singapore now have similar debt capital market infrastructures that are effective in most respects but scale of use.[87]

The justification for this public policy effort arises from basic elements, against which can be assessed practical costs and strategic disadvantages.[88] These gains are

---

[86] Jiang, Tang & Law (*op cit*).

[87] Limitations in each case relate to permitted issuers, free use of proceeds (Singapore), differential tax treatments *vis-à-vis* corporate and other issuers, and restrictions on purchases by certain investor classes.

[88] Bond markets arguably require health warnings. Some commentators argue that sophisticated markets may intensify or distribute volatility, rather than act as the dampener that capital market proponents generally expect. Such critics suggest that debt market new issue activity is positively correlated with bank credit expansion, lessening the markets'

shown in the sections that follow, together with some primary challenges. Structural change is essential for some of these benefits to be captured successfully. For example, if policy intends to broaden financing sources for medium-scale enterprises then some form of innovation in financial architecture is necessary, either to create a new channel of funds and for risk appraisal, or to encourage changes in bank lending, funding or liability management practices. Some market reforms may be limited; others may demand ambitious cooperation for which the region may not be fully prepared or which would provoke a drain of sympathy from other competing national interests. The European Union's experience during the 1980s of creating a single market for trade and services may be useful in this respect for Asian policymakers since the framework preceded Europe's moves towards more extensive confederal integration, including the formation of the euro.[89]

5.1.1. Welfare: The economic and social value of using Asian savings in Asia.

Accepted. Yet proponents of market development may not always quantify associated direct and hidden costs. (For example, in terms of Asian savers' preferences for stable risks, which may need to adjust to accommodate new Asian debt issuers in the absence of external credit enhancement).

5.1.2. Risks I: Active financial markets may help avoid systemic risks of crises of confidence; their impact on the banking sector and the 'real' economy.

Whether bond markets help circumvent collapses in bank liquidity depends upon their being an uncorrelated alternative. Conversely, debt markets may provide efficient media for contagion to worsen a crisis. Highly developed markets demonstrate a direct positive correlation between bond issuance and private sector bank credit expansion. The U.S. domestic debt market is no exception, yet is lauded for its effectiveness in backing up the banking system in times of crisis, and vice-versa.

5.1.3. Risks II: Operating risk management, for example, having efficient markets promote efficient portfolio management by investors and of official reserves.

This point is generally accepted though neglected in official circles because of the political value historically associated with high levels of international reserves.

---

effectiveness as alternative financing channels to mitigate the contagion effects of banking crises. Jiang, Tang & Law (*op cit*) and Yoshitomi & Shirai (*op cit*) are examples.

[89] Discussed in the wider sense of all securities markets by Arner (2002b).

5.1.4. Risks III: Competition, the promotion of optimal allocations for long-term investment, and lower capital costs available through dispersed risk-sharing.

Effective, well-regulated banking systems may better promote resource allocation than financial markets, due to asymmetry in information gathering and skilled risk management. Yet this is belied by recurring herd behavior by banks. Market distortions (for example, national accounting differences, fiscal incentives or concessionary funding) may also discourage banks from fully appraising higher risks.

5.1.5. Secondary benefits: New funding channels assist complementary financial sectors (for example, banking, equity markets, direct investment, project finance or recycling impaired assets).

It is impossible to legislate for such vague factors. The effects on the competitiveness and risk profile of the banking system in Asia cannot be fully judged, especially if changes to capital adequacy rules based upon value at risk assessments or credit ratings are introduced under proposed Basel II guidelines.

This section has summarized the patchy evolution of Asia's domestic debt markets and how official opinion may now be resolved to create workable reforms, especially with regional initiatives for cooperation in the sharing of new constructions and the removal of market impediments. It has described East Asia's participation in the international bond markets, and how this has served as a semi-substitute for capable domestic or regional markets for a limited subset of Asian borrowers and investors. If the development cost issues associated with pro-market policies are considered to be satisfactory then how best can the region encourage the building of domestic markets? The question most often asked has been whether there exists a model for Asia to follow or adapt. The response is unclear, as the remainder of the chapter will show: East Asia's domestic and international financing patterns are unique in the contemporary world.

6. Appraising Asia's Debt Capital Markets

Previous sections in this chapter have shown how the region's markets are often well-developed but poorly used. Hong Kong and Singapore may be praised for establishing well-integrated systems but like the hidden spare tyre, these markets' use is latent; how they perform in stress is unknown. Liquidity is not present by any accepted measure, with only ephemeral exceptions. The markets are ineffectual as an alternative channel to the banking sector and thus fail to lessen the risk of contagion. They are poor in primary financial resource allocation and to date they have been of limited use in recycling impaired financial assets except in Korea and Malaysia.

All that is universally accepted is that Asia's debt markets are sub-optimal: there is no exception in respect of market usage or investor confidence, even in Korea or Taiwan, where trading can be intense and market capitalization has become substantial, because of controls and market segmentation or impediments. Thus in some cases new issue growth has been robust since the Asian crisis but the markets remain illiquid, opaque and subject to variations in regulation, taxation or legal status that deter many investor classes, may prevent others from becoming established, and constrain natural savings and investment flows within the region. Concomitantly, bond markets are important but inessential. This encapsulates why public policy has failed to achieve adequate energy and why past private sector initiatives have never wholly succeeded. As with Japan in its post 1940s industrialising era, East Asia lacks not funding, but efficient financial systems. Some national irregularities are shared: a theme of this report is to identify common policy remedies to correct such problems. This section is an outline of where reform should be applied.

6.1. Tasks for reform

Policy formation will need to address a series of characteristics and impediments, of which the following are the most common and important.

6.1.1. Micro-level impediments

Common barriers to steady growth in bond market activity in the review countries, notably issuance volumes and secondary trading liquidity.[90] These especially include obstacles in relation to withholding taxes, differentials in the application of taxes, restrictions on settlement or custody, arbitrary differences in creditor status that constrain institutional investment, legal risks for investors, creditor claims, and property rights generally and specifically in receivership or bankruptcy.

6.1.2. Regulatory restrictions

Institutional blockages, including the framework and application of regulatory guidelines for banks, pension and mutual funds, insurance companies and borrowers, and how they hinder activity.

6.1.3. Securitization

Policy reforms to facilitate structured finance involving asset transfer. If securitization is effective in promoting balance sheet restructuring and to provide ongoing supply for Asia's bond markets, does it require specific corrective legal measures or in civil code jurisdictions the enactment of 'umbrella' legislation as was completed by post-crisis Korea and Thailand? Are there other ways to enhance the creditworthiness of Asian borrowers and open funding alternatives for medium-scale

---

[90] Accepted indicators of liquidity are beyond measure if the market tends always to trade 'bid-only'.

businesses, including structured solutions such as credit enhancement with over-collateralization or external support?[91]

6.1.4. Governance

Cultural factors that cause obstructions relating to corporate governance and ownership. Is Asia's concentration of family-controlled or closely-held companies and conglomerate structures a product of the absence of a deep debt capital market? Has the lack of such markets resulted from these aspects of ownership and governance?[92] Asia's exporting economies are aggregates of mainly medium-scale enterprises in which ownership is comparatively closely-held, and for which related party transactions are thought relatively important, resulting in poor disclosure and a regulatory environment lacking credibility and confidence. For similar reasons, the work of local rating agencies (none established before 1990) has been erratic and in some cases their coverage has been conflicted. All these factors can make structured transactions impossible.[93] Where corporate credit risk might be enhanced by securitization the law has often been inadequate, especially if asset transfers to a special purpose vehicle (SPV) may be challenged or subjected to *ad valorem* taxation. Data records will often be inadequate to sustain an economic transaction. In this context, how has Asia nurtured an equity culture but not admitted traded debt? A majority owner's desire for control provides the most plausible explanation, with minority shareholders accepting risk with a (theoretically) limitless return and some semblance of a shared interest with the owner.[94] For such recalcitrant companies, issuing public debt instruments would compel both disclosure and a contractual coupon. In the long run true corporate debt markets will assist the equity markets by stimulating fuller disclosure.

6.1.5. Accounting

Poor accounting standards and inadequate disclosure, especially non-consolidation in reporting, including corporate leverage hidden by related-party transactions, off-

---

[91] Arner (2002a) gives a contemporary view of this issue.

[92] One survey shows that whether a company uses external finance may not be a function of the financing alternatives available in its host economy, although the form it takes typically is. Further, the size of companies is an important determinant of the extent of that choice being realistically available (Beck, Demirgüç-Kunt, & Maksimovic 2002).

[93] The 1990s saw pioneering securitized or asset-backed transactions close in Indonesia, Korea, the Philippines, Thailand and Asian countries outside the review group. In most cases, these transactions were not repeated, despite all intentions and heavy development expenditure.

[94] Herring & Chatusripitak (*op cit*).

balance sheet financing and cross-guarantees.[95] Uncertain disclosure of derivatives or contingent liabilities. Unrecorded exposure to currency risks from short-term foreign borrowing and unstated use of hedging instruments.

6.1.6. Loan classification

For banks and finance companies, qualitative classification and poor disclosure of sectoral risk concentrations, delinquent loans, provisioning, non-accruing assets and 'voluntary' rescheduling with new advances.

6.1.7. History and culture

Last, how Asia's financial sectors differ from those of advanced economies, whether intrinsically or purely in terms of relative stage of development. This question affects policy implementation in that governments risk promoting capital markets because of their assumed value while neglecting fair competing interests and a variety of other costs. Today's bond markets may be underdeveloped mainly because their host economies are themselves youthful: greater sophistication will flow naturally from further economic growth bringing institutional development. It has been suggested that Asia is now in the second, semi-sophisticated stage of three distinct phases of financial development, and that its systems for funding and intermediation are in their 'natural' state on an evolutionary path.[96] Even if correct, it remains likely that external effort is needed to induce Asia's markets to the third stage of sophistication: this inevitably demands policy reform.

6.2. Other reform considerations

6.2.1. China factors

Reviews of the Asian crisis often neglect China's success in avoiding output losses in 1997-98[97] while noting that a substantial 1994 devaluation and a pre-crisis external current surplus left China free of the stresses placed on Korea and Southeast Asia in mid-1997.[98] That China's border halted the contagion may owe much to its economy's limited natural credit culture. Market techniques have grown steadily

[95] 'Asymmetric information—the situation in which some people have greater access to knowledge relevant to a decision—appears always to have limited the scope and use of financial markets', Baskin (1988), reviewing 300 years of market evolution.

[96] Yoshitomi & Shirai (*op cit*). The analytical framework is especially due to Goldsmith (1969).

[97] Real GDP grew by 7.8 per cent in 1998.

[98] Although China's devaluation may have increased the probability of subsequent falls in other Asian currencies.

more important since the 1980s but financial institutions do not yet operate in the fullness of market forces. This has two consequences for China's banks. First, they continue to suffer external direction and may be unable to extend or withdraw credit from state sector borrowers as freely as most banks would prefer. Second, banks are protected from external shifts in sentiment. The sector cannot be attacked rapidly even though the scale of its impaired assets and weak capital bases is accepted. China's continuing market liberalization and prudential re-regulation will eventually make those pressures less susceptible to semi-official resistance; it is essential for China to create a true debt capital market to guard against destabilization. This is also a question of funding efficiency for China's private enterprise sector, which hitherto has relied on internal funding and received minimal external financing support.[99]

6.2.2. 'Original sin'

A recent debate asks why an economy cannot use its own currency to borrow abroad, or to borrow domestically for long maturities.[100] With this 'incompleteness', financial fragility is unavoidable because all investments will suffer either a currency or maturity mismatch. Critically, these mismatches exist not because of imprudent hedging but because a country whose external liabilities are denominated solely in foreign exchange is unable to hedge.[101] Deeper capital markets lessen the problem, as the early 20th century proved for the U.S. and several other leading industrial economies. The key in the progression of 'older' economies to become free to issue external debt in their own currencies (or having local currency debt bought by non-residents) was their response to shocks on the scale of war or the 1930s depression. In this respect the U.S. debt market evolved more rapidly than those in Europe because of the size of its host economy. This produced a vast investor need for domestic debt and made it less risky for investors to hold bonds (despite a phasing out of convertibility).[102] Until the 1960s investment in foreign debt securities was most often undertaken through a limited number of financial centers that were home to prominent investor communities, but there is no longer any correspondence between a bond's currency of issue and its place of issue or listing. In Asia it is clear that future bond market development is more truly a domestic question, for the critical need is to admit or establish prominent local currency investors at home, as

---

[99] Gregory & Tenev (2001) surveyed over 600 private Chinese enterprises.

[100] Initiated by Eichengreen & Hausmann (1999). This condition has been termed 'original sin' (ironically unknown in Asian traditions).

[101] Since no investor is willing to acquire this local currency, it is assumed that hedging instruments are likewise unavailable (Eichengreen & Hausmann, *op cit*).

[102] Prior to 1933 bonds typically provided for repayment in gold at the investor's option (Bordo, Meissner & Redish, 2003).

well as abroad.[103] Research[104] and anecdotal evidence show that large countries are better able to attract foreign investment to their domestic currency issues; market depth is an important corollary to an economy's size.

6.2.3. Regional initiatives

Does Asia's debt capital market development require regional impetus? There may be fears that collective action by national authorities may lead to non-commercial solutions or duplicate wastefully what may safely be left to the private sector. The same view advocates an evolutionary approach to financial market development, leaving each local market to grow alone to maturity.[105] It is doubtful whether even greatly expanded Asian economies would support liquid domestic bond markets adequate for both non-bank investor activity and intermediation that militates against financial market contagion. Indeed, certain substantial economies have never produced sophisticated debt markets. Between the end of the Bretton Woods agreement in 1971 and the 1999 creation of the single currency, Western Europe included comparatively prosperous states that maintained prolonged budget deficits, some with well-developed government debt markets. In France, Germany and the Netherlands, for example, those markets were self-sustaining but among current EU states robust markets for corporate debt existed only at intervals prior to the adoption of the euro (although generally in the UK). In many cases government funding was reliant on overseas core currency issues: for long periods this was true for Belgium, Denmark, Ireland, Italy, Spain and Sweden. A regional initiative in Asia appears to be essential, both to harmonies reform and give appropriate momentum to market development while respecting the primacy of commercial conditions.

Asia's government bond markets are likely to evolve further but they will be deficient with neither budget deficits to fund nor principle to support in the form of welfare and efficiency.[106] This is a current concern of several regional official working groups established by intergovernmental bodies such as ASEAN or APEC.[107]

Whether governments issue bonds to raise funds or for the operation of monetary policy the practice must have clarity and predictability. Too often this is not the case and investors and intermediaries suffer impromptu withdrawals of auctions of notes

---

[103] This accords with the second precept of the analysis, whether an economy is supported by long-term domestic local currency investors (Eichengreen and Hausmann *op cit*).

[104] Bordo, Meissner & Redish (*op cit*).

[105] Exemplified by Yoshitomi & Shirai (*op cit*). North (1995) plainly states the anti-evolutionary case, 'throughout history, there is no necessary reason for this development to occur.' p102.

[106] China's 2004 decision to promote reform of its domestic debt markets may mean that its profound funding needs are catalytic for growth and participation throughout the region.

[107] Described in detail in Chapter 8. APEC is the Asia-Pacific Economic Cooperation forum; ASEAN is the Association of Southeast Asian Nations.

or bonds. The same argument can be made of international financial organisations issuing in Asian currencies, often failing to contribute to liquidity with regular issues (there are many examples of supranational borrowers making single visits to emerging bond markets).[108] The absence of a well-developed market may have costs for any economy (in terms of efficiency and capital allocation[109]) but in Asia this has been seen most acutely for investors. Competition among banks for major relationships has often been so extreme that creditworthy borrowers have generally not lacked external funding, and few budget deficits have become endemic. With a more developed financial infrastructure, the near-term gains will be most apparent from the investor's perspective, whose resulting behavior could provide a practical counter to future contagion. This results from a lack of defensive investments increasing instability in volatile conditions. When rational, risk averse investors (domestic or foreign) wish to reduce their holdings of local currency assets of any type, they may ordinarily seek to acquire defensive short-term instruments in the same currency. Core currency markets make this choice possible by allowing non-bank investors to hold liquid money market instruments (or wholesale money market funds), usually without fiscal penalty. Such alternatives are available in no Asian currency except yen, and prudence limits the use of local currency bank deposits by institutional investors.

6.2.4. Product innovation

Regulatory or system arbitrage frequently become drivers of product innovation, particularly in rule-based economies. This has mostly clearly been seen in the global banking and securities markets responses to the initial 1988 Basel Accord on capital adequacy, the effects of which were to propel enormous growth in credit risk transfer and the creation of capital-efficient assets, much taking place through new instruments. However, the growth of markets will not succeed without reform, however much it may be desired by participants. Governments need to legislate wherever necessary to remove or correct obstacles and inconsistencies, as well as agreeing new wholly practical elements (as radically new as the U.S. mortgage or German *pfandbrief* markets once were). If debt market reform is a goal of public policy, then the aim is to promote the role of bonds in Asia as a broadening of financial intermediation. Public policy's task must therefore be to promote usage and may involve significant expansions in government issuance. It may also involve the creation of national or regional agencies to facilitate change. For many of these issues the IFC has a reliable view given its experience in fundraising in developing markets. It has argued that not every country will be able to develop active markets

---

[108] To the extent that these issues are held by commercial banks, it is arguable that they also represent a negative market distortion due to favourable risk-asset weightings, and as such form part of Asia's risk averse post-crisis portfolio adjustment (Crockett *op cit*).

[109] 'The financial superstructure, in the form of both primary and secondary securities, accelerates economic growth and improves economic performance to the extent that it facilitates the migration of funds to the best user.' Goldsmith (1969 *op cit*) p400.

for reasons of volition or scale.[110] This further supports a solution involving a hub approach by which system resources are pooled. Behavioral factors are critical in achieving market usage and since this takes time to become manifest[111] it must be recognized that creating financial infrastructure alone does not bring usage, nor achieve the broad benefits of bond markets. No policymaker can countenance encouraging market development as a mark of a sophisticated economy.

6.2.5. Objectives

Liquid debt markets engender a culture of enquiry, for they demand accepted standards of exchange and information. Reliable domestic markets will ease the World Bank's three current concerns.[112] Asia's performance record is remarkable but far from immaculate, for reasons that are widely discussed.[113] A post-1998 output resurgence has resolved certain issues, some structural as conceived by critics of the region's growth record, and others relating to the quality of regulatory insight and observance. The most pertinent policy task is to solve permanently a crisis overhang of non-performing or impaired financial assets, and instigate practices that lessen the true occurrence of such assets and provide a means to deal with new cycles of loan losses and recovery. Fully-functional debt markets are part of Asia's prescription, not least in their giving banks a means to raise local currency regulatory capital and broaden their funding and asset refinancing. Governments may become better able to fund themselves securely, with fewer risks of flight capital leading to contagion and chronic illiquidity; active markets will offer greater real choices for both borrowers and investors.

The issue of feasibility cited at the beginning of this report is addressed by the two following summary tables. Fully functioning and active markets are desirable and feasible but will not be achieved without dedicated effort and agreement to remove structural, legal and regulatory blockages. Furthermore, it is unlikely that the needs of each review economy are sufficient to maintain a debt capital market effective in all respects. This report's proposals for collaboration in policymaking and in detailed aspects of implementation are based upon these conclusions, in particular for the creation of formalized regional financing arrangements through a new offshore capital market. Table 3-10 assesses the present strengths of domestic and offshore markets for debt securities in terms of how participants are served by each market. Most commonly, the domestic markets provide adequate means for governments to borrow and conduct monetary policy, albeit that each may be limited

---

[110] Harwood (2000 *op cit*), introduction.

[111] Similar to the market evolution concept (Yoshitomi & Shirai, *op cit*).

[112] Section 3.3 (*supra*).

[113] Including corruption, crony capitalism, self-induced moral hazard, over-investment, unhedged foreign currency borrowing, poor exchange rate management, inadequate risk analysis by bankers and project sponsors, and government 'interference' in the economy. Arner, Yokoi-Arai & Zhou (2001) show that such problems are not uncommon elsewhere and have been regularly identified in crisis analysis.

in ambition. No market offers value in risk management or for all corporate borrowers or investors. Six core questions as to overall feasibility are considered in Table 3-10.

7. Market Characteristics

This section indicates the more important attributes of Asia's bond markets, identifying their principal features and those that most require reform. It illustrates conditions and activity in both domestic markets and for aspects of offshore issuance and trading, and isolates concerns to which attention is needed. No attempt is made to extend beyond certain key points: descriptive comprehensiveness is ephemeral and subject to continual coverage by private sector sources. The factors shown also address questions arising for non-bank institutional investors in assessing any developing market.

7.1. Common issues and concerns

- A recurring concern is the effect on general liquidity and price transparency of government securities (and in some cases other instruments) being held by the domestic banking sector as part of an overt or indirect regulatory regime.
- The scale of domestic markets in terms of available debt instruments. How freely do these securities trade and with what degree of liquidity?[114] Measures of turnover may be unreliable in unsophisticated markets but outstanding capitalization can never be the sole criterion by which a market is assessed.
- Regulatory restrictions on issuance and external constraints on investor activity.
- How withholding taxes apply to bonds and money market instruments. Do these and other taxes differ in their impact on types of instrument or classes of investor, domestic or foreign? Are banks (domestic or offshore) or foreign investors able to lessen or offset the incidence of withholding taxes?
- The impact of exchange controls on cross-border investors and fundraising. Are there differences between the legal and practical incidence of exchange controls?
- Do domestic dealing and settlement processes differ between debt instruments? Are domestic and foreign investors offered clear unitary settlement models using delivery against payment and for custody?

---

[114] Measures of liquidity are uncontroversial but never absolute. For example, dealing (bid-offer) spreads can faithfully show competitive liquidity only if convention requires continual market-making. Relative turnover and the effect of single trades on prevailing prices are helpful indicators for less-developed markets but are clearly subjective. The most comprehensive survey of East Asian liquidity is by Mohanty (2002) but covers only government securities.

***Table 3-10.* How current markets affect participants**

	Market beneficiaries	Market omissions
China	Central government as borrower; and in monetary policy operations Infrastructure project promoters	Fund managers and insurers Banks needing to recycle impaired assets Non-state corporate borrowers and medium-scale enterprises Central government as risk manager
Hong Kong	Central government as borrower; and in monetary policy operations Supranational borrowers	Fund managers and insurers All corporate borrowers Central government as risk manager
India	Central government as borrower, and monetary policy operations Banks and public sector investors	Fund managers and insurers Major corporate borrowers and medium-scale enterprises Central government as risk manager
Indonesia	Central government in monetary policy operations	Central government as borrower; and as risk manager Fund managers and insurers All corporate borrowers
Korea	Central government as borrower, and in monetary policy operations Major borrowing companies Banks needing to recycle impaired assets	Fund managers and insurers Medium-scale enterprises Central government as risk manager
Malaysia	Central government as borrower, and in monetary policy operations Public sector investors and pension funds	Major corporate borrowers Fund managers and insurers Medium-scale enterprises Central government as risk manager
Philippines	Central government as borrower Short-term corporate borrowers Banks as investors	Central government as risk manager All non-bank investors Medium-term borrowers Infrastructure project promoters
Singapore	Central government as borrower, and in monetary policy operations Major local companies Public sector investors	Supranational and foreign borrowers Fund managers and insurers Medium-scale enterprises
Taiwan	Central government as borrower, and in monetary policy operations	Companies of all kinds Fund managers and insurers
Thailand	Central government as borrower, and in monetary policy operations Prominent, well-rated companies	Banks needing to recycle impaired assets Medium-scale enterprises Infrastructure project promoters
Offshore	Well-rated sovereign, public sector and major corporate borrowers Banks as borrowers Inactive investors	Non-investment grade borrowers Governments as risk managers Banks as regulatory capital issuers Active investors and hedge funds

Table 3-11. **Feasibility of true debt capital markets in Asia**
Feasibility of true debt capital markets in Asia

Do Asia-Pacific's established patterns of finance make mature bond markets infeasible in a conventional sense?	Not infeasible but new markets will not develop naturally.
Are weak Asian markets chiefly indicative of the region's relative development?	The markets' current disposition reflects funding and spending choices and historic priorities.
Can debt capital markets be developed effectively without an active risk-free benchmark yield curve?	With difficulty, but providing regulatory discretion allows interest rate derivatives to generate a continuous swap yield curve.
Will new financial structures (regional or shared among several markets with common objectives) facilitate effective bond issuance, investment and trading?	Giving system reliability, issuer predictability, and prospects for improving credit ratings, investors and other new users will proliferate.
Can such new structures assist the funding of medium-scale businesses, and widen the use of securitization for continuing funding and asset recovery?	This is demonstrable in the case of NPLs. Funding SMEs is feasible if complex (compared to applying securitization to homogenous assets such as home loans); banks must be encouraged to accelerate SME lending in return for arms' length refinancing through securitization.
Do potential net gains in economic welfare justify active investment to strengthen Asia's bond markets?	The potential gains in terms of a shield against instability are real, universal, but unquantifiable. The pooling of resources or cooperation in regional solutions will require new political effort.

- How secure and actionable is the sale of financial assets, transfer of creditor claims or of associated collateral between unconnected parties? Do taxes or duties affect such transfers so as to threaten the integrity of conventional structured finance transactions, including those for NPLs?
- Path dependence exists in the institutional development of all markets, for example, in the way that the treatment of property rights affects asset-backed securities (ABSs). Rights created recently in law to facilitate privatisation programmes may not be fully appropriate for reliable ABS issues.
- Legal impediments concentrate on areas most affecting investor confidence and the structuring of ABS transactions or programmes. Circumventing these problems with complex (or synthetic) ABS transactions is not a sufficient solution.
- The quality and reliability of mandatory issuer disclosure requirements.
- The availability and price transparency of interest rate swaps and other important OTC or exchange traded derivatives and hedging products.

7.2. Summary and explanation

Table 3-12. Summary characteristics

China	Substantial government and state sector issuance. Negligible trading activity. Directional, allocated market with centrally determined interest rates. Reform of all kinds under close official scrutiny. Modest illiquid foreign currency issuance (hampered by credit concerns and post 1997 defaults).
Hong Kong	Sophisticated, potentially substantial but underused market. Non-bank investors often lack confidence.
India	Structurally flawed market with substantial government issuance. Investible assets are scarce, especially for non-bank investors. Generally highly regulated. Reform is desired but slow in implementation.
Indonesia	Modest market that grew after the Asian crisis due to government funding needs connected to banking sector recapitalization. Limited corporate debt market.
Korea	Sizeable market made resourceful and sophisticated since 1999 by considerable legal and regulatory innovation. High corporate and ABS issuance. Risks of systemic volatility may threaten usage. Controls on cross-border usage.
Malaysia	Effective but under-used market, the product of significant systemic innovations.
Philippines	Financial sector dominated by government funding needs and a strong banking sector. No traditional of non-governmental debt issuance except in money market instruments.
Singapore	Post-1998 policy changes led to a considerable increase in all market activity; this has not been sustained. New applications and greater foreign interest may be needed. Highly effective systems.
Taiwan	Dominant domestic banking sector has led to a semi-active, closely regulated debt market with little true liquidity. Reform has now allowed ABS transactions but the speed of all such change is slow.
Thailand	Expanding corporate debt market including active private placement issuance. Growing but irregular government and public sector issuance. All activity constrained by close regulatory control.

7.3. Available instruments

References are to domestic markets for local currency debt securities unless stated.

7.3.1. China

Central government issues fixed and floating rate treasury bonds and sanctions financial institution bonds on a similar scale (and state enterprise bonds in smaller amounts) most of which are bought by commercial banks for liquidity requirements.

A growing non-bank financial institutional sector has a lesser passive investment role. Modest secondary dealing split between the Shanghai or Shenzhen exchanges and an interbank market: the untraded yuan bond market is thus substantial. Primary sales have been made by auction since 2002-03 but the process is closed and only part of the state's issuance plans is typically declared. Scheduled or pre-announced auctions have been cancelled at short notice. Bonds are placed or bought by direction, so the market lacks infrastructure for information purposes, open regulation, trading and settlement.

7.3.2. Hong Kong

Government has issued debt sporadically. The Hong Kong Monetary Authority regularly issues Exchange Fund notes (12 months or less) and bonds (10 years or less), the main use for which is as liquidity regulation instruments through a discount window, and to provide the private debt market with a benchmark yield curve. Open auction used for these quasi-government securities with a declared issuance programme. The amounts in issue have traditionally been limited by Hong Kong's quasi-currency board structure but this restriction could be overcome if agreed. Statutory bodies issue medium-term bonds regularly but never prolifically.

In each case, secondary markets can be liquid, but conducted largely by banks: non-bank institutional investors have little continual access to paper. Non-government sector bonds follow eurobond market issue and trading practice: issuers are mainly supranational organisations (for tax reasons), banks in Hong Kong. Local and foreign corporates are far less active. A liquid market for commercial paper existed in the early 1990s until crowded out by the Exchange Fund notes. Hub for medium-term note (MTN) issuance based on semi-liquid derivatives market. Retail targeted debt issues popular since 2002 due to low nominal interest rates. Since 1997, government agency Hong Kong Mortgage Corporation encourages banks to securitize residential mortgage loans and is itself an issuer in local and core currencies. Sporadic core currency public issuance by major corporates.

7.3.3. India

Market dominated by government sector (central and government and public corporations) as issuers; banks (and the central bank) as investors. Government sector needs reform to consolidate debt issues. No fully open auction or declared issuance programme for government primary issues (but short-term issues are announced semi-annually). Little general liquidity in government issues due to liquidity requirements and historic legal constraints on issuance. Central government auctions treasury bills (up to 12 months), and notes of up to 10 years; state government securities can be similar. Central and state governments also guarantee bonds (up to 15 years) to assist infrastructural financing. Corporate bonds and commercial paper are bought by banks and (bonds) to a limited extent by domestic retail investors.

In a first rupee issue for a foreign borrower in February 2004, the ADB raised $ 110 m equivalent in 10 year notes, 60 per cent bought by commercial banks, the remainder by non-bank institutions. Foreign borrowing and outward investment very closely regulated.

7.3.4. Indonesia

Money markets are liquid and well established, with government and public sector bills and commercial paper held or traded prior to the Asian crisis, mainly due to central bank issuing short-term notes (SBIs) for funding and liquidity management, and state companies borrowing for longer periods. Commercial bank demand for SBIs is governed by regulatory requirements. Several very large medium-term government debt issues arranged after 1998-99, mainly to support the recapitalization of the public sector and newly nationalized banking sector. Currently, an open auction exists for new government securities but there is no issuance programme or guidance: a firm institutional framework for issuance is lacking. Legislation enacted in 2002 is intended to give a formal setting for government issuance, and will be tested when the outstanding post-1999 transactions are refunded.

Medium-term corporate debt issues have begun to increase in number since 2001-02, following legislation encouraging mutual fund investment in debt securities.

7.3.5. Korea

Market size and activity overstated before 1998, since when reforms have fed growth in government, corporate and ABS volumes and usage, much of the expansion assisting post-crisis financial reconstruction. Government issues traditionally account for a relatively small share of total market capitalization. Despite the scale of the overall market, non-bank investors often find acceptable instruments scarce, in part because Korea has a comparatively large insurance sector. Central government issues several security types (including treasury, monetary stabilisation and foreign exchange stabilisation bonds) in maturities of up to 10 years, and historically guaranteed other public sector borrowers, producing an unnecessarily fractured market and benchmark yield curve. Coupled with bank regulatory requirements, such fragmentation greatly lessening liquidity. Open auction for government securities and declared issuance programme. ABS growth sourced successively from banks, finance companies and corporates. Foreign issuers not generally permitted despite the Won market's size. Overseas core currency issuance by Korean borrowers is sizeable and generally well-traded.

7.3.6. Malaysia

Despite improvements in systems and a long history of market initiatives, Malaysia's domestic bond markets suffer illiquidity and a lack of issuer usage. Government and public sector instruments take many forms, while the core of outstanding central government issues is compulsorily acquired and held by public sector provident funds.

Government issues securities directly (with open auctions and a declared issuance programme) and through the central bank, and include guaranteed Islamic notes of up to 10 years. Liquidity requirements for financial institutions further constrain trading in Government of Malaysia treasury bills and bonds. The government has long recognized the problem, and caused federal agencies to issue securities that domestic investors would regard as government risk: Cagamas founded in 1986 as a national mortgage agency, and Khazanah Nasional, a state investment company since 1993 that issues state guaranteed notes that serve to provide a benchmark zero coupon yield curve. Market innovation is healthy and money market activity is liquid. The corporate debt market is effective but modest (there is a history of bank-guaranteed corporate issues). Foreign investors have also been deterred by capital controls (1998-2000). Bar to issuance by foreign borrowers.

7.3.7. Philippines

Government issues dominate the debt and money markets. Recurrent public sector fiscal deficits have led to heavy government issuance. Government auctions notes and bills, and has issued up to 25 year bonds through underwritten transactions, but most have tenors of up to 1-3 years. Except in short-term bills, liquidity is slight as most issues are held to maturity. Liquidity in government bond markets heavily constrained by bank liquidity requirements. Open auction for government securities through a relatively large group of primary dealers but there is no declared issuance programme, and retail issue methods are ineffectual. Structural weaknesses in the long-term domestic debt market have historically made the state equally dependent on foreign currency debt. There is no tradition of domestic corporate debt other than in very short maturities. No real attempt to create a long-term market, although pending ABS legislation may lead to constructive change. Credit concerns prevent the development of a market for public sector risk similar to the U.S. municipal bond market despite announced intentions. Government sector foreign borrowing erratic and colored by rescheduling history since 1980s, but foreign borrowing has been essential due to domestic market shortcomings.

7.3.8. Singapore

Money markets have been liquid for some years but the medium-term debt market was shallow and illiquid until 1999 (except for equity-linked issues favored by local corporates). Government debt was modest and simply absorbed in the state-sponsored provident fund. In a series of 1998-99 reforms, government began an appreciable increase in bond issuance and secondary activity with an enlarged government debt programme, the relaxation of controls on foreign issuers and with targeted incentives to participants. Central government overfunding produced a substantial growth in outstanding (tradable) government bonds, raising liquidity and giving an effective term benchmark yield curve for the first time, and encouraged domestic and foreign corporate new issues, some of which have been sizeable. Foreign issuance has been more diverse than in Hong Kong. Open auction for government securities. Declared 12 months issuance programme but subject to variation. Foreign issuance encouraged, although there are restrictions on the use of proceeds. The market has strongly supported commercial property securitizations and bank regulatory capital transactions. However, market growth has now stalled and may need to be stimulated with further more modest reform: for example, foreign (especially regional) participation could be encouraged. Singapore could become a source of regulatory capital for ASEAN banks. The domestic market would be further helped by new instruments (CLOs) to assist SME finance and adjustments to the working of the mandatory provident scheme.

7.3.9. Taiwan

Highly regulated government debt market and the financial system is dominated by banks. Closed auction for government securities (since 1992). Issuance programme announced irregularly and at short notice. No reliable benchmark yield curve due to general lack of liquidity. Government bonds and notes important in bank and financial institution liquidity requirements; heavy emphasis on repurchase trading, partly for tax reasons. Government bonds issued in maturities of up to 20 years, a majority for either 5 or 10 years. For an open, active government market to grow and encourage a transparent corporate debt market, there may need to be changes in the focus and importance of the banking sector. A limited number of supranational borrowers have issued fixed rate bonds in the domestic market. Corporate fundraising orientated to banks and equity markets.

7.3.10. Thailand

All issuance has grown markedly since the recovery from Asian crisis due to investor demand, disintermediation from banking sector and high state funding requirements and for bank recapitalization.

Irregular (but sizeable) government issuance except short-term instruments. Hence despite growing demand for government and corporate issues, there is no reliable benchmark yield curve and the corporate debt market has a bias to private issues and short maturities (3-5 years). Government issues or sponsors a variety of bills, bonds and public sector instruments that would benefit from consolidation. Open auction for government securities and issuance programme disclosed but not consistent other than for bills. Generally excess demand for government issues for liquidity purposes and from public sector provident schemes.

7.4. Legal impediments[115]

Legal issues include general problems and specific concerns hindering securitized transactions, notably the feasibility of true sales and creation of bankruptcy remote vehicles, risks of set-off, whether the sale of receivables is treated as secured lending to an asset originator, and matters of notice or registration that materially lessen the feasibility or simplicity of any such transaction.

---

[115] Chapter 8 deals in detail with the incidence and effects of legal, fiscal, systemic and regulatory market impediments.

7.4.1. China

Historically, property and securities law are not comprehensive and subject to administrative rulings. New contract (1999) and trust laws (2001) provide for true sale and allow single transactions, but property rights, effectiveness of transfer, and the creation of bankruptcy remote vehicles for ABS issues require further reform and refinement (hence offshore ABS structures have been preferred to date). Quantitative constraints on corporate issuers now prevent the use of onshore SPVs for structured transactions. Enforcement uncertainties are common and may vary between provinces. Four asset management companies were set up after 1997 to dispose of bank impaired assets: foreign participation in such sales has been minimal despite great interest, partly due to pending legal and regulatory uncertainties. These problems are acknowledged by government and its main regulators.

7.4.2. Hong Kong

Common law framework generally amenable to securities markets.

Delayed reform of law on administration and bankruptcy.

Listing rules may deter non-Chinese foreign companies.

7.4.3. India

The transfer of receivables is valid but real property rights may be constrained or subject to delay in transfer. Limits to foreign ownership of domestic companies.

7.4.4. Indonesia

Legal system is less accommodative to market-based securities than Asian common law systems, and may require comprehensive legislation of the kind introduced by Korea after the Asian crisis. There is uncertainty in the enforcement of foreign and domestic judgements, and in the acceptance by the courts of the choice of foreign law for contracts or collateral deeds. Current receivables may be transferred by assignment but there are doubts as to necessary notices and consents. Law permitting ABS issues was enacted in 1997 but domestic SPVs cannot issue without a trading record. Law allowing the transfer of receivables to an onshore vehicle passed in 1998. Unclear that courts respect contractual priorities among secured creditors in restructuring, but secured creditors have retained rights over collateral. Further uncertainty exists in respect of new bankruptcy law.

7.4.5. Korea

Korea appears a model for successful civil law financial reform but long-term impact on activity cannot yet be judged. Strong controls remain on all Korean issuers and largely prohibit non-Korean Won issues. Despite ABS growth it is unclear whether originators may service loans, but this has not been disputed. True sales are allowed under ABS legislation but SPVs are often placed offshore to safeguard true sales.

7.4.6. Malaysia

The legal framework generally does not hinder market development but post-crisis enforcement has been questioned.

7.4.7. Philippines

Several efforts since the 1990s to enact securities, regulatory and financial sector reform have suffered extensive political delay.

Securitization impossible despite central bank having introduced transaction guidelines in 1998. A new enabling act currently awaits presidential ratification.

True sale may be treated as a secured loan to a seller of assets.

Unclear how courts treat contractual and other priorities among secured creditors and with unsecured creditors.

Controversy as to court enforcement of regulatory compliance matters.

7.4.8. Singapore

Singapore's common law framework is generally amenable to securities markets.

7.4.9. Taiwan

Non-equity markets have been undergoing deregulation at a slow rate for more than 10 years but the legal background needs reform for debt market activity to improve significantly. Securitization legislation enacted in 2002 is the first such example: so far it is little used and may not be fully effective in tax implications and perfection of title.

Legislation to allow real estate investment trusts was proposed in 1998 but not enacted.

7.4.10. Thailand

Weak rules covering corporate new issue disclosure and documentation, based largely on 1992 legislative framework that initiated a market regulatory environment.

Provisions relating to transfer are unclear in some respects despite ABS legislation, including notice requirements and the unwinding of sales. Market confidence not assisted by the frequent use of decrees compared to changes in primary legislation.

Uncertainty as to principles adopted by the central bankruptcy court in adjudicating settlements. Other aspects of enforcement have been unreliable. Effects of external capital controls on all offshore borrowing is tightly controlled.

7.5. Taxation

7.5.1. China

Withholding taxes on interest payable offshore and to domestic non-bank investors.

7.5.2. Hong Kong

No withholding taxes but corporate debt issues costs are treated unequally for profits tax purposes compared to banks, public sector and supranational issuers: this has historically deterred both local and foreign corporate issuance. Non-bank traders and investors may be similarly disfavored, although this anomaly was lessened in 2003.

7.5.3. India

Withholding tax is typically 20 per cent of interest due to non-resident investors. A tax treaty with Mauritius has been used by non-resident Indians and domestic borrowers to eliminate withholdings. Government has sought unsuccessfully to impose capital gains taxes in lieu of withholdings taxes. Stamp duty applies to CDs which limits money market trading. Ad valorem stamp duties apply to the transfer of receivables.

7.5.4. Indonesia

Withholding tax applies to interest from debt securities but with differing domestic and foreign exemptions. Foreign investors may be subject to taxes on capital gains. A limited number of tax treaties only lessen minimum effective rates of deduction. Stamp duty applies to the transfer of collateral assets (this has led to unnecessarily complex structures to create reliable ABS issues).

7.5.5. Korea

General 25 per cent withholding tax on interest. Banks actively use foreign tax treaties.

7.5.6. Malaysia

15-20% withholding tax imposed on investments for all non-bank investors, but some instruments are tax exempt, including Government treasury bills, zero coupon bonds and identified corporate bonds rated by RAM. Investors often use a Labuan conduit to avoid or lessen domestic taxes (Labuan investors generally buy domestic instruments free of tax).

7.5.7. Philippines

Stamp duty levied on trades in non-government securities.

The withholding tax regime is complex and deters inward portfolio investment.

7.5.8. Singapore

Offshore withholding tax exemption on 'qualified debt securities'

7.5.9. Taiwan

Transaction tax is a continuing deterrent to market growth.

A punitive 20 per cent withholding tax and differentials in tax treatment distort trading activity and lessen active involvement by non-bank investors.

7.5.10. Thailand

Withholding taxes on interest and imposts on asset transfer are generally complex, affecting confidence and investor costs. Withholdings on public sector issues will be waived under 2004 decrees and the waiver extended to a variety of issues to assist activity. However, there is uncertainty over retroactive coverage in the event of the concession's withdrawal.

7.6. Rating agencies

7.6.1. China

Historically, over fifty firms have been known. The matter is under regulatory study. Two national firms have limited roles; one may have official support.

7.6.2. Hong Kong

None. International agencies are active.

7.6.3. India

Listed corporate issues must be rated (at investment grade) by two local agencies.

7.6.4. Indonesia

Ratings are mandatory for public corporate issues.

The established rating agency has ties to a sister agency in Malaysia and technical assistance agreement with an international agency.

7.6.5. Korea

Three agencies, each with an international link. Ratings mandatory for public issues.

7.6.6. Malaysia

Two private domestic agencies have external ties to the ADB and Standard & Poor's Corp. Ratings mandatory for all public issues.

7.6.7. Philippines

Domestic agency concerned mainly with short-term corporate commercial paper.

7.6.8. Singapore

None. International agencies are active.

7.6.9. Taiwan

Established domestic agency. Ratings are mandatory for public issues.

7.6.10. Thailand

Well-established agency has limited resources.

Ratings mandatory for public issues since 2000.

7.7. Securitization

7.7.1. China

Since 2003 several domestic or foreign currency issues completed using NPLs but only with full or partial recourse to the asset seller, or enhanced with well-performing assets. China Banking Regulatory Commission (CBRC) and People's Bank of China issued new outline ABS regulations in April 2005, which will be subject to pilot legislation. Many more transactions planned or announced.

7.7.2. Hong Kong

No substantial omissions or anomalies.

7.7.3. India

Recently enacted securitization law, not yet tested.

7.7.4. Indonesia

Handful of single transactions since 1996-97 supported by foreign monoline cover. Legal framework for onshore transactions in need of correction (except those using credit card receivables). Acute enforcement problems have made conventional ABS expansion hazardous for domestic investors and almost impossible for offshore transactions.

7.7.5. Korea

New laws in 1998-99 permit ABS and mortgage-backed issues by help create a simple means of transfer and public notification. As a result the government's NPL recycling body (KAMCO) has been highly effective since 2000 in assisting the financial and corporate sectors in disposing of impaired and restructured assets, financed with ABS issues. All KAMCO assets were acquired with recourse. Overseas ABS issues have been generally successful, relying on monoline credit wrap support becoming more freely available with Korea's credit rating recovery after 1998. Primary (non-synthetic) CLOs and MBS issues successfully completed since 1999-2000.

7.7.6. Malaysia

Cagamas issues pass-through securities to fund mortgage purchases. Two public entities (Danaharta Nasional and Danamodal Nasional) were established after the Asian crisis, respectively to acquire and recycle NPLs, and to assist bank re-capitalization. 1999 securitization guidelines led to a new law governing ABS issues in 2001 but this has been little used, perhaps due to regulatory caution as to the originator's control or influence over a new SPV.

7.7.7. Philippines

Guidelines 1998. Never effective. Securitization act became law in March 2004 but is untested.

Most announced offshore transactions have never been completed, often due to contractual or legal problems.

7.7.8. Singapore

Central bank maintains comprehensive regulatory guidelines.

Commercial property securitization popular since 1998.

7.7.9. Taiwan

ABS provisions enacted in 2002. The law is little tested but may now be effective.

Since April 2003, non-bank investors permitted to invest in listed ABS issues.

7.7.10. Thailand

Single ABS transactions completed since 1999 (using car loans, credit card receivables and mortgage loans) but all have been highly structured. 1997 ABS legislation allows onshore SPVs but is ambiguous as to notice requirements in transfer.

Central agency created 1998 to recycle banking sector assets.

7.8. Derivatives & bond financing

This category refers to the domestic market's product capabilities. Not considered here are offshore derivatives (mainly interest rate products) based upon non-deliverable forward contracts, intended to mimic domestic instruments that are non-existent, illiquid or unavailable to foreign counterparties. Regulators commonly prohibit some or all domestic market participants from using such OTC products in their home currency, despite their being freely traded offshore.

7.8.1. China

Bond repurchases allowed since 2003. Draft derivative regulations issued by CBRC in 2004 clarify counterparties for onshore foreign currency trades. Not yet known what yuan products will be permitted, nor who may use derivatives and for what purposes.

7.8.2. Hong Kong

OTC hedging instruments (especially interest rate swaps and options) are well traded. The exchange based market in interest rate products is more limited.

7.8.3. India

Restrictions on short sales, bond futures and bond options.

Negotiated, semi-liquid OTC interest rate derivative market.

7.8.4. Indonesia

Securities financing and short sales permitted but little used.

No onshore market in interest rate swaps; no exchange traded interest rate contracts.

7.8.5. Korea

Limits on bond repurchases. Interest rate and currency derivatives generally permitted and the domestic swap market has been encouraged recently by the authorities. Domestic investor demand likely to increase the use of structured products.

7.8.6. Malaysia

Bond repurchases permitted. Short selling and securities lending barred.

Bond options market permitted from 2004. Semi-liquid onshore market in interest rate swaps. Onshore synthetic instruments and credit derivatives are growing but may become subject to new central bank regulation.

7.8.7. Philippines

Bond and note repurchases subject to capital charge.

Foreign banks trade money market based OTC derivatives.

7.8.8. Singapore

Free use except securities lending.

Strong exchange traded derivatives. Local interest rate swap market not consistently liquid (which dissuades foreign issuers) but has received central bank support.

7.8.9. Taiwan

Restrictions on securities lending, short sales, bond futures and bond options.

Bond repurchases limited by transaction tax on corporate issues.

Limited exchange traded products and illiquid OTC derivatives.

7.8.10. Thailand

Restrictions on short sales by non-banks.

No exchange traded bond option or futures markets. Limited domestic market in interest rate swaps and other OTC hedging instruments.

7.9. Trading, settlement & custody

This sub-section considers transparency for users, the degree of mandatory settlement centralisation, whether dealing or settlement is fractured by being subject to choice, variations in settlement days, the reliability of delivery against payment procedures (if extant), and systemic links between settlement and payments.

7.9.1. China

No mandatory central securities depositary. Limited provision for delivery against payment settlement. Trading days vary between instruments, and if bonds are listed.

7.9.2. Hong Kong

Integrated, well established systems and bridges to overseas clearing houses. Central securities depositary is linked to payments system for HK and US dollar securities.

7.9.3. India

No central securities depositary for all instruments. Central government issues settle through an automated system operated by the central bank, which also acts as a depository. Limited provision for delivery against payment settlement. Settlement trading days vary by instrument. Physical delivery persists in some cases.

7.9.4. Indonesia

Use of central securities depositary is not mandatory for all instruments. Limited delivery against payment settlement. Settlement trading days vary.

7.9.5. Korea

Centralized settlement and custody but not mandatory.

Delivery against payment settlement since 1999 but not universal.

7.9.6. Malaysia

Central settlement and depositary mandatory for government, Cagamas and Khazanah bonds, but feasible for all listed debt securities, as is delivery against payment settlement. Settlement trading days may vary.

7.9.7. Philippines

Generally fragmented. Use of central securities depositary is not mandatory for all instruments. No delivery against payment settlement. It is common for securities to be transferred by serial assignment to avoid stamp duties, making ownership unreliable.

Settlement trading days varies. Certain settlement rules for government securities are inconsistent (for example, same day settlement conflicts with transfer mechanism).

7.9.8. Singapore

Effective central securities depositary linked to domestic payments system.

7.9.9. Taiwan

Use of central securities depositary is not mandatory for all instruments.

Limited delivery against payment settlement.

Settlement trading days varies.

7.9.10. Thailand

Use of central securities depositary not mandatory for all instruments.

Partial use of delivery against payment settlement.

7.10. Regulatory issues

7.10.1. China

Unclear division of responsibilities among securities, banking and insurance regulators, and historically between the central bank, finance ministry and National Development and Reform Commission. There is strong recognition of the need for regulatory clarity among all central authorities. Offshore borrowing and investment is tightly controlled.

7.10.2. Hong Kong

Issuer disclosure and reporting is a concern for many investors. Unclear relationship between securities regulators.

7.10.3. India

There is no unambiguous regulation of debt securities issuance.

Bank liquidity requirements are comparatively high, which depresses market liquidity.

7.10.4. Korea

The regulatory environment developed since the Asian crisis has clear divisions of roles but future reform may concentrate on questions of corporate disclosure and reporting. As a primary CLO market expands (probably based upon SME loans and finance company receivables) then the regulatory treatment of interest rate and credit derivatives will need clarification and be made consistent with capital regulation. Unclear also that all public intervention has been market-driven, for example, in 2001 state bodies were encouraged to assist in engineering a recovery in the market for corporate bonds.

7.10.5. Philippines

No clear regulatory regime for debt securities.

All securitization, corporate issuance and foreign borrowing is tightly controlled, needing central bank approval.

7.10.6. Singapore

Restrictions on the overseas use of Singapore dollars and on domestic fundraising by foreign financial institutions.

7.10.7. Taiwan

Full effects not yet seen of financial holding company legislation in 2001, separating bank shareholding in related companies from lending decisions.

History of restrictions on portfolio inflows.

Disclosure requirements needing attention.

SEC must approve all domestic issues; offshore borrowing is tightly controlled.

7.10.8. Thailand

Government has a promising outlook on reform but has yet to improve disclosure. Government bond consolidation is vital. Close informal control by finance ministry of most aspects of financial market activity, including transactional approvals and investment policy.

Thai Bond Dealers' Center is unusual in Asia as a self-regulatory organisation representing securities houses and regulating trading, but its core authority is unclear, and competition exists among other regulatory bodies.

Controls on outward investment and portfolio inflows.

7.11. Announced and intended reforms

7.11.1. China

World Trade Organisation commitments suggest liberalization will occur in the coming 2-3 years but many reforms are political. China's State Council gave a commitment to debt market reform in 2004. Many reforms have been mooted or announced for markets and to deal with NPLs. Approval for non-bank money market funds was announced in 2003, which could assist liquidity. It is likely that government issuance will become market-orientated in stages, allowing interest rates to cease being centrally determined.

7.11.2. Hong Kong

Approval for real estate investment trusts (REITS) and retail orientated debt issues has yet to take full market effect due to a lack of tax incentives. Slight legal uncertainty following 2004-05 litigation for LINK privatization issue, but generally attributed to failure of due diligence.

7.11.3. India

Securitization, related issues of taxation and stamp duty have been under discussion since 1999. Existing offshore borrowing controls were tightened in November 2003 to encourage domestic borrowing.

7.11.4. Indonesia

General intention to support capital market reform with further legislation. Rules announced in 2003 for more comprehensive disclosure by issuers.

General intention to create a new unified regulatory authority.

7.11.5. Korea

Proposed separation of ownership and financing.

7.11.6. Malaysia

A 'master plan' for reform adopted in 2001 aims to improve the use and functioning of all capital markets by 2010. Most of the systemic reforms are in place. Regulatory changes affecting banks and investors being are progressively introduced, including greater freedom for state provident funds: this may eventually cause market activity to expand to its potential.

7.11.7. Philippines

Financial sector legal and administrative reform have long been characterized by delay.

7.11.8. Singapore

Further changes to listing and corporate disclosure rules.

7.11.9. Taiwan

ABS law became effective in 2003.

7.11.10. Thailand

Caution in all post-crisis reform has slowed development.

Foreign (initially supranational) issues to be permitted subject to ceilings 2004.

References

Akhtar, S., 2001, 'Institutional investors in Asia', OECD Financial Trends, October.

Allen, F., Qian Jun & Qian Meijun, 2002, 'Law, finance and economic growth in China', Wharton Financial Institutions Center working paper 02-44; Journal of Financial Economics, 2005.

Arner, D., 2002a, 'Emerging market economies and government promotion of securitization', 12 Duke J. Comp. & Int'l L. 505.

Arner, D., 2002b. 'Globalization of financial markets: an international passport for securities offerings?', 35 Int'l Law. 1543.

Arner, D., M. Yokoi-Arai & Z. Zhou, (eds.), 2001, 'Financial crisis in the 1990s', London, British Institute of International & Comparative Law.

Aziz, J. & C. Duenwald, 2002, 'Growth-financial intermediation nexus in China', IMF working paper 02/194.

Baskin, J., 1988, 'The development of corporate financial markets in Britain and the United States, 1600-1914: overcoming asymmetric information', Business History Review 62(2,.

Beck, T., Demirgüç-Kunt, A. & Levine, R, 2002, 'Law and finance: why does legal origin matter?', World Bank policy research working paper 2904.

Beck, T., Demirgüç-Kunt, A. & Maksimovic, V., 2002, 'Financing patterns around the world: the role of institutions', World Bank policy research working paper 2905.

Bhagwati, J. 1996, 'The miracle that did happen: understanding East Asia in comparative perspective', keynote address to Cornell University conference, May.

Bordo, M., Meissner, C. & Redish, A., 2003, 'How 'original sin' was overcome: the evolution of external debt denominated in domestic currencies in the United States & the British dominions 1800-2000', National Bureau of Economic Research working paper 9841.

Borio, C., 2003, 'Market distress and vanishing liquidity: anatomy and policy options', in Persaud, A., ed, 'Liquidity black holes understanding, quantifying and managing financial liquidity risk', London, Risk Books.

Cai Hongbin, Liu Qiao & Xiao Geng, 2004, 'Does Competition Discipline Firms? The Case of Corporate Profit Hiding in China, Hong Kong Institute of Economics and Business Strategy working paper 1126.

Cerra, V. & C. Saxena 2003, 'Did output recover from the Asian crisis?', World Bank working paper 03/48.

Corsetti, G., P. Pesenti & N. Roubini, 1998, 'What caused the Asian currency & financial crisis?', parts I & II, National Bureau of Economic Research.

Crockett, A., 2002, 'Capital flows in East Asia since the crisis', speech in Beijing to ASEAN+3 group, BIS, October.

Eichengreen, B. & Hausmann, R., 1999, 'Exchange rates and financial fragility', National Bureau of Economic Research working paper 7418.

Eichengreen, B., R. Hausmann & U. Panizza 2002, 'Original sin: the pain, the mystery, & the road to redemption', presentation at conference 'Currency & maturity matchmaking: redeeming debt from original sin', Inter-American Development Bank.

Emery, R., 1997 'The Bond Markets of Developing East Asia', Boulder, CO, Westfield Press.

Fernald, J. & Babson, O., 1999, 'Why has China survived the Asian crisis so well? What risks remain?', Federal Reserve System international finance discussion papers 633.

Gerschenkron, A., 1962, 'Reflections on the concept of 'prerequisites of modern industrialization', in 'Economic backwardness in historical perspective', Cambridge MA, Belknap Press.

Goldsmith, R., 1969, 'Financial structure and development', New Haven CT, Yale University Press.

Goldsmith, R., 1983, 'The financial development of Japan, 1868-1977', New Haven CT, Yale University Press,.

Greenspan, A. 2000, 'Global Challenges', speech to Financial Crisis Conference, Council on Foreign Relations, Washington, DC, available at http://www.cfr.org/.

Gregory, N., & S. Tenev, 2001, 'The financing of private enterprise in China', IMF 'Finance & Development', March.

Harwood, A., 2002, 'Building corporate bond markets in emerging market countries', presentation to OECD/ World Bank workshop on bond markets.

Harwood, A., ed, 2000, 'Building local bond markets, an Asian perspective', International Finance Corporation.

Herring, R. & Chatusripitak, N., 2000, 'The case of the missing market: the bond market & why it matters for financial development', Asian Development Bank Institute working paper.

Jiang, G., N. Tang & E. Law, 2001, 'Cost-benefit analysis of developing bond markets', Hong Kong Monetary Authority Quarterly Bulletin, November.

King, M., 2001, 'Who triggered the Asian financial crisis?', Review of International Political Economy 8(3,.

Krugman, P., 1994, 'The myth of Asia's miracle', Foreign Affairs, Nov-Dec.

Lejot, P., D. Arner & Liu Qiao, 2004, 'Making markets: reforms to strengthen Asia's debt capital markets' Hong Kong Institute For Monetary Research Working Paper 13.

Liu Qiao & Lu Zhou, 2004, 'Earnings management to tunnel: evidence from China's listed companies', Hong Kong Institute of Economics and Business Strategy working paper 1097.

Liu Qiao & Xiao Geng, 2004, 'Look Who Are Disguising Profits: An Application to Chinese Industrial Firms', Hong Kong Institute of Economics and Business Strategy working paper 1095.

McCauley, R., Fung, S.S. & Gadanecz, B., 2002, 'Integrating the finances of East Asia', BIS Quarterly Review, December.

Mohanty, M., 2002, 'Improving liquidity in government bond markets: what can be done?' BIS papers 11.

North, D., 1995, 'Some fundamental puzzles In economic history/ development', Economics Working Paper Archive at WUSTL No 9509001.

Oh, G.T., Park, D.K., Park, J.H. & Yang, D.Y. 2003, 'How to mobilize the Asian savings within the region: securitization & credit enhancement for the development of East Asia's bond market', Korea Institute for International Economic Policy working paper 03-02, Seoul.

Pettis, M., 2000, 'The risk management benefits of bonds', in Harwood, 2000, *op cit*,.

Pomerleano, M., 1998, 'The East Asia crisis and corporate finance—the untold micro story', World Bank policy research working paper 1990.

Rajan, R., 2002, 'Is there a case for an Asian bond fund? It depends!', University of Adelaide mimeo.

Rhee, S. Ghon, 2000, Rising to Asia's Challenge: Enhanced Role of Capital Markets, in Rising to the Challenge in Asia: A Study of Financial Markets, Volume 1 Manila, Philippines: Asian Development Bank, 2000, 107-174.

Stiglitz, J., et al, 1999, transcript of press conference to introduce World Bank development report 1999/2000, 15 September.

Takagi, S., 2000, 'Fostering capital markets in a bank-based financial system', Asian Development Review 19/1.

World Bank, 2003, 'Global development finance', Washington, DC.

Xiao Geng, 2004, 'People's Republic of China's round-tripping FDI: scale, causes and implications', Manila: Asian Development Bank Institute discussion paper No. 7.

Yoshitomi, M. & Shirai, S., 2001, 'Designing a financial market structure in post-crisis Asia; how to develop corporate bond markets', Asian Development Bank Institute working paper 15.

Young, A., 1995, 'The tyranny of numbers: confronting the statistical realities of the East Asian growth experience', Quarterly Journal of Economics, August.

Part II

The Role of Reform

Chapter 4

Institutional Reform and Economic Development

Paul Lejot[1], Douglas Arner[1] & Frederick Pretorius[2]

[1]*Asian Institute of International Financial Law and Faculty of Law, University of Hong Kong;* [2]*Asian Institute of International Financial Law and Department of Real Estate and Construction, University of Hong Kong*

1. Introduction

This chapter seeks to relate the modern dilemma of Asia's underdeveloped bond markets to certain transforming phases of financial history, by isolating the qualities and value of well-functioning markets. It considers the economic welfare, resource allocation and risk management qualities of effective debt capital markets, and asks if those potential benefits to the region are clear and sufficient, especially when weighed against a variety of opportunity costs and risks associated with promoting market reform, especially for indigenous banks and other lenders and in the funding needs of East Asian infrastructure and medium-scale enterprises. As part of this review, the chapter examines pertinent applications of contemporary law and finance theory to the most notable features of today's well-established major markets and seeks to identify implications for market reform in Asia.

Asia made its leap to prolific economic growth from the 1970s without the support or succor of active domestic bond markets. The region's banks provided ample financing for the private and public sectors—sometimes with state prodding, often funded by international loans—much as predicted by then conventional financial development opinion.[1]

History's paramount lesson for Asia is that a profound scale of need is essential for effective markets to develop. While the region lacked that imperative in its formative period of rapid growth when reliant on a dominant banking system, a greater impetus may have emerged in the immediate post-crisis years since 1997-98. This has provided policymakers with an unusual opportunity for market reform to be

[1] See especially Gerschenkron (1962) or Enke (1963, p261 *et seq.*). Each uses the growth framework created a decade earlier by W.W. Rostow (1953).

planned and introduced in a deliberate way involving cooperation among non-Japan Asia's leading economies, supported by their shared conviction that future financial contagion is to be avoided or limited.

The chapter contains two themes. The first is that the existence of bonds is not of itself important to their host economies, nor to the majority of individual financial agents. If this were the case then the scale of domestic state sector issuance in China since 1998 would be a paragon for all intending reformers. Bonds of all kinds are merely a means to evidence financial claims, and neither their creation nor characteristics denotes anything about the quality of financial intermediation. Rather, it is the market that results from their transparent and continual transfer that offers value in the aggregate and for potential individual users, whether they be borrowers, investors, or interested outsiders.

The second theme is a lesson from history, that however sophisticated is an economy, and whatever the objectives of the actors and agents that play within it, no well-functioning bond market has emerged and been sustained without material, compulsive need. That want has most commonly been the desire of the state to fund military spending, which has usually been beyond its concurrent fiscal means. Contemporary Asia may have lacked any such scale of need until it began to register the costs and implications of the 1997-98 financial crisis, and in particular sought to identify a reliable means by which the waves extending from a similar shock might be dampened, and prevented from carrying infection elsewhere.

2. What Makes Markets?

The bondless economy lacks market-determined interest rates to benchmark capital costs, lacks hedging instruments for risk management, restricts savers' choice and constrains institutional investment (it is less clear that borrowers in a bondless economy necessarily face higher costs of funds). It will undergo periodic banking sector strains. These circumstances describe Asia's least developed securities markets in China or Indonesia but may not imply that all economies can sustain active bond markets.[2] It has been further argued that any economy inadvertently unable to borrow abroad in its own currency or borrow at home in long maturities will suffer unavoidable fragility, for all investments then entail unhedgeable currency or maturity mismatches.[3] The same view holds that 'older' economies became able to sell bonds offshore due to their response to significant shocks. Yet this may not be consistent: until the 1960s investment in foreign bonds was made through hubs that were home to investor groups but there is no longer a correspondence between currency and place of issue. Market development in Asia is mainly a domestic question, for the critical need is to engage prominent home and regional investors,

---

[2] Harwood (2000: 1-37 *passim*).

[3] The debate over 'original sin': Eichengreen and Hausmann (1999).

and large countries better attract foreign investment to their domestic issues:[4] Market depth is an important corollary to an economy's size.

These are grounds for market-based policy innovation, though not without cost, most immediately in improving corporate governance and regulatory enforcement. Asia's leading companies are generally able to issue public debt at home and abroad, so this is not an immediate funding problem but one of the interests of investors. For small and medium-scale enterprises (SMEs) that constitute most of Asia's commercial population, poor disclosure will deny access to an imposed debt market but they would be unlikely issuers even if standards were high. Indeed, this is a cause of illiquidity as important as issues of system architecture, law, taxation and investor behavior. Natural or enhanced creditworthiness is critical to an expanded market and upon this depends the risk management benefits of bonds.

2.1. Generic qualities

Classically, bonds are widely-held, tradable medium or long-term securities. The vast majority represent unsecured unsubordinated claims on a borrower, even when issued as part of asset-backed or securitized arrangements.[5] In the real world they can be none of these: a significant share by volume of Asia cross-border issues since 2001 have been small transactions arranged as substitutes for loans, intended for purchase by limited groups of commercial banks and, like most financial assets, merely transferable rather than tradable.[6] This section looks at the origins and features of developed markets and what they might offer a developing or newly industrialized economy in which the banking sector is dominant.

Accepted theory and market practice may converge but never meet. The modern U.S. bond market pre-dates its seminal writings by at least 20 years,[7] yet all practitioners know that government bond yield curves provide risk-free rates for every corporate investment decision and a pricing formula for comparable debt securities.[8]

---

[4] Bordo, Meissner and Redish (2003).

[5] Secured bonds (except covered bonds) tend to be transaction-specific, narrowly-held and in some jurisdictions may be transferable only at the risk of impairment.

[6] Up to US$50m or its equivalent. A similar qualification applies to instruments issued by frequent international borrowers in Asian currencies under medium-term note programmes and which typically rely on the efficiency of swap arbitrage to provide low cost funding in the borrower's base currency.

[7] For example, on specific issues such as term structure and duration, Fisher (1930), Hicks (1939), Lutz (1940) or Macaulay (1938). The first acknowledged work describing formal aspects of bond trading appeared only in 1972 (Homer and Leibowitz).

[8] Government yield curves are tools of description, not pricing. Market practice prices new issues relative to a matrix of outstanding comparable bonds, and references to benchmarks are typically made for brevity in describing terms or to suggest trading conditions at the time of launch.

Almost all the commonly accepted features of liquid bond markets can be contradicted, as the following examples suggest:

- The most well developed government bond markets conceal substantial sectoral illiquidity and price discontinuities; the majority of corporate bonds are typically traded for only a fraction of their full lives.
- Active markets help improve financial sector efficiency and competitiveness. Nonetheless, new issue cartels operated for many years among domestic U.S. investment banks to control transaction fees.
- Debt securities enhance the stability of the system by creating funding alternatives to banks, reducing the sector's power and lessening moral hazard. Can this be reliable when banks manage all new issues, make markets in securities and are perennial long-term bond investors?
- Bond markets serve as a communication medium between policymakers and markets, and with the economy at large. This may be only partly true of the Japanese government bond market; the world's second largest by volume.
- Domestic government debt denominated in the issuer's fiat currency is deemed risk-free. Yet there are contemporary examples of overt defaults on such issues (for example, by Russia in 1998) that suggest the concept is suspect, even if taken solely as implying a yield offering no premium for risk.

2.2. Theory vs. *practice*

In this way, market reality is most easily seen as a blend of theory and assumed practice. Mainstream corporate finance theory suggests that long-term investment is best financed by long-term capital. It also asserts that banks are not providers of such capital. Yet loans may have long-term contractual features, which when combined with interest rate or other derivatives will offer full certainty as to long-run cost (applicable also to bank liabilities); while corporate bonds can be inadvertently short-term or cost uncertain, given that embedded options or event covenants may trigger prepayment or changes in commercial terms.

Project loans made by banks before the Asian crisis often financed wasteful schemes—observers recall the many skylines of idle cranes—but at fault were risk appraisal and choice, not the instrument of funding. For some years in the U.S. and now globally, loans and bonds have become increasingly alike: loans are traded or acquired by non-bank investors, especially as the use of standard credit and loan transfer documentation becomes increasingly widespread. In developed banking markets, including parts of East Asia, there is a growing separation between bank-customer relationship management and the retention to maturity of financial assets by banks. Loans and bonds are evolving into instruments with common features but different origins, making it hazardous to identify a financing tool with a market segment.

The availability of total return swaps and credit derivatives—especially credit default swaps—make this process irreversible. Among professional participants, price transparency will increasingly apply equally to both loans and bonds. It thus becomes necessary to ask whether such developments in derivatives and loan trading make contagion less likely?[9] For Asia, regretfully, the probability is low until disclosure and risk appraisal generally improve.

Fungibility among instruments is similar to the severing of the early 20th century connection between financial centers and the currency they offer to the borrower: markets increasingly distinguish solely between risks, not the means by which those risks are intermediated.[10] In the same way, credit and currency risks are increasingly regarded as distinct: this also has consequences for the relationship between domestic and core currency bond issuance and investment, and what may be needed to promote active markets.

Thus only certain generic features of debt securities markets are accepted, given limiting conditions. At the very least, active bond markets will improve competitive practices within the banking sector by offering an alternative means of intermediation, strengthening investor choice and assisting risk transfer and risk management. Any contribution to financial policy formation must distinguish between in principle needs (which are not wholly proven) and an acceptable balance of probability. Developing or newly-industrialized economies deprived of effective bond markets will lack market-determined interest rates, leading firms to fail properly to measure their capital costs. The bondless economy offers no simple hedging instruments to assist appropriate risk management, restricts portfolio choice for its savers and constrains institutionalized savings.[11] This in turn encourages short-termism in capital investment and the acceptance of undue foreign exchange risk. Worse, the bondless economy will undergo periodic banking sector strains. These circumstances can be said to describe China and Indonesia, which sustain the region's least developed securities markets.

---

[9] The accelerating ease and sophistication of credit risk transfer has been cautiously welcomed by financial regulators, encouraged by a notable Bank for International Settlements (BIS) study (2003). The report's conclusion (that ease of transfer leads to a welcome diversification of credit risk and thus limits the threat to financial institution capital) may have been borne out by events in 2004-05 concerning the deteriorating credit ratings to sub-investment grade of Ford Motor Co. and General Motors Corp., both prolific global bond issuers. Substantial trading in credit protection through credit default swaps and other derivatives may have prevented a collapse in the corporate debt market due to forced selling by investors unable to hold sub-investment grade claims. Thus the credit derivative markets performed ably in widely spreading risk. See also section [ ] *infra*.

[10] Highlighted in the 'original sin' debate as to blockages to the offshore sale of domestic currency bonds. See footnote 3.

[11] It is less clear that its bondless borrowers face higher effective costs of funds.

2.3. Essential conditions

For a major rating agency effective debt capital markets require several cardinal conditions:[12]

- Strong, independent regulator of securities issuance and trading, with sound rules.
- An extended period of macroeconomic stability.
- Strong legal system and bankruptcy procedures.
- Coordinated, advanced payment, settlement, and custodial systems.
- Developed base of natural buyers of long-dated securities, specifically pension funds and insurance companies.

Even so, only the last condition truly existed in Britain or the U.S. at the start of the 20th century when their respective modern markets began periods of extraordinary growth.[13] This practical framework draws on a more formal analysis, which is ably summarized in the suggestion that four preconditions exist for a securities market to function well:

> 'the availability of accurate information, the existence of a broad base of investors with access to this information, legal protection of these investors' rights, and a liquid secondary market unencumbered by excessive transaction costs or constraints'.[14]

Others have looked for specific indicators of sophistication while accepting that the optimal market exists only on paper.[15]

More broadly, differences in national financial development may be explained by a range of factors, including legal origins, treatment of investor or property rights, or how legal systems adapt to commercial circumstances[16] but the formation of today's prominent, actively-traded markets has received relatively little attention in the extensive historical and empirical analysis of the influence of financial innovation on

---

[12] Standard & Poor's Corporation (2003). One further condition is contentious: to require standard resolution mechanisms in new issue documentation, including collective action clauses. The latter have been commonplace in international and Euromarket practice for which English law predominates but is historically far more rare in transactions governed by New York law, including the bulk of core currency bond issues for Latin American borrowers.

[13] Even so, continuous, active, transparent, competitive debt markets are a contemporary phenomenon in North America, Europe and Australasia that date back only to the 1970s when cheapening and accessible computer processing capacity allowed a great acceleration in product innovation and system reliability.

[14] Avolio, Gildor and Shleifer (2001: 125-126).

[15] Herring and Chatusripitak (2000).

[16] Beck, Demirgüç-Kunt and Levine (2002).

economic development. Observations on pre-1950s debt market turnover and liquidity are largely anecdotal and resist empirical analysis. However, taking the view that financial development precedes and stimulates growth,[17] it is reasonable to identify prominent exogeneities associated with market development. In the long-run growth may influence an economy's 'institutional framework', including the functioning and nature of its financial system;[18] earlier, Gurley & Shaw (1955) argued that the 'development of financial institutions (...) is both a determined and a determining variable in the growth process'.

Otherwise, no contemporary body of theory holds that primary causation flows from growth to finance. Robinson's widely quoted statement 'enterprise leads finance'[19] is alone of its kind but is taken literally by many.[20] It was nonetheless almost certainly unrelated to financial markets, for the nature of 'finance' is entirely a modern concern, perhaps a product of mass media attention on stock market performance. The substantial work postulating strong casual links between financial and economic development[21] is not unquestioned, for example, empirically[22] or qualitatively, especially for its use of partial liquidity or credit as proxies for systemic financial development.

2.4. *Value of active markets*

The root value of true, active, participatory debt capital markets stems from their multifarious nature. Whereas the commercial banking sector performs one function (credit creation) in a multiplicity of ways,[23] well developed bond markets have the distinct roles cited in the preceding paragraphs. Asia would now welcome the means for stresses to be lifted from its banking systems; a reform that may become imperative while risk taking and money transmission commingle in banks, especially given the openness of many of the review economies. Only China, India, Malaysia and Taiwan maintain significant capital controls: these were also the countries least directly affected by the Asian crisis.

If effective, well-utilized bond markets promote efficiency and general welfare,[24] has output growth been impeded by the absence of fully developed markets? The Asian crisis resulted in part from an overdependence on external debt acquisition under fixed rate exchange regimes. Yet outside China there were few restrictions

[17] From Hicks (1969).

[18] North (1995: 2).

[19] Robinson (1953: 86).

[20] Including Levine (1997), Rousseau & Sylla (2001) and Fase (2003).

[21] From Goldsmith (1969); Shaw (1973); to King & Levine (1993).

[22] Favara (2003).

[23] Ignoring money transmission and non-capital attracting activities.

[24] Herring & Chatusripitak (*op cit*).

prior to 1997 on the availability of domestic credit from banks and finance companies. While this may not have been ideal it was not always inefficient. Would East Asia's recent problems have been less severe had its economies not relied so heavily on banks as their principal means of financial intermediation? In a crude sense the use of mismatched and unhedged U.S. dollar liabilities to fund domestic baht loans would always have reached a limit and halted lending by Thailand's banks; but did the Thai economy also need to collapse? With a functioning capital market, the outcome might well have been far more benign, providing that the market was uncorrelated in operations with the domestic banking sector. The existence of multiple avenues of financial intermediation is common to high income economies; for example, working effectively in the U.S. both during a late 1980s credit contraction and after Russia's unpredicted debt default in 1998.

While the absence of an effective market may make an economy more prone to crisis, it is unclear that such reasoning alone provides sufficient foundation for all countries to sustain active bond markets. These are grounds for market-based innovation, though not without cost, most immediately in improving corporate governance and regulatory enforcement. Asia's leading companies are generally able to issue public debt at home and abroad, so this is not a pure funding question for well-rated credits but more a matter of the interests of investors. For medium-scale enterprises that constitute the majority of Asia's commercial population, narrow ownership and poor disclosure and reporting will deny access to an 'imposed' debt market but they would be unlikely issuers even if such standards were high.[25] Indeed, this is a cause of illiquidity equally important as issues of system architecture, law, taxation and investor behavior. Natural or enhanced creditworthiness is critical to the market's functioning and to this is tied the effective risk management benefits of bonds.[26]

Whether the bond market becomes a panic-spreading mechanism depends on the quality of its flows of information and how sensitive are the regulatory requirements it faces. Also, if there is leakage between the bond and loan markets then creating a corporate bond market serves only to absorb bank capital, with banks substituting bond purchases for lending. This has represented a cheap source of revenue for many Asian banks in the post-crisis recovery. Without a non-bank investor base such leakage can eliminate secondary liquidity even in a bond market with noticeable new issue volume. It characterizes most Asia-Pacific domestic debt markets prior to 1997.

From a policy viewpoint, 'co-movement' between bank lending and bond purchasing may erode the value of capital markets as market-dampening mechanisms, for example, to provide corporate liquidity in times of stressed banking markets. The same features in the cross-border debt markets may lead to contagion: a withdrawal of bank credit taking place simultaneously with a cessation of new debt issues and collapse of secondary prices, although there is no agreement on the

---

[25] Corporate issues are taken as more costly for the borrower than the deployment of internal funds due to the high agency costs associated with asymmetry of information, a problem that is almost always more acute for SMEs.

[26] The main system impediments to properly functioning markets in Asia are described in Chapter 7.

result.[27] In the long-run, sound regulation and risk management are more effective in preventing contagion of any kind than financial innovation is in its cause.[28] The International Finance Corporation (IFC) has assessed these types of costs and its judgment is highly practical, not least as the most experienced offshore user of emerging debt markets.[29]

2.5. Roots of modern markets

Germany shows that economies maintaining a strong relationship banking model can be consistent with effective debt capital markets. More generally, the early lives of sophisticated markets may show whether they share common roots.

The history of government borrowing is a story of transaction techniques no less sophisticated than deployed by contemporary investment banks. Soon after emperors or monarchs found it possible to tax their subjects[30] they learned to raise loans collateralized by streams of expected revenues, and both French and Spanish rulers grew used to financing state spending with forward sales of projected income. These pass-through structures were unreliable: European monarchical credit risk was uniformly volatile in the Middle Ages and the creditor's life consequently unstable. Only in the 17th century when costly standing armies became obligatory did European tax raising become continual and not wholly arbitrary. In an institutional sense, the modern bond—and the standardisation it implies—dates from the same era.

Trade in short-term government loans began in 16th century Antwerp, though the sale of public annuities in Europe dates from the late Middle Ages.[31] Pools of investors willing to fund the state existed in much of the continent by the mid-17th century, most effectively in the Dutch United Provinces.[32] Yet real markets existed nowhere until 1693, when Antwerp's earlier innovation of negotiability for trade

---

[27] McCauley, Fung & Gadanecz (2002).

[28] Discussed by Arner & Lin (2003).

[29] Harwood (2002) is an example. Only the benefits are stated, not the costs, nor whether the presumed benefits might be achieved in other ways.

[30] Taxation by tribute probably appeared in the 9th century 'for the declared purpose of defending the realm from outside attack' (Ormrod & Barta, 1995 p57).

[31] Van der Wee (1977 p352 *et seq*).

[32] Kindleberger (1984 p156). Some argue that Spain's Netherlands provinces developed the first 'permanent public debt market' (Rousseau & Sylla, *op cit*) but van der Wee (*op cit*) shows that the trade was confined to short-term public finance loans: annuities were cumbersome to transfer. Antwerp invented negotiable trade bills by 1547 but failed to apply similar principles to create a long-term public debt market (*ibid* p323 *et seq*), and may thus have begun to cede Europe's financial leadership to London. Amsterdam remained a force in international lending through much of the 18th century, but its flagship position was yielded to London soon after England's Glorious Revolution of 1688 (see also Wilson (1941).

bills was applied in London to the sale of the first transferable long-term government bonds. Central to their success was continual, non-arbitrary taxation, giving confidence to bondholders that future resources would service their claims, and secure creditor rights in transfer to reconcile the time horizons of debtor and creditor. Such innovation made feasible regular large-scale borrowing, and the states adopting these changes were the most able to raise funds.[33]

The first transferable long-term bonds were introduced in London in the late 17th century soon after the founding of the Bank of England, the creation of which emphasized 'that its securities were not considered to represent merely the monarch's personal debt.'[34] As new instruments allowed those in power to spend increasingly freely, the growth of issuance by the leading European nations and later the U.S. would accelerate.[35]

Throughout the 18th and 19th centuries, military spending was the critical determinant of state issuance: most governments sought to reduce indebtedness in times of peace but issued debt without restraint in the order of several multiples of contemporary national output when preparing for war.[36] Voracious war spending created demand for innovative financing instruments; the amounts raised were of a new order to those available from any bank, state contractor or moneylender, each of which was constrained by capital or personal prudence. The need to finance military spending instigated the first public securities markets by the 1750s[37] and subsequently allowed other borrowers (initially, British canal builders and American railroads) to follow in using these new funding techniques.[38]

---

[33] Dickson shows that England's 'financial revolution' after 1688 made possible a public bond market, the absence of which 'would have effectively stopped [the state] from borrowing on the scale it needed.' (1967: 457). England's 1689 Bill of Rights is to North an essential change: 'A capital market [...] will simply not evolve where political rulers can arbitrarily seize assets or radically alter their value.' (1991: 101). These problems persist in 20th century post-crisis Asia.

[34] Baskin (1988) p206.

[35] For Brewer (1989), efficient fundraising created the 'fiscal-military states' of the Dutch United Provinces, France and Spain by the early-17th century and England after the 'Glorious Revolution' in 1688.

[36] Ferguson (2001).

[37] 'The urgent need to raise enormous sums created by the American Civil War [from 1861] was instrumental in the development of mass markets in securities, much as the Napoleonic wars [from 1799] had been earlier in Britain.' (Baskin *op cit* p207).

[38] Davis & Gallman (2001) ch2. In an early analysis of the determinants of economic growth Rostow (1953) writes that 'war emerges ... in real terms as a national economic enterprise, a form of communal capital investment' (p161), which has never been controversial, but then states more specifically that 'A striking aspect of the sequence of British war finance is the relationship between war and the development of the capital market.' (p162), and suggests that the same pattern later applied in the US.

The unprecedented expense of the Great War of 1914-18 was ruinous for all combatants but the U.S.. Shortly afterwards, Britain's treasury calculated that the marginal cost of the 'financial effort' of the war was £8.9bn, of which £7.2bn (81 per cent) was financed by borrowing of all kinds at home and overseas.[39] At the outbreak of war Britain's total outstanding public debt was approximately £645m; at the close of fiscal 1918-19 the amount had risen twelve-fold to £7.9bn.[40] War's absolute, inviolable demand is the root of modern debt capital markets.[41] The official historian of Britain's national debt conceded in the 1930s that while the financing of the war produced financial problems of 'an entirely new order' it would be mistaken 'to suppose that the nation is now confronted with a situation to which there is no parallel in its own history'.[42]

Historically, scale and momentum appear to be crucial to the making of a successful, usable market. Asia's foreseeable funding needs (compatible with creditworthiness) are far smaller in real terms than the amounts borrowed by the Great Powers in 1914-18 but its overall demands must be sufficient to be convincing to market participants. It is arguable that until 1997-98, Asia had no need for developed bond markets. Only the wish to guard against future instability or contagion will provide that essential momentum, rather than gradual increases in public borrowing.

The advanced economies that have elected to build fully developed debt capital markets are those with a history of financing organized conflict, and generally later chose in the Great Depression or after 1945 frequently to maintain fiscal deficits, whether because of military or welfare spending.[43] If Asia is to be an exception it must establish a contemporary need as compelling as war. The crisis and its aftermath provides motivation: ignoring the loss in output in Korea and Southeast Asia, the direct costs to central governments of supporting stricken banking sectors

---

[39] Including the UK's first foreign currency debt issue, jointly and severally with France, a US$500m 5 year fixed rate bond launched in October 1915 in the domestic US market via JP Morgan & Co. The issue was poorly received: much of the transaction was left with the underwriters (Wormell, 1999), a fate known to all modern issuers.

[40] Ramsey (1918 in Wormell, *op cit* pp181-6). Without the benefit of macroeconomic national income accounting, the calculated marginal cost of the war was an under-estimate; the volume of debt issued was accurate.

[41] Ferguson (*op cit*) gives a similar picture for other western issuers. This point ignores the strategic considerations of an enemy's awareness of its protagonist's shortage of financial resources. Recalling the exhaustion of Britain's foreign reserves in 1916, Keynes (1930 pp339-340) considered it 'rather strange' that 'the acuteness of this problem of foreign finance should not have been more vivid to the imagination of our enemies.'

[42] Hargreaves (1930 in Wormell, *op cit* p230). London's financing of the Napoleonic wars was a test of financial engineering.

[43] 'Welfare' in this context means non-contributory public spending on education, employment, health, social security or social infrastructure.

were enormous[44] and an overhang of impaired assets has not been fully realized, especially in China and parts of Southeast Asia. In the longer-term, further substantial needs may originate from infrastructural and social requirements.

Asia must establish a comparable need: the crisis and its aftermath may provide sufficient motivation and create grounds for cooperation. Output losses and the cost of supporting stricken banking sectors were enormous and an overhang of non-performing loans (NPLs) is far from removed. One year after the Asian crisis began, Hong Kong's financial secretary asked impassionedly, 'how is it that we in Asia have never been able to replicate the eurobond market success...?'[45] He might privately have welcomed the crisis as providing suitable reason: if market activity is stirred so as to assist in solving the banking sector's post-1997 burden of impaired assets the ongoing result will be depth and liquidity of the order envisaged by the most optimistic participants, and systemic reform that will constrain future post-shock contagion and support future economic development.

2.6. Technical omissions

Thus a history of conflict or profound funding needs ultimately explains the existence of corporate debt markets, not only a benchmark risk-free yield curve. If public borrowing is inadequate to sustain a government bond market that is liquid throughout the term structure, are fully synthetic yield curves feasible in Asian currencies, given that state funding is generally constrained? This is usually regarded as unlikely with a foundation of illiquid derivative and money markets, where trading spreads will be volatile and futures contracts non-existent or little used. However, contemporary techniques may soon allow the building of a synthetic yield curve based upon several references and informed by sovereign credit differentials.

Government's role in supporting benchmarking is always valuable, shown by the markets of Hong Kong and Singapore, yet synthetic instruments can increasingly replace traditional aspects of financial market architecture. It will soon no longer be necessary to have a standard risk-free yield curve in sophisticated markets and the trend may spread to their newer counterparts in Asia and elsewhere. Supply conditions in certain mature government bond markets have recently caused term interest rates to fall below the 'true' nominal risk-free yield curve.[46] How may companies then estimate the risk-free rate for investment decisions, and how will non-government issues be priced by the market?

---

[44] Estimated as shares of GDP in the 12 months to July 1998 to be 17 per cent for Indonesia; 2 per cent for Korea; 13 per cent for Malaysia; and in the 12 months to July 1999 22 per cent for Thailand (Lindgren, Tomás, Baliño, Enoch, Gulde, Quintyn & Teo, 1999).

[45] Donald Tsang, speech to Asian Bond Market conference, 4 July 1998.

[46] For example, in Australia, the UK and the US. Cooper & Scholtes (2001) discuss *inter alia* the effects on advanced corporate bond markets of a diminishing supply of 'risk-free' government bonds.

In each case, the market already provides an effective answer, by using interest rate swap rates as a substitute for government bond yields. Arrangers of new issues in all major markets use the trading level of comparable outstanding bonds and the yield curve of interest rate swaps (actual, imputed or implied) for guidance, with launch pricing quoted as a spread above a government benchmark solely for convenience, if at all. While the trend of the vanishing benchmark has been confined to certain major currency markets, the principle applies to the issue and trading of domestic Hong Kong non-government bonds, which are priced in relation to Hong Kong and U.S. dollar swap rates and expected credit spread differentials.

Less sophisticated East Asian markets could follow a similar approach, especially if cross-border investment activity grows within the region. A liquid government bond market is not an absolute prerequisite for a deep and effective corporate debt securities market, providing that an adequate interest rate derivative market exists in the national currency and is not prohibited by government. Early private sector initiatives to open a long-term debt market in parts of East Asia were hampered, not only by non-existent government yield benchmarks, but also by the relative youth of all interest rate swap markets. This is not to dispense with active and efficient government markets but rather to find a solution to illiquidity that is appropriate to the region by which sovereign issuance can be adequate if insufficient, and yet encourage a corporate and securitized market to grow.

Soon after the inception of the 1997-98 crisis, the BIS reported that:

> 'Government debt markets are especially important [...] where the fiscal costs of resolving systemic problems in the banking sector will be significant, and capital markets are needed to facilitate the restructuring and recapitalization of banks and non-bank corporations. In such countries, the upgrading of both debt and equity market infrastructure is a high priority.'[47]

History suggests that momentum is equally important in fostering market innovation and growth. New issue scale and regularity will promote liquidity and encourage institutional investors, even the most risk preferring of which craves predictability.[48] As the institutionalization of savings increases through mandatory provident schemes and commercial insurers, then debt products will doubtless be generated to meet their needs.

2.7. Policy needs

Regulatory or system arbitrage drives innovation, particularly in rule-based economies, but the growth of markets will not occur without reform, however much it may be desired by participants. Governments must legislate wherever necessary to remove or correct obstacles and inconsistencies, as well as sanctioning wholly practical elements as radical as the original U.S. mortgage or German pfandbrief

---

[47] Bank for International Settlements (1998 p17).

[48] Flandreau & Sussman (2002).

markets. Does debt market development require regional impetus? There may be fears that collective action may breed non-commercial solutions or duplicate what may safely be left to the private sector. History makes it doubtful that even greatly expanded Asian economies would support liquid markets adequate for both non-bank investor activity and intermediation to militate against contagion. Indeed, certain substantial economies have never produced sophisticated debt markets. From the collapse of Bretton Woods in 1971 to the birth of the euro in 1999, France, Germany and the Netherlands maintained well-developed government debt markets but elsewhere in Europe governments relied for long periods on overseas core currency issues (Belgium, Denmark, Ireland, Italy, Spain and Sweden). Except generally in Britain, robust markets for corporate debt existed only at intervals. A regional initiative in Asia appears to be essential, both to harmonize reform and give momentum to market development while respecting commercial primacy.

Government issuance must have predictability. Asian investors and intermediaries are accustomed to impromptu withdrawals of auctions or sales of notes or bonds. A similar criticism applies to multilateral organizations using Asian markets but failing to contribute liquidity with regular issues. If public borrowing is inadequate to sustain a government bond market that is liquid throughout the term structure, are fully synthetic yield curves feasible in Asian currencies, given constrained state funding? This is traditionally implausible but synthetic yield curves can increasingly be constructed using multiple references and credit differentials. Government's role in benchmarking is central, yet synthetic instruments will gradually supplant the conventional.

3. Policy Needs and Recommendations

Earlier chapters describe the efforts rehearsed by private and official interests in building viable international and local capital markets for Asian debt before and since the 1997-98 crisis; how the results are sparse except in offering a means for conspicuous issuers to borrow, central banks to influence money market activity (often in limiting ways that lessen price transparency) and how these hopeful markets are thus subject to regular questioning. Asia's fixed income markets are of scant use to many potential participants, including most classes of non-bank investors and a majority of aspiring borrowers, and fail to induce sufficient non-core currency issuance of adequate risk quality to satisfy regional and domestic investors. Above all, they provide no guard against crisis or ensuing contagion, nor act as a balance to banking systems that are susceptible to complex monopoly, distortions in resource allocation and to event risk.[49] Too little collaborative public effort has been made to stir activity: specific action beyond exhortation or planning is needed from Asia's governments and the official groups now deliberating on their behalves.

---

[49] Consumer finance has become highly competitive in Asia in the last decade but complex monopolies widely exist in SME financing and retail deposit taking, whereby two organisations maintain a sizeable joint market share or a larger number act as an effective cartel.

Left to grow alone, Asia's domestic markets will fail to generate adequate liquidity or activity. The world's most sophisticated debt markets sprang from the most essential needs, enabled by reform and product innovation, and would otherwise have evolved neither as far nor fast. Only economies with a history of financing organized conflict or extensive state welfare programmes have nurtured fully developed debt capital markets.[50] Nowhere else has the need been as large or the motivation as great. Asia must recognize a contemporary need with as great an imperative as war: the shocks of 1997-98 and their aftermath may have created such motivation, especially when taken together with a regional need for improved resource allocation and investment in infrastructure.

3.1. Guidelines for reform

This section advances policy suggestions and recommendations for reform, all appropriate to the region and intended to promote supply and usage and to widen participation. The most important elements are set out in the following ten paragraphs.

3.1.1. Standardisation

- For each currency sector and regionally, standardize and broaden the range of available feasible debt instruments, especially as to issuers and maturities.

3.1.2. Benchmarks

- Establish and consolidate benchmarks (normally single obligor government or quasi-government securities) across a declared range of maturities; introduce and adhere to visible debt issuance programmes, nationally or regionally.

3.1.3. Remove historic restrictions

- Remove restrictions on trading techniques, including bond or note repurchases on all investment grade issues, short selling, and the freest use of OTC (over-the-counter) or exchange traded interest rate and currency derivatives compatible with declared exchange rate policy.

---

[50] While the conception of those markets dates from the late-18th century their modern (liquid) form is highly contemporary (from no earlier than the mid-1970s) so that on a developmental timeline Asia is not far 'behind'. The eurobond market experienced prolonged spells of chronic illiquidity at recently as the late 1980s.

3.1.4. Clearing and settlement

- Standardize clearing (real-time book entry settlement and delivery) systems and custody requirements to provide reliability, eliminate principal risks in the settlement process and promote market integrity so as to encourage investor confidence. Remove obstacles to the use of securities financing by conventional bond and note repurchase and lending, so to support efficient trading techniques and safeguard settlement liquidity.

3.1.5. Maintain liquidity

- Where necessary, require market-makers to provide trading liquidity in benchmark notes and bonds. Ensure that bank liquidity requirements and day-to-day central bank operations do not generally hinder liquidity in benchmark securities (through an over-reliance on bond repurchases). Ensure that trading systems allow an open, efficient price discovery mechanism that is fully visible to end users, rather than a closed circle of central and commercial banks.

3.1.6. Securitization

- Promote securitization and other credit transfer mechanisms through regulation or legislation (and consultation with all established credit rating agencies) to allow the dependable structured pooling of risks (generating both short and medium-term instruments) to enhance weak credits and assist risk and liability management by banks.

3.1.7. Investor restrictions

- Remove regulatory restrictions that prevent non-bank institutional investors from acquiring or trading in term debt securities of any kind, subject only to agreed credit rating floors that are purposefully harmonized, and in money market instruments whether or not rated.

3.1.8. Enforcement issues

- Where necessary, remove common barriers that prevent investors to establish a legal basis for trading, ownership and settlement.

3.1.9. Taxes

- Remove (or as a minimum standardize and simplify) withholding taxes on securities, collateral assets and their sale; eliminate differential treatments among interest-bearing and other debt instruments; and remove differential source taxation of identical investments by banks and non-bank institutional investors.

3.1.10. Accounting standards

- Support common portfolio accounting standards among investor groups, in particular to apply similar requirements among banks and non-bank financial institutions.

These needs are optimal, non-parochial but not infeasible.[51] It is unreasonable to expect even incomplete reforms to be introduced speedily throughout the region. Were agreement to emerge from today's platoon of working groups then attendant legislation is still unlikely to pass quickly and untroubled.[52] This paper's proposals balance the most desirable reforms with recognition of an inevitable resistance to change by government and other entrenched interests. For example, the institutional structures proposed later in this section could be used to bring into effect all the detailed prescriptive measures described in chapter 7, though without demanding that hesitant governments of less-developed markets relinquish full authority to those untrammeled forces of which they may be suspicious, in some cases correctly.

4. Future regulatory concern

The perception of a favorable outlook for credit risk transfer described earlier in this chapter[53] is neither unqualified, nor likely to remain unaltered. Indeed, the next decade may see a global move towards institutional and market reform that would coincide with the emancipation of the markets in Asia for bonds, interest rate products and credit derivatives.

Regulatory interest in the use and risk management implications of credit derivatives is profound; first, because they are yet to be tested as volume instruments

---

[51] Proxies may eventually develop for the factors listed here; for example, using cash swap curves as a substitute for conventional risk-free benchmark yield curves (*supra*). Common standards for corporate disclosure are beyond the direct scope of this chapter. 'Asymmetric information [..] appears always to have limited the scope and use of financial markets', Baskin (*op cit*), reviewing 300 years of market evolution.

[52] Whether by design, Taiwan's 2002 Financial Assets Securitisation Law was enacted in haste and is widely regarded as deficient save for limited use.

[53] Section 2.2.

through a complete interest rate or credit cycle; second, as their use by unregulated 'non-banks' and hedge funds questions the application of regulation and the ways in which sophisticated credit risk transfer assists and impedes the functioning and stability of financial markets.

This section explains where such attention is most likely to focus.

4.1. Background to credit risk transfer

4.1.1. Widening applications of derivatives

Trends in financial globalization are commonly seen as manifested in a blurring of divisions, most commonly market segments or national borders. What has been termed the 'End of Geography' is a not a target but a progression along which financial activity is increasingly less acquainted with any particular place.[54] At the same time, many distinct financial products increasingly assume qualities of fungibility historically associated with cash. Just as corporate shares in any single class are perfect substitutes, so new instruments or applications may give *de facto* ownership rights to a creditor, or priority of claim to a stockholder, even while debt and equity claims may wholly differ in tradition and law. These transformations are made possible by derivative instruments that involve changes over time in combinations of expected risk and return for market participants, whether associated with credit risk, currencies, insurance, commodities, interest rates, shares or financial indexes, and whether contracted singly or in combinations or buried unseen in structured transactions. Certain derivatives have been known for centuries:[55] primitive commodity forward contracts were bought and sold in medieval Europe and organized futures or options markets existed in Japan by the late sixteenth century. Other instruments come and go according to fashion.[56] All are more easily characterized by use or availability rather than defined as a market segment.

The risk management techniques that lead to their creation, aggregation and maintenance may be immensely sophisticated. Financial derivatives draw on the language of differential calculus, and many are priced using differential mathematical functions to imply instruments whose value is determined as a function of an underlying contract, security or index, but this may not always be true, and the original integrand may be long lost to history. For example, simple fixed-floating interest rate swaps were once derived from continuous chains of forward short-term interest rates and a comparison of the conventional borrowing costs of two dissimilar counterparties: today's global interest rate swap markets are so large and liquid that

---

[54] O'Brien (1992).

[55] Writing in the fourth century BCE, Aristotle describes an option strategy involving the forward purchase of olive oil pressing capacity; *Politics* I xi: 4 (1259^{a}6-23).

[56] Typified by structured instruments notes issued under medium-term note programmes that have periodic coupons designed to meet the interest rate expectations of specific investor classes in particular prevailing conditions.

the swap yield curve is itself the dominant source of pricing for loans and bonds. In this evolution is seen the challenge for law and regulation to keep pace with product development.

Most derivatives are subject to some form standardisation that results from their either being traded on a commodity or futures exchange, or made to conform with the global harmonization of market practices brought about by the sector's self-regulatory organization (SRO), the International Swaps and Derivatives Association Inc. (ISDA). They can be distilled into four types according to how they are bought and sold and whether they are based on forward or option contracts. Over the counter (OTC) derivative contracts are dealt and settled among financial institutions and their clients. Trades are entered into directly between counterparties, so the nature of counterparty credit risk differs from that associated with exchange traded contracts. OTC derivatives lack standardized margin requirements but financial institutions often require that their clients maintain liquid collateral against the mark-to-market valuation of the contract whenever it represents a net credit risk to the institution.

4.1.2. Credit derivatives

Credit derivatives are an innovation of the mid-1990s that have become the third most important aspect of the global OTC derivatives market. Used for credit risk transfer, they center on the buying and selling of protection against single or multiple credit risks. The three elemental types of credit derivative can each be used singly, in arrays and with other financial instruments to achieve various forms of credit risk transfer, once possible only with the outright sale of securities or loans. All three provide a means for a credit protection seller to acquire, avoid or amend credit risk exposure without need for a direct agreement with the credit risk subject; each offers a form of insurance to the buyer and a risk to the seller; some give highly leveraged credit risk exposure with a minimal deployment of capital and funding.

The three main instrument types are:

- Credit default swaps (CDSs), which most commonly relate to single credit risks but also to groups of risks (basket default swaps').
- Credit-linked notes (CLNs), debt securities for which repayment is linked to the performance of a defined reference asset such as an outstanding bond or a pool of assets such as loans or receivables.
- Total return swaps (TRSs), by which two counterparties exchange obligations linked to the market performance of an underlying reference asset, most commonly a bond or loan.

The value of these derivatives is a function of the performance of their underlying credit risks, which is indicated by the market price of cash market assets or determined by conditions—including the events that trigger certain payments under CDSs—that form part of the derivative contract.[57]

[57] In almost all cases the 'ISDA Master' swap umbrella agreement and annexes.

Survey data suggests that Asia currently accounts for around 10 per cent of global turnover, with Hong Kong and Singapore together contributing approximately 4 per cent of the total.[58] Local and foreign banks in the region began using credit derivatives in the late-1990s primarily as sellers of credit protection through CDSs and CLNs, but now engage in broader trading activity.[59] CDS use dominates the two other instruments but the volume of new transactions in each has grown markedly since 2000.[60] As at end-August 2005, CDSs were traded on only 30 single name risks (corresponding to the region's most common borrowers) and 3 regional indexes from non-Japan Asia, according to a leading provider of index data for credit derivatives.[61] This implies that Asian banks engage heavily in credit derivatives linked to non-Asian risks.

While the transfer of credit risks within and from the banking sector among an increasing number and diversity of investors may have systemic benefits, it also raises questions of the effects of information flows on transparency, control and moral hazard[62] and illustrates how regulation has needed to adapt from its traditional institutional and segregated focus.

Credit derivative have a myriad of uses and applications that spring from portfolio configurations that are for the most part private to the investor or liability manager. This phenomenon also has significant implications for risk transfer and leverage. National banking regulations commonly set quantitative limits to banks' credit risk exposure, for example, with single obligor limits or industry limits, usually in relation to assets or capital, real or risk-adjusted. The mechanism became instrumental to the development and widespread use of syndicated loans in the banking sector as a tool to allow substantial lending business to be captured even more broadly.

For users, employing derivative instruments can be seen as a way to influence the expected risks and returns associated with a portfolio of assets or liabilities, whether by seeking higher rewards, lower borrowing costs, a new balance of credit risks, or better to achieve an objective mix of risk and return than would be feasible with other financial instruments. This section considers the main types of risk associated with financial derivatives and key aspects of current risk management practice,

---

[58] British Bankers' Association Credit Derivatives Report 2003-04, available at www.bba.org.uk/.

[59] See for example, Hong Kong Monetary Authority 'Credit risk transfer using derivatives and implications for financial market functioning' 2003, report available at http://www.info.gov.hk/hkma/eng/research/CDS.pdf.

[60] Fitch Ratings' Global Credit Derivatives Survey. September 2004, available at http://www.fitchratings.com. CDS trades are thought to represent around 50-55 per cent of the current market.

[61] iTraxx, part of Deutsche Börse affiliate International Index Company (http://www.indexco.com).

[62] Explained in F. Mishkin (1997).

especially in day-to-day valuations of OTC contracts. Both topics strongly influence regulatory thinking and its application.

4.2. Future concerns

This pattern of market development is likely to lead to two main regulatory pressures, although they may accepted nationally or globally only after the forthcoming Basel II Capital Accord has taken effect and seen 'in action' by its designers. These will be:

4.2.1. Increased transparency.

The world's national and international bond markets are very often highly transparent compared, for example, with the bank credit sectors, but the measure is typically taken among single classes of existing participants. All those banks or institutional investors that engage actively in buying and selling notes or bonds are likely to do so from a well-briefed platform, in which price and credit information is easily available and quickly transmitted. The same is not always true for less frequent users, or small investors, for which the bond markets can appear opaque in comparison to equity or futures markets.[63]

Second, the entry by means of efficient credit risk transfer of lightly regulated investors and traders into the business realm of highly regulated banks is eventually likely to add to a demand for a general increase in transparency. Whether these pressures will erode the value seen, for example, by the BIS[64] is unpredictable, but an eventual evening of the disclosure burden among classes of participants would seem likely.

Third, the gradually increasing direct participation of retail investors in different forms of debt instrument will accelerate the effects of the two foregoing factors. This will be seen at an early stage in Asia, where governments have chosen to market domestic (usually illiquid) bond issues as a form of conventional savings instrument, and where the structure of the forthcoming local currency Asian Bond Fund (ABF2) has a similar emphasis.[65]

4.2.2. Outcomes

These forces could become manifest in several ways:

---

[63] But note that even the constantly reported US stock markets may not be associated with adequate information. One study found a decline in such standards despite the effect of technological growth to assist its dissemination (D'Avolio, G., E. Gildor, & A. Shleifer *op cit*).

[64] Credit risk transfer (2003 *op cit*).

[65] Discussed in detail in Chapter 8.

- A general harmonization of regulation among different classes of financial sector, so that hedge funds, institutional investors and banks are treated increasingly similarly in respect of defined investment or trading activity.
- Pressure for certain OTC derivatives to be traded on an exchange, particularly where non-bank participants are involved. ISDA has lobbied successfully against this type of regulatory change since the mid-1980s but the final result may not have been seen. The change would be supported by investor protection advocates if it were to widen market disclosure.
- Market and regulatory pressure for improved standards of corporate governance and reporting in relation to all public and transferable issues of debt, including bonds and loans. This could be the greatest challenge in Asia in planning a successful enlargement of its local currency debt markets.

References

Arner, D. & J. Lin (eds), 2003, 'Financial regulation: a guide to structural reform', Hong Kong, Sweet & Maxwell.

Bank for International Settlements, 2003, 'Credit risk transfer', Basel.

Bank for International Settlements, 1998, 'Reports on the international financial architecture: report of the working group on strengthening financial systems', Basel, October.

Baskin, J., 1988 'The development of corporate financial markets in Britain and the United States, 1600-1914: overcoming asymmetric information', Business History Review 62(2).

Beck, T., A. Demirgüç-Kunt, & R. Levine, 2002, 'Law and finance: why does legal origin matter?', World Bank policy research working paper 2904.

Bonney, R. (ed.), 1995, 'Economic systems & state finance', Oxford, Clarendon Press.

Bordo, M., C. Meissner, & A. Redish, 2003, 'How 'original sin' was overcome: the evolution of external debt denominated in domestic currencies in the United States & the British dominions 1800-2000', National Bureau of Economic Research working paper 9841.

Brewer, J., 1989, 'The sinews of power: war money and the English state, 1688-1783', London, Unwin Hyman.

Cooper, N. & C. Scholtes, 2001, 'Government bond market valuations in an era of dwindling supply', BIS papers 5.

D'Avolio, G., E. Gildor, & A. Shleifer, 2001, 'Technology, information production, and market efficiency', paper presented at Federal Reserve Bank of Kansas City symposium, Jackson Hole, Wyoming, 'Economic Policy for the Information Economy', available at http://www.kc.frb.org.

Davis, L. &. R. Gallman, 2001, 'Evolving financial markets and international capital flows: Britain, the Americas, and Australia, 1865-1914', Cambridge, Cambridge University Press, pp35-56.

Dickson, P., 1967. 'The financial revolution in England: a study in the development of public credit 1688-1756', London, Macmillan.

Eichengreen, B. & R. Hausmann, 1999, 'Exchange rates and financial fragility', National Bureau of Economic Research working paper 7418.

Enke, S., 1963, 'Economics for Development', Englewood Cliffs, NJ, Prentice-Hall.

Fase, M., 2003, 'Financial environment & economic growth in selected Asian countries' Journal of Asian Economics 14.

Favara, G., 2003, 'An empirical reassessment of the relationship between finance and growth', IMF working paper wp03/123.

Ferguson, N., 2001, 'The cash nexus: money and power in the modern world 1700-2000', London, Basic Books.
Fisher, I., 1930, 'The theory of interest', New York, Macmillan.
Flandreau, M. & N. Sussman, 2002, 'Old sins: exchange clauses & European foreign lending in the 19th century', presentation at conference 'Currency & maturity matchmaking: redeeming debt from original sin', Inter-American Development Bank.
Gerschenkron, A., 1962, 'Reflections on the concept of 'prerequisites of modern industrialization', in 'Economic backwardness in historical perspective', Cambridge MA, Belknap Press.
Goldsmith, R., 1969, 'Financial structure and development', New Haven CT, Yale University Press.
Gurley, J. & E. Shaw, E., 1955, 'Financial aspects of economic development', American Economic Review 45(4).
Hargreaves, E., 1930, 'The national debt', in J. Wormell (*op cit*).
Harwood, A., 2002, 'Building corporate bond markets in emerging market countries', presentation to OECD/ World Bank workshop on bond markets.
Harwood, A. (ed.), 2000, 'Building local bond markets, an Asian perspective', International Finance Corporation.
Herring, R. & N. Chatusripitak, 2000, 'The case of the missing market: the bond market & why it matters for financial development', Asian Development Bank Institute working paper.
Hicks, J., 1969, 'Theory of economic history', Oxford, Clarendon Press.
Hicks, J., 1939, 'Value and capital', Oxford, Oxford University Press.
Homer, S. & M. Leibowitz, 1972, 'Inside the yield book', Englewood Cliffs NJ, Prentice-Hall.
Keynes, J.M., 1930, 'The draft convention for financial assistance by the League of Nations', in D. Moggridge (ed.) 'The collected writings of John Maynard Keynes', XX pp338-341, London, Macmillan, 1981.
Kindleberger, C., 1984, 'A financial history of Western Europe', New York, Oxford, University Press.
King, R. & R. Levine, R., 1993, 'Finance & growth: Schumpeter might be right', Quarterly Journal of Economics 108.
Levine, R., 1997, 'Financial development and economic growth: views and agenda', Journal of Economic Literature 35(2).
Lindgren, C., J. Tomás, J Baliño, C. Enoch, A. Gulde, M. Quintyn & L. Teo, 1999, 'Financial sector crisis & restructuring: lessons from Asia', IMF occasional papers.
Lutz, R., 1940, 'The structure of interest rates', Quarterly Journal of Economics 55.
Macaulay, F., 1938, 'Some theoretical problems suggested by the movements of interest rates, bond yields and stock prices in the United States since 1856', New York, National Bureau of Economic Research.
McCauley, R., S.S. Fung, & B. Gadanecz, 2002, 'Integrating the finances of East Asia', BIS Quarterly Review, December.
Mishkin, F., 1997, 'Causes and propagation of financial instability: lessons for policymakers', paper presented to Federal Reserve Bank of Kansas City symposium 'Maintaining Financial Stability in a Global Economy' Jackson Hole, Wyoming, August, 1997, available at http://www.kc.frb.org/.
North, D., 1991, 'Institutions', Journal of Economic Perspectives 5(1).
North, D., 1995, 'Some fundamental puzzles In economic history/ development', Economics Working Paper Archive at WUSTL No 9509001.
O'Brien, R., 1992, 'End of Geography', London, Royal Institute of International Affairs.

Ormrod, W. & J. Barta, 1995, 'The feudal structure & the beginnings of state finance', in Bonney (*op cit*).
Ramsey, M., 1918, 'Memorandum by the Treasury as to the financial effort of Great Britain and the cost of war', in J. Wormell (*op cit*).
Robinson, J. 1953, 'The rate of interest and other essays', London, Macmillan.
Rostow, W., 1953, The Process of Economic Growth, Oxford.
Rousseau, P. & R. Sylla, R., 2001, 'Financial systems, economic growth and globalization', National Bureau of Economic Research working paper 8323.
Shaw, E., 1973, 'Financial deepening in economic development' New York, Oxford.
Standard & Poor's Corporation, 2003, 'How domestic capital markets can help sovereign creditworthiness', New York.
Van der Wee, H., 1977, 'Monetary, credit & banking systems' in Rich, E. & Wilson, C. (eds) 'The Cambridge economic history of Europe; vol V, economic organization of early modern Europe', Cambridge, Cambridge University Press.
Wilson, C., 1941, 1966, 'Anglo-Dutch Commerce & Finance in the Eighteenth Century', Cambridge.
Wormell, J. (ed.), 1999, 'National debt in Britain 1850-1930', London, Routledge.

Chapter 5

Reforming China's Bond Markets[1]:
Development prospects and the effects of corporate behavior

John Board[1], Paul Lejot[2] and Stephen Wells[3]

[1]ISMA Centre, University of Reading; [2]Asian Institute of International Financial Law, Faculty of Law, University of Hong Kong; [3]tba

1. Introduction

A sketch of the emerging or newly-industrialized East Asian economy would show high domestic savings rates, great investment needs, large gross capital inflows and outflows, and financial systems that have been especially vulnerable to shocks and in which banks are dominant. China is pictured no differently, and shares with most of its neighbors a desire for reform in many aspects of financial market structure and operation. However, China's systemic needs greatly exceed those of other Asian economies: in particular, the adoption from 21 July 2005 of a more liberal currency regime necessitates the creation of a market-orientated monetary policy, for which debt capital market reform will be essential.[2]

---

[1] This chapter draws on research undertaken in 2005 by the ISMA Centre, University of Reading, in cooperation with the Futures and Options Association, as part of a technical assistance project commissioned by the United Kingdom's Department of Trade and Industry, whose assistance the authors acknowledge.

[2] Unless stated, this chapter uses an exchange rate of US$1=Rmb8.0924, taken as at 12 September 2005. Between 1994 and July 2005 the US$/Rmb rate was fixed at 8.28.

1.1. Desire for reform

The 'Nine Opinions' promulgated in January 2004 by China's governing State Council set three objectives for capital market development, including:[3]

> 'Actively and steadily develop bond markets. On the basis of the strict control of risks, encourage enterprises conforming required conditions to fund through issuing corporate bonds, reduce the lag of development in bond financing, enrich the variety bond market products, and promote the coordinated development of capital markets. Formulate and consummate relevant rules and regulations on corporate bond issuance, trade, information disclosure, and credit rating, establish the fully functional credit safeguard mechanisms, such as asset collaterals and credit guarantees. Gradually establish the centrally regulated, unified, and interconnected bond markets.'
>
> and
>
> 'Establish the market-oriented securities innovation mechanism. Research and develop new equity and bond products and related derivatives. Enhance the development of low-risk fixed income securities products, provide investors with alternative investment securities besides the savings. Actively explore and develop asset securitisation products.'

Such firm statements indicate that reform is intended, unqualified and well underway. Issuance of government debt has been increasingly prolific since 1998, to some extent for funding needs and to siphon personal savings into the financial system; to a great degree since 2000 as a function of the need to sterilize domestic credit expansion arising from a managed exchange rate policy. If China succeeds in creating active, reliable debt securities markets then the impact elsewhere in Asia could be profound.

1.2. The current market

Outstanding debt securities market capitalization was $ 483.3 billion as at end-2004, of which 63.3 per cent and 33.6 per cent were central government and financial issues, respectively. Net issuance in 2004 was $ 42.9 billion (2003 $ 63.2 billion), ignoring non-negotiable retail targeted bonds (around one-third of the gross amount in issue). Annual gross treasury bond issuance since 2001 exceeds $ 70.0 billion.

Central government issues fixed and floating rate treasury bills (2-5 years) and bonds (since 2002 of up to 30 years' tenor) and sanctions financial institution bonds.

---

[3] Gazette of the State Council of the People's Republic of China, no. 9/2004. The State Council's formal role is to put into effect administrative regulations in accordance with China's constitution and laws enacted by the National People's Congress and the latter's Standing Committee.

Most of this debt is bought by commercial banks for liquidity requirements or under a system of mandatory allocation. A growing non-bank financial institutional sector has a lesser investment and trading role.

Government bonds have discounted, fixed or floating-rate coupons, annual or semi-annual payment dates, and accrue interest on an actual/365 day basis. Treasury bills of 2-5 years tenor are zero coupon discounted issues.

Financial bonds are issued by the four state development banks, priced at spreads above a comparable benchmark yield. For example, earlier this year China Development Bank's 3.39 per cent bond due 2013 was priced at 53 basis points above the 10 year treasury yield, which itself is derived not from pure market influences but as a spread to the 12 month deposit rate. Corporate bonds, mainly issued by state controlled organisations, are scarce. Current practice now allows 10-15 transactions each year. Most are issued by the more important state-owned enterprises (SOEs) and guaranteed by large state banks. There is virtually no secondary market in corporate debt. Primary practice is to price these issues with reference to the 12 month fixed deposit rate, regardless of tenor.

1.3. Chapter outline

This chapter examines the prospects for modern, effective bond markets to develop in China as a result of waves of pressure for reform that have swelled in the last 3-5 years. China's external commitments to the World Trade Organization (WTO) provide some of the motivation for change in the financial services sector, but the momentum has been increasingly supported by policymakers and is prodigiously well-informed by foreign commercial and official sources. The chapter first examines the salient aspects of previous initiatives, which are of more importance than elsewhere in Asia. It assesses how market development may be impacted by the financing behavior of government and the commercial sectors, and by a web of legal and practical impediments and obstacles. Finally, the chapter looks at the main strategic alternatives available to China is bringing reform to fruition.

2. History

> 'Economic explanations are more convincing if they acknowledge culture; cultural explanations are more convincing if they acknowledge the market forces of economics.'[4]

This section examines the history, policy sequencing and sectoral considerations associated with markets for bonds and associated derivative instruments in China.

[4] Redding (1990).

2.1. Market characteristics

Virtually all analysis of the 1997-98 Asian financial crisis favors the nurturing of active domestic debt capital markets.[5] East Asia is generally free from non-cyclical aggregate shortages of capital but its capability to apportion financial resources is suspect. Broad, liquid debt securities markets exist nowhere outside Japan, even though bills, notes or bonds are issued throughout the region. The consensus of analysis is that active bond and interest rate derivative markets will improve national resource allocation by providing an unbiased, visible price mechanism, widen the choices available to investors and diminish the contagion effects of market instability.[6]

Asia's largest bond markets are also those most subject to impediments and restrictions that limit participation by investors and issuers.[7] Among these, China's use of bonds is substantial but one-dimensional: bonds provide a borrowing device for central government but fail to fulfill other functions typical of liquid markets, and are generally unavailable to the important growth sectors of the economy.

China's debt capital market comprises substantial volumes of medium and long-term bonds, almost entirely due from central government and state sector banks. The bond market is Asia's third largest by nominal capitalization after Japan and Korea, and at end-2004 represented 30.0 per cent of domestic debt securities issued in the nine largest economies of non-Japan Asia. At $ 483.3 billion, China's stock of domestic securities ranked 12th overall, of the same order as those of Belgium and Denmark.[8] This results from a growth in issuance begun in 1994-95 that has become associated with exchange rate and capital account policies which demand sterilization of domestic credit expansion.

Trading activity of all issues is negligible, the markets for bills and bonds are directional and the primary market for new issues is largely allocated, and interest rates set centrally by fiat. Bond issuance is a healthy source of funding for central government and certain infrastructural projects, but the markets provide no value for

---

[5] Eichengreen and Luengnaruemitchai (2004), Harwood (2000), Herring and Chatusripitak (2000), Jiang and McCauley (2004), Lejot *et al* (2003), McCauley (2003), Rhee (2004), Schinasi (2003), World Bank (2005), and many others. A minority holds that large-scale reform is unwarranted since organic development will be sufficient for the purpose (Yoshitomi and Shirai, 2001), a view often shared in Asian official circles.

[6] Exemplified by Jiang *et al* (2001), notably from an official setting.

[7] China, Korea and Taiwan, measured by US dollar equivalent outstanding market capitalization as at end-2004 (source http://www.bis.org/statistics/index.htm).

[8] These Bank for International Settlements (BIS) data exclude certain China retail savings bonds. Some published measures of domestic market capitalization may thus be higher than given in this chapter.

other users or purposes; onerous and capricious new issue requirements for corporate bonds ensure that they are few in number.[9]

These weaknesses are well known to central policymakers and financial regulators.[10] Legal and regulatory reform of China's financial sectors has been increasingly discussed (or implemented) since 1999, partly benchmarked by national WTO accession undertakings. The range of official attention includes issuance and trading of government and state sector debt, participation by non-state investors, and the permissibility of new instruments, notably securitised risks, corporate debt, and interest and exchange rate derivatives.

Throughout Asia, financial market reform is not without complication and risk. While most major economies have made progress since 2000 in fostering more efficient debt markets, the objectives of these reforms often offend sectional interests. Rent-seeking participants that are well-served by a partly-effective system inevitably fear that reform will lessen its value. They can include commercial banks and governments in their lending and borrowing activity, respectively. In China, bonds exist as a borrowing medium and a home for directed investment so that liquidity is available reliably only to state banks.[11] Similarly, the non-state sector, which accounts for the largest share of contemporary national growth has no reliance on traditional external finance.[12] Non-state enterprises (NSEs) are forced or may choose to be self-financing, or use informal sources of external funding not directly visible in the banking system.[13]

The use of derivative instruments is constrained and slender, and while the authorities plan to allow banks more freedom in using over-the-counter (OTC) exchange rate swaps and options, the permissible use of interest rate and credit-linked products is limited. Some OTC swap trades take place between securities houses with the floating leg set to the government's fiat short-term lending rate, and in forward fixed income trading but this is regarded as experimental, and since bond financing is not permitted, short-selling is not openly found. Although the People's

---

[9] Unless stated, 'corporate' includes both state and non-state firms. Scott and Ho summarize most laws and regulations affecting corporate issuance (2004: 29-34).

[10] For example, Wu (2005), and China Securities Regulatory Commission (2004).

[11] This applies widely in East Asia. Jiang and McCauley (*op cit*) observe that '[t]he "investible" portion of Asia's debt markets is much smaller than the total outstanding amount, but not inconsequential', using as an illustration a composite local currency bond index published by HSBC. 'Investible' is undefined but the index's capitalization is adjusted for impediments and illiquidity. AIIFL and HSBC estimates indicate that the US dollar equivalent index capitalization now represents 32 per cent of the unadjusted total of its ten constituents. China now represents around 7 per cent of the index weighting (shown at http://www.hsbcnet.com/hsbc/home/global-markets/asian-local-bond-index).

[12] Allen *et al* (2002).

[13] Non-state enterprises are those in which the state does not own a majority of shares.

Bank of China (PBoC) now allows forward dealing by banks in government bonds[14] it is clear that introducing substantive reforms requires a conventional market-driven interest rate structure, and regulatory sympathy to the use of derivatives in risk management.

Appraisals of China's financial sector published since the early-1990s generally show the non-state sector to be funded inadequately from external sources, despite its remarkable importance in economic performance, with bank lending directed at and solely accustomed to dealing with SOEs.[15] More recent research suggests that NSEs of all kinds rely for finance on internal funds and informal external sources.[16] The weakness of the system is certain and while the restricted use of funds by the growth sector may also reflect a range of issues in corporate governance, accounting standards, risk appraisal and transparency, the need for reform is crucial.

Market development must be made to accord with China's related objectives, notably:

- Overhauling domestic monetary policy, especially the introduction of market-determined interest rates. Short-term interest rates are currently set centrally, and the government risk-free yield curve is discontinuous and ambiguous in all maturities due to fractured trading and price reporting.
- Improving other channels for financial intermediation, including addressing the severe accumulation of impaired assets in the state banking sector. Beijing now sees Korea's post-crisis experience as a model: promote structured finance to help recycle assets and bequeath a mechanism for both securitised and corporate risks to be issued and traded.[17]
- China is committed to market-orientated reform, both by conviction and under its WTO commitments. However, officials may be nervous as to the pace and scale of implementation, and of the unknown implications of change, thinking influenced by China's having suffered no material loss in welfare during the Asian financial crisis due to its centralized network of controls.

---

[14] PBoC announcement (2005) No 9, 'Administrative rules on forward bond transactions in the national inter-bank bond market', May.

[15] For example, Fernald and Babson (1999), Goldie-Scott (1995), Gregory *et al* (2000), Herring and Chatusripitak (*op cit*), Harwood (*op cit* 2000, 2002), Kumar *et al* (1997) and many supranational studies.

[16] Allen *et al* (*op cit*). The authors are unspecific as to how volition affects these patterns but others show that NSEs enjoy few financing alternatives (Liu Qiao and Xiao Geng, 2004), see section 3 *infra*.

[17] Explained by Oh *et al* (2003).

- The sequencing of reform is held critical to political success and to avoid systemic fragility leading to losses of confidence and welfare.[18] Beijing is also determined that financial reforms should not lead to fragmentation of the kind seen in other industries.[19] Last, it is anxious to avoid disruption of the kind caused by 1990s policy failures in the financial sector, including abortive bond trading and activity in exchange-traded bond derivatives unrelated to an underlying cash market, which were associated with fraud, corruption, the collapse of participants, widespread losses by investors, and proved costly for government.

The introduction of a new foreign exchange regime in July 2005 will have profound long-term implications for the formation and operation of monetary policy, including the creation or enhancement of tools to allow its effective functioning.[20]

2.2. Past and current reforms

Conventional debt issuance by central and state government and financial institutions began in the early-1980s, but has suffered hiatuses caused by economic, institutional or irregular shocks. Its contemporary form has evolved only since 1994. While issuance by central government and state organisations has become substantial, a true market for notes and bonds has always been modest, with only peripheral trading liquidity available to investors of all types. Corporate bonds have an irregular history: state organisations were permitted to issue bonds in a semi-regulated fashion in the mid-1980s and the results became chaotic.[21] Similarly in the early-1990s, markets in exchange-traded and OTC interest rate and bond futures and options were wholly speculative in use, became discredited and were prohibited by 1995. Issuance by SOEs is now modest, NSE issuance trivial and secondary trading virtually non-existent. New interest rate and exchange rate derivatives will be permitted with the eventual implementation of reform guidelines announced in 2004.

---

[18] Seen in Beijing's reaction to a 2002-04 APEC study of asset securitisation (Arner, 2004). A resulting administrative framework issued in April 2005 by PBoC and China Banking Regulatory Commission (CBRC) uses a pilot model intended both to secure State Council legislative consent and encourage the undisruptive introduction of single transactions.

[19] Young (2000) describes China's silk industry being released from central control, not to a market orientation but one that became fragmented, corrupt and subject to the parochial interests of local officials.

[20] Typical is 'China's ultimate aim is to transform the monetary policy platform into a market-based framework, rather than one centered on administrative directives. The CNY regime shift is the first step in the process of shifting emphasis from the exchange rate to interest rates in formulation of monetary policy.' (Jen, 2005).

[21] Scott and Ho (*op cit*) identify four separate phases of issuance of non-government, non-financial bonds since 1980, encouraged by two competing sets of laws and at least three waves of regulation.

The growing breadth of financial intermediation in China means that professional and investor interest in issuance and trading is profound, and a limited number of approved investment firms now engage in trading state sector debt issues with the considerable sophistication known in major markets, despite general illiquidity.[22] Their success on an observable scale requires the loosening of symbiotic links between state banks and government typical of Asia's domestic money markets, where banks and their regulators form a circle that restricts the use of debt instruments by other parties.[23]

The consequence is pervasive compensating behavior by public and private sector savers and borrowers. Investors circumvent blockages and legal weaknesses by moving funds overseas; aspiring borrowers take funds from informal sources of credit when access to bank financing is limited.[24] These actions may be condoned by the authorities: PBoC gave permission in May for large SOEs to issue unsecured short-term notes in the inter-bank market, a non-transparent concessionary reform that may remain informal.

Reviews of the Asian financial crisis often neglect China's success in avoiding output losses in 1997-98.[25] That China's border halted the contagion may owe much to a limited domestic credit culture. Market techniques have grown steadily important since the 1980's but financial institutions are prevented from operating in the fullness of market forces. This has two consequences for China's banks. First, they suffer external direction and may be unable independently to extend or withdraw credit from certain borrowers. Second, banks are protected from external shifts in sentiment. The sector cannot be attacked rapidly even though the scale of its impaired assets and weak capital bases is universally known. China's insidious deregulation will eventually make those pressures less susceptible to semi-official resistance; it is essential for China to create a true debt capital market to guard against destabilization, and open funding alternatives for China's larger NSEs, which rely on internal funding and receive minimal external financing support.[26]

---

[22] Li (2003) is an early and influential example.

[23] A problem addressed by Mohanty (2002).

[24] Aziz and Duenwald (2002). Allen *et al* (*op cit* pp4-5) postulate 'effective, non-standard financing channels' funding private companies, including 'privately placed bonds and loans' (*ibid* p32).

[25] Real GDP grew by 7.8 per cent in 1998. A substantial 1994 devaluation and pre-crisis current external surplus left China free of the stresses placed on Korea and Southeast Asia in mid-1997.

[26] First shown in a survey of over 600 larger private Chinese enterprises (Gregory and Tenev, 2001).

Since 2002-03, China's central authorities[27] have accumulated a strong understanding of the practicalities of building robust market and issuance infrastructures for debt instruments of all kinds, not least due to massing attention of foreign and multinational organisations and transaction-seeking private sector banks. However, there is a profound need for commensurate legal and regulatory reform, both enabling in nature and specific to markets or instruments. The speed at which implementation can occur is limited by competing political interests, the outcomes of past quasi-market developments, the need for policy sequencing, and by the timetable for China's service sector WTO obligations, which set more demanding and hasty agendas for banking and insurance reform than for changes in the securities industry. CSRC and PBoC policy heads are also aware that time pressure may be subsumed to the tactics needed to secure new legislation.

Policy sequencing is taken as critical to success and to further central government's dedication to stability. This means, for example, that a market-orientated monetary policy involving interest rate reform cannot precede the creation of a transparent infrastructure for the issuance of government debt by auction or placement,[28] nor the means to allow a volume increase in OTC trading of all such instruments with open participation by a broad range of investors.[29]

The solution adopted by agencies such as CSRC and PBoC is threefold. First, to use a problem-solving approach, seeking legislative support in the National People's Congress for pilot projects or single transactions, so as to demonstrate their value and to make clear the need for overarching reform that accords with prior declarations of intent by the State Council. Second, to prevent reform leading to shocks and uncertainty by combining the creation of modern debt markets with the pressing need for a market structure to recycle impaired assets from the balance sheets of state banks. Third, to conduct a pragmatic engagement with non-Chinese academic, professional and regulatory resources that are seen to have established value.[30]

Thus the authorities intend that the creation of a non-government bond market be led by the structured finance model used successfully in Korea, creating a pricing mechanism to assist in the disposal of non-performing loans (NPLs) without a loss of

---

[27] Especially China Securities Regulatory Commission (CSRC), PBoC, Ministry of Finance and National Development and Reform Council (NDRC, which until 1995 was the lead bond regulator, then losing status after market failures). Early in 2004 China's State Council endorsed the principle of modern markets for government and corporate debt, and in the regulated use of commodity, interest rate and equity derivatives. All initiatives require new legislation.

[28] Bond auctions began in 2002 with a primary dealer network of selected state banks.

[29] Reform has been opposed by participants fearful of losing rents, including central government interests that value the efficient capturing of personal savings via state bank liquidity.

[30] Regulators have been informed by many official and commercial sources since 1994. Certain US interests have been especially active in promoting resources and training, notably the Securities and Exchange Commission.

confidence or the elimination of fictitious bank capital, and eventually establishing a platform for subsequent corporate debt issuance.[31] A similar tactic favored in several emerging Asian bond markets has been to allow international organisations to issue domestic local currency bonds to prove their feasibility. China intends to allow the Asian Development Bank, International Finance Corporation and others to do likewise.

This conservative, staged approach to policymaking has a risk with which Beijing is familiar: that non-transparent administrative orders delay legislative reform.

2.3. Market impediments

Impediments in the structure or operation of capital debt markets may be said to have legal, fiscal, systemic or regulatory origins.[32] Attacking these problems requires solving intentional or implied restrictions, omissions of law or practice, and unnecessary inconsistencies.

The most damaging features are obstacles and omissions, since discrepancies can be reflected in the pricing of risk, but legal irregularities are damaging and poorly compensated in ratings, risk or pricing. Obstacles are specific factors, not all of which are deliberate, and aspects of market practice that deter institutional participation. The following tables show the comprehensiveness of impediments affecting China's financial system.

Table 5-1. **Legal impediments**

Obstacles	**Omissions**	**Disparities**
Reliable transfer of rights, the rights of creditors in proceedings for bankruptcy or debtor restructuring, and taxes and duties penalizing reputable financial transaction structures.	Especially questions of enforcement, and the penalizing of transactions, notably asset-backed issues.	Conflicts of law. Treatment of creditor classes and between domestic and foreign claims. Fracture of property rights from effective enforcement.

These questions determine the reliability of sale of financial assets, and transfer of creditor claims or associated collateral between unconnected parties; practices not yet comprehensively developed in China as relevant civil procedures are recently enacted. Legal clarity is important to safeguard the enforcement and transfer of

[31] In APEC-led discussions, Thailand's finance ministry has suggested China adopt a portfolio securitisation approach to funding NSEs (Chaipravat and Chaipravat, 2003). Only Japan and Korea among Asian APEC members have attempted something similar.

[32] Examined in detail in Lejot, Arner and Liu (2004); see also chapter 7. Schinasi (*op cit*) notes that impediments may arise within the financial sector 'most often from market power in the financial industry that stifles access to securities markets or impedes the functioning of securities markets.'

legitimate claims, and avoid qualified acceptance of ownership and property rights, or limits to such rights in relation to investor classes, barriers to the certain sale of property or financial assets, limitations on collateral rights in bankruptcy or reorganization, and limits to enforcement against public organisations through the arbitrary extension of sovereign immunity. Such obstacles help explain the existence of informal corporate credit markets where non-institutional sources supply external finance, or when legal or regulatory limits lead to the disguising of claims in an officially acceptable or more enforceable form.

Historically, property and securities law are not comprehensive and subject to administrative rulings. New contract (1999) and trust laws (2001) provided for the true sale of financial claims and allow single transactions, but property rights, effectiveness of transfer, and the creation of bankruptcy remote vehicles for asset-backed issues require further reform and refinement. Quantitative constraints on corporate issuers prevent the use of onshore special purpose vehicles for structured transactions. Enforcement uncertainties are common and may vary between provinces. Debtor notice requirements can also affect the reliability of transfer of creditor claims. China's pilot asset securitisation measures are unclear as to detail but may require that extensive notice be given prior to the sale of assets into a securitisation pool. Incomplete or flawed notice may additionally result in the risk of borrower set-off in asset sales.

***Table 5-2.* Fiscal impediments**

Obstacles	Omissions	Disparities
Taxes and duties penalizing reputable financial transaction structures or transfer.	Matters relating to information, especially clarity in the application of taxes, duties and allowances.	Disparities between classes of creditor, obligor or financial institutions, and between local and foreign participants.

Withholding tax affects most Asian debt markets. It complicates dealing and investment practice, and raises or obscures transaction costs. The tax and duty regime in China is currently unclear by application, tariff, amelioration or the reliability of collection, except for government bonds, which are tax exempt for certain holders. Taxes on transfer threaten the integrity of both corporate and structured transactions, including those using impaired assets.

***Table 5-3.* Regulatory impediments**

Obstacles	Omissions	Disparities
Prohibitions on investment by non-bank financial institutions. Quantitative corporate issuer and coupon restrictions (inequitably affecting contract integrity).	Markets for risks or instruments that are closed to classes of investor, either deliberately or by default. Independent role for credit rating agencies.	Differences in the treatment of investor activity are a source of market distortion. The resulting lack of clarity deters investor participation. Regulatory rivalry.

Corporate bond issuance is subject to an unusually restrictive process originally designed to encourage borrowers to raise funds elsewhere. Approvals are required of NDRC, PBoC and CSRC for all issues, commercial terms and the use of proceeds. Rules introduced after investor losses in the early-1990s require that corporate issues are guaranteed by banks or 'parent' SOEs.

China will shortly permit issuance by designated foreign entities but transaction feasibility cannot be equated to the opening of a market that lacks other substantive infrastructure.

Most debt derivative instruments have been prohibited since the 1990s. The authorities intend gradually to reverse this outright ban by allowing the use of selected instruments and new contracts, although there are likely to be continuing restrictions on eligible users.

While the central authorities recognize the need for regulatory clarity the division of responsibilities is unclear among securities, banking and insurance regulators, and historically between the central bank, finance ministry and agencies of the State Council.[33]

***Table 5-4.* Systemic impediments**

Obstacles	Omissions	Disparities
Aspects of financial structure, regulation or enforced practice that deter institutional activity.	Absence of continuous, transparent, market-driven yield curves.	Conflicts between exchange and OTC transfer, trading and settlement practices. Market fragmentation.

The absence of a declared or consistent benchmark issuance programme is crippling to corporate bond market development. Government issuance must have predictability, and flawed auction mechanisms lead to a weakened pricing formula, poor visibility and inconsistent interest rates. Primary sales have been made by auction since 2002-03 yet the process is closed and only part of the state's issuance plans is typically declared. Scheduled or pre-announced auctions have been cancelled at short notice. Bonds are placed or bought by direction, so the market lacks infrastructure for information purposes, open regulation, trading and settlement.

The nominal amounts of government bonds available to investors without a large price impact has been estimated at under Rmb125 million ($ 15.5 million)[34] but this represents a range of purchases drawn from outstanding issues: the non-disruptive amounts available in any single issue, whether or not considered a benchmark, would be far less or trivial. There is confusion as to the functions of the Shanghai and Shenzhen stock exchanges in debt issues and between the exchanges and the inter-bank market, all of which produces a duplicated, non-contiguous government yield

[33] Notably CBRC, China Insurance Regulatory Commission, CSRC and NDRC.

[34] By HSBC in compiling the index described in footnote 9 (*supra*).

curve. The bond market is closed to foreign investors, although approved joint venture investment vehicles may in principle buy exchange-listed bonds.[35]

3. Corporate characteristics and financing

China's modern economy has sustained high rates of growth and a considerable rolling back of central control, but lacks a market-orientated infrastructure. Financial reforms thus need to recognize the characteristics and funding dynamics of China's corporate sectors, which will inform the value, nature and feasibility of any active corporate bond market, as well as its path to introduction. The practices explained in this section are well-developed (and not unknown elsewhere), representing quasi-Coasian solutions to the restrictions and inadequacies of a controlled economy undergoing the profoundest change.[36] They include a forced reliance on equity funding, manipulation of corporate behavior and reporting by controlling shareholders, heavy use of informal or disguised external sources of funds, cross-border round tripping of domestic funds, and pronounced management of earnings.[37]

The stock markets were first organized to allow SOEs to raise capital and improve operating performance, with government retaining predominant access to debt market financing.[38] China's listed companies look to the public equity markets for two practical reasons. First, the banking sector is undercapitalized and historically weak in assessing corporate risk and needs, which constrains firms' external financing. Second, until recently equity financing has been comparatively inexpensive and accompanied by light disclosure requirements. This has reinforced incentives for firms to manipulate their performance and neglect minority interests. Dominant shareholders typically hold a far higher proportion of shares than are listed, and have scope to manage firms to their sole benefit without fear of minority rights being upheld by law.

---

[35] Available rarely, or at distorted prices. An offshore OTC market in yuan non-deliverable forward contracts has a daily trading volume of approximately $ 100mm but can reach around $ 500mm. The maximum tenor is 3 years; liquidity concentrates in maturities of up to 12 months. Activity is constrained by official disapproval, and negative interest spreads to US dollar rates due to expectations of a yuan revaluation. Source: Deutsche Bank.

[36] See in particular Allen *et al* (*op cit*), Cai *et al* (2004), Fan *et al* (2005), Liu (2003), Liu and Lu (2004), Liu and Xiao (*op cit*), and Xiao (2004). Others examine general capital mobility and how resource allocation is retarded by the system, whether or not local savings are scarce (Boyreau-Debray, 2003). Prominent informal sources of funds are not unique to China, nor elsewhere in East Asia. They reflect *inter alia* induced responses to legal and regulatory obstacles of the kind discussed in section 5 (*supra*).

[37] Not explicitly included is a discussion of weak corporate governance, poor corporate financial performance, weak accounting and reporting standards, and the general lack of a credit risk and credit rating culture, that require attention as part of the creation of a successful market for corporate debt.

[38] Stock market underperformance has made this strategy increasingly redundant.

Firms' external funding can generally be predicted by ownership: the main flow of bank credit is to SOEs while NSEs rely for funds on cashflow and informal sources. That schism does not necessarily show that NSEs face an aggregate lack of short or long-term funding.[39] From this first evidence alone it cannot be predicted how the creation of an active corporate bond market would affect the private sector but recent research may show what special factors need to be considered.

NSEs now provide most of the economy's growth. Since the non-state sector has sustained high rates of growth with few resources from the banking system it is possible that informal financing exists on a large scale in China, of which under-reported or disguised profits are an important source. Evidence relating profit disguising to firms' external financing constraints may also show how developing corporate bond and securitised debt markets would offer a means for NSEs to relieve those constraints. Also, if firms with greater financing constraints tend to hide more of their true results then revealing the extent of under-reporting may help in the development of active financial markets.

The central National Bureau of Statistics (NBS) classifies firms among six main ownership categories: SOEs, collective firms, private firms, mixed firms, foreign firms, and those from Hong Kong and Taiwan.[40] NBS maintains a database for national income purposes containing firm-level information based on accounting reports of large and medium-sized industrial firms since 1995. Recent research[41] using NBS source data extends the early conclusion to indicate other sectoral characteristics.

The sectoral patterns seen in these data and elsewhere have been taken to recommend one suggested approach to policy sequencing, in which provision is made for structured finance involving securitisation to address China's NPL problem and provide in due course a platform for true corporate issuance.

3.1. Disguised profits

Profit disguising is explained by tax evasion, the incentive to overcome financing constraints, and circumventing behavior prompted by insecure property rights and weak leverage in the conventional domain among creditors and shareholders.

Firms with tighter financing constraints tend to disguise more profits. Hiding sales revenue seems to be the preferred means to conceal profits. Smaller firms are more inclined to hide profits than larger firms.

Competition increases the incentive to hide profits, and firms at a comparative competitive disadvantage have a stronger propensity to hide profits.[42]

---

[39] Allen *et al* (*op cit)*.

[40] Green (2004) gives an explanation of the roots and consequences of the categorization of Chinese enterprises.

[41] Cai *et al* (*op cit*), Liu and Lu (*op cit*), Liu and Xiao (*op cit*), and Xiao (*op cit*).

[42] Cai *et al* (*op cit*). The authors suggest that their findings support 'strengthening institutional infrastructure'.

3.2. Public sector reporting

Local officials in China have tended to overstate the growth of output in the area for which they are responsible. This may suggest a weaker profit disguising propensity among SOEs.[43]

Informal sources include true funds ultimately sourced from state banks, but which will have passed outside the banking sector and financial risk management or credit processes.

3.3. Informal funding channels

Informal sources also include cross-border funding (largely from Hong Kong and Taiwan) that is treated as foreign direct investment (FDI) but which essentially is disguised debt. In effect this is an informal placement market that circumvents capital and regulatory controls. It may also widen investor participation in unlisted NSEs.

A large part of China's capital outflows is held offshore prior to returning as investment funding to domestic users. Such 'circular' FDI has been estimated at 20-30 per cent of the total exported. Thus China contributes to its overall FDI inflows, based on domestic funds made available overseas through flight capital and over-invoicing for imported goods. The ultimate source of these funds are domestic firms whose risk averse owners are hoping to obtain better protection of property rights from offshore, usually from a comparatively stable legal environment in Hong Kong, or take advantage of domestic fiscal and administrative incentives offered to foreign investment.[44] Eliminating the circular process requires removing incentives inherent in close regulation, and building credible domestic financial markets that lessen incentives to divert into other jurisdictions.[45]

3.4. Institutional and agency conflicts

Agency conflicts between owners and minority shareholders are the fundamental drivers of earnings management. Earnings management is mainly induced by the controlling shareholders' incentive to tunnel, that is to conceal or expropriate value from the minority.[46]

---

[43] Young (*op cit*).

[44] Xiao (*op cit*).

[45] *Ibid*; Global Development Finance 2002 p41.

[46] Liu and Lu (*op cit*).

Finally, funding constraints help explain the use of corporate pyramid structures in both NSEs and SOEs.[47] NSEs use pyramid structures to help disguise earnings, while for local or provincial government, pyramids give scope to transfer ownership rights in SOEs to third parties without infringing limits on the disposal of state sector assets. Differing limits to rights affecting the two sectors lead to different incentives and compensating behavior.

4. Today's Capital Markets

China's capital markets have developed rapidly since liberalization of the economy that began in the early 1980's. However it remains primarily an equity market with a limited, though growing government bond market, an insignificant corporate bond market (where all issues are, in effect, government guaranteed) and no financial derivatives market (though commodity futures are traded on three exchanges).

4.1. Equity markets

Listed companies—almost all of which are SOEs—issue several types of share. The largest categories are legal person shares and state shares that are held by the government or state agencies and are not tradable. Tradable shares represented 35 per cent of total shares issued at end-2003, [48] which is a major development challenge given the potential for dilution of outstanding tradable shares. The government began in mid-2005 to bring forward proposals for legal person and state shares to be converted into tradable shares. The market value of listed tradable shares at end-2003 was Rmb1,500 billion ($ 185.4 billion).[49]

Securities law recognizes two intermediary types, comprehensive and brokerage firms. Comprehensive firms may undertake a full range of investment banking services and are required to maintain appropriate capital. Brokerage firms are allowed to engage in a more limited spread of activities. Some comprehensive firms may engage in fund management, and will face higher capital requirements. As at mid-2005 there were 127 operating firms with a combined asset base approaching Rmb500 billion ($ 61.8 billion). CSRC has continuing problems with insolvency of brokerage firms and in the year to end-June 2005 has forced the closure or merger of 10 firms.

There are stock exchanges in Shenzhen and Shanghai. The allocation of listings between them is decided centrally, with larger enterprises typically listed in Shanghai. Corporate bonds are also listed on the exchanges and traded through their respective order-driven trading systems. Clearing and depositary transfer functions

---

[47] Fan *et al* (2005) examined 750 and 62 newly listed firms, respectively majority-owned by Chinese local governments and private sector entrepreneurs.

[48] Source: CSRC.

[49] Source CSRC; Deutsche Bank.

for shares and listed corporate bonds are carried out by the China Securities Depositary and Clearing Corporation (CSDCC). The market is organized on a cash basis, so that investors must demonstrate the required cash or stock and deposit assets with their broker before any transaction can be struck. Brokerage firms may manage substantial balances of third party client cash, either as transaction balances or entrusted assets that are effectively under discretionary management.

In recent years the market has been falling partly because of the overhang of legal person shares and partly from weak confidence. As a consequence, revenue among traditional securities firms—derived from commissions, proprietary trading and underwriting—has been squeezed, and caused the failure or compulsory reorganization or merger of a number of firms.

4.2. Sources of funding

In the pre-reform command economy, corporate finance concerned itself mainly with the mechanics of transferring state funds to state enterprises, and in some cases remit surpluses from enterprises to the government. The state banking sector was the sole conduit. It remains the dominant funding conduit though the nature of banking has changed to a more conventional model of deploying deposit to support lending. A general reliance on bank funding has been a feature of Asian economies and an overdependence on easily-given bank credit was a major factor underlying the 1997-98 crisis. Since then Asian economies have sought with varying success to diversify their sources of enterprise funding.

Figure 4-1 illustrates the contributions of funding sources in 2003 for a range of Asian economies and certain developed markets. From this it becomes clear that China has a significantly higher proportion of bank debt (80 per cent) than the Asian average (ex-China, at 29 per cent, reduced from 39 per cent in 1998). In addition, the share of bank debt (excluding China and Hong Kong) ranges from 25 per cent to 40 per cent. The range in the selected developed markets is higher because of a high level in Japan, extending from 23 per cent in the US (reflecting a traditionally fragmented banking system) to 50 per cent in Japan.

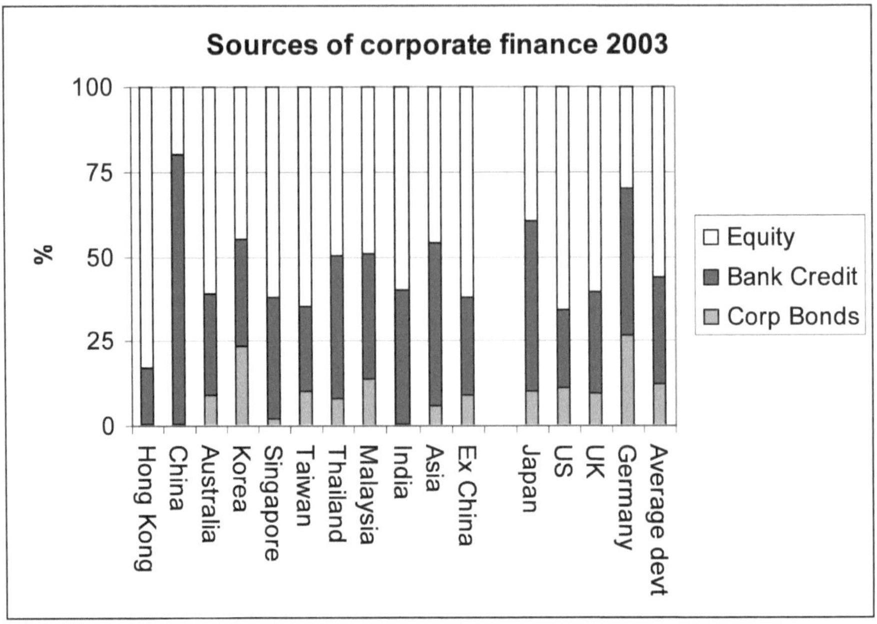

Figure 5-1. **Sources of external funding 2003**

It is clear that the accumulation of delinquent, impaired and non-performing loans and other assets on the balance sheets of China's state banks is high, not only in absolute terms but in relation to the total of all financial assets within the formal economy.

Data reported to the BIS for bonds issued and market capitalization are shown in Table 5-5

Table 5-5. **Summary Rmb bond issuance (excluding retail bonds) US$ billion**

	Outstanding (end period)			Net annual issuance	
Issue sector	**2004**	**2003**	**% change**	**2004**	**2003**
Government	331.8	287.4	15.4	44.4	44.4
Financial	183.7	140.8	30.5	42.9	18.8
Corporate	12.2	12.2	0.0	0.0	0.0
Total	527.7	440.4	19.8	87.3	63.2

4.3. State sector bonds

Government debt issuance encompasses 'true' government bonds (T-Bonds) and Finance Bonds issued by state financial institutions, mainly development banks.

Almost all bonds are bought and held by commercial banks to meet compulsory liquidity requirements. Outstanding debt grew by 19.8 per4e cent in 2004 to exceed $ 500 billion for the first time with annual issuance of $ 87.2 billion split approximately equally between T-Bonds and Finance Bonds.

The Ministry of Finance's treasury division manages all issuance. Since 2001 new issues have been made largely by sealed bid Dutch auction through a group of 50 appointed primary dealers. An annual issuance schedule covers around 80 per cent of the expected total, with the remaining amount treated as special issues and updates issued quarterly. The ministry reserves the right to intervene and reject unwanted bids. The dominance among the primary dealers of the four large commercial banks has encouraged observers to believe the process to be subject to collusion. Issuance now covers a range of maturities as long as 30 years: prior to 2001 a 7 year maximum prevailed. In a market sensitive innovation, the finance ministry may now reopen outstanding issues during auctions in order to consolidate issues and enhance liquidity.

Trading takes place on an opaque interbank market operated by PBoC and separately on the two stock exchanges. Some issues are dealt only on one market and all investors are limited to participating in one market segment. Commercial banks trade their bond holdings very little but are active in the interbank repurchase (repo) market: bond repurchases have been allowed by banks since 2003. Trading segmentation diminishes liquidity that is already modest and leads to unpredictable prices differences in any single issue.

Primary dealers have no market-making obligations and are not required to quote bond prices. Short-selling is prohibited by law. The finance ministry has examined ways to improve liquidity but the ban on short selling and the dominant position of the large banks makes difficult any piecemeal reform. The finance ministry is known to have considered allowing new bond derivative instruments to develop but has concluded that the underlying market is insufficiently robust, doubtless influenced by past experiences.

4.4. Corporate debt

The modern corporate bond market dates originally from 1980 when SOEs first issued bonds to the public. From 1987 PBoC was the lead regulator for the market. Issuance by a variety of entities including regional governments increased rapidly and peaked in 1992 at nearly Rmb70 billion ($ 8.7 billion). The market was largely unregulated, the quality of issuers uncontrolled, and the result appeared in numerous defaults, with in many cases delinquent payments finally satisfied by the banks that had distributed the defaulted issues. After 1992, government sought a more controlled and orderly market and the role of PBoC was reduced.

The events of 1993 were traumatic, not least due to significant state losses. Among other measures, the government prohibited regional government issuance, although they continue to do so indirectly through captive development companies. There remains considerable political caution as to the reopening of corporate bond markets despite the enthusiasm of public pronouncements.

4.4.1. Instruments

Corporate bond issuance has varied very considerably during the liberalization period, following changes in policy and the fortunes of the market. In 2003, bond issuance totaled Rmb35.8 billion ($ 4.4 billion) and involved 15 issuers.[50] Maturities ranged from 3 to 30 years, the majority being of 10 years. All issuers in the current market phase have been state entities, including municipal development corporations. Bonds are invariably issued to finance infrastructure projects. Regulation requires all bonds to carry bank guarantees, which are normally provided by the four main state commercial banks. For practical purposes bonds are government guaranteed with no perceived risk of default. All issues are required to be rated but (unsurprisingly given their guarantees) almost all are rated triple-A. One half of 2003 issues were listed but this is not compulsory.

4.4.2. Investors

The large four state banks account for the greatest share of total bank assets.[51] Banks are limited by regulation to the provision of basic banking services and officially may not own non-banking financial subsidiaries. UP to three-quarters of household savings are deposited with banks and individual savers regard the main banks as entirely safe and generally willing to sacrifice deposit returns for security. Banks may invest in government bonds and finance bonds but are not permitted to hold or trade corporate issues.

China's insurance sector has been traditionally dominated by two organisations, large domestic insurers but WTO demands make radical change inevitable before 2008. Liberalization of the sector began in 2000-01, since when revenue from premium income and net investments have risen rapidly. At end-2003 insurance company investment may have reached Rmb30-Rmb40 billion ($ 3.7-$ 4.9 billion).[52] Until 2002 insurers were barred from investing in corporate securities but they now hold at least 50 per cent of outstanding corporate bonds, albeit a small portion of their investment portfolios.

China introduced a three pillar pension find structure in 1997. The first pillar is a pay-as-you-go defined benefit system. The second pillar is contributory at centrally set rates and, at least in theory, is funded. The third pillar is voluntary and fully funded but at an early stage of development and so the funds deployed are modest. Some enterprises offer pension schemes under the third pillar. Life insurers also offer similar schemes. The National Social Security Fund (NSSF) was endowed with state funds to provide cover for deficits in the Pillar 1 schemes. Both Pillar 3 schemes and NSSF may invest in corporate securities. Corporate funds and NSSF may invest up to 30 per cent and 10 per cent, respectively, of total assets in corporate bonds but the impact so far has been small.

---

[50] For clarity, the issues described in this section are retail bonds and omitted from BIS data.

[51] Around 86 per cent in 2002 according to the Economist Intelligence Unit.

[52] Source : Deutsche Bank.

Collective investment schemes are growing rapidly and have become significant equity investors. Together, open-ended and closed funds managed Rmb110-Rmb120 billion ($ 13.6-$ 14.8 billion) of market assets as at end-2003. No bond funds currently exist, but neither do regulatory barriers, and China's first exchange-traded fund to invest in domestic debt securities has been launched in 2005 as a single currency fund contributor to the regional central bankers' second Asian Bond Fund (ABF2).[53] The fund's impact will not be known until it becomes clear how easily will bonds be available for purchase.

Securities companies engage in asset management mainly for large SOEs and typically invest only in equities. These funds involved are of the order of Rmb30 billion ($ 3.7 billion).

Trust and investment companies were key investors in China's formative capital markets and grew rapidly for lack of any competition of assets. Most experienced losses in the early 1990's and a number were dissolved. They face a lack of public confidence and competition from other fund management companies.

Qualified Foreign Institutional Investors (QFIIs) may invest in local currency assets including corporate bonds up to an absolute total limit. To date they have not been attracted to corporate bonds.

Thus most retail savings are currently placed with banks but the emergence of mutual funds, insurance schemes and pension products against a background of growing enrichment among a widening urban population suggests that the investment infrastructure to support a corporate bond market is developing but is severely constrained by lack of investible instruments.

4.5. Issuance

The new issue process is merit-based, complex, slow and restrictive, not least since at least three regulators each directly influence issuance (NDRC, PBoC and CSRC). For corporate bonds it entails two main phases:

- An annual borrowing plan is mandated by the State Council. Historically this seeks to ensure that investment went to the sectors that accorded with government priority but it also now reflects a perceived need to limit capital investment for deflationary motives. NDRC has responsibility for implementing the borrowing quota. Aspiring issuers submit proposals as part of the annual planning process to NDRC, which tries to ensure that the declared use of the issue proceeds is consistent with state industrial policies and the overall annual quota. This means that only infrastructure and a few debt restructuring proposals are approved by NDRC. The borrowing plan and qualified issuers list is subject to State Council approval.
- Individual issue proposals are submitted to PBoC, which regulate bond yields. Corporate coupons may be no more that 140 per cent of the fixed bank rate for deposits of the same term, itself administered by PBoC. In practice bank rates

[53] See chapter 8.

do not exceed 5 years, whereas bonds have longer maturities but effectively bonds of a given maturity have identical yields based on deposit rates. PBoC's decision is subject to NDRC approval.

PBoC has recently allowed bank deposit and lending rates to vary: rates seen as fixed may now be subject to variation. This benefits bond issuers as prevailing yields are currently below bank lending rates—as at end-July 2005, 5 year bank loan rates were 5.25-5.76 per cent while 5 and 10 year bond yields were 3.77 per cent and 4.26 per cent, respectively.[54] PBoC will also permit issuance of floating rates notes when restrictions on yields make issuance otherwise infeasible.

Bonds need not be listed on an exchange but to access the official trading market requires a listing. Listing proposals are dealt with by CSRC to ensure compliance with disclosure requirements as well as by a stock exchange. Initial and ongoing disclosure requirements are not rigorous, but investors currently see the bond guarantor as their primary obligor. All issues are made as public offers: there is no provision for private placements, shelf-registration or fast-track procedure for seasoned bond issuers.

The issuance process takes over 12 months in the first stage and a further 1-2 months in the second. Issuers risk interest rate changes, which have become more frequent under an active monetary policy and are likely to be made an increasing feature of a PBoC strategy configured to post-July 2005 exchange rate policy. New issue coupons can only be changed after further PBoC approval. Issuers are yet to suffer: most bonds are placed with captive investors at sub-market yields due to the acute shortage of supply.

4.6. Secondary market trading and settlement

To date trading has been limited, depositary arrangements fragmented, and issues may or may not be listed on an exchange. In practice about 50 per cent of bonds are listed. Most new issues are initially lodged with a central depositary,[55] but on subsequent listing a portion of the issue will be held in accounts in the China Securities Depositary and Clearing Corporation (CSDCC), the settlement vehicle for equities.

The volume of government bonds designated for the interbank market greatly exceeds that for the two stock exchanges but interbank turnover is low by comparison. Bonds sold into the interbank market tend to be held to maturity and need not be accounted for as marked-to-market, unlike exchange-traded bonds. The result is price confusion throughout the yield curve.

The two stock exchanges are the only legal venues for dealing in corporate bonds. Both exchanges use conventional order-driven systems but most trading takes place electronically or by telephone and reported to the exchange, as in many other countries. The system offers immediate post-trade publication. Block trades can be

[54] Corporate bonds are subject to 20 per cent income tax, government bonds are tax exempt.

[55] Unlisted bonds issued by securities companies are deposited at CSDCC at issue.

transacted at the end of the day at prices that fall within the day's range. Exchange turnover is high in corporate issues, partly as the exchanges allow repurchases to facilitate bond borrowing. Repo trading is negligible in Shenzhen but in Shanghai is far more active than the cash bond market, implying active bond borrowing and frequent renewals of outstanding trading positions.

Government bond issues and those of China International Trust and Investment Corporation (CITIC) are dealt on the interbank market operated and regulated by PBoC. In addition, substantial OTC trading takes place business by private negotiation and settled between counterparties, which is both unregulated and technically illegal. Given that the period between issue and listing is typically several months, bonds may not be legally traded during the time when trading would be expected to be most active, so the existence of a curb market and unofficial practices is unsurprising. Trading also takes place in this market in subordinated issues of Bank of China and China Construction Bank and certificates of indebtedness of smaller banks and insurers. Some observes have seen this market—which inevitably will be known to the authorities—as an unofficial trial of an expanded corporate bond sector without the regulatory authorities being seen as complicit in the event of problems or defaults.

4.7. Securitisation

Since 2003 several domestic or foreign currency transactions have been completed using pools of NPLs but all with full or partial recourse to the asset seller, or enhanced with well-performing assets. New draft regulations were issued by PBoC and CBRC in April 2005,[56] providing for a pilot programme of issuance by China Construction Bank and China Development Bank, using residential loans and infrastructure loans, respectively. The resulting bonds will be traded only on the interbank market.

4.8. Credit rating agencies

China has hitherto lacked a ratings culture, not least due to the requirement that all non-government and finance sector issues be guaranteed. It is home to over fifty firms engaged in credit rating and related advisory activity but only five are effectively engaged in rating new issues and none was reliably established or officially recognized until 2004. The role of independent rating agencies is now under regulatory study, with preference given to China Chengxin Credit Rating Co., with which Fitch Ratings was associated. Beijing has indicated for several years that it will license foreign agencies to operate in the domestic arena but this has yet to take proper form.

---

[56] People's Bank of China & China Banking Regulatory Commission Announcement [2005] No. 7, available at http://www.pbc.gov.cn/english//detail.asp?col=6400&ID=548..

4.9. Derivative instruments

China's commodity futures markets are regulated by CSRC, which licenses exchanges and brokers. A forward market for corporate bonds has begun to develop that could become substantial, for example, if used by borrowers seeking to hedge liabilities. There is currently an unresolved debate as to whether futures contracts might be treated as securities, and thus eventually be traded on an existing exchange. The State Council 'Nine Opinions' refers briefly to the development of futures markets but this referred solely to commodity contracts.[57] While the newly-announced exchange rate policy may encourage the adoption market-orientated instruments to assist monetary operations, including interest rate futures and options, the authorities are wary of their predecessors' experience in 1992-94, when a speculative market in bond futures collapsed with losses that were finally borne by central government.

5. Market Underdevelopment

Several questions, often interlinked, will affect the progress made in building effective government and corporate debt capital markets, the more critical of which are reviewed in this section.

5.1. Need for benchmark yield curve

China's government bond market is relatively underdeveloped and small in scale, though issuance has risen and may continue to do so.[58] More problematically, liquidity is limited and new issue pricing is not market determined. Thus primary and secondary bond yields may diverge significantly. A yield curve is published that is based on exchange reported prices but neither interbank prices nor repurchase rates are taken into account in its compilation.

5.2. Lack of true borrower demand

It has been argued by certain practitioners since SOEs may borrow cheaply from state banks without the firm expectation of being required to repay the loan, no incentive exists for the larger or more creditworthy entities as feasible public issuers to make use of the corporate bond market, bringing the attendant effort of laboriously gaining approvals and ultimately having no choice but to service the debt. The alternative view takes a more positive outlook on banking sector reform,

---

[57] See introduction, *supra*.

[58] Subject to the consequences of new exchange rate policies in relation to domestic credit expansion.

arguing that bank credit practices will improve materially through a combination of foreign participation, better internal governance, investor pressure due to bank new listings and competition from smaller but financially stronger banks. The result may be that SOEs gradually lose access to loans on 'soft' terms.

5.3. Credit substitution by guarantee

All corporate bonds must carry a full bank guarantee, and investors have typically believed that guarantors are supported by government. At the same time, guarantors offer guarantees only for issues that they see as risk-free. Taken with a restrictive issuance process, this means that only a handful of companies regarded as secure have been permitted to issue bonds. Even the largest such SOEs may not be creditworthy in themselves, with weak financial reporting and no independent credit rating system, which again necessitates that potential issues carry a bank (quasi-government) guarantee.

This system is known to be infeasible and detrimental to market development since it clearly offends the concept of a corporate bond market where prices and yields properly reflect risk. It is also inconsistent with the desire of the government to transfer commercial risk on to the private sector. If the capital market is to have a functioning corporate bond market then it must abandon guarantees and establish a proper credit culture.

This in turn requires a creative willingness among investors. Historically, credit substitution by guarantee in not uncommon in East Asia, especially in Korea and Taiwan. Korea's post-crisis experience may be instructive in this context. Prior to 1997 most Korean bond issues were guaranteed, at first by banks and later by two state-owned guarantee funds. Bank credit capacity evaporated in the 1997-98 crisis, and in the following year the two state guarantee funds became insolvent due to credit-induced losses.

In late 1999, the Korean government legislated to allow the development of a securitisation, initially using credit card and home loan risks, and later with corporate bonds and loans, with government providing partial guarantees for asset-backed new issues. Korean asset-backed issuance rose in 2002 to account for more than 50 per cent of the substantial domestic corporate bond market. In this case, structural reforms removed the need for blanket guarantees for new issues, and provided a stimulus to Korea's credit infrastructure, for example, in helping stimulate the creation of independent and professional rating agencies. The results were noteworthy in Korea and elsewhere in Asia, and appear now to be seen favorably by policymakers in Beijing.

5.4. Credit assessment infrastructure

State banks have until recently lacked many credit assessment resources, and institutional investors have traditionally not needed properly to assess credit risk. Yet there are few disclosure requirements for unlisted corporate bonds and generally lax enforcement of reporting with listed issues. Poor information will become an increasingly serious hindrance if a wider spectrum of bonds is issued. Weaknesses in disclosure will hinder the development of effective rating agencies and other credit infrastructure.

5.5. Inadequate bankruptcy procedures

The concept of bankruptcy is relatively new to China, not well understood and as yet the associated legal structures are frail. Clear winding-up procedures are critically important for successful corporate bond markets. This is even more critical important in markets for higher risk bonds. A new bankruptcy law will replace the current interim law, which has proved difficult to interpret in practice since it requires petitioners to prove three demanding points; poor management, substantial losses and an inability to pay liabilities when due. The draft law reduces the grounds for bankruptcy to two: an inability to discharge debt as it becomes due, and insufficient assets to meet liabilities. The second factor may be difficult to prove given the complexity and opacity of corporate structures. For the draft legislation to be effective it must be accompanied by several associated reforms.

5.6. Regulatory uncertainty and competition

The speed and extent of change has led to considerable regulatory uncertainty: practitioners operate without legal sanction (OTC interbank bond trading, for example) and the functions of so many regulators have changed such that rules made by one body are now policed by a second, with confusion as a sole result. Several regulators share responsibility for the bond markets, notably NDRC, PBoC and CSRC, while the finance ministry is closely involved as state debt manager and issuer. Other central and regional government entities become involved in the markets in various ways as sponsors of potential borrowing from infrastructure projects. Successfully functioning markets will require more clarity in these arrangements.

6. Assessment

China's capital markets exhibit both great potential for successful transformation, and profound challenges to that future. The assessment in this section is based not only upon conventional analysis, but includes anecdotal support from market observers and regulators in China and in interested offshore centers.

- Recent growth in the number and operational scale of institutional investors is encouraging. Most of the requirements for this sector now seem to be in place, although in the long-term it may be counterproductive to limit too tightly how banks may hold state or corporate bonds. The prevailing discount of corporate bond yields to loan rates suggest there is excess investor demand for fixed income instruments which would be highly supportive of a reformed market.

- The issuance process must be redesigned. A merit-based system means that most potential non-governmental issuers are denied access to the bond market; disclosure provisions and monitoring are poor; new issue timetables are far too protracted. At a later time, the requirement to list all new bonds may deter specialist investors from acquiring higher risk issues.
- Administered and controlled interest rates are a clear barrier to a true and effective debt capital market, even though PBoC has allowed limited flexibility in terms. It is not known whether the authorities would eventually accept the high yield spreads associated with lesser qualities issuers.
- The government market is underdeveloped: in particular, the auction process for new issuance is unreliable and controlled and secondary trading is fractured, even though a semi-reliable yield curve can now be said to exist in the main maturities.
- Secondary market trading is unduly restricted and the respective regulatory environment is confused. Regulatory recognition of the active OTC government bond secondary market would benefit overall liquidity.
- Regulatory confusion and legal uncertainty are widespread. In part this is the result of a furious speed of change in a limited period: most of the reforms described in this chapter were conceived after 2000. It may also be a deliberate style of policy to allow experimentation without giving legal sanction, then to allow the result to encourage legislation to be passed without controversy. Many commercial participants may see this matter as offering a manageable risk.

References

Allen, F., Qian Jun & Qian Meijun, 2002, 'Law, finance and economic growth in China', Wharton Financial Institutions Center working paper 02-44; *Journal of Financial Economics*, 2005.

Arner, D., 2004, 'Second report of the China panel of experts', APEC Initiative on Development of Securitisation and Credit Guarantee Markets, made available to APEC finance ministers working group, unpublished.

Aziz, J. & C. Duenwald, 2002, 'Growth-financial intermediation nexus in China', Washington: IMF working paper 02/194.

Barth, J., R. Koepp & Zhou Zhongfei, 2004, 'Banking reform in China: catalyzing the nation's financial future', mimeo; Hong Kong: *China Review*, forthcoming.

Boyreau-Debray, G., 2003, 'Financial intermediation and growth: Chinese style', Washington: World Bank policy research working paper 3027.

Boyreau-Debray, G. & Wei Shang-jin, 2005, 'Pitfalls of a state-dominated financial system: the case of China', Washington: National Bureau of Economic Research working paper 11214.

Cai Hongbin, Liu Qiao & Xiao Geng, 2004, 'Does competition discipline firms? The case of corporate profit hiding in China, Hong Kong Institute of Economics and Business Strategy working paper 1126.

Chaipravat, O. & T. Chaipravat, 2003, 'Securitisation: an alternative SME financing' Fiscal Policy Research Institute, Ministry of Finance, Thailand, mimeo presentation to Asian Bond Market Forum, University of Hong Kong, November, available at http://www.aiifl.com.

China Securities Regulatory Commission, 2004, 'China's securities and futures markets', Beijing.

Eichengreen, B. & P. Luengnaruemitchai, 2004, 'Why doesn't Asia have bigger bond markets?', Washington: National Bureau of Economic Research working paper 10576.

Fan, Joseph P.H., Wong, T.J. & Zhang Tianyu, 2005, 'The emergence of corporate pyramids in China' Chinese University of Hong Kong.

Fernald, J. & Babson, O., 1999, 'Why has China survived the Asian crisis so well? What risks remain?', Washington: Federal Reserve System international finance discussion papers 633.

Goldie-Scott, D., 1995, 'China's financial markets', London, Financial Times Publishing.

Green, S., 2004, 'The privatisation two-step at China's listed firms', China Project working paper 3, London, Chatham House Asia Programme.

Gregory, N. & S. Tenev, 2001, 'The financing of private enterprise in China', Washington: IMF Finance and Development, March.

Gregory, N., S. Tenev & D. Wagle, 2000,'China's emerging private enterprises: prospects for the new century', Washington: International Finance Corporation.

Harwood, A. (ed.), 2000, 'Building local bond markets, an Asian perspective', Washington: International Finance Corporation.

Harwood, A., 2002, 'Building corporate bond markets in emerging market countries', presentation to OECD/ World Bank workshop on bond markets.

Herring, R. & Chatusripitak, N., 2000, 'The case of the missing market: the bond market and why it matters for financial development', Manila: Asian Development Bank Institute working paper 11.

Jen, S., 2005, 'China: CNY: 'Regime shift to lead to monetary orthodoxy', Morgan Stanley Global Economic Forum, 9 September, available at http://www.morganstanley.com/.

Jiang Guorong & R. McCauley, 2004, 'Asian local currency bond markets', Basel: *BIS Quarterly Review*, June.

Jiang Guorong, N. Tang and E. Law, 2001, 'Cost-benefit analysis of developing debt markets', *Hong Kong Monetary Authority Quarterly Bulletin,* November.

Kim, Y.B., I. Ho & M. St. Giles, 2003, 'Developing institutional investors in the People's Republic of China', Washington: World Bank.

Kumar, A., Jun Kwang, A. Saunders, S. Selwyn, Sun Yan, D. Vittas & D Wilton, 1997, 'China's emerging capital markets', Hong Kong: FT Financial Publishing Asia Pacific.

Lejot, P., D. Arner & Liu Qiao, 2004, 'Making markets: reforms to strengthen Asia's debt capital markets' Hong Kong Institute For Monetary Research Working Paper 13.

Lejot, P., D. Arner, Liu Qiao, M. Chan & M. Mays, 2003,) 'Asia's debt capital markets appraisal and agenda for policy reform', Hong Kong Institute of Economics and Business Strategy working paper 1072.

Li Huaizhong, 2003, 'Challenges to and opportunities for investing in China bond markets' mimeo presentation to Asian Bond Market Forum, University of Hong Kong, November, available at http://www.aiifl.com.

Liu Qiao, 2003, 'Financing China's medium-scale enterprises' mimeo presentation to Asian Bond Market Forum, University of Hong Kong, November, available at http://www.aiifl.com.

Liu Qiao & Lu Zhou, 2004, 'Earnings management to tunnel: evidence from China's listed companies', Hong Kong Institute of Economics and Business Strategy working paper 1097.

Liu Qiao & Xiao Geng, 2004, 'Look who are disguising profits: an application to Chinese industrial firms', Hong Kong Institute of Economics and Business Strategy working paper 1095.

McCauley, R., 2003, 'Unifying government bond markets in East Asia', Basel: *BIS Quarterly Review*, December.

Mohanty, M., 2002, 'Improving liquidity in government bond markets: what can be done?', Basel: BIS papers 11.

Park, J., 2004, 'Study on Korea's corporate bond market and its implications on China's bond market development', Washington: World Bank.

Oh, G.T., Park, D.K., Park, J.H. & Yang, D.Y., 2003, 'How to mobilize the Asian savings within the region: securitization and credit enhancement for the development of East Asia's bond market', Korea Institute for International Economic Policy working paper 03-02, Seoul.

Redding, S., *The Spirit of Chinese Capitalism*, Berlin: W. de Gruyt, 1990.

Rhee, S. Ghon, 2004, 'The structure and characteristics of East Asian bond markets', in 'Developing Asian bond markets', T. Ito and Park Y.C. (eds.) Canberra: Asia Pacific Press.

Schinasi, G., 2003, 'The development of effective securities markets', mimeo presentation to Asian Bond Market Forum, University of Hong Kong, November, available at http://www.aiifl.com.

Scott, D. & I. Ho, 2004, 'China's corporate bond market', Washington: World Bank.

World Bank, *passim*, China Quarterly Update, Beijing.

World Bank, 2002, Global Development Finance, Washington, D.C.

World Bank, 2005, Global Development Finance, Washington, D.C.

Wu Xiaoling, 2005, 'Develop corporate bond market to improve financial asset structure', speech to the ninth forum of China's Capital Market, Beijing, 17 January, available in English translation at http://www.bis.org/review/r050216i.pdf.

Xiao Geng, 2004, 'People's Republic of China's round-tripping FDI: scale, causes and implications', Manila: Asian Development Bank Institute discussion paper No. 7.

Yoshitomi, M. & S. Shirai, 2001, 'Designing a financial market structure in post-crisis Asia; how to develop corporate bond markets', Manila: Asian Development Bank Institute working paper 15.

Young, A., 2000, 'The razor's edge: distortion and incremental reform in the People's Republic of China', *Quarterly Journal of Economics* 115(4).

Chapter 6

Improving the Policy Environment for Private Sector Participation in the Development of Local Currency and Regional Bond Markets in APEC: *Report of a financial sector survey*

Julius Caesar Parreñas[1]

[1]*Chinatrust Financial Holding Company and Taiwan Institute of Economic Research*

1. Introduction

In May 2004, the APEC Business Advisory Council (ABAC) and the Pacific Economic Cooperation Council (PECC) convened a conference in Taipei on the development of Asia-Pacific bond markets.[1] Private sector participants identified conditions that are necessary to promote private sector investment and issuance in the region's local currency bond markets and the emergence of a commercially viable regional bond market.

As a next step, ABAC and PECC, with the collaboration of the Asian Bankers' Association (ABA), conducted a survey among Asia-Pacific private financial sector institutions on the areas of improvement identified in this conference. The survey, which was conducted in March-April 2005, draws attention to a number of considerations on the issue of improving the policy environment for private sector participation in bond market development in APEC emerging markets. The following are the major conclusions of this survey.

First, the survey results reveal wide disparities within the region with respect to providing such a favorable policy environment, as seen from the private sector.

[1] *Developing Bond Markets in APEC: Moving Forward through Public-Private Sector Partnership*, May 10-11, Taipei, co-organized by the APEC Business Advisory Council and the Pacific Economic Cooperation Council. More information on this conference, including the conference report, are available at the conference website http://www.tier.org.tw/pecc/conference/bondmarket2004.htm.

These disparities, however, are very much in line with the varying levels of development of local currency bond markets among the region's economies as indicated by the size of these markets relative to GDP and their respective levels of general economic development.

This is consistent with the view that economic development goes hand in hand with the development of market-supporting institutions, including those that support financial markets such as reliability of contract enforcement and certainty of investor rights. This would imply that achieving the scale needed for deep and liquid bond markets necessitates attaining a certain level of economic development to set the stage for further improvements in the policy environment that, once undertaken, eventually lead to the growth of these markets.

To what extent and how rapidly such improvements in the policy environment are made, however, is decided within each economy. A number of emerging markets in the region have particularly made significant advances in developing relatively robust policy and regulatory frameworks, market infrastructure, and key components of deep and liquid bond markets. However, the majority of the region's emerging markets still belong to a second category where many of these requirements are far from adequately met, or where fundamental issues are yet to be sufficiently addressed.

Second, progress toward a favorable policy environment for private sector participation in bond market development is also uneven with respect to its various components. On a general level, the region as seen from the private sector perspective has done relatively well in addressing issues related to the reporting framework as well as the political and macroeconomic environment, reflecting the impact of reforms undertaken by a number of economies in response to the 1997-98 Asian financial crisis.

However, much remains to be done, particularly in the less developed emerging markets, to address market infrastructure issues and to build up key components of deep and liquid bond markets, such as derivatives and secondary bond markets, benchmark treasury yield curves with a broad range of maturities, a significant domestic retail investor base, the variety of product types, credible credit rating systems, and credit enhancement facilities that reflect market prices. Even in the more advanced emerging markets, further work is needed in many of these areas.

One area where the less developed emerging markets have significantly lagged behind their more developed counterparts is the development of an adequate regulatory framework. A number of weaknesses continue to hinder greater private sector activity in local currency bond markets, particularly with respect to the legal framework governing asset securitization, effective enforcement of capital market rules, disclosure, the balancing of interests of market participants, and the consistency of tax rules with the goal of market development.

Furthermore, the private sector views some basic reforms as important in closing significant gaps between the less developed and more developed emerging markets. These include the improvement of the legal framework governing the protection of creditor rights and its enforcement, the progressive removal of restrictions on economic activities in all industries, the establishment of effective competition regulators, and further reforms to strengthen financial system stability.

Third, private sector financial institutions believe that the reforms most critical to facilitate private sector participation in bond market development within the region are those related to ***capital market development***, as well as those with respect to the ***regulatory framework*** in the case of the less developed emerging markets. The survey identified the key objectives, the attainment of which needs to be prioritized in the view of the private sector.

Objectives that are critical in most of the markets surveyed are:

- the existence of a deep and liquid secondary market in local currency bonds;
- the existence, for an appropriately lengthy period, of a benchmark treasury yield curve across a broad range of maturities; and
- a developed domestic retail investor base with broad participation in capital markets.

Objectives are critical for the less developed emerging markets are:

- the existence of clearly defined creditor rights, insolvency and informal workout processes;
- the effective enforcement of creditor rights; and
- consistency of regulations and laws promoting capital market activities, in particular with respect to taxation.

Objectives that are critical for the more developed emerging markets are:

- the opening of the market to many players, domestic and foreign alike;
- healthy cooperation between financial officials as well as regulators and the private financial sector;
- continuity in economic policies; and
- an exchange rate regime that is conducive to efficient capital flows and payments.

Objectives that are less critical than those above, but that less developed emerging markets must meet to close the gap with their more developed counterparts, are:

- effective enforcement of rules and penalties governing capital market activity;
- market regulation and supervision that effectively balances the interests of all market participants;
- the existence of a credible and apolitical credit rating system for local currency bonds;
- an effective legal framework for asset securitization;
- a competition regulator with full authority to act against anti-competitive market activity;
- a robust system of clear, complete, timely and meaningful disclosure;
- a wide variety of product types available to investors; and
- the removal of restrictions on economic activities for all industries.

Fourth, the survey identified a number of priorities for policy reforms and capacity-building based on public-private sector partnership in some of the above-mentioned critical areas to improve the environment for private sector participation in bond market development. The proposed ***policy reform priorities*** (which would vary in mix in accordance with specific characteristics of each market) are as follows:

- relaxing regulations on market participation, new financial products, repo transactions, short-selling and the use of derivatives;
- reform of accounting and investment rules, tax and insolvency laws, banking and capital market regulations and administrative procedures, as well as pension systems;
- addressing basic issues such as judicial independence, the application and enforcement of laws and property rights;
- frequent regular issuance of public sector bonds to build a benchmark treasury yield curve across a broad range of maturities;
- improving coordination among domestic agencies involved in bond market development; and
- undertaking concrete steps toward flexible exchange rate regimes.

The proposed priorities for ***regional cooperation and capacity-building*** efforts, based on public-private sector partnership, are as follows:

- providing ***technical assistance***, particularly with expanded support from multilateral and regional development and financial institutions, for efforts to reform legal frameworks governing capital markets (including securitization) and the protection of creditor rights, and to promote region-wide convergence of credit rating, accounting and credit guarantee systems;
- expanding ***regional-level discussions*** among capital market regulators, relevant officials from all branches of government, with the participation of industry associations and private sector experts and market players, to share experiences and expertise on the development of secondary, derivatives and asset-backed securities markets and the effective protection of creditor rights within domestic and cross-border contexts;
- developing ***regional-level programs*** for creating new financial products and credit enhancement facilities, promoting investor education, deepening awareness and expertise among policy makers and regulators on global best practices in capital market rules and regulations, and strengthening risk management practices in financial institutions; and
- undertaking ***initiatives to develop the domestic retail investor base*** with broad participation from public and private sectors, including banks and public sector entities issuing paper of interest to retail investors.

Reflecting the significant disparities within the region, the focus of policy reform and capacity-building efforts would have to vary with the level of development of individual markets. For those at the early development stages, more attention needs to be focused on the more fundamental issues such as exchange rate, basic accounting, regulatory, legal and creditor rights issues. For those at the more advanced stages, reforms and capacity-building could focus more on market issues.

Ultimately, the success of any effort to develop local currency bond markets will hinge on the commitment of the relevant authorities in each individual economy to thoroughly carry out the necessary policy and regulatory reforms. It was also underscored that a commercially viable regional bond market would have as prerequisites robust legal, policy and regulatory frameworks and market practices consistent with global standards underpinning vibrant domestic capital markets. Efforts to address these issues would be important for the success of initiatives to develop new debt instruments and mechanisms for a regional bond market.

Finally, the survey highlights the importance of cooperation between emerging and advanced markets as well as between the public and private sectors, and the central role that APEC can play in this process.

The development of bond markets in the Asia-Pacific region has been the focus of recent efforts among governments and regional organizations, including the Asia-Pacific Economic Cooperation (APEC) forum and the Association of Southeast Asian Nations (ASEAN) Plus Three grouping.[2] APEC began substantial work on *local currency* bond markets in the wake of the 1997-98 Asian financial crisis. In 2003, both APEC and ASEAN Plus Three initiated work on the development of a *regional* bond market.[3] Various initiatives are currently being undertaken, but governments recognize that private sector investors and issuers must eventually assume the lead role for these efforts to succeed.

2. Background

In May 2004, the APEC Business Advisory Council (ABAC) and the Pacific Economic Cooperation Council (PECC) convened a conference in Taipei on the development of Asia-Pacific bond markets.[4] A total of 150 participants representing the region's major market players attended the event. They identified conditions that are necessary to promote private sector investment and issuance in the region's local

---

[2] Other organizations that have also undertaken significant efforts in this area are the Executives' Meeting of East Asia Pacific Central Banks (EMEAP) and the Asia Cooperation Dialogue (ACD). For an overview of current issues and debates related to the development of a regional bond market in Asia, refer to Takatoshi Ito and Yung Chul Park, "Overview—Challenges and Strategies," Takatoshi Ito and Yung Chul Park (Eds.), *Developing Asian Bond Markets* (Canberra, Asia-Pacific Press 2004), pp. 1-15. The rationale and alternative directions for an Asian bond market are also discussed in Jeffrey Len-Song Koo, "Asia Needs a Robust Bond Market," (May 18, 2000) *Asian Wall Street Journal*.

[3] A brief overview of recent policy reforms and initiatives is given in "East Asian Local Currency Bond Markets: Seven Years after the Crisis," (November 2004) *ADB Asia Bond Monitor*, pp. 20-23.

[4] *Developing Bond Markets in APEC: Moving Forward through Public-Private Sector Partnership*, May 10-11, Taipei, co-organized by the APEC Business Advisory Council and the Pacific Economic Cooperation Council. More information on this conference, including the conference report, are available at the conference website http://www.tier.org.tw/pecc/conference/bondmarket2004.htm.

currency bond markets and the emergence of a commercially viable regional bond market. [5] Private sector participants expressed their willingness to work in partnership with the public sector to help develop these markets.[6]

As a next step in promoting this partnership, ABAC and PECC, with the collaboration of the Asian Bankers' Association (ABA), conducted a survey among Asia-Pacific private financial sector institutions on the areas of improvement identified in this conference. The survey questionnaire is attached as *Annex A*. The survey, which was conducted in March-April, 2005, aimed to form a basis for (a) an assessment of the current policy environment for private sector participation in the development of local currency bond markets in APEC as well as in promoting the emergence of a regional bond market; and (b) concrete proposals on priorities for capacity-building involving public-private sector partnership toward these goals. This report analyzes the results of this survey.

The survey aimed to solicit responses with respect to 16 APEC member economies, which are classified as emerging markets.[7] A total of 40 responses were received. Over two-thirds of these were provided by banks. The rest were divided among asset management firms, credit rating agencies, an insurance company as well as financial sector and banks' research institutions.

The survey responses covered 14 out of the 16 APEC member economies.[8] Responses were not evenly distributed among the 14 economies. Some economies had better coverage, such as Chinese Taipei, Hong Kong, China and Indonesia, while six economies were covered by only one response each.

The survey questionnaire was divided into three parts.

The ***first part*** aimed to assess the current policy environment for promoting private sector participation in the region's local currency bond markets and the emergence of a commercially viable regional bond market. The questionnaire presented respondents with 39 objectives[9] (henceforth referred to in this report as *key objectives*) identified in the 2004 Taipei ABAC/PECC conference as crucial in this process, and asked them to rate the extent to which they deem each of these key objectives were met in the economy they are assessing.

---

[5] As a PECC study discusses, institutional investors are likely to determine what types of bonds can be issues and traded and play a major role in the development of market competition and infrastructure, see Daekeun Park and Yung Chul Park, "Creating regional bond markets in East Asia: rationale and strategy," Takatoshi Ito and Yung Chul Park (Eds.), *op.cit.*, p. 43.

[6] See also "Developing Bond Markets in the APEC Region: Need and Agenda for Public-Private Sector Partnership," (2004) *Issues@PECC.*

[7] These are Brunei, Chile, China, Hong Kong, Indonesia, Republic of Korea, Malaysia, Mexico, Papua New Guinea, Peru, Philippines, Russian Federation, Singapore, Thailand, Chinese Taipei and Vietnam.

[8] The two economies not covered were Brunei Darussalam and Papua New Guinea.

[9] See Part I of Annex A.

Table 6-1: **Breakdown of survey responses by source**

Source	Responses
Banks	27
Financial sector/bank research institutions	5
Asset management companies	4
Credit rating agencies	3
Insurance companies	1
TOTAL	40

Table 6-2: **Breakdown of survey responses by economy covered**

Economy Covered	Responses
Chinese Taipei	9
Hong Kong, China	6
China	5
Indonesia	4
Malaysia	3
Singapore	3
Korea	2
Vietnam	2
Chile	1
Mexico	1
Peru	1
Philippines	1
Russia	1
Thailand	1
TOTAL	40

This was accomplished through the use of scores on a scale of 1-4, corresponding to the following levels of attainment of each of the key objectives:

1 = *To develop* (no work has yet been initiated)

2 = *Partially met* (some work carried out; much improvement needed)

3 = *Mostly met* (substantial work carried out, slight improvement needed)

4 = *Fully met* (all necessary work carried out; no significant improvement needed)

The 39 key objectives were distributed among 5 major areas relevant to the development of bond markets, which are as follows:

- the macroeconomic and political environment;
- the regulatory framework;
- the reporting framework;
- public-private sector partnership; and
- capital market development.

The ***second and third parts*** of the questionnaire aimed to identify concrete proposals on priorities for capacity-building involving public-private sector partnership to promote bond market development. In the second part, the questionnaire asked the survey respondents to identify, among the key objectives previously presented to them, the 3 most critical ones in facilitating the development of local currency bond markets, and to rank them in order of importance. In the third part, the respondents were asked to identify policy changes and capacity-building measures that would be helpful in the achievement of these critical objectives. In this report, these two parts will be consolidated into one section.

3. Survey Results

3.1. The Policy Environment for Private Sector Participation in Bond Market Development in APEC Emerging Markets

For analytical purposes, the 14 markets have been divided into two groups using an indicator of the level of bond market development based on the size of the local currency bond market and per capita GDP.[10] Following this criterion, Chile, Hong Kong, Korea, Malaysia, Singapore and Chinese Taipei make up the more developed emerging markets (MDEMs). China, Indonesia, Mexico, Peru, Philippines, Russia, Thailand and Vietnam make up the eight less developed emerging markets (LDEMs).

Due to the significantly uneven distribution of responses across economies, this report will not emphasize comparisons of individual economies, but will focus on analysis at the regional and group (MDEMs and LDEMs) levels. However, scores assigned to individual economies are made available for reference in *Annex A*.

The survey results yielded a strong positive correlation between the level of bond market development and overall scores for the attainment of key objectives, considered as a measure of how favorable the policy environment is for promoting

[10] This indicator is derived by multiplying the amount of local currency bonds outstanding at end-2003 as a percentage of GDP with the 2003 per capita GDP for each market.

private sector activity in the region's bond markets.[11] Overall, key objectives for a favorable policy environment were mostly met in the MDEMs on average, and only partially met in the LDEMs.

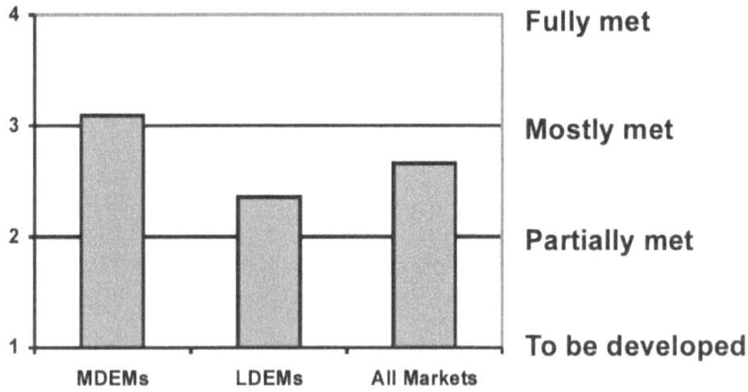

MDEMs: Chile, Hong Kong, Korea, Malaysia, Singapore, Chinese Taipei
LDEMs: China, Indonesia, Mexico, Peru, Philippines, Russia, Thailand, Vietnam

***Figure 6-1.* Overall scores for the attainment of key objectives (average for the two groups and all markets)**

Out of the total 39 key objectives, an average of 37 (95%) were mostly met in the case of MDEMs. In contrast, only 8 (20%) key objectives on average were mostly met in the case of LDEMs; the rest being only partially met. The average for all markets is 29 (74%) mostly met and 10 (26%) key objectives partially met, as shown in Figure 6-2. These figures disguise very significant differences among these markets. In some individual economies, a number of key objectives have been fully met, while in others, no work has yet been done to meet some of them, as shown in Figure 6-3. Overall, however, a considerable amount of work remains to be done to improve the policy environment, even in the more developed markets.

MDEMs consistently scored higher than LDEMs in the five major areas relevant to bond market development. The largest gap between the two groups was in the area of regulatory framework, while the smallest was in public-private sector partnership. MDEMs as a group achieved the highest average scores equally for both regulatory and reporting frameworks. LDEMs as a group attained the best score in the area of reporting framework. MDEMs had their lowest scores for public-private sector partnership, LDEMs for capital market development.

[11] Computing for the Pearson Product-Moment Correlation Coefficient *r* (Pearson's *r*) for the two variables, the resulting value is statistically significant at r(38) = 0.773041, p < 0.01 (with degree of freedom df = 38, the alpha level set at 0.01 indicating a 99% confidence in the existence of a relationship, and the corresponding level of significance p = 0.418).

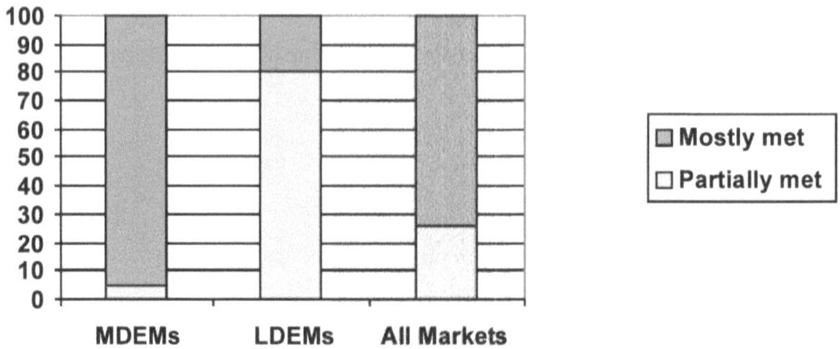

MDEMs: Chile, Hong Kong, Korea, Malaysia, Singapore, Chinese Taipei
LDEMs: China, Indonesia, Mexico, Peru, Philippines, Russia, Thailand, Vietnam

***Figure 6-2.* Level of attainment of key objectives (number attained at each level as a percentage of all 39 key objectives), average for the two groups and all markets**

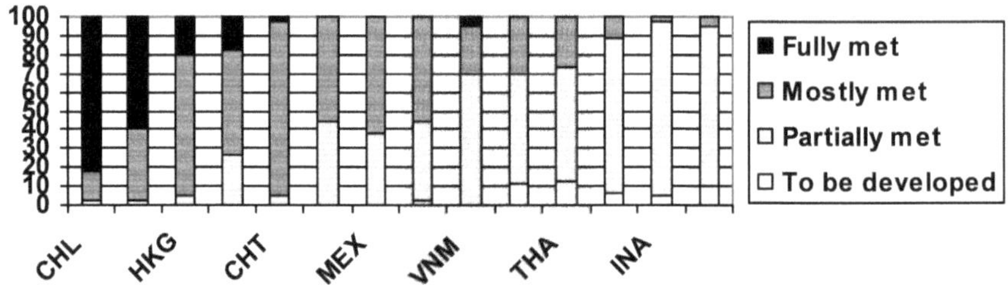

***Figure 6-3.* Level of attainment of key objectives (number attained at each level as a percentage of all 39 key objectives), by individual markets**

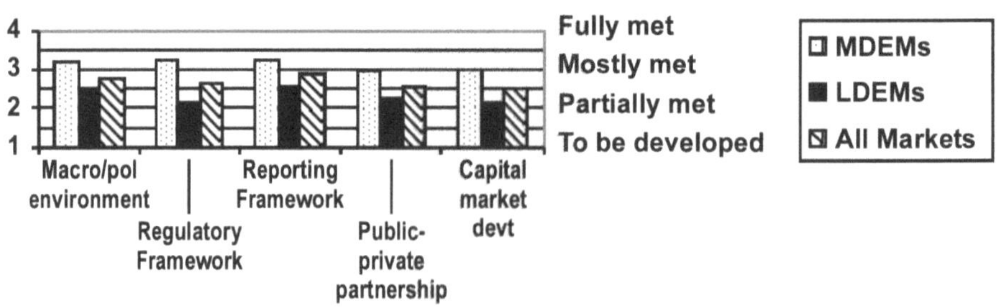

MDEMs: Chile, Hong Kong, Korea, Malaysia, Singapore, Chinese Taipei
LDEMs: China, Indonesia, Mexico, Peru, Philippines, Russia, Thailand, Vietnam

***Figure 6-4.* Average scores for the 5 key areas, average for the two groups and all markets**

Looking at the individual markets, the reporting framework was the most developed among the five key areas throughout the region, with the exception of transition economies. As seen in Table 6-3, capital market development and public-private sector partnership were the areas most needing further attention.[12]

***Table 6-3:* Average scores for the 5 key areas by individual economies**

	CHL	CHN	HKG	INA	KOR	MAL	MEX	PER	PHP	RUS	SIN	THA	CHT	VNM
A	✓✓✓	✓	✓✓	✓	✓✓	✓✓	✓✓	✓	✓✓	✓	✓✓✓	✓✓	✓✓	✓✓
B	✓✓✓	✓	✓✓	✓	✓✓	✓✓	✓✓	✓	✓	✓	✓✓✓	✓	✓✓	✓
C	✓✓	✓	✓✓	✓✓	✓✓	✓✓	✓✓	✓✓	✓✓	✓	✓✓✓	✓✓	✓✓	✓
D	✓✓	✓	✓✓	✓	✓	✓✓	✓	✓	✓✓	✓✓	✓✓	✓	✓✓	✓
E	✓✓✓	✓	✓✓	✓	✓	✓✓	✓	✓	✓	✓	✓✓	✓	✓✓	✓✓

Legend:

✓✓✓ Fully met
✓✓ Mostly met
✓ Partially met

Table 6-4 lists the ten key objectives with the highest incidence of attainment within the region. In most markets, financial institutions judged the objective of ***robust and transparent accounting standards*** to have been mostly met (and fully met in Chile, Malaysia and Singapore). The private sector also gave high scores to the region's emerging markets for ***stable financial systems*** (fully met in Chile, Hong Kong, Singapore and Chinese Taipei) as well as ***stable political systems*** (fully met in Chile, Malaysia, Singapore and Vietnam).

Financial institutions also viewed most of the markets surveyed as by and large having ***no capital controls*** that have a significant impact on capital flows (fully met in Chile and Singapore and mostly met in the others with the exception of 3 markets). ***Clearing and settlement systems*** were judged as generally efficient (an objective fully met in Chile, Hong Kong and Malaysia) and mostly met in others except in 4 markets. ***Continuity of economic policies*** was seen as having been fully or mostly met in all but 3 markets.

Other key objectives that have been mostly or fully attained in most of the markets surveyed included a ***market that is open*** to multiple domestic and foreign players; ***healthy cooperation*** between domestic officials and the private sector; and an ***exchange rate regime*** that is conducive to efficient capital flows and payments. The more developed emerging markets have also attained sufficient progress in

[12] For a detailed comparative overview of the characteristics of several East and Southeast Asian markets, refer to the factsheet in "Development of East Asian Local Currency Bond Markets—A Regional Update," (April 2005) *ADB Asia Bond Monitor 2005*, pp. 25-28.

establishing ***effective legal frameworks*** for asset securitization significantly ahead of less developed markets.[13]

Table 6-4. **Top ten (Key objectives with highest incidence of attainment)**

Rank	Key objective	Scores		
		All Markets	MDEMs	LDEMs
1	Robust and transparent accounting standards	3.00	3.37	2.67
2	Stable financial system	2.96	3.44	2.54
3	Stable political system	2.95	3.44	2.54
4	No significant capital controls	2.93	3.19	2.69
5	Efficient clearing and settlement systems	2.93	3.32	2.56
6	Continuity in economic policies	2.84	3.07	2.58
7	Market open to many players, domestic and foreign	2.83	3.16	2.54
8	Healthy cooperation bet. officials and private sector	2.83	3.14	2.53
9	Exchange rate regime conducive to capital flows	2.82	3.05	2.59
10	Effective legal framework for asset securitization	2.81	3.27	2.29

**Shaded area: Key objectives mostly met*

MDEMs: Chile, Hong Kong, Korea, Malaysia, Singapore, Chinese Taipei
LDEMs: China, Indonesia, Mexico, Peru, Philippines, Russia, Thailand, Vietnam

The ***domestic retail investor base*** was seen as still very much underdeveloped in most markets; only in 4 of these economies (Chile, Hong Kong, Singapore and Chinese Taipei) were they viewed by the private sector as sufficiently attained. ***International consultative mechanisms for public-private sector partnership*** in developing a regional bond market are likewise seen as underdeveloped in the region (only partially or not at all met in 10 markets), although financial institutions acknowledged that some efforts were being made toward developing them.

Another major issue is the lack of ***deep and liquid secondary markets*** in local currency bonds. The objective of having such markets was seen as only partially met in 10 economies, which even include a number of more developed emerging markets. Financial institutions also considered ***credit enhancement facilities*** in most of the region's emerging markets (8 out of 14) as not sufficiently reflecting the market price of capital.

---

[13] This appears consistent with the existence of significant gaps between more developed and less developed emerging markets with respect to the effective protection of creditor rights, which is a major requirement for a sound asset-backed securities market, see John Hawkins, "Bond markets and banks in emerging economies," *BIS Papers* No. 11, pp. 46-47.

Other objectives viewed as insufficiently met by the private sector in most of the markets surveyed include the ***removal of restrictions on short-selling and repo transactions***; the existence of a ***benchmark treasury yield curve*** across a broad range of maturities for over a sufficiently long period of time; clear rules for ***credit enhancement mechanisms***; and the existence of a ***competition regulator with full authority*** to act against anti-competitive market activity.

Table 6-5: **Bottom ten (Key objectives with lowest incidence of attainment), from the bottom up**

		Scores		
Rank	**Key objective**	**All Markets**	**MDEMs**	**LDEMs**
39	No restrictions on derivatives	2.10	2.56	1.65
38	Inter-governmental coordinating mechanism for domestic/regional bond market development	2.15	2.29	2.00
37	Developed domestic retail investor base	2.18	2.63	1.79
36	International public-private sector consultative mechanism	2.24	2.59	1.85
35	Deep and liquid domestic bond secondary market	2.27	2.67	1.95
34	Credit enhancement facilities reflect market prices	2.27	2.49	1.99
33	No restrictions on short-selling and repo transactions	2.36	2.79	2.01
32	Benchmark treasury yield curve across broad range of maturities for over a sufficiently long period	2.39	2.81	2.04
31	Clear rules for credit enhancement mechanisms	2.41	2.72	2.08
30	Competition regulator with full authority	2.43	2.93	1.95

**Shaded area: Key objectives mostly met*

MDEMs: Chile, Hong Kong, Korea, Malaysia, Singapore, Chinese Taipei
LDEMs: China, Indonesia, Mexico, Peru, Philippines, Russia, Thailand, Vietnam

The survey also helped identify those key objectives where the gap between MDEMs and LDEMs were widest, as shown in Table 6-6. Most of these (8 out of 12) were key objectives related to the regulatory framework, in particular the protection of creditor rights, the effective enforcement of capital market and competition rules, the availability of financial information, the legal framework for asset securitization and consistency of laws and regulations, especially taxation. Others relate to capital market development, in particular the presence of credible credit rating agencies and a wide variety of product types for investors in the market, deregulation of economic activities and the general stability of financial systems.

The above key objectives also represent areas with considerable potential for regional capacity-building partnership in developing bond markets. LDEMs stand to benefit from policy dialogues and seminars where regulators, market players and other key private sector representatives from MDEMs and other advanced economies can share their experiences and expertise in these areas.

***Table 6-6.* Key objectives with widest gaps between the scores of MDEMs and LDEMs**

		Scores		
Rank	**Key objective**	**All Markets**	**MDEMs**	**LDEMs**
1	Clearly defined creditor rights, insolvency processes	3.35	2.19	1.16
2	Effective enforcement of creditor rights	3.27	2.12	1.15
3	Effective enforcement of capital market rules	3.11	2.05	1.06
4	Market regulation and supervision effectively balances interests of market participants	3.14	2.10	1.04
5	Credible and apolitical credit rating system	3.28	2.29	0.99
6-8	Effective legal framework for asset securitization	3.27	2.29	0.98
	Competition regulator with full authority	2.93	1.95	0.98
	Robust disclosure system	3.18	2.20	0.98
9-10	Wide variety of product types available to investors	3.05	2.10	0.95
	No restrictions on economic activities (all industries)	3.23	2.28	0.95
11-12	Stable financial system	3.44	2.50	0.94
	Consistent regulation and laws (incl. taxation) promoting capital market activities	3.13	2.19	0.94

**Shaded area: Key objectives* <u>*mostly met*</u>

MDEMs: Chile, Hong Kong, Korea, Malaysia, Singapore, Chinese Taipei
LDEMs: China, Indonesia, Mexico, Peru, Philippines, Russia, Thailand, Vietnam

Table 6-7. Most critical objectives required to facilitate private sector participation in bond market development: More developed emerging markets (MDEMs)

Rank	Key Objectives	Score*
1	Deep and liquid domestic bond secondary market	2.67
2	Benchmark treasury yield curve across broad range of maturities for over a sufficiently long period	2.04
3	Market open to many players, domestic and foreign	3.16
4	Healthy cooperation between officials and private sector	3.14
5–6	Continuity in economic policies	3.07
	Exchange rate regime conducive to capital flows	3.05
7	Developed domestic retail investor base	2.63

**Attainment score*

Shaded area: Key objectives mostly met

MDEMs: Chile, Hong Kong, Korea, Malaysia, Singapore, Chinese Taipei

***Table 6-8.* Most critical objectives required to facilitate private sector participation in bond market development: Less developed emerging markets (LDEMs)**

Rank	Key Objectives	Score*
1	Clearly defined creditor rights, insolvency processes	2.19
2	Deep and liquid domestic bond secondary market	1.95
3	Effective enforcement of creditor rights	2.12
4–6	Developed domestic retail investor base	1.79
	Stable political system	2.54
	Consistent regulation and laws (incl. taxation) promoting capital market activities	2.19
7	Benchmark treasury yield curve across broad range of maturities for over a sufficiently long period	2.04

**Attainment score*

Shaded area: Key objectives mostly met

LDEMs: China, Indonesia, Mexico, Peru, Philippines, Russia, Thailand, Vietnam

3.2. Critical Areas for Capacity-Building in the Development of Local-Currency and Regional Bond Markets

The survey highlighted areas that in the view of financial institutions are critical to facilitate private sector participation in the development of local currency bond markets and the eventual emergence of a regional bond market and should be prioritized. The responses yielded varying results for the MDEMs and LDEMs, and the respective results are listed below in Tables 6-7 and 6-8. In the case of MDEMs, the critical areas were mostly related to capital market development, while in the case of LDEMs both capital market development and the regulatory framework were equally emphasized.

In the case of MDEMs, the critical objectives have been mostly met with a few exceptions. The objective of having a benchmark treasury yield curve across a broad range of maturities for over a sufficiently long period remains partially met for most, and secondary market depth and liquidity as well as the domestic retail investor base are not yet well-developed in one or two of these markets. In these latter areas, some work remains to be done.

For LDEMs, however, most of the critical objectives are at best only partially met, with the exception of political stability, which financial institutions consider mostly attained. Much work needs to be done, especially with respect to developing the domestic retail investor base, promoting secondary market depth and liquidity, and developing a benchmark treasury yield curve.

From these results, a number of implications for capacity-building can be drawn. The role of the private sector in the development of local-currency bond markets and the emergence of a regional bond market may be substantially enhanced if capacity-building efforts are focused on meeting a number of critical objectives. A first set of these objectives is made up of areas related to capital market development that financial institutions have identified as ***critical to both LDEMs and MDEMs***, which are:

- the existence of a deep and liquid secondary market in local currency bonds;
- the existence, for an appropriately lengthy period, of a benchmark treasury yield curve across a broad range of maturities; and
- a developed domestic retail investor base with broad participation in capital markets.

A second set of objectives is composed of areas related to the regulatory framework that are ***critical to LDEMs*** but where MDEMs have been able to forge ahead and could provide advice and expertise together with advanced APEC member economies. These are:

- the existence of clearly defined creditor rights, insolvency and informal workout processes;
- the effective enforcement of creditor rights; and
- consistency of regulations and laws promoting capital market activities, in particular with respect to taxation.

A third set of objectives involves policy reforms that the private sector has identified as being ***critical to MDEMs*** and where MDEMs and advanced APEC member economies could provide useful advice in policy dialogues to LDEMs. These objectives are:

- the opening of the market to many players, domestic and foreign alike;
- healthy cooperation between financial officials as well as regulators and the private financial sector;
- continuity in economic policies; and
- an exchange rate regime that is conducive to efficient capital flows and payments.

A fourth set of objectives includes areas that are ***less critical*** than those named above, but where ***LDEMs significantly lag behind MDEMs***, which are:

- effective enforcement of rules and penalties governing capital market activity;
- market regulation and supervision that effectively balances the interests of all market participants;
- the existence of a credible and apolitical credit rating system for local currency bonds;
- an effective legal framework for asset securitization;
- a competition regulator with full authority to act against anti-competitive market activity;
- a robust system of clear, complete, timely and meaningful disclosure;
- a wide variety of product types available to investors; and
- the removal of restrictions on economic activities for all industries.

Respondents proposed a number of priorities for policy reforms and capacity-building based on public-private sector partnership in some of the above-mentioned critical areas to improve the environment for private sector participation in bond market development. Table 6-9 lists the proposed policy reforms while Table 6-10 enumerates their proposals on capacity-building measures. The critical areas covered by these proposals are related to the depth and liquidity of secondary markets, creditor rights, development of the retail investor base, consistency of regulations and laws, and exchange rate regimes.

The proposed policy reform priorities focused on the following:

- relaxing regulations on market participation, new financial products, repo transactions, short-selling and the use of derivatives;
- reform of accounting and investment rules, tax and insolvency laws, banking and capital market regulations and administrative procedures, as well as pension systems;
- addressing basic issues such as judicial independence, the application and enforcement of laws and property rights;
- frequent regular issuance of public sector bonds to build a benchmark treasury yield curve across a broad range of maturities;

- improving coordination among domestic agencies involved in bond market development; and
- undertaking concrete steps toward flexible exchange rate regimes.

The different proposals were submitted by each respondent with the needs of the particular market being surveyed in mind. It should be underscored that the mix of policy reform priorities required to accelerate bond market development would have to differ for economies at varying levels of market development. In the case of markets at the early development stages, attention has to be given to fundamental issues such as exchange rate, basic accounting, regulatory, legal and creditor rights issues. For economies at the more advanced stages, priorities can shift to market issues.

Proposals on priorities for regional cooperation and capacity-building efforts, based on public-private sector partnership, focused on the following:

- providing ***technical assistance***, particularly with expanded support from multilateral and regional development and financial institutions, for efforts to reform legal frameworks governing capital markets (including asset securitization) and the protection of creditor rights, and to promote region-wide convergence of credit rating, accounting and credit guarantee systems;
- expanding ***regional-level discussions*** among capital market regulators, relevant officials from all branches of government, with the participation of industry associations and private sector experts and market players, to share experiences and expertise on the development of secondary, derivatives and asset-backed securities markets and the effective protection of creditor rights within domestic and cross-border contexts;
- developing ***regional-level programs*** for creating new financial products and credit enhancement facilities, promoting investor education, deepening awareness and expertise among policy makers and regulators on global best practices in capital market rules and regulations, and strengthening risk management practices in financial institutions; and
- undertaking ***initiatives to develop the domestic retail investor base*** with broad participation from public and private sectors, including banks and public sector entities issuing paper of interest to retail investors.

Some respondents emphasized that, ultimately, the success of any effort to develop local currency bond markets will hinge on the commitment of the relevant authorities in each individual economy to thoroughly carry out the necessary policy and regulatory reforms. It was also underscored that a commercially viable regional bond market would have as prerequisites robust legal, policy and regulatory frameworks and market practices consistent with global standards underpinning vibrant domestic capital markets. Efforts to address these issues would be important for the success of initiatives to develop new debt instruments and mechanisms for a regional bond market.

Table 6-9. Proposed policy reform priorities in critical areas to improve the environment for private sector participation in bond market development

To develop deep and liquid secondary markets in local currency bonds:
▪ Relax existing regulations to allow more participants (domestic and foreign investors and market makers) into the market, especially for corporate debts. ▪ Develop sound credit rating and accounting systems in order to attract foreign investors, including convergence toward global accounting standards based on timetables. ▪ Encourage the development of new financial products, including those from abroad, including through more flexible legal frameworks. ▪ Develop a trading platform for bonds while liberalizing access and participation in over the counter (OTC) markets. ▪ Relax restrictions on repos and short-selling. ▪ Maintain a tax regime and administrative procedures that encourage domestic bond trading activities. ▪ Undertake frequent regular issuance of public sector bonds at different maturities to build a benchmark treasury yield curve across a broad range of maturities. ▪ Relax restrictions on the use of derivatives within a framework of the ability of banks to do so within their own risk taking appetites and to monitor these risks. ▪ Encourage the development of a domestic institutional investor base, including through pension reform, reform of investment and tax rules and investor education. ▪ Move away from discriminatory treatment of foreign and domestic capital.
To develop clearly defined creditor rights and effective insolvency and informal workout processes:
▪ Reform, strengthen and modernize insolvency and banking laws and capital market regulations, moving toward globally accepted standards. ▪ Address basic issues related to the independence of the judiciary and the application and enforcement of laws. ▪ Develop the institutional framework for efficient functioning of markets starting with property rights, especially where there is a large informal sector. ▪ Address the issue of cross-border insolvency in the region.
To develop the domestic retail investor base with broad participation in capital markets:
▪ Relax existing restrictions on retail investors' participation in capital markets. ▪ Use tax incentives to encourage domestic retail investors to participate in markets.
To promote consistency of regulations and laws (including taxation) encouraging capital market activity:
▪ Establish and maintain coordination among agencies involved in local currency bond markets through a high-level central coordinating body. ▪ Reform tax laws related to capital market instruments, ensuring that decisions to invest and issue instruments will be based on judgment calls rather than arbitrage opportunities.
To develop an exchange rate regime that is conducive to efficient capital flows and payments:
▪ Move toward a floating exchange rate regime while strengthening financial systems against volatility.

Table 6-10. Proposed capacity-building priorities in critical areas to improve the environment for private sector participation in bond market development

To develop deep and liquid secondary markets in local currency bonds:
▪ Provide technical assistance in creating more flexible legal frameworks to facilitate the development of new products and securitization, and enable greater domestic and foreign investor participation in the market. ▪ Organize regional conferences, seminars and visiting programs for regulators and industry associations to share experiences and expertise in the formulation and implementation of policies and regulations to develop the secondary market, including reforms to promote derivatives and asset-backed securities markets, in coordination with market players and private sector regional organizations. ▪ Collaborate in creating new products and develop credit enhancement facilities, building on the experiences of ABF and ABF-2. ▪ Develop programs to enhance sound interest rate risk evaluation, risk management and market pricing in financial institutions, especially commercial banks, within the region. ▪ Develop technical assistance programs and regional policy dialogue to strengthen and promote region-wide convergence of credit rating, accounting and credit guarantee systems.
To develop clearly defined creditor rights and effective insolvency and informal workout processes:
▪ Encourage regional level discussions among officials from the executive, legislative and judicial branches of government to address critical issues, including cross-border insolvency and region-wide convergence toward globally accepted standards, with the participation of the private sector. ▪ Expand the activities of multilateral and regional development and financial institutions in this area, including technical assistance to regional public and private organizations and individual economies and reform advocacy among policy makers and opinion leaders.
To develop the domestic retail investor base with broad participation in capital markets:
▪ Develop programs and enhance regional cooperation to promote the education of investors and policy makers involved in the formulation and implementation of rules and regulations affecting capital markets. ▪ Promote public-private sector collaboration in developing the domestic retail investor base.
To promote consistency of regulations and laws (including taxation) encouraging capital market activity:
▪ Develop programs to more widely expose policy makers and regulators to global best practices in capital market rules and regulations, with active support from advanced economies, multilateral/regional development institutions and the private sector. ▪ Finance and undertake in-depth research on the effect of rules on market participants.

In the view of private sector financial institutions, developing economies stand to benefit more from cooperation with advanced economies that have well-developed capital markets, rather than among themselves. This highlights the potential role that regional cooperation within APEC can play in this process, as this would allow regulators and policy makers from developing Southeast Asian and Latin American economies to have access to the expertise and experience available in the advanced markets of North America, Oceania and the existing East Asian financial centers.

4. Conclusions

This survey draws attention to a number of considerations on the issue of improving the policy environment for private sector participation in bond market development in APEC emerging markets. ***First,*** the survey results reveal wide disparities within the region with respect to providing such a favorable policy environment, as seen from the private sector. These disparities, however, are very much in line with the varying levels of development of local currency bond markets among the region's economies as indicated by the size of these markets relative to GDP and their respective levels of general economic development.

This is consistent with the view, supported by empirical research,[14] that economic development goes hand in hand with the development of market-supporting institutions, including those that support financial markets such as reliability of contract enforcement and certainty of investor rights. This would imply that achieving the scale needed for deep and liquid bond markets necessitates attaining a certain level of economic development to set the stage for further improvements in the policy environment that, once undertaken, eventually lead to the growth of these markets.

To what extent and how rapidly such improvements in the policy environment are made, however, is decided within each economy. A number of emerging markets in the region have particularly made significant advances in developing relatively robust policy and regulatory frameworks, market infrastructure, and key components of deep and liquid bond markets. However, the majority of the region's emerging markets still belong to a second category where many of these requirements are far from adequately met, or where fundamental issues are yet to be sufficiently addressed.

Second, progress toward a favorable policy environment for private sector participation in bond market development is also uneven with respect to its various components. On a general level, the region as seen from the private sector perspective has done relatively well in addressing issues related to the reporting framework as well as the political and macroeconomic environment, reflecting the impact of reforms undertaken by a number of economies in response to the 1997-98 Asian financial crisis.

However, much remains to be done, particularly in the less developed emerging markets, to address market infrastructure issues and to build up key components of deep and liquid bond markets, such as derivatives and secondary bond markets, benchmark treasury yield curves with a broad range of maturities, a significant domestic retail investor base, the variety of product types, credible credit rating

---

[14] See for example the study by Barry Eichengreen and Pipat Luengnaruemitchai, "Why Doesn't Asia Have Bigger Bond Markets?" (June 2004). *NBER Working Paper No. W10576.*

systems, and credit enhancement facilities that reflect market prices. Even in the more advanced emerging markets, further work is needed in many of these areas.

One area where the less developed emerging markets have significantly lagged behind their more developed counterparts is the development of an adequate regulatory framework. A number of weaknesses continue to hinder greater private sector activity in local currency bond markets, particularly with respect to the legal framework governing asset securitization, effective enforcement of capital market rules, disclosure, the balancing of interests of market participants, and the consistency of tax rules with the goal of market development.

Furthermore, the private sector views some basic reforms as important in closing significant gaps between the less developed and more developed emerging markets. These include the improvement of the legal framework governing the protection of creditor rights and its enforcement, the progressive removal of restrictions on economic activities in all industries, the establishment of effective competition regulators, and further reforms to strengthen financial system stability.

Third, private sector financial institutions believe that the reforms most critical to facilitate private sector participation in bond market development within the region are those related to ***capital market development***, as well as those with respect to the ***regulatory framework*** in the case of the less developed emerging markets. The survey identified the key objectives, the attainment of which needs to be prioritized in the view of the private sector.

Objectives that are critical in most of the markets surveyed are:

- the existence of a deep and liquid secondary market in local currency bonds;
- the existence, for an appropriately lengthy period, of a benchmark treasury yield curve across a broad range of maturities; and
- a developed domestic retail investor base with broad participation in capital markets.

Objectives are critical for the less developed emerging markets are:

- the existence of clearly defined creditor rights, insolvency and informal workout processes;
- the effective enforcement of creditor rights; and
- consistency of regulations and laws promoting capital market activities, in particular with respect to taxation.

Objectives that are critical for the more developed emerging markets are:

- the opening of the market to many players, domestic and foreign alike;
- healthy cooperation between financial officials as well as regulators and the private financial sector;
- continuity in economic policies; and
- an exchange rate regime that is conducive to efficient capital flows and payments.

Objectives that are less critical than those above, but that less developed emerging markets must meet to close the gap with their more developed counterparts, are:

- effective enforcement of rules and penalties governing capital market activity;
- market regulation and supervision that effectively balances the interests of all market participants;
- the existence of a credible and apolitical credit rating system for local currency bonds;
- an effective legal framework for asset securitization;
- a competition regulator with full authority to act against anti-competitive market activity;
- a robust system of clear, complete, timely and meaningful disclosure;
- a wide variety of product types available to investors; and
- the removal of restrictions on economic activities for all industries.

Fourth, the survey identified a number of priorities for policy reforms and capacity-building based on public-private sector partnership in some of the above-mentioned critical areas to improve the environment for private sector participation in bond market development. The proposed ***policy reform priorities*** (which would vary in mix in accordance with specific characteristics of each market) are as follows:

- relaxing regulations on market participation, new financial products, repo transactions, short-selling and the use of derivatives;
- reform of accounting and investment rules, tax and insolvency laws, banking and capital market regulations and administrative procedures, as well as pension systems;
- addressing basic issues such as judicial independence, the application and enforcement of laws and property rights;
- frequent regular issuance of public sector bonds to build a benchmark treasury yield curve across a broad range of maturities;
- improving coordination among domestic agencies involved in bond market development; and
- undertaking concrete steps toward flexible exchange rate regimes.

The proposed priorities for ***regional cooperation and capacity-building*** efforts, based on public-private sector partnership, are as follows:

- providing ***technical assistance***, particularly with expanded support from multilateral and regional development and financial institutions, for efforts to reform legal frameworks governing capital markets (including securitization) and the protection of creditor rights, and to promote region-wide convergence of credit rating, accounting and credit guarantee systems;
- expanding ***regional-level discussions*** among capital market regulators, relevant officials from all branches of government, with the participation of industry associations and private sector experts and market players, to share experiences and expertise on the development of secondary, derivatives and

asset-backed securities markets and the effective protection of creditor rights within domestic and cross-border contexts;

- developing ***regional-level programs*** for creating new financial products and credit enhancement facilities, promoting investor education, deepening awareness and expertise among policy makers and regulators on global best practices in capital market rules and regulations, and strengthening risk management practices in financial institutions; and
- undertaking ***initiatives to develop the domestic retail investor base*** with broad participation from public and private sectors, including banks and public sector entities issuing paper of interest to retail investors.

Reflecting the significant disparities within the region, the focus of policy reform and capacity-building efforts would have to vary with the level of development of individual markets. For those at the early development stages, more attention needs to be focused on the more fundamental issues such as exchange rate, basic accounting, regulatory, legal and creditor rights issues. For those at the more advanced stages, reforms and capacity-building could focus more on market issues.

Finally, the survey underscores the importance of building a regional bond market on the foundations of robust legal, policy and regulatory frameworks and market practices consistent with global standards underpinning vibrant domestic capital markets in each individual economy. This highlights the importance of cooperation between emerging and advanced markets as well as between the public and private sectors, and the central role that APEC can play in this process.

Annex A

Average Scores of Individual Economies for Part I of the Survey Questionnaire

	CHL	CHN	CHT	HKG	INA	KOR	MAL	MEX	PER	PHP	RUS	SIN	THA	VNM	*ALL*
A. Macroeconomic and Political Environment															
1	4.00	2.80	2.78	3.33	2.50	2.92	4.00	2.00	1.00	3.00	2.00	4.00	3.00	4.00	*2.95*
2	3.00	2.80	3.00	3.17	2.25	2.71	3.00	2.00	2.00	3.00	0.00	4.00	3.00	3.00	*2.84*
3	4.00	2.00	3.67	3.67	2.00	2.83	3.33	3.00	3.00	3.00	2.00	4.00	2.00	3.00	*2.96*
4	4.00	2.00	2.78	3.67	2.25	2.96	3.00	3.00	2.00	2.00	2.00	3.67	2.00	3.00	*2.74*
5	4.00	1.80	2.78	3.67	2.25	2.96	2.67	3.00	3.00	3.00	2.00	3.33	2.00	2.50	*2.78*
6	4.00	2.00	3.00	3.33	2.50	2.92	2.67	3.00	3.00	3.00	2.00	3.67	3.00	3.00	*2.93*
7	4.00	2.00	2.89	3.17	2.25	2.71	2.67	3.00	2.00	3.00	3.00	3.33	3.00	2.50	*2.82*
8	4.00	2.20	2.44	2.67	2.25	2.46	3.00	3.00	2.00	3.00	2.00	3.67	2.00	2.50	*2.66*
9	1.00	1.80	2.13	2.60	1.67	2.13	2.33	3.00	1.00	3.00	1.00	4.00	3.00	1.50	*2.15*
Ave	3.56	2.16	2.83	3.25	2.21	2.73	2.96	2.78	2.11	2.89	2.00	3.74	2.56	2.78	*2.75*
B. Regulatory Framework															
1	4.00	2.00	3.13	3.50	2.00	2.75	3.50	2.00	2.00	3.00	2.00	4.00	2.00	2.50	*2.74*
2	4.00	1.80	3.11	3.33	1.67	2.50	3.50	2.00	2.00	3.00	2.00	4.00	2.00	2.50	*2.67*
3	4.00	1.80	2.89	3.50	1.67	2.58	2.50	3.00	3.00	2.00	2.00	4.00	2.00	2.50	*2.67*
4	4.00	1.80	2.89	3.50	1.75	2.63	3.50	3.00	3.00	2.00	0.00	4.00	2.00	2.50	*2.81*
5	4.00	1.60	2.44	3.50	1.67	2.58	2.50	3.00	0.00	2.00	2.00	3.67	2.00	2.00	*2.54*
6	4.00	1.60	2.89	3.17	2.00	2.58	3.00	3.00	2.00	3.00	2.00	4.00	2.00	2.00	*2.66*
7	4.00	1.80	2.67	3.00	1.67	2.33	3.50	3.00	2.00	3.00	2.00	4.00	2.00	3.00	*2.71*
8	4.00	1.60	2.89	3.33	1.75	2.54	3.00	2.00	2.00	2.00	0.00	3.67	2.00	3.00	*2.60*
9	4.00	1.80	2.67	3.17	2.00	2.58	3.00	3.00	2.00	2.00	2.00	4.00	2.00	2.00	*2.59*
10	4.00	2.00	2.78	3.33	2.00	2.67	3.00	3.00	2.00	2.00	2.00	3.67	2.00	2.50	*2.64*
11	4.00	1.40	2.89	3.33	1.67	2.50	2.00	3.00	2.00	2.00	2.00	3.67	1.00	2.50	*2.43*
Ave	4.00	1.75	2.84	3.33	1.80	2.57	3.00	2.73	2.20	2.36	2.00	3.88	1.91	2.45	*2.63*
C. Reporting Framework															
1	4.00	2.00	3.22	3.17	2.33	2.75	3.50	3.00	3.00	3.00	2.00	4.00	3.00	3.00	*3.00*
2	3.00	1.40	3.00	3.17	2.33	2.75	3.00	3.00	0.00	3.00	2.00	4.00	3.00	2.00	*2.74*
3	3.00	1.80	3.00	3.20	3.00	3.10	3.00	3.00	0.00	2.00	2.00	0.00	3.00	2.00	*2.68*
Ave	3.33	1.73	3.07	3.18	2.56	2.87	3.17	3.00	3.00	2.67	2.00	4.00	3.00	2.33	*2.85*

Average Scores of Individual Economies for Part I of the Survey Questionnaire *(continued)*

	CHL	CHN	CHT	HKG	INA	KOR	MAL	MEX	PER	PHP	RUS	SIN	THA	VNM	*ALL*
D. Public-Private Sector Partnership															
1	3.00	2.00	3.11	3.17	2.25	2.71	3.33	2.00	3.00	3.00	3.00	4.00	2.00	3.00	*2.83*
2	3.00	1.75	3.00	2.60	2.33	2.47	3.33	3.00	2.00	3.00	0.00	3.00	2.00	1.50	*2.54*
3	4.00	1.80	2.56	2.80	1.67	2.23	2.50	2.00	1.00	3.00	0.00	2.00	2.00	1.50	*2.24*
Ave	3.33	1.85	2.89	2.86	2.08	2.47	3.06	2.33	2.00	3.00	3.00	3.00	2.00	2.00	*2.56*
E. Capital Market Development															
1	4.00	1.80	2.78	3.00	2.00	2.50	3.00	3.00	2.00	2.00	2.00	3.50	2.00	2.00	*2.54*
2	4.00	2.40	3.22	2.67	2.00	2.33	3.00	2.00	2.00	2.00	3.00	3.33	2.00	2.50	*2.60*
3	4.00	1.60	2.67	2.67	1.75	2.21	1.67	2.00	1.00	2.00	2.00	3.00	2.00	2.00	*2.18*
4	4.00	1.80	2.78	3.33	2.50	2.92	3.33	3.00	2.00	2.00	3.00	3.00	3.00	3.00	*2.83*
5	4.00	1.80	2.50	2.67	2.00	2.33	2.67	2.00	2.00	3.00	2.00	3.00	1.00	2.50	*2.39*
6	4.00	1.60	2.88	2.17	2.00	2.08	2.33	2.00	2.00	3.00	2.00	2.67	1.00	2.00	*2.27*
7	4.00	1.60	2.56	2.50	2.00	2.25	2.33	2.00	3.00	2.00	2.00	3.33	1.00	2.50	*2.36*
8	3.00	1.20	2.56	3.00	1.50	2.25	2.67	2.00	2.00	1.00	2.00	2.67	1.00	2.50	*2.10*
9	4.00	1.60	3.00	2.80	1.00	1.90	2.50	2.00	2.00	2.00	2.00	3.00	2.00	4.00	*2.41*
10	4.00	1.40	2.63	2.80	1.00	1.90	1.50	2.00	2.00	2.00	2.00	3.00	3.00	2.50	*2.27*
11	4.00	1.80	2.67	3.17	1.75	2.46	2.67	3.00	3.00	3.00	2.00	3.33	2.00	2.50	*2.67*
12	4.00	1.60	3.25	3.33	2.25	2.79	3.33	3.00	3.00	3.00	1.00	3.50	2.00	2.50	*2.75*
13	4.00	2.20	3.33	3.67	2.25	2.96	3.67	3.00	3.00	3.00	2.00	3.00	2.00	3.00	*2.93*
Ave	3.92	1.72	2.83	2.91	1.85	2.38	2.67	2.38	2.23	2.31	2.08	3.10	1.85	2.58	*2.49*
OVERALL	***3.63***	***1.84***	***2.89***	***3.10***	***2.10***	***2.60***	***2.97***	***2.64***	***2.31***	***2.65***	***2.22***	***3.54***	***2.26***	***2.43***	**2.66**

For a list of the individual key objectives corresponding to the numbers listed under the five major areas, refer to Part I of the survey questionnaire (Annex B).

What the scores signify:

1 = To develop (no work has yet been initiated)
2 = Partially met (some work has been carried out; much improvement needed)
3 = Mostly met (substantial work has been carried out, slight improvement needed)
4 = Fully met (all necessary work has been carried out; no significant improvement needed)
0 = Not applicable

Annex A

Financial Sector Survey on Asia-Pacific Economies' Preparedness for Developing Local Currency and Regional Bond Markets

In May 2004, the APEC Business Advisory Council (ABAC) and the Pacific Economic Cooperation Council (PECC) convened a conference in Taipei on the development of Asia-Pacific bond markets.* A total of 150 participants representing the region's major market players attended the event. They identified conditions that are necessary to promote private sector investment and issuance in the region's local currency bond markets and the emergence of a commercially viable regional bond market.

This survey of Asia-Pacific financial sector executives focuses on the areas of improvement identified in this conference. It seeks to form a basis for (a) a private sector assessment of the current policy environment for the development of local currency bond market activities in the region and (b) concrete proposals on capacity-building involving public-private sector partnership.

Economies covered by this survey (including those that are yet without an operational local currency bond market) are the following:

- Brunei
- Chile
- China
- Hong Kong, China
- Indonesia
- Republic of Korea
- Malaysia
- Mexico
- Papua New Guinea
- Peru
- Philippines
- Russian Federation
- Singapore
- Thailand
- Chinese Taipei
- Vietnam

We request your kind cooperation in answering the questionnaire below. The identity of respondents will be kept confidential. You should complete one questionnaire for each economy, from the list above, on which you wish to provide comments.

Please return your responses on or before Friday, April 29, 2005, preferably *by e-mail* to:

Dr. J.C. Parrenas
c/o Chinese Taipei Pacific Economic Cooperation Committee (CTPECC)
16-8 Tehui St., Taipei, Taiwan
Email: jcparrenas@tier.org.tw

---

* *Developing Bond Markets in APEC: Moving Forward through Public-Private Sector Partnership*, May 10-11, Taipei, co-organized by the APEC Business Advisory Council and the Pacific Economic Cooperation Council. More information on this conference, including the conference report, are available at the conference website http://www.tier.org.tw/pecc/conference/bondmarket2004.htm

Fax: +886 2 2594 6528
Tel: +886 2 2594 6316 or +886 2 2586 5000 Extension 504

Your cooperation will go a long way toward accelerating the expansion of business opportunities in our region's financial markets. We thank you very much in advance.

Financial Sector Survey on Asia-Pacific Economies' Preparedness for Developing Local Currency and Regional Bond Markets

Survey Questionnaire

Economy covered (*one per questionnaire, please choose one from list on previous page*):	________________
Your name*	________________
Name of your organization/firm*	________________
Your position	________________
Your e-mail address	________________
Your telephone number (*with country/city code*)	________________

**Identity of respondent and organization/firm will be kept confidential.*

Part I

Please rate the extent to which you feel that each objective was met by typing the corresponding number on the blank column after each item, using the following scale:

1 = **To develop** (*no work has yet been initiated*)
2 = **Partially met** (*some work has been carried out; much improvement needed*)
3 = **Mostly met** (*substantial work has been carried out, slight improvement needed*)
4 = **Fully met** (*all necessary work has been carried out; no significant improvement needed*)
0 = **Not applicable**

Example:

If you think the goal of a stable financial system was fully met, type "4" in the column after the statement.

Stable financial system; banking systems and capital markets are strong. **4**

A. Macroeconomic and Political Environment

1. Stable political system; no major internal social upheavals are expected. ____
2. Continuity in economic policies; no major economic policy reversals in last 10 years. ____
3. Stable financial system; banking systems and capital markets are strong. ____
4. No restrictions on economic activities, trade and foreign investment (for all industries). ____
5. No restrictions on trade in financial services and foreign investment in financial sector. ____
6. No capital controls which significantly impact on capital flows. ____
7. Exchange rate regime which is conducive to efficient capital flows and payments. ____
8. Existence of domestic coordinating mechanism among government agencies to develop local currency bond market. ____
9. Existence of mechanism to coordinate development of local currency and regional bond markets with other governments. ____

B. Regulatory Framework

1. Clearly defined creditor rights, insolvency and informal workout processes. ____
2. Effective enforcement of creditor rights. ____
3. Tax and administrative procedures conducive to holding and trading of bonds. ____
4. Effective legal framework for asset securitization. ____
5. Cross border securities transactions are unhindered. ____
6. Robust system of clear, complete, timely and meaningful disclosure. ____
7. Clear and sound rules on corporate governance, financial controls and market integrity. ____
8. Effective enforcement of rules and penalties governing capital market activity. ____
9. Market regulation and supervision effectively balances interests of all market participants
10. Consistent regulations and laws (including taxation) promoting capital market activities. ____
11. Competition regulator with full authority to act against anti-competitive market activity. ____

C. REPORTING FRAMEWORK

1. Robust and transparent accounting standards for financial and non-financial institutions. ______
2. Convergence of domestic accounting standards with the IFRS. ______
3. Existence of time-framed plan for converging domestic accounting standards with IFRS. ______

D. PUBLIC-PRIVATE SECTOR PARTNERSHIP

1. Healthy cooperation between finance officials/regulators and the private financial sector. ______
2. Existence of domestic consultative mechanism between public and private sectors to develop local currency bond markets. ______
3. Existence of international consultative mechanism between public and private sectors to develop a regional bond market. ______

E. CAPITAL MARKET DEVELOPMENT

1. Wide variety of product types available to institutional and retail investors. ______
2. Developed domestic institutional investor base. ______
3. Developed domestic retail investor base with broad participation in capital markets. ______
4. Market is open to many players, both domestic and foreign. ______
5. Existence, for an appropriate lengthy period, of benchmark treasury yield curve across a broad range of maturities. ______
6. Existence of deep and liquid secondary market in local currency bonds. ______
7. No restrictions on short-selling and repo transactions. ______
8. No restrictions on use of derivatives across the range of maturities and currencies (e.g., swaps, options, forwards, futures). ______
9. Existence of clear rules for deployment of credit enhancement mechanisms. ______
10. Credit enhancement facilities reflect market price of capital; non-subsidized. ______
11. Availability of timely, useful and reliable financial information to guide investment decisions in the local market. ______
12. Existence of a credible and apolitical credit rating system for local currency bonds. ______
13. Efficient clearing and settlement systems. ______

Part II

Of the above items (A.1 – E.13), identify three (3) where reform is most critical to facilitate the development of the local currency bond market. Rank the 3 items in order of importance, by typing the number of the item on the corresponding blank column below.

Example:

If you believe that the three most critical items which ought to be the subject of priority reform in order of importance are (1) efficient clearing and settlement systems (item E.13 above); (2) no restrictions on short-selling and repo transactions (item E.7) and (3) no capital controls (item A.6 above), type the number of the item on the corresponding blank column as follows:

Most critical	**E.13**
Second most critical	**E.7**
Third most critical	**A.6**

THE 3 MOST CRITICAL ITEMS

Most critical	______
Second most critical	______
Third most critical	______

If there is another item (or items) not identified in this survey which you consider more critical than any of the 3 items you have chosen, please identify it (them) by typing in the blank below.

Additional Critical Item(s) (*PLEASE TYPE YOUR ANSWER IN THE SPACE BELOW.*)

Part III

To achieve progress in the 3 most critical items you have identified, (a) what policy changes are necessary and/or (b) what capacity-building (e.g., technical assistance, public-private sector partnership, regional cooperation) measures would you consider helpful? ***(Please type in your answers to the questions below.)***

For the Most Critical Item
1. What policy changes are necessary?
2. What capacity-building measures would you consider helpful?

For the 2nd Most Critical Item
1. What policy changes are necessary?
2. What capacity-building measures would you consider helpful?

For the 3rd Most Critical Item
1. What policy changes are necessary?
2. What capacity-building measures would you consider helpful?

<u>If you have identified an additional critical item, please answer the questions below:</u>

Additional Critical Item
1. What policy changes are necessary?
2. What capacity-building measures would you consider helpful?

Part IV

Other comments you wish to make (Please write them in the box below.)

WE THANK YOU VERY MUCH FOR COMPLETING THIS QUESTIONNAIRE.

Part III

Strategies for Development

Chapter 7

Essential Changes in National Law and Regulation:
Impediments to cross-border investment in Asian bond markets

S. Ghon Rhee[1], Paul Lejot[2] and Douglas Arner[2]

[1]Asia-Pacific Financial Markets Research Center and College of Business Administration, University of Hawaii; [2]Asian Institute of International Finanical Law and Faculty of Law, University of Hong Kong

1. Introduction[1]

Reforms to encourage the development of Asian domestic bond markets have received growing official priority since the end of the 1997-98 crisis, as a result of their being seen both as a vehicle for savings mobilization and a means to mitigate mismatches of currency and maturity in lending and funding. However, firm policy achievements have been persistently elusive. One reason is inappropriate policy sequencing in efforts to support regional integration. So far, much effort has focused on harmonization of regulations while the elimination of impediments to capital flows is too often overlooked.[2] To hope to create regional markets prior to eliminating impediments to cross-border capital flows is likely to be forlorn.[3] However laudable, harmonization is neither a necessary nor sufficient condition for

[1] Some analysis in this chapter was prepared for the APEC Finance Ministers' technical working group meeting, June 2005 in Gwangju, Korea and a conference on 'Developing Bond Markets in APEC: Toward Greater Public-Private Sector Regional Partnership', June 2005 in Tokyo, Japan, organized by the APEC Business Advisory Council, Asian Development Bank Institute and Pacific Economic Cooperation Council. The authors are grateful to the Korean Ministry of Finance and Economy for financial support. Certain data is drawn and updated from the Asian Bond Monitor, prepared while Rhee was senior consultant to the Asian Development Bank in 2004.

[2] See Asian Development Bank (2003); Asami and Mori (2001); and Lynch (2000).

[3] Rhee (2004a).

financial market integration, even though it may assist in the process.[4] Instead, placing emphasis on harmonization may delay progress towards otherwise feasible financial sector alignment or integration.

Given the limited level of activity associated with foreign investment in Asian bonds and the supply of local currency or foreign currency denominated bonds issued by foreign borrowers in Asia, this chapter identifies impediments to cross-border investment in Asian bonds, some of which apply to other market segments. Section 2 gives a current overview of Asia's bond markets and examines regional capital flows so as to explain cross-border investment activity. Section 3 describes the many effects of market impediments on investor and borrower behavior, with the causes shown in detail in section 4. Section 5 closes the chapter.

2. Reforms and constraints

2.1. Recent history

If measured by cross-border investment, the appeal of Asian bonds is apparently insignificant. Less than one per cent of local currency bonds outstanding are held by overseas investors in Korea and Thailand, even though their domestic bond markets are theoretically open to foreign investment. The same observation can be made for other Asian economies: foreign ownership accounts for approximately one per cent of outstanding local currency bonds in Hong Kong, Indonesia, and Malaysia.[5] Even Japan, which has the world's largest amount of government bonds outstanding ($ 4.8 trillion as at the end-2004), is no exception. Foreign holdings of Japanese government bonds account for no more than 4 per cent of the total.

Local currency bonds issued by foreign borrowers could be an important means to promote cross-border investment activities. So far, foreign institutions have issued local currency bonds in no more than eight national markets: Australia, Hong Kong, Japan, Korea, Malaysia, Singapore, Taiwan and Thailand.[6][7] The relative magnitude of local currency denominated bonds issued by foreign institutions is small with the exception of Australia and Hong Kong. Samurai bonds—yen bonds issued in Japan by foreign borrowers—accounted for less than one per cent of Japan's local currency bonds outstanding in 2004, although the volume issued has apparently risen in 2005; foreign obligor Singapore dollar bonds represented less than 1.5 per cent of the total

---

[4] Steil (2002); Lejot, Arner & Liu (2004).

[5] Takeuchi (2004). One proviso is that international HK dollar issues may be widely held.

[6] This ignores Indonesia and Macau, both of which have seen a handful of foreign issues. China announced new rules in March 2005 to allow multilateral financial institutions to issue domestic yuan bonds. In December 2004, the finance ministry had approved ADB, IFC and JBIC as potential issuers.

[7] New Zealand is unusual in that its domestic investors mainly purchase non-government bonds from liquid offshore markets including Australia.

market. The share of won-denominated 'Arirang' bonds issued in Korea by foreign issuers is a mere 0.0001 per cent of the total. Arirang bonds have been used as a financing source by foreign subsidiaries of Korean firms, and the market has been unable to serve the financing needs of foreign institutional or corporate borrowers. Foreign currency issues targeted at domestic investors have yet to develop in a consistent way: Japan's Shogun bond market (domestic foreign currency issues) has been largely dormant since 1994.

International Financial Institutions (IFIs) have often piloted the earliest foreign issues in local currency markets but few of the results are liquid: institutional investors buy and hold such bonds to take advantage of withholding tax exemptions and as a result none provide practical benchmarks other than for the same issuer. It is unsurprising that questions are raised about the true contributions of IFI issuance to market development.[8] If anything, their main benefit in 'new' markets may materialize in revealing market impediments and idiosyncrasies, which the IFI could itself address through technical assistance. However, IFIs are treated favorably in this context and as a result this potential benefit is lost.

2.2. *Market dimensions*

Excluding Japan, the size of local currency bond markets in the East Asian economies more than tripled from $ 402 billion in 1997, the first year of the Asian financial crisis, to $ 1.42 trillion in December 2004, at an annual growth rate of 20 per cent, some 2.5 times the average growth rate of global markets as reported in Table 7-1[9] The annual growth rate of the East Asian bond markets compares with 7.2 per cent for Latin America, 6.9 per cent for the United States, 7.2 per cent for the European Union, and 11.5 per cent for Japan. In Asia, Indonesia exhibited the highest growth rate of 45 per cent in long-term bonds outstanding between 1997 and December 2004, followed by Thailand with 29.5 per cent and China and Korea, each with 23 per cent.

Local currency bonds outstanding worldwide were $ 44.0 trillion at the end of December 2004. Excluding Japan, the market shares of East Asian economies were 1.6 per cent (or $ 402 billion) in 1997 and 3.2 per cent (or $ 1.42 trillion) in 2004 of aggregate global domestic bonds. This seems slender for two main reasons. First, non-Japan Asia contributes 8.3 per cent of global output, so that a 3.2 per cent market share in outstanding domestic bonds could more appropriately have at least doubled. Second, the relative size of Asian bonds outstanding as a share of GDP amounted to 43.3 per cent as at end-2004. This ratio is far lower than Japan (189 per cent), the United States (157 per cent) or the EU (94 per cent).

---

[8] Rhee (2004b). In February 2004 ADB issued Rs5.0 billion 10 year bonds in the Indian domestic market, using the proceeds to fund private sector loans. Nevertheless, Indian domestic bonds are extremely illiquid. See Hoschka (2005a, 2005b) and Bestani and Sagar (2004) for local currency financing.

[9] Market statistics are taken from Bank for International Settlements (BIS) data on domestic debt securities. For consistency, no adjustments are made for discrepancies in national data.

Table 7-1. **Domestic bond market capitalization (US$ billion)**

End-period data	Market capitalization	% of GDP	Market capitalization	% of GDP	Annual growth rate (%)	% of World
United States	1,999.60	144.50	19,186.60	157.37	6.9	43.56
EU	7,013.10	84.84	11,385.00	94.17	7.2	25.85
Latin America	467.8	31.47	651	-	7.2	1.48
Japan	4,148.30	103.98	8866.7	189.36	11.5	20.13
Non-Japan Asia	401.7	17.70	1,419.80	43.33	19.8	3.22
China	116.3	12.89	483.3	29.11	22.6	1.10
Hong Kong	41.1	23.69	46.5	29.25	1.8	0.11
Indonesia	4.3	1.81	57.8	22.40	44.9	0.13
Korea	130.3	25.06	568.4	83.59	23.4	1.29
Malaysia	57.0	56.36	106.6	90.34	9.4	0.24
Philippines	18.4	22.29	25.2	29.33	4.6	0.06
Singapore	23.7	24.84	66.3	61.96	15.8	0.15
Thailand	10.6	6.73	64.9	38.29	29.5	0.15
World	25,420.20	85.49	44,048.70	109.83	8.2	100.00

Source: BIS securities data, Asian Development Bank, national sources.

Note: EU data excludes Luxembourg and post-2004 accession states. Latin America here comprises Argentina, Brazil, Chile, Colombia, Mexico and Peru.

In addition, the composition of Asian bonds outstanding as illustrated by Figure 7-2 indicates that post-crisis market growth of Asian bonds is attributed to government issuance and not new corporate bonds.

The development of corporate bond markets is uneven. Only Korea and Taiwan support robust issuance. Corporate bonds outstanding in non-Japan Asia as at end-2004 amounted to under 8 per cent of aggregate, while Japanese and U.S. corporate bonds outstanding represented 17 per cent and 21 per cent, respectively of GDP.

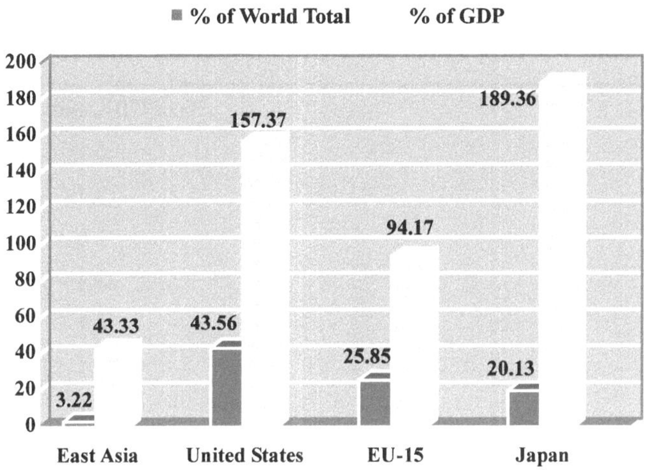

Figure 7-1. **Relative size of East Asian bond markets (end-2004, source BIS)**

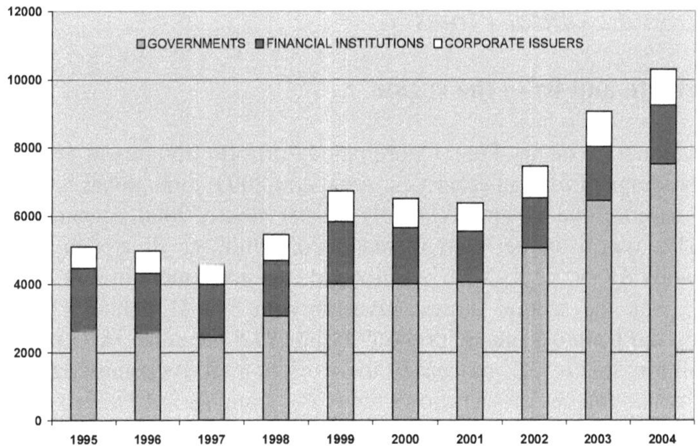

Figure 7-2. **Composition of Asian bonds (source BIS)**

***Table 7-2.* Size of corporate bond market (source BIS)**

	% of GDP, end-2004
China	0.7
Hong Kong	3.7
Indonesia	1.6
Korea	23.4
Malaysia	38.1
Philippines	0.1
Singapore	5.1
Thailand	11.7
Non-Japan Asia	7.7
Japan	16.9
United States	21.2

2.3. Regional Capital Flows

2.3.1. Flows to and from the region

The International Monetary Fund Coordinated Portfolio Investment Survey compiles domestic holdings of foreign securities. As at end-2003, total global bond investment was \$ 9.1 trillion, that is, approximately 22 per cent of total outstanding domestic bonds.[10] This was a 30 per cent increase from 2002 as illustrated in figure 7-3. Approximately 61 per cent (\$ 5.61 trillion) of this investment in 2003 was from the EU; Japan was the second largest investor with \$ 1.41 trillion (15.0 per cent) followed by the United States with \$ 869 billion (9.5 per cent). Asia invested a total of \$ 232 billion, that is, 2.5 per cent of the world's total. As summarized in Table 7-3, the two major sources of such flows are Hong Kong (\$ 154 billion) and Singapore (\$ 52 billion). The EU is the largest recipient of global bond investment with \$ 5.4 trillion (59 per cent), followed by the United States with \$ 1.6 trillion (18 per cent). Asia's share of this aggregate was \$ 190 billion, no more than two per cent of global investment in long-term debt securities.

[10] The composite figures are based on 70 participating economies in the IMF survey. These economies invest in 239 countries and international organizations.

Table 7-3. **Inter-regional capital flows in long-term bonds (US$ billion)**

	Investment by the world in each economy 2002 (inflow)	Investment by the world in each economy 2003 (inflow)	Investment by each economy in the world 2002 (outflow)	Investment by each economy in the world 2003 (outflow)	Net bond investment 2002	Net bond investment 2003
China	4,008	4,098	0	0	4,008	4,098
Hong Kong	7,294	9,149	123,528	154,096	(116,234)	(144,947)
Indonesia	3,025	4,244	703	1,715	2,322	2,529
Japan	126,097	107,528	1,135,519	1,407,173	(1,009,422)	(1,299,645)
Korea	25,330	24,586	9,608	13,833	15,722	10,753
Malaysia	11,073	14,381	471	800	10,602	13,581
Philippines	8,326	11,680	1,476	2,202	6,850	9,478
Singapore	8,171	11,472	51,524	57,580	(43,353)	(46,108)
Thailand	2,778	3,106	1,344	2,224	1,434	882
East Asia	196,202	190,461	1,324,173	1,639,623	(1,127,971)	(1,449,162)
US	1,308,105	1,636,683	705,237	868,948	602,868	767,735
EU	4,008,650	5,358,700	4,191,079	5,614,652	-182,429	(255,952)
World	6,998,266	9,127,804	6,998,266	9,127,804	0	0

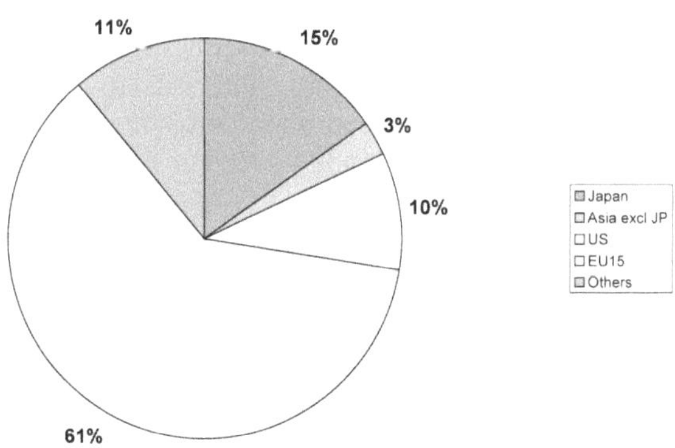

Figure 7-3. **Global investors in domestic bond markets (2003 value $ 9.1 trillion; source IMF)**

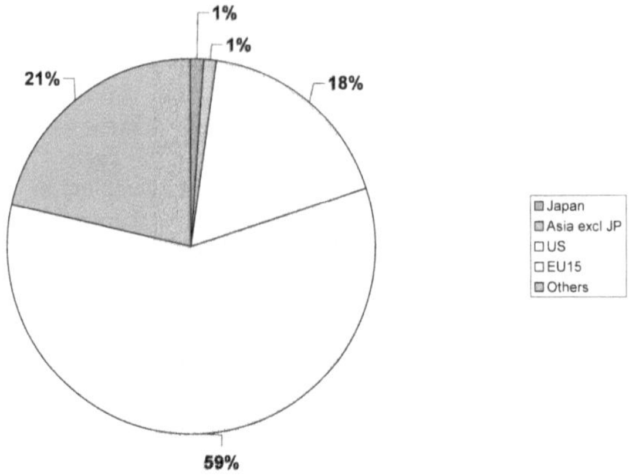

Figure 7-4. **Recipients of global bond investment (2003 value $ 9.1 trillion; source IMF)**

As summarized in table 7-4, the investment profile in table 7-3 illustrates the following:

- Positive net capital flows amounted to $ 768 billion for the United States, which indicates that long-term capital investment in the U.S. long-term bond markets was greater than the U.S. investment in the rest of the world.
- In contrast, negative net capital flows were recorded for Japan ($ 1.3 trillion) and EU ($ 256 billion).
- Hong Kong and Singapore were the only two economies with negative net capital flows among East Asian economies, with $ 145 billion and $ 46 billion, respectively.
- The rest of East Asia received more investment in domestic bond markets than their investments made overseas.

A similar pattern was seen in both 2002 and 2003. Figure 5 presents global investments in East Asian debt. Total global investment in Asian bonds was $ 190.5 billion in 2003, marginally less than in 2002. The EU was the largest investor with $ 70.2 billion or 43 per cent of the total, followed by the United States with $ 53.8 billion (28 per cent). Japan was the largest recipient of global inflows with $ 107.5 billion, with Korea a distant second with $ 24.6 billion, followed by Malaysia ($ 14.4 billion), Philippines ($ 11.7 billion), Singapore ($ 11.5 billion), and Hong Kong ($ 9.1 billion).

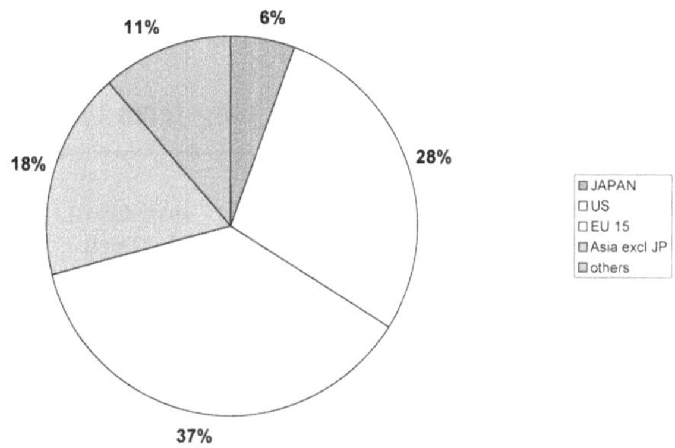

Figure 7-5. **Global investors in Asian bonds (2003, source IMF)**

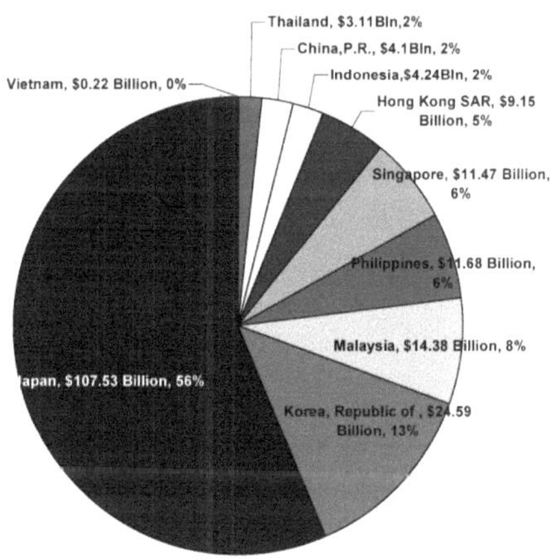

Figure 7-6. **Recipients of global investment in Asian bonds (2003, source IMF)**

2.3.2. Flows within the region

The summary in table 7-4 suggests that Hong Kong is the largest regional investor in local currency Asian bonds with annual investment of \$ 22.3 billion in 2003 and \$ 15.8 billion in 2002. Japan's share was smaller, at \$ 10.76 billion in 2003 and \$ 11.76 billion in 2002. In contrast, investments by other East Asian economies in long-term bonds issued by Hong Kong, Japan, and Singapore were \$ 3.69 billion, \$ 7.96, and \$ 4.40 billion, respectively, in 2003. Thus these three economies showed negative net bond investment flows, which indicates that they are Asia's only capital exporters. Korea had a positive net bond investment flow of $ 14.0 billion, followed by Malaysia with $ 6.1 billion. China, Philippines, and Thailand collected $ 2.4 billion, $ 2.0 billion and $ 1.4 billion, respectively.

Table 7-4. **Intra-regional flows in long-term bonds (US$ million)**

	Investment by East Asia in Each Economy in 2002 (Inflow)	Investment by East Asia in Each Economy in 2003 (Inflow)	Investment by Each Economy in East Asia 2002 (Outflow)	Investment by Each Economy in East Asia 2003 (Outflow)	Net Bond Investment (2002)	Net Bond Investment (2003)
China	2,164	2,399	0	0	2,164	2,399
Hong Kong	3,031	3,693	15,761	22,264	(12,730)	(18,571)
Indonesia	1,010	1,019	88	202	922	817
Japan	6,745	7,957	11,586	10,758	(4,841)	(2,801)
Korea	11,936	15,176	1,181	1,083	10,755	14,093
Malaysia	6,237	6,205	138	122	6,099	6,083
Philippines	2,569	2,330	130	243	2,439	2,087
Singapore	2,779	4,396	9,070	9,916	(6,291)	(5,520)
Thailand	1,471	1,430	20	49	1,451	1,381
Non-Japan Asia	31,229	36,680	26,388	33,879	4,841	2,801
Total	37,974	44,637	37,974	44,637	0	0

To place intra-regional investment activities in perspective, figure 7-7 presents the size of investments in Asian bonds by each economy relative to its total investment in bonds. Japan and Thailand invested disproportionately small amounts in Asian bond markets with 0.8 per cent and 2.2 per cent, respectively, in 2003, while holdings by Singapore and Malaysia amounted to 17.2 per cent and 15.3 per cent, respectively. Few differences are observed in the intra-regional investment behavior of any member of this group, prompting the question as to why intra-regional investment in Asian bonds remains insignificant?

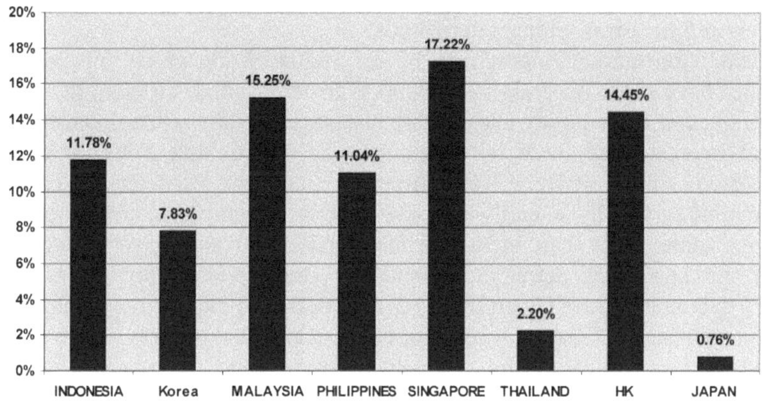

***Figure** 7-7.* **Domestic Asian bond investment as a share of total investment (2003)**

3. Impediments to Market Activity

The preceding section showed how cross-border investment in Asian currency bond markets is unusually low, both comparatively and in relation to the scale of regional trade-related flows.

3.1. Implications of cross-border trade flows

Contemporary studies of Asian bond market capitalizations relative to national income concur with the law and finance school's view that country size, economic growth, creditor rights and certain risk factors are important determinants of bond market size.[11] The region's lack of large debt markets may also reflect conservative fiscal policies and historic cultural factors, or insufficient will, at least until recently.[12,13] Since 1999, national governments have been understandably keen to guard against new crises, so that a pro-market consensus has gradually been established with little dissent: active bond markets may lessen the impact and contagious ripples of future shocks. They might further promote efficiencies in

[11] Eichengreen and Luengnaruemitchai (2004) and Burger and Warnock (2004) respectively examine 41 and 49 local currency debt markets, 11 and 14 respectively from Asia. Both studies acknowledge data limitations hindering analysis of the determinants of market turnover, and in suggesting reverse causality. Law and finance theory is exemplified in La Porta, López-de-Silanes, Shleifer & Vishny (LLSV) (1997, 1998).

[12] Eichengreen and Luengnaruemitchai (*op cit*).

[13] Lejot *et al.* (2003) argue that Korea's extraordinary post-crisis restructuring imperative may have provided such determination.

capital raising, investment appraisal and resource allocation, and provide both borrowers and investors with greater choice.

Implementing market reform may be hazardous. While nearly all major Asian economies have made progress since 2000 in fostering more efficient debt markets, the objectives of these policy changes are distant, especially when they often offend sectional interests, the force of which may be overarching even in markets as sophisticated as those of Hong Kong, Korea or Singapore. Rent-seeking participants that are well-served by a partly-effective system inevitably fear that reform will lessen its value. They can include commercial banks and governments in their lending and borrowing activity, respectively. The capitalizations of Asia's local currency debt markets are generally larger than ever, and include a widening array of risks and instruments. Yet the breadth of benefits afforded by truly active markets is captured only sporadically, and rarely by most regional cross-border issuers and investors. Bonds exist as a borrowing medium and a home for passive investment (with increasing emphasis given by governments to structures and distribution orientated towards retail investors) but fitfully for active risk-averse fund managers, or as risk management, treasury or capital investment appraisal tools. Liquidity is a dynamic quality, not merely a function of market size, and is generally not reliably available to aspiring non-bank participants.[14]

Some observers seem more optimistic. The World Bank declared in early 2005 that since the Asian financial crisis:

> 'government bond issuance has grown significantly in a few countries, such as Malaysia and Thailand, where government issues have not only served as a vehicle for government financing, but also have developed into benchmarks for pricing corporate bonds'.[15]

Here, 'significantly' is not necessarily connotative of depth, absolute scale or liquidity, and the second part of the assessment would be contentious to many market participants for whom a true 'benchmark' suggests continuity rather than a one-time comparison. Furthermore, it is unclear that the volume of corporate

---

[14] McCauley (2004) observes that '[t]he "investible" portion of Asia's debt markets is much smaller than the total outstanding amount, but not inconsequential', using as an illustration HSBC's Asian composite local currency bond index. 'Investible' is undefined but the index's capitalization is adjusted for sectoral impediments and illiquidity. The authors' and HSBC estimates indicate that the US dollar equivalent index capitalization currently represents approximately 30-32 per cent of the 'true' aggregate of its ten constituents. Nonetheless, this is an index that cannot be tracked by all investors except with synthetic instruments (however useful it may be in indicating trends). McCauley makes the valuable point that market quality allows liquidity in Australia, for example, greatly to exceed the considerably larger domestic markets of China and Korea.

[15] Global Development Finance (2005: 79).

issuance in the two cited markets has shown any substantive aggregate trend change since 2001.[16]

Asia's bond markets thus remain constrained as alternative channels for intermediation and to assist in public risk management policy: a virtual world for many potential users, known to exist but frequently unreachable. This section examines constraints on usage not seen in efficient debt markets, regardless of whether they serve "bank-based" or "market-based" economies.[17] It also considers the influence on debt markets of organizations involved in cross-border trade and non-portfolio investment.[18] Last, it points towards essential measures in law, regulation, taxation and system architecture that will remove impediments to market participation and growth, and encourage eventual harmonization and regional usage by a range of participants.[19]

---

[16] There was no material growth in net issuance of corporate debt securities in either Malaysia or Thailand compared to pre-crisis levels, other than in Malaysia during the third quarter of 1999 and first quarter of 2003, which both saw irregularly large issuance by public agencies linked to economic restructuring. The amounts outstanding in each case have risen by accretion and are not a reaction to increased government issuance. These data are presented in US dollars but cover periods subsequent to the 1997-98 collapses in Asian currencies. Malaysian corporate issues include those of Cagamas Bhd, a state-sponsored mortgage financing vehicle which until September 2004 was treated as a non-guaranteed arm of central government with a favorable 10 per cent risk-asset weighting for bank capital adequacy purposes. Note that domestic government debt securities outstanding have materially risen by amount and proportionately only in China, India, Indonesia, Korea, Thailand and Taiwan, in each case beginning during 1998-99. Sources: Tables 16 and 17A in http://www.bis.org/statistics/secstats.htm, Euroweek (passim) and International Financing Review (passim).

[17] A distinction associated first with Gerschenkron (1962) and Goldsmith (1969). Levine (1997, 2002) is notable among authors who point to the absence of an 'optimum' financial framework that would suggest either system is inherently favored.

[18] In addition, cross-border equity portfolio managers typically have natural recurring demand for liquid, low risk domestic currency money market instruments for liquidity, synchronization and risk management purposes. Asia's conventional non-synthetic markets provide no scope in this respect, giving conservative offshore fund managers no means of holding temporary local currency liquidity other than as retail bank deposits.

[19] Berkowitz *et al.* (2004) find data from 55 countries indicates that the quality of domestic legal and regulatory institutions has an important positive impact on international trade flows. They suggest this is largely explained by such regimes offering a reliable means to enforce private sale of goods contracts against an exporter. It has yet to be shown if similar links may exist between capital flows and institutional quality, and in such a case that the domestic legal and regulatory environment associated with cross-border capital flows is predominantly that of the user of funds.

3.2. Activities most subject to constraint

Asia's markets' constraints affect a wider community than conventional investors in notes and bonds. There is an affinity between the mechanics of international trade and cross-border capital flows more intricate than a presiding macroeconomic identity. It concerns the nature and housing of those flows, the facilitation of trade, decisions at firm level as to fixed capital formation and non-portfolio direct investment, and to the choices available to non-bank financial market participants, that is, organizations (or individuals) other than intermediating financial institutions that transact in those markets for reasons to which their trading is ancillary.[20] Non-bank participants tend to enter foreign debt capital markets (issuing, buying or selling) to assist four main functions:

- Liquidity management
- Hedging of financial risks
- Short-term investment
- Local currency borrowing.

These are typically not ends in themselves, nor are they speculative.[21] They represent activities undertaken in pursuit of the participant's primary commercial goals, and apply equally to onshore and cross-border activity. The list excludes more specialist dealings commonly undertaken through major financial centers, such as the hedging of credit, commodity or weather related risks. These functions would generally be associated with day-to-day (non-financial) trading, mitigating foreign exchange exposure and risks associated with the timing of capital expenditure. In most cases, the participants would hope to trade without incurring significant additional risks (including unforeseen costs) related to custody, settlement, taxation, payment timing, liquidity or counterparty default. None of the world's markets is perfectly configured, so that non-financial participants will always operate under constraints, yet when access to foreign financial markets is compromised there will be few usable alternatives that are not time-consuming, highly illiquid or costly to transact.

Cross-border borrowers need to know whether and how non-domestic issuance is permitted in their target currency, and what restrictions will influence the timing of payments, taxation parameters, limits on the use or transfer of proceeds and the market regulator's initial and ongoing disclosure requirements. Do new issue rules

---

[20] The financial choices of such parties are examined less often than those of conspicuous participants: banks, governments and funded investors. This may reflect both the variability of data and the tendency of most schools in economics and finance to ignore or assume away the nature of financing.

[21] King (2001) suggests that inflows to Asia of foreign capital from non-bank institutions remained positive until after July 1997 when the Thai baht collapsed, helping to fund a withdrawal of foreign bank lending and portfolio equity sales. All private capital inflows became negative throughout the region in the fourth quarter of 1997.

differ between class or status of borrower, and are restrictions placed upon the exchange of proceeds between counterparties, so that an eligible issuer may raise funds on behalf of a foreign end-user? Does the market offer an appropriate framework for pricing new issues, and hedging local currency interest rate risks? Foreign investors need to know whether the target market gives free or limited access, how it deals with custody, settlement timing, and risks in settlement, and what debt instruments are available to purchase and sell, both theoretically and feasibly. Procedures for dealing may vary by issue type and timing, as will the effects of taxation of all kinds during the period of holding an investment and upon its sale, and any means by which dealing is assisted (such as bond financing, repurchases or lending) may have consequences in the pricing and availability of securities. How will the proceeds of sale be treated? Will the cross-border investor be regarded in law equally with other holders of like claims?

Market blockages or distortions may result in the trading or issuance of bonds becoming infeasible, impractical, excessively costly, protracted or unreliable. These problems may emerge at the time of a potential transaction or recur over a period, imposing ongoing costs. For investors or borrowers the consequences will be wasteful and risk-enhancing, rather than efficient. The severest examples lead to general illiquidity in local currency instruments by rendering them unavailable or unusable, so that even where such securities exist and their sale not restricted by law or regulation, non-bank participants may be unable to rely on their effective existence or scope of use, even for accounting purposes. In the same way, foreign potential borrowers may find it impermissible or largely infeasible to issue debt or make free use of new issue proceeds.

Academic and regulatory circles discuss market quality more frequently in relation to exchange-traded instruments than those dealt over-the-counter (OTC) between participants. The result is that the prevailing liquidity of debt capital markets and availability of debt instruments relies in some measure upon the merit of market data and the sophistication of any single product sector. Exchanges provide single-source data but regulatory bodies, industry associations and clearing and settlement organizations collect data on well-traded OTC markets but their coverage may be haphazard when transaction reporting is unreliable, and when settlement involves elements of choice. Correcting for shortfalls in the quality of market data may require structural or procedural change. While operational aspects of system architecture in Asia have been subject to extensive review since 2000, there have been few assessments of the market quality regime faced by investors.[22,23] Data on overall investor activity is similarly limited. A once-published OECD review of institutional investment patterns used survey material from a financial magazine as its data source, and the IMF's Coordinated Public Investment Survey is incomplete in its national coverage.[24]

---

[22] Most notably Akamatsu (2004).

[23] Mohanty's survey (2002) of short-term government securities markets is an exception.

[24] The OECD's report remains unique, although banking and consulting sources regularly undertake surveys of investor behavior (Akthar, 2001).

3.3. Implications

Under-utilized markets are inefficient in two particular respects: from the resources absorbed by both public and private sectors in their operation, and in the high marginal costs of transaction execution for participants. Asia's semi-liquid domestic markets carry all the costs but not all the true benefits associated with debt capital markets. No financial market functions perfectly at all times; the most well developed government bond markets conceal liquidity and price discontinuities at intervals along their yield curves, and most major currency corporate bonds can be expected to be traded for only a fraction of their full lives. One consequence is that the quality of information offered to investing or borrowing participants is fractured or substandard, for example, as to prevailing yields or the credit risks of certain issuers.

Nowhere are markets constant and wholly impartial (even the largest) but those considered effective can be considered generally reliable for issuers and investors, without restrictions that offer support to rent-seeking participants, such as banks selling scarce cash securities or opaque synthetic products to circumvent law or regulation. The growing wish to use Asian currency bond instruments as freely as possible then leads to the use of alternatives, notably synthetic instruments and those involving embedded non-deliverable currency contracts, that can serve only a partial purpose and are likely to be shallowly regulated or supervised.

Prior to the Asian financial crisis, this often took the form of US dollar or yen asset swaps based on local currency claims and sold to international investors, usually commercial banks. In the time since the recovery there has been a broader increase in non-conventional debt claims sold offshore, including loans (for which harmonized transfer and contractual standards continually increase liquidity), private placements and credit derivatives.[25] Low-risk local currency money market instruments are often available only transiently to non-bank institutional investors (and never to money market funds). This typically increases portfolio management costs, deters foreign and domestic investors and may ultimately encourage post-shock contagion, for a lack of defensive investments increases instability in volatile conditions. Trade flows and streams of direct or portfolio investment generate natural demand for short and long-term debt instruments, hedging products and tools to assist capital asset benchmarking. When rational, risk averse investors (domestic or foreign) wish to reduce their holdings of local currency assets of any type, they may ordinarily seek to acquire defensive short-term instruments in the same currency. Core currency markets make this choice possible by allowing non-bank investors to hold liquid money market instruments (or wholesale money market funds), usually without fiscal penalty. Such alternatives are available in no Asian currency except yen, and prudence limits the use of local currency bank deposits by institutional investors, both at home and from overseas.

---

[25] Growth in the volume of non-deliverable forward exchange transactions indicates demand for private cross-border synthetic debt transactions, notably for markets where restrictions make simpler investments less feasible in China, India, Indonesia, Korea, Philippines and Taiwan (Ma *et al.*, 2004).

Banks and their regulators are known in some markets to form an enclosed circle that restricts the use of otherwise liquid debt instruments from other parties. The determinants of bank liquidity include subjective treasury risk management objectives such as the precautionary retention of reserves to help offset the impact of runs on retail deposits or the unavailability of wholesale money market funds. In domestic and foreign operations, banks will hold a sizeable part of their liquidity buffers in debt instruments acceptable to a monetary authority as lender of last resort or manager of some form of discount facility, such instruments typically including all notes and bonds of certain durations issued by or for central government, and in certain countries by non-government issuers meeting credit rating or status criteria. The approach adopted by any bank is likely to be informally known by some or all of its national peers, and may be guided by rule or informally by its respective regulatory authority. Bank runs have taken place far more recently in Asia than in most OECD economies, for example, being known in the fifteen years prior to 1997 in sophisticated markets such as Hong Kong and Korea.

Taken with the shocking experience of the region's financial system in 1997-98, this may help explain a strong risk-averse approach to bank liquidity management that is endorsed by both the region's banks and their supervisors. A further interest is vested in maintaining the exclusivity of the system to commercial and central banks: the competent national authority feels itself better able to supplant system liquidity to correct for the effects of exogenous losses of confidence by purchasing eligible securities or conducting reverse repurchase operations with banks within its designated circle, likely to be those with access to the window of the lender of last resort. Finally, the existence of the liquidity reserve cushion may make the competent authority operate more efficiently as lender of last resort, or convince the authority that it could so do.

The result can be further forms of compensating behavior. Investors seek to circumvent restrictions and blockages; aspiring issuers look to banks as a source of funding, or seek funds from informal sources of credit.[26] These alternatives are not restricted to the sophisticated investor or borrower. EMEAP's local currency Asian Bond Fund (ABF2) appears to be a similar creation, for its activity in those markets where investment is restricted will be to circumvent the key impediment facing a direct investor.[27] ABF2 will comprise a series of open-ended mutual funds, each of which will invest in money market instruments of a designated Asian currency. A separate "umbrella" fund will later invest in each of these single currency funds as well as directly in other Asian currency money market instruments. Thus the announced single currency and regional index funds are effectively a means to lessen problems associated with direct investment in local currency instruments by offshore

---

[26] Aziz and Duenwald (2002). As one example, in China where domestic and foreign-owned non-state enterprises have limited access to bank financing, Allen *et al.* (2002: 4-5) postulate 'effective, non-standard financing channels' funding private companies, including 'privately placed bonds and loans' (*ibid* 32). Much foreign direct investment to China may be loans disguised to avoid exchange controls (Fernald and Babson, 1999). See Chapter 5.

[27] EMEAP is the Executives' Meeting of East Asia and Pacific Central Banks. Its two Asian bond funds are assessed in Chapter 8.

investors and certain domestic investors, such problems relating to custody, enforcement of rights, reliability of transfer, taxation and other matters, which exist in all cases to varying degrees except in Hong Kong and Singapore. ABF2 is a market-based solution meant to circumvent problems of the type described in this study, and the most likely method by which it will influence reform could be by encouraging the supply of new issues and making those impediments and costs more apparent and thus in need of removal.

3.4. Blockages

The most salient and common issues of detail that crimp Asia's markets are explained in section 4 of this chapter. They constitute real or effective bars to growth in debt market activity, notably the volume of issuance and liquidity in secondary market trading. These include obstacles in relation to withholding taxes and duties, differentials in the application of taxes, restrictions on settlement or custody, arbitrary differences in creditor status constraining institutional investment, legal risks for investors, creditor claims and property rights in receivership or bankruptcy, the framework and application of regulatory guidelines for banks, pension and mutual funds, insurance companies and borrowers, and how they collectively hinder activity. Truly active markets will demand the solving of three types of problem: intentional or implied restrictions, omissions of law or practice, and unnecessary inconsistencies within and among national domains, embracing issues of law and regulation, taxation, and system design or operation. These issues characterize how cross-border issuance and investment is blocked, modified or made to look away. Some features are widely known to governments and market participants, especially since risk-preferring traders welcome price discontinuities as sources of rents but the severest problems are obstacles and omissions because a price may adjust to market discrepancies but seldom fully compensate for legal irregularities. These issues are those that the ABF2 plan will attempt partly to circumvent.[28] Until now, reform has rarely been devised sufficiently specifically to guide legislative or rule changes. National authorities may become accustomed to changing rules by fiat, which can deny certainty to local or foreign participants over retroactive coverage for the later withdrawal of any concession.

Meeting these objectives requires three problems to be solved: intentional or implied restrictions, omissions of law or practice, and unnecessary inconsistencies within and among national bond markets. The most damaging features are obstacles and omissions, since market discrepancies can often be reflected in the pricing of risk, but domestic irregularities relating to matters of law are also damaging and not fully compensated in ratings, risk or pricing. Obstacles are specific factors, not all of

---

[28] Lejot *et al.* (2004) propose the hastening of national reforms by governments sanctioning a regulated market for regional, domestic and non-Asian use, allowing the trading and settlement of new and outstanding bonds in a hub meeting agreed standards, free of withholdings, duties and capital controls, subject to common regulation and available to all investors and approved issuers.

which are deliberate, and aspects of local market practice that deter institutional and professional activity. Omissions are critically, a lack of continuous, market-driven yield curves, whether conventional risk-free government yield curves or alternatives (fair value, zero coupon, interest rate swap, implied forward). Disparities are system disparities which encourage an arbitrage orientation, discourage regional institutional investment, lessen confidence, and penalize asset classes within markets.

3.5. Methodology and consequences

Certain specific legal and regulatory concerns relate to findings or in contemporary law and finance theory that legal environment, and jurisdictional or regulatory differences in investor protection are strong determinants of the effectiveness of financial systems, including capital markets, and will influence economic performance.[29] A second thread argues that legal traditions significantly influence investor protection and market sophistication, including the view that common law traditions better support creditor rights and effective markets than civil law jurisdictions, and conversely that the protection of such rights improves the functioning of capital markets because the quality of enforcement varies with legal systems. If the nature of legal systems is a strong, timeless determinant of financial development, then market weaknesses identified in this chapter may be intrinsic, incapable of piecemeal remedy, and harmonized reform unable to fashion a feasible outcome.[30]

Practice is unlikely to produce so rigid a result. There are accepted examples in Asia (and elsewhere) of civil law economies that sustain flourishing debt capital markets and of common law jurisdictions that fail so to do.[31] Experiences within the EU since 1986 suggest that harmonization to minimum standards, coupled with mutual recognition, can be effective across economies with differing legal and

---

[29] LLSV 1997 (*op cit*) and 1998 (*op cit*); Beck & Levine (2003).

[30] Aspects of law and finance theory are difficult to test. Creditor data are erratic (equity claims are simpler to identify); the determined variable 'debt' is commonly taken as the sum of bank claims against the non-banking sector and disclosed or public non-financial bond issues (LLSV, 1997 *op cit* & 1998 *op cit*) and may exaggerate sophistication in bank-based systems. It may also confuse aspects of rights relating to the enforcement of collateral since (except in the US) a higher proportion of bank claims are secured than those of bondholders. Data weaknesses erode the view that the treatment of claims denotes effective markets. 'Financial development' often fails to distinguish between the availability of or growth in credit, and the sophistication of the system. Empirical problems in assessing comparative creditor rights suggest that the theory intrinsically uses a common law perspective. The scale of bank assets (LLSV, 1997 *op cit*) cannot alone signal sophistication in Asian markets (anticipated by Goldsmith, 1969 *op cit*) for bank cartels are widespread; large companies may borrow in all environments, at home or abroad (acknowledged by LLSV, 1997 *op cit*: 1148). Further, certain analyses aggregate debt and equity claims, despite differences in their respective rights and agency problems being associated mainly with equity claims.

[31] Compare Japan or Korea with India and Malaysia, for example.

institutional settings. Further, unsecured rights attaching to debt claims are different in character to the corporate governance issues linked to equity claims, where agency concerns are direct and permanent. In addition, empirical problems associated with assessing comparative creditor rights may suggest that the theory is advanced from a common law perspective, for example, as the choice of proxy variable cannot easily control for common law systems inherently encouraging commercial dispute at law. The role of debt is less easily examined by the law and finance school than rights and obligations associated with equity claims,[32] although they have been taken in aggregate to signify degrees of national investor protection. Last, law and finance theory studies that amalgamate in analysis the claims of banks and outstanding non-financial sector bondholders presume in so doing that debt creditors have collateral rights that are typically absent from contemporary debt issues.

From a pro-reform perspective, the scale of bank assets in an economy[33] cannot signal financial market sophistication.[34] Lending cartels are widespread; large companies may choose to raise funds offshore; indeed, large companies are able to obtain debt in all environments.[35] As an example, the most dynamic part of the contemporary Chinese corporate sector has been found to have no reliance on traditional external finance;[36] this sector accounts for the largest share of contemporary national growth. Chinese non-state enterprises are largely self-financing or have access to informal sources of external funding not visible in the domestic banking system, and the public sector is almost wholly responsible for China's outstanding domestic and foreign debt issues.

If constraints exist on general reform in the most pressing financial systems, how can public policy effectively promote market usage? The optimal approach may be to recognize that the issues cited in section 4 are objectives to which all concerned governments must strive, accepting that the overall legal framework within which they approach reform may not be conducive to specific changes, however necessary, or at worst may make repealing existing rules unreliable. The approach taken by Korea and Taiwan in promoting laws to allow securitization may be models for broader initiatives.[37] Public policy must also promote risk-averse reform rather than allow liberalization of the type seen often before 1997, which contributed to the scale

---

[32] Compared to equity, debt claims are less heterogeneous and complete associated data are less consistently available, either at national income accounting or transaction levels. Public (listed) issues are usually traded in ways that are wholly transparent only for professional counterparties; exchange listings for bonds usually entails only token reporting of buying, selling or prices.

[33] For example, measured against national income, corporate revenue and cashflow (LLSV 1997 *op cit*).

[34] Anticipated by Goldsmith (1969 *op cit*) prior to data becoming even partially available.

[35] Acknowledged by LLSV (1997 *op cit*) p1148.

[36] Allen *et al* (*op cit*).

[37] Recognizing that in Korea legislation is longer-established and has been put to far greater use.

of the Asian crisis and contagion. More radical proposals may require improvements in the regulation of issuers and investors, and the taxation of issuers, banks and investors. In helping to shape policy reform each will have corollary effects on the development of Asia's banking sectors, particularly in risk management and product innovation, in lessening the contagion effects of future crises of confidence, and in reducing the occurrence of moral hazard in inherently conflicted bank-dominated economies.

There is considerable value to a harmonized regional approach to reform despite inherited institutional obstacles that make common objectives achievable only in different ways.[38] First, joint efforts over an agreed period show purpose to market participants. Second, the sharing of intelligence and resources is valuable despite intrinsic national differences in systems and solutions. Third, collective action will support future intra-regional non-core currency investment and trading. The subsidiarity principle of the EU may be a guide for this purpose: the 1987 Single European Act sought to liberate capital movements among member states only by providing common minimum standards for implementation through national legislation to make the reform effective, which varied among those signing the Act. Mutual recognition became the second stage of reform on the basis of those common standards.

The success of all pro-market reform will be limited if governments fail to address a compendium of impediments that deter activity and penalize participants throughout East Asia, even in markets regarded as advanced. The measures listed in this chapter are examples of essential changes, without which activity will not develop to its potential, institutional investors will be constrained and forego opportunities, and the region will continue to lack the dependable risk averse macroeconomic characteristics of active, non-contiguous debt capital markets.

Successful markets are sustained by accommodative legal systems and bankruptcy procedures, and are regulated independently with clarity and fairness. No aspect of market issuance or trading distinguishes unreasonably between classes of issuer or investor. Systems providing for data gathering or dissemination, settlement, payments and custody are simple in use, coordinated and risk-minimizing, and the market is supported by a core of institutional buyers of term securities. No such markets properly exist within the EMEAP circle except in Australia and Japan.[39] Reform has seldom been proposed in a fashion sufficiently specific to provide reliable guidance for legislation or rule changes. One reason is the opacity of existing rules: for example, most Southeast Asian withholding tax regimes are unclear, whether by application, tariff, amelioration or the reliability of collection. Banks are favored in this respect over other financial institutions that have fewer chances to exploit fiscal loopholes or claim treaty exemptions made freely available to the

[38] This may be the greatest benefit of a successful EMEAP local currency bond fund.

[39] Hong Kong and Singapore approach international standards but suffer anomalies, restrictions and a lack of turnover in many instruments.

banking sector.[40] Withholding taxes can create long-term distortions in resource allocation; they generate substantial revenue in no review economy and would not do so in any purely domestic capital market even with substantially increased turnover.

Policy formation must address all significant institutional blockages and how they hinder activity, including the framework and application of regulatory guidelines for banks, pension and mutual funds, insurance companies and borrowers. It must lessen obstacles in relation to withholding taxes, differentials in the application of taxes and tax treaties, restrictions on settlement or custody, arbitrary differences in creditor status that constrain institutional investment, legal risks for investors, creditor claims and property rights generally and specifically in receivership or bankruptcy. It must also examine cultural factors that may cause obstructions relating to corporate governance, disclosure and ownership. Last, for structured finance techniques to become a significant aspect of capital market activity, each legal, regulatory, taxation and accounting system must provide simply for the true sale of financial claims and associated collateral assets, and minimize title uncertainties arising from set-off, the incidence and collection of duties, the giving of notices, permissible foreign ownership, and concerns as to partial enforcement or contract integrity. Restrictions and legal uncertainties that impede securities financing (mainly bond and note repurchase and bond lending) will lessen dealing and settlement liquidity for all investors and professional traders.[41] Regulators have often sought to dampen trading regarded as destabilizing but limitations on market techniques that are generally considered legitimate may heighten volatility by inducing unwarranted selling. Domestic and foreign investors are hindered in both long-term investment and day-to-day trading by the poor availability of local currency short and long-term hedging products and supportive credit risk procedures for risk netting and collateralization. Similarly, low risk instruments to house investors' short-term liquidity are available only in core currencies. Asian money market instruments may not exist, are taxed at source, or are artificially scarce, effectively held within a closed circle of central banks and their domestic banking acolytes. This lessens choice, efficiency and reduces price (interest rate) transparency.

Meeting these objectives requires three problems to be solved: intentional or implied restrictions, omissions of law or practice, and unnecessary inconsistencies within and among national bond markets. The elements in this matrix of market

---

[40] The interplay between withholding taxes and associated tax treaties may cause a net transfer to the offshore banking sector that distorts the pricing of credit risk and can stimulate short-term capital flows from offshore. For example, it was influential in the accumulation by many European banks never represented in Asia of relatively high levels of Korean and Southeast Asian risk assets prior to the 1997-98 crisis.

[41] Securities financing refers chiefly to repurchase arrangements, securities lending and to collteralization. Bond or note repurchases ('repos') are a trading tool most common in use in Asia by central banks influencing day-to-day liquidity and may be used by professional traders for the same motive. Investors lend or borrow securities to increase portfolio returns or facilitate short sales; securities lending thus affects settlement liquidity. Collateralization using debt securities is integral to managing counterparty credit risk in interest rate swaps and other medium-term OTC derivatives.

obstacles and omissions divide into four categories: legal, fiscal, regulatory and systemic, the aggregate effect of which is to prohibit or deter issuance and investment. Section 4 lists issues within this framework for which attention is most needed and especially where that need is common to several of the review countries. They apply to both government and corporate long-term debt markets, and to a majority of the review economies' domestic money markets. Some of these problems and disparities are widely known, especially in the sense that those risk-preferring organizations dealing in Asian bonds welcome credit and price discontinuities and the trading anomalies that they create: this is true in measure of the proprietary activities of banks and private funds. Until these questions are resolved general trading activity will be permanently constrained to the detriment of wider interests within the financial sector and notably in terms of regional crisis containment. The most damaging features are obstacles and omissions, since market discrepancies can often be reflected in the pricing of risk, but domestic irregularities relating to matters of law are also damaging and not fully compensated in ratings, risk or pricing.

If Asia accepts the need for change to promote market-based activity, its first step is to agree a precise intention and require national authorities to proceed with more complex mechanics. Section 4 shows specific topics for the region's policymakers to address. All the points shown in section 4 demand attention although their respective importance varies among the review economies. Many factors are manifested through a lack of investor confidence that is pervasive across markets. Significant commitments of time, resources and political determination will be needed for these measures to be addressed everywhere in the region. Active, integrated debt securities markets will not otherwise be seen in Asia.[42]

4. Market Impediments

This section identifies and describe market impediments of two basic types, problems relating to law and taxation and those arising from regulatory or systemic sources. In each case, the issues are divided into obstacles, omissions and discrepancies in a way intended to guide the formation of national or regional policy. Within these categories, specific matters are listed in groups, and followed by a series of comments or examples.

4.1. Legal and fiscal impediments

4.1.1. Obstacles

The most common and serious obstacles relate to the reliable transfer of rights, the rights of creditors in proceedings for bankruptcy or debtor restructuring, and taxes

[42] '[T]he evolution of the legal framework underlying efficient market economies was a long incremental process [...]. If the legal framework doesn't already exist or only partially exists it must be created.' North (1995: 11).

and duties penalizing reputable financial transaction structures. Legal clarity is important especially to safeguard the enforcement and transfer of legitimate claims.

- Qualified acceptance of ownership and property rights, and limitations of such rights in relation to investor classes.
- Barriers to the certain sale of property or financial assets.
- Limitations on collateral rights in bankruptcy or reorganization.
- Bars to non-portfolio foreign ownership and associated asset transfers.

Legal impediments of this kind are particularly corrosive for investor confidence. Such restrictions are typically related to enforcement of secured creditor claims, and impact the feasibility and efficiency of asset-backed transactions, and in matters relating to corporate bankruptcy. Circumventing such problems with complex (or synthetic) asset-backed transactions is not typically a sufficient solution.

These obstacles partly help explain the existence of substantial informal corporate credit markets (for example, in China, India and Thailand), where non-bank, non-institutional sources are prominent in supplying external finance, or when legal or regulatory limits leads to the disguising of claims in an officially acceptable form.

- Legal threats to the integrity of asset transfer.
- Debtor notice requirements affecting the reliability of transfer of creditor claims.
- Onerous registration requirements for the transfer of simple claims evidenced by notes or bonds.

How secure and actionable is the sale of financial assets, transfer of creditor claims or of associated collateral between unconnected parties? (It is common to adopt synthetic structures using credit derivatives if the sale of claims is suspect).

The effectiveness of the transfer by assignment of claims, including property rights and securities, may be affected by the circumstances under which notice is required to be given to a debtor. This has generally been the case in non-common law jurisdictions, including Japan, Indonesia, Korea, Philippines, Thailand and Taiwan. The practice has not yet been comprehensively developed in China, where the relevant civil procedures are relatively recently enacted.

In Japan, Korea and Taiwan, new securitization legislation has removed a general notification requirement towards pooled debtors in asset-backed securities but the alternatives have not become fully established. China's pilot measures to allow asset securitization, published in April 2005, are unclear as to detail but notice is likely to be demanded prior to the sale of assets into a securitization pool.

Incomplete or flawed notice may additionally result in the risk of borrower set-off in asset sales (usually requiring additional credit enhancement in asset-backed securities).

- Restrictive enforcement of local judgments.
- Limits to enforcement against public organizations; arbitrary extension of sovereign immunity.
- Enforcement of court-sanctioned restructurings.

- Inability of or refusal by courts to enforce applicable foreign commercial judgments.

Common law jurisdictions are generally more amenable to the creditor in these respects, but only Hong Kong and Singapore maintain consistent standards generally acceptable in international practice.

Enforcement problems are most known in China, Indonesia and Thailand, applying both to the enforcement of foreign judgments and the satisfying of domestic awards against foreign or foreign-owned claimants.

- Effect of restrictions on currency and capital movements on cross-border fundraising in local currency debt instruments. (See also regulatory restrictions on the use of proceeds, the effect of which represents a further curb to issuance, for example in Singapore or Thailand, section 5 *infra*).

Most comprehensive in China, India, Korea and Taiwan; of some significant effect also in Indonesia, Malaysia, Philippines and Thailand.

There may also be differences in the legal and practical incidence of exchange controls, that constitute highly effective bars to the later repatriation abroad of funds raised onshore.

Legal obstacles to issuance by designated foreign entities have generally been eased since 2000. This has enabled organizations such as the ADB and IFC to issue local currency debt in markets hitherto closed to foreign public debt issuance of any kind, including India, Malaysia and Taiwan. Other jurisdictions have stated their intention to do likewise, including China and Philippines. However, in principle transaction feasibility must not be equated to the opening of a market that lacks other substantive infrastructure, infra.

Thailand has allowed foreign-owned entities in Thailand to issue local currency instruments since the mid-90s but subject to restrictions on use of proceeds and an onerous and opaque approval process. The number of issues completed is correspondingly few, most originating in the banking and consumer finance sectors.

Capital and currency controls may also impact on the permissibility (either for banks or all counterparties) of domestic currency interest rate and currency swaps and related derivatives, which is a material deterrent to issuance.

- Currency and capital restrictions: impact of exchange controls on cross-border investors, covering inflows, reinvestment and capital repatriation.

This obstacle affects both cross-border investment and foreign ownership of domestic investment vehicles.

In both cases, restrictions are most comprehensive in China, India, Philippines, Korea and Taiwan, and until recently in Malaysia, especially in relation to foreign portfolio investors.

Note that the largest markets of those reviewed in this chapter, measured by absolute market capitalization and relative to national income, are also those with the most restrictive law and regulation on cross border investing, that is, China, India, Korea and Taiwan.

Foreign owned domestic investors are freely permitted to establish in Hong Kong, Indonesia, Malaysia and Singapore, but may not necessarily raise funds domestically. Elsewhere, severe restrictions exist on foreign participation and control of investment vehicles of any kind, notably in China, India, Korea, Philippines, Thailand and Taiwan.

Omissions

Questions of enforcement, the penalizing of transactions, notably corporate and asset-backed issues, issues of clarity in the application of taxes, duties and allowances.

- Inadequate or unreliable creditor rights in bankruptcy or reorganization, including failure of priority rights, unpredictable rules on foreclosure and status of collateral assets, and insecure priority rights after reorganizations.

These omissions may lead to the arbitrary dismissals of claims and are a hazard for creditors, particularly those that are foreign or foreign-owned. The issue now most concerns the perfection of structured finance techniques as a significant aspect of capital market activity, as in post-crisis Korea.

Legal issues include general problems and specific concerns hindering securitized transactions, notably the feasibility of true sales and creation of bankruptcy remote vehicles, risks of set-off, whether the sale of receivables is treated as secured lending to an asset originator, and matters of notice or registration that materially lessen the feasibility or simplicity of any such transaction.

National legal, regulatory, taxation and accounting systems must provide simply for the dependable and enforceable sale of financial claims and associated collateral assets, and minimize title uncertainties arising from set-off, the incidence and collection of duties, the giving of notices, permissible foreign ownership, and concerns as to partial enforcement or contract integrity. Recent enabling legislation to allow asset securitization in Indonesia, the Philippines, Thailand and Taiwan has failed completely so to do. China and India announced this year their intention to provide a legal framework for creating and trading securitized debt instruments.

- Absence of clarity and consistency in settlement, custody, funds netting, securities transfer and the treatment of securities in transit.

Legal risks for investors, creditor claims and property rights generally, and specifically in matters linked to receivership or bankruptcy. Counterparty risks and uncertainties can be introduced inadvertently into conventional securities dealing.

The lack of clarity in these questions typically raises actual or perceived transaction costs for investors and thus deters cross-border participation.

- Failure to recognize trusts or equivalent insubstantive onshore or offshore entities.

This presents a hindrance to fund managers and to the reliability of asset-backed issues. Recent legislation in Korea, Philippines and Taiwan addresses the problem in specific (though important) contexts, rather than generally.

- Recognition of ISDA master agreements and definitions; permissible set-off and netting in swap and derivatives contracts.
- Custodian recognition and market admissibility of ISMA general master repurchase agreements and ISDA general collateral agreements.

The status of these accords in relation to private contracts is unclear for domestic currency obligations governed by national law except generally in Hong Kong and Singapore, even where acknowledged or adopted by local financial industry associations, such as in Korea and Thailand. This has created uncertainty, for example, with regard to interest rate determination, especially in Southeast Asia.

- Clarity in the imposition of taxes on asset sales or the transfer of creditor claims.
- Absence of commitments to tax neutrality for securities.
- Homogeneous treatment of interest, interest deductions and accruals.

National authorities may from time-to-time impose restrictions or penalties on investment activity or payments other than sanctioned transparently by the competent regulatory authority.

4.1.3. Disparities

These are common in the treatment of creditor classes, between domestic and foreign claims, and in differences in the taxation or duty treatment of classes of creditor, obligor or financial institutions, or between local and foreign parties.

- Impact of withholding taxes; assessment rates, and differentials in the application of taxes and tax treaties.
- Withholding tax complexity in assessment, application, collection or exemption.
- Taxes imposed, applied or lifted by fiat without grandfathering, as to instruments, issuers or investor classes.
- Duties, taxes and penalties imposed upon the transfer of financial assets and claims, and associated collateral rights.
- Incidence of stamp duties and other ad valorem taxes.

Withholding tax affects most Asian debt markets, either for cross-border investors or for all. It complicates conventional dealing and investment practice, and raises or obscures transaction costs. Most withholding tax regimes are unclear, whether by application, tariff, amelioration or the reliability of collection: this applies to China,

India, Korea, Philippines and Taiwan, while in Indonesia, Malaysia and Thailand the effect is usually a simple direct cost.

Tax reform requires abolition or clarification by law, rather than by directive, as in recent exemptions decreed in Malaysia and Thailand. Even where tax rates are low or apply only to certain classes of security, any lack of clarity as to the incidence of withholdings deters investors, as will complexity associated with paying or (where feasible under double taxation treaties) recovering tax due. Only Hong Kong and Singapore are generally free of withholding taxes (but in each case gross income accruing on certain securities to domestic investors can be subject to general taxation).

Capital account restrictions may complicate the process of repatriating overseas interest income and capital gains. Most jurisdictions examined in this section require withholding tax to be paid before repatriation while others require prior approval.

- Withholding taxes and other imposts applied asymmetrically to investor groups, domiciles, instruments, coupon types or issuers.
- Securities financing by repurchase or lending treated as an outright sale for tax purposes.
- Taxes and impositions that recur within single transactions, for example, in the sale of assets or claims between special purpose vehicles or trusts used in asset-backed transactions.

How withholding taxes apply to bonds and money market instruments: do these and other taxes differ in their impact on types of instrument or classes of investor, domestic or foreign? Are banks (domestic or offshore) or foreign investors able to ameliorate or compensate for the incidence of withholding taxes? Is the application of allowances under double taxation treaties inconsistent? Do such treaties have non-universal applications, for example in effecting concessions for banks vis-à-vis other financial institutions, in granting allowances for write-offs, interest deductions, access to double taxation treaties, and the use of offshore funding centers.

Banks are typically favored in this respect over other financial institutions that are less able or prevented from exploiting fiscal loopholes or claiming treaty exemptions made freely available to the banking sector.

Withholding taxes can create long-term distortions in resource allocation, and generate substantial revenue in none of the review jurisdictions.

Taxes and duties payable on transfer may threaten the integrity of conventional and structured transactions, including those for impaired assets. This has been problematic for certain classes of security in India, Indonesia, Korea, Philippines and Taiwan. The position in China is currently uncertain.

- Arbitrary differences in creditor status that constrain institutional investment.
- Creditor status: uncertainty as to whether courts will enforce or dissolve private contractual creditor priorities.
- Uncertainty in priority of claim and secure title.

Path dependence exists in the institutional development of all markets, for example, in the way that well-established national provident funds may be preferred in terms of market access and rights in bankruptcy, or in the treatment of property rights affecting the collateral associated with asset-backed securities. Such practices may introduce moral hazards to the market, for example, in that indigenous investors may perceive no difference in the status of differing government sector instruments or of privileged 'official' investors.

Rights in law created in recent years to facilitate national privatization sales may not be fully appropriate for reliable asset-backed issues, nor umbrella securitization legislation for other similar applications involving the use of trusts or the transfer of financial assets.

- Rules on usury (excluding systemic prohibitions, for example, under Islamic legal structures).

These apply especially to penalties, and to new issue interest rate, total return or coupon restrictions, and where evident will constitute a distortion or ban to commercial issuance.

- Imprecision or conflicts of law.

In relation to disputes as to cross-border settlement and to securities custody, these cause problems of uncertain priority and title, and impact upon transaction costs. They can exist in all cases where settlement and custody procedures are not consolidated into a single or unified system. The Hague Convention No. 36, currently under ratification, on rights relating to securities held in custody has yet to be adopted by Indonesia, Philippines, Thailand and Taiwan.

4.2. Regulatory & Systemic Impediments

4.2.1. Obstacles

Most damaging are prohibitions on local currency investment, usually by non-bank financial institutions. Issuer restrictions hope to block immediate or subsequent capital outflows. These restrictions impact inequitably upon the integrity of freely-entered private contracts.

- Prohibitions and constraints on issuers, including non-guaranteed, corporate and foreign entities.
- Regulatory restrictions on issuance and external constraints on investor activity.

Certain local markets require corporate debt issues to carry bank guarantees, irrespective of the primary obligor's credit risk. The practice is usually induced by the state sector or by monopolistic banks and is unfavorable to capital market development.

Each jurisdiction's objective would best be to create a consistent framework for the application of regulatory guidelines for investment and trading in securities by banks, pension and mutual funds, insurance companies, including as few discretionary limits as possible and common standards for portfolio accounting.

- Initial and ongoing disclosure requirements.

In domestic markets where foreign issues are generally permitted (Hong Kong, Japan, Korea, Singapore and Thailand), compliance with listing requirements for issuer disclosure may be unreasonably difficult, even where new issues would not be directed (or made available easily) to retail investors.

Hong Kong has begun to address this problem by implementing proposals for shelf disclosure by debt issuers. Korea's domestic Arirang market for foreign issuers was created with the 1999 Foreign Exchange Market Liberalization Act but involves unusually heavy documentation and disclosure demands more associated with primary share listings, that together deter most foreign potential borrowers. The market is therefore small, and used almost exclusively by foreign affiliates of Korean organizations. This example represents confusion as to the role of stock exchanges in debt issues that extends on a lesser scale to China, Indonesia, Singapore and Thailand.

- Restrictions on the borrower's use of proceeds.

These exist in varying forms and for reasons with different roots in Indonesia, Malaysia, Philippines, Singapore, Thailand and Taiwan, and act as a constraint on new issues by foreign borrowers and to the liquidity of local currency interest rate and currency swap markets.

- Investor constraints on permissible asset holdings and risks.
- Limits on access to money market, short-term or other eligible instruments.

Together with inconsistent rules on mark-to-market accounting, these external constraints reduce the choices available to non-bank investors.

A related concern for liquidity in government securities markets (and in some cases for other instruments) arises from their being concentrated in the domestic banking sector as part of an overt or indirect regulatory regime. Asia's money markets are dominated by government notes but lack the liquidity that established markets offer to non-bank participants. Closed relationships in the money market between banks and governments can be a distortion and potential moral hazard. Likewise, an irregular or fractured supply of government issues may not meet both liquidity regulatory requirements and institutional investor demand.

- Restrictions on settlement or custody.

This includes custody controls, directed settlement, and rules on sub-custody for foreign investors. The cost of appointing a local custodian can make cross-border investments unattractive.

- Ease of establishing and operating foreign owned investment funds.

Foreign-owned investment vehicles are permitted only with varying degrees of difficulty, ignoring conventional regulatory procedures associated with the management of third party funds. The burden is extensive in China, India, Korea and Taiwan, and notable in Malaysia, Philippines and Thailand, and includes restrictions that limit or prohibit investing and trading in certain instruments, and restrictions on cross-border capital movements. Foreign-owned investors face liquidity constraints and impediments to dealing that worsen ongoing and pre-entry transaction costs.

- Regulatory responsibilities divided among competing authorities.
- Unpredictable or political reviews of judicial decisions.

Regulation should be transparently free from political influence and conflicts among competing national authorities, with the aim of maintaining agreed standards for market practice.

Changing rules by fiat may deny certainty or transparency to both local or foreign participants over retroactive coverage for the withdrawal of any concession. For example, in the last 12 months Thailand has waived withholding taxes on certain government bond issues solely by finance ministry decree.

- Prohibitions on securities lending and short-sales.

Restrictions and legal uncertainties that prevent securities financing will lessen dealing and settlement liquidity for all investors and professional traders. However, securities financing may improve settlement liquidity but lessen overall market liquidity and price transparency. Markets must operate openly for all investors to benefit from such techniques.

Securities financing consists of repurchase arrangements, securities lending and collateralization. Bond or note repurchases (repos) are a trading tool most commonly used in Asia by central banks to influence day-to-day liquidity, and by banks and other investors for individual motives. Investors lend or borrow securities to increase returns or facilitate short sales; securities lending thus affects settlement liquidity. In established markets, collateralization using debt securities is integral to managing counterparty credit risk in interest rate swaps and other medium-term OTC derivatives.

- General illiquidity

The nominal amounts of instruments (particularly government notes and bonds) available to investors in each national secondary market without a "large price impact" is estimated by HSBC to range from under US$15m equivalent in China, Indonesia, the Philippines and Thailand to over US$130m in Hong Kong and Singapore and at least US$860m in Korea. However, in each case these estimates represent a range of purchases drawn from outstanding issues of over 12 months remaining maturity, so that the non-disruptive amounts available in any single issue, whether or not considered a benchmark, would thus be far less, and in some cases trivial.

- Inequitable qualifications or restrictions on dealing.

Regulators may wish to dampen trading regarded as destabilizing but limitations on market techniques that are generally considered legitimate may heighten volatility by inducing unwarranted selling. This would be the case with imposed minimum effective holding periods.

4.2.2. Omissions

Markets for risks or instruments that are closed to classes of investor, either deliberately or by default. These omissions reflect action or inaction by central banks, market and investor group regulators, listing authorities or accounting regulators.

- Absence of declared or consistent benchmark issuance programs.

Government issuance must have predictability. Asian investors and intermediaries are accustomed to impromptu withdrawals of auctions or sales of notes or bonds (a criticism similar to that offered to those supranational organizations that fail to contribute to liquidity with regular issues, infra). Flawed auction mechanisms lead to a weakened pricing formula, poor visibility and inconsistent interest rates.

Given that usable local currency synthetic benchmark yield curves are currently infeasible throughout the region, if public borrowing is inadequate to sustain a government bond market that is liquid throughout the term structure then attempts must be made to overhaul and consolidate national debt management, consider overfunding as a market-supportive strategy (as used at intervals in Singapore), and promote the use of asset-backed structured transactions to assist meeting investor needs (as in Korea, and in the future in China). The result otherwise is for local market practice to become eccentric to the exclusion of foreign interests: for example, the use as pricing references of non-contiguous interest rates or bond yields. The most extreme cases involve long-term bonds priced by reference to short-term interest rates, which may themselves not be freely determined.

- Transparent and declared objectives for monetary policy.
- Coordination between national debt management strategy and monetary policy.

This concerns the scale of domestic markets in terms of available debt instruments. How freely do such securities trade and with what degree of liquidity? Measures of turnover may be unreliable in unsophisticated markets but outstanding capitalization is not the sole criterion by which a market is assessed. Low risk instruments to house investors' short-term liquidity are available only in core major currencies. Asian money market instruments may not exist, are taxed at source, or are artificially scarce, effectively held within a closed circle of central banks and their domestic banking counterparties.

National governments need to assess their debt management techniques so as to lessen discrimination among market participants, and avoid confusion with similar money market instruments being issued by different arms of the state.

- Availability and price transparency of interest rate swaps and similar hedging instruments.

Domestic and foreign investors are hindered in both long-term investment and day-to-day trading by the poor availability of local currency short and long-term OTC or exchange traded derivatives and supportive credit risk procedures for risk netting and collateralization.

- Poor settlement practices and associated risks in settlement.

This chiefly involves a lack of book entry operations, and real-time settlement and reporting. Systems providing for data gathering or dissemination, settlement, payments and custody must be unified, simple in use, coordinated and risk-minimizing. The optimal system has centralized reporting of bond prices and trades, and is built upon consistent use of centralized arrangements for settlement.

Domestic and foreign investors need an optimal clear, unitary settlement model using delivery against payment and for custody. Dealing and settlement processes must differ as little as possible for classes of debt instruments.

- Lack of regulatory oversight.

Host authorities are ideally subject to observation and scrutiny by an independent advisory body, but have central day-to-day oversight of issuance, trading, securities settlement and custody.

- Oversight of credit rating agencies.

National regulators will in future need to consider the appraisal and credit monitoring standards and practices of local credit rating agencies if their findings become relevant to ratings based risk asset weightings under the Basel II capital accord.

- Quality and reliability of mandatory issuer disclosure requirements.

Including inadequate accounting standards compared to IOSCO recommendations for best practice in accordance with IAAP or IFRS.

Weak issuer reporting and disclosure and weak oversight are common. Listing rules and prospectus requirements need to be framed appropriately for debt issues, and where advantageous to allow for issuance programs or "shelf" issues. These remarks should not be taken to suggest dilution of requirements for issues directed towards retail investors. Credit rating requirements linking new issues to regulations affecting investors need to be made transparent, with domestic credit rating organizations encouraged to adopt and disclose standard methodology.

- Incomplete practice framework for derivatives.

Regulators commonly prohibit some or all domestic market participants from using OTC derivatives in their home currency, despite their being widely available offshore. As a result, there is a sizeable lightly regulated market in offshore mainly interest rate products based upon non-deliverable forward foreign exchange contracts, intended to mimic domestic instruments that are non-existent, illiquid or unavailable to foreign counterparties.

Disparities

Differences in the regulatory treatment of conventional investor activity are a weakening source of market distortion. The resulting lack of clarity leads to a sacrifice in investor participation.

- Settlement and custody anomalies.

The most common examples are elective use of central depositaries for settlement or custody and elective physical delivery of bond certificates. In some cases delivery against payment is applied inconsistently across instruments or classes of issuer.

The issuer's domicile may affect transaction conditions, including fiscal treatment, eligibility as collateral for repurchase agreements or permissibility in regulatory reserves.

The aim in each market must be to offer clarity and reliability transparency to all users, the centralization and unification of settlement procedure, no variations in settlement days, reliable delivery against payment and sound links in transfer, custody and payment.

- Preferential treatment of foreign and other issuers.

Since the early 1990s, initially in Hong Kong, certain supranational borrowers have been granted access to national markets, often in ways that compare favorably in some manner with other feasible domestic issuers. Such issues are now known in Hong Kong, India, Indonesia, Korea, Malaysia, Singapore, Thailand and Taiwan, and have often been seen as developmental and market-supportive in nature. However, except in Hong Kong at intervals, issuance has never been consistent, and is therefore not necessarily replicable by other borrowers, domestic or foreign. Such issues may be welcome to investors due to comparatively high credit ratings but their developmental value has been exaggerated. This problem is compounded by issue infrequency, and by the tendency of most supranational issuers to seek in any single new issue to equalize their average and marginal borrowing costs in US dollar Libor terms. Unless these issues increase in frequency to become substitutes for liquid risk-free debt programs, they may act as cushions against legal and market reform. The contrary argument, that single inaugural transactions serve to "open" markets to new issuers, is suspect.

In a similar example of reform in late 2004, Malaysia ended certain preferential regulatory treatments for its residential mortgage financing vehicle Cagamas so as to encourage more transparent market pricing and widen investor access to the agency's issues.

5. Policy Implications

For Asia's markets to flourish and deliver their full value (given that these are agreed policy goals among national governments and within regional groupings such as the Association of South East Asian Nations, Asia-Pacific Economic Cooperation forum and elsewhere) governments must stimulate usage, not only with specific reforms, fiscal, regulatory or legal, but with suasion, innovation and example, especially in their debt management and approach to funding.

References

Akamatsu, N., 2004, Cross-border settlement and regional bond market integration, World Bank Financial Sector Operations & Policy Department, mimeo.

Akhtar, S., 2001, Institutional investors in Asia, *Financial Trends*, October. Paris, OECD.

Allen, F. Qian Jun & Qian Meijun, 2002, Law, finance and economic growth in China, Wharton School working paper; *Journal of Financial Economics*, 2005.

Asami, T. & J. Mori, 2001, Regional cooperation in developing bond markets: harmonization and standardization of the regions bond markets, Institute for International Monetary Affairs, Japan.

Asian Development Bank, 2003, Harmonization of bond markets: rules and regulations, background study for APEC Finance Ministers Process.

Aziz, J. & C. Duenwald, 2002, Growth-financial intermediation nexus in China, IMF working paper 02/194.

Benink, H. & S. Ghon Rhee, 2004, Why Asia must think global for financial markets, *Financial Times*, August 6.

Berkowitz, D., J. Moenius & K. Pistor, 2004, Legal institutions and international trade flows 26 *Mich. J. Intl L.* 163.

Bestani, R. & A. Sagar, 2004, The local currency financing revolution, *Asia Pacific Review of Project Finance International*.

Burger, J. & F. Warnock, 2004, Foreign participation in local currency bond markets, Federal Reserve System International Finance discussion paper No. 794.

Eichengreen, B. & P. Luengnaruemitchai, 2004, Why doesn't Asia have bigger bond markets?, National Bureau of Economic Research working paper 10576.

Goldsmith, R., 1969, *Financial Structure and Development*, New Haven, CT: Yale University Press.

Gerschenkron, A., 1962, *Economic Backwardness in Historical Perspective: A Book of Essays*, Cambridge, MA: Harvard University Press,.

Hoschka, T., 2005a, Local currency financing: next frontier for MDBs?, Asian Development Bank ERD working paper No. 68.

Hoschka, T., 2005b, Developing the market for local currency bonds by foreign issuers: lessons from Asia, Asian Development Bank ERD working paper No. 63.

Jiang, G. & R. McCauley, 2004, Asian local currency bond markets, *BIS Quarterly Review*, June, 67-79.

King, M, 2001, Who triggered the Asian financial crisis? *Review of International Political Economy* 8(3), 438-467.
La Porta, R., F. López-de-Silanes, A. Shleifer & R. Vishny, 1997, Legal determinants of external finance, *Journal of Finance* 52(3), 1131-1150.
La Porta, R. F. López-de-Silanes, A. Shleifer & R. Vishny, 1998, Law and finance, *Journal of Political Economy*, 106(6), 1113-1155.
Lejot, P. & D. Arner, 2004, Well-intentioned Asian bond fund wont work, 23 *International Financial Law Review* 23(9).
Lejot, P., D. Arner & Liu Qiao, 2004, Making markets: reforms to strengthen Asia's debt capital markets, Hong Kong Institute For Monetary Research Working Paper 13.
Lejot, P., D. Arner, Liu Qiao, M. Chan, and M. Mays, 2003, Asia's debt capital Markets appraisal and agenda for policy reform, Hong Kong Institute for Monetary Research working paper 19.
Levine, R., 2002, Bank-based or market-based financial systems: which is better?, National Bureau Of Economic Research working paper 9138.
Levine, R., 1997, Financial Development & Economic Growth: Views & Agenda, *Journal of Economic Literature* 35(2) 688-726.
Lynch, D., 2000, *Asian Bond Markets*, International Banks and Securities Association of Australia.
Ma G., C. Ho & R McCauley, 2004, The markets for non-deliverable forwards in Asian currencies, *BIS Quarterly Review*, June, 81-94.
McCauley, R., 2003, Unifying government bond markets in East Asia, *BIS Quarterly Review*, December, 89-98.
Mohanty, M., 2002, Improving liquidity in government bond markets: what can be done? BIS papers 11.
Rhee, S. Ghon, 2004a, Why Asian Bond markets initiative may fizzle out?, *Financial News*, December 19,.
Rhee, S. Ghon, 2004b, The structure and characteristics of East Asian bond markets, in *Developing Asian Bond Markets*, edited by T. Ito and Y.C. Park, Canberra: Asia Pacific Press, 112-128.
Rhee, S. Ghon, 2000, *Rising to Asia's Challenge: Enhanced Role of Capital Markets, in Rising to the Challenge in Asia: A Study of Financial Markets*, Vol. 1 Manila: Asian Development Bank, 2000, 107-174.
Steil, B., 2002, *Building a Transatlantic Securities Market*, Zurich: International Capital Markets Association.
Takeuchi, A., 2004, Identifying impediments to cross-border bond investment and issuance in Asian countries, Bank of Japan Working Paper.
World Bank, 2005, *Global Development Finance*, Washington, DC.

Chapter 8

Policy Concerns and the Value of Regional Markets

Paul Lejot[1], Douglas Arner[1] and Qiao Liu[2]

[1]*Asian Institute of International Financial Law and Faculty of Law, University of Hong Kong;* [2]*Faculty of Business and Economics, University of Hong Kong*

1. Introduction

This chapter examines progress towards market reform made since 1998 in Asia's many official regional economic policy forums, considers the most tangible results of those deliberations, and puts forward a proposal for a new, deliberate harmonized approach to create a regional market for bonds and notes. If implemented, the plan would represent a considerable and workable success for intergovernmental groupings, whose results may not always appear substantive to the financial sector spectator.

The central plan presented here is for a collaborative pan-Asian public market for local and major currency bond issues, monitored by confederal regional regulation in an established financial centre. Its intentions would be to encourage overall activity and hasten the reforms needed in each domestic market, especially the removal of unreasonable legal and regulatory impediments of the kinds identified in chapters 6 and 7.

The governing aims are to promote the supply of new issues and widen the scope and nature of participation in the region's existing markets. While this may have become an objective shared by the region's policy officials, it is unclear that it will be achieved by the central bank sponsored local currency Asian Bond Fund (ABF2), established in 2005 and the most tangible result of post-crisis joint governmental efforts. Regardless of investment objectives, ABF2 will be constrained in its currency composition and freedom to invest without changes of detail at national levels for which this proposal would give momentum. The operational obstacles that ABF2 faces are discussed at the end of the chapter.

The proposal described here seeks to balance the optimal with a recognition of national parochial interests and the inevitable caution of government in passing authority to forces of which it may be suspicious. Most critically, the proposal offers a substantive means to stimulate bond market reform and activity in a way that recognizes the limitations of prevailing regional politico-economic structures.

It also offers a considered means to introduce prescriptive measures. For example, Taiwan's 2002 securitization law was enacted hastily and is thought by practitioners to be limited in use; similar questions exist of recently enacted Philippines and Thai legislation. The simplest means to remove widespread legal, regulatory or systemic obstacles to development of the kind itemized in chapters 6 and 7 would be to sanction a collaborative offshore market for which from inception no impediment can exist.

The result has already been seen elsewhere:

> 'The rapid emergence in the 1960s of a worldwide Eurocurrency market [...] resulted from the peculiarly stringent and detailed official regulations governing residents operating with their own national currencies.'[1]

While this proposal favors open price mechanisms in an institutional sense, it should not be taken as suggesting that there is intrinsic superiority in either bank or market-centered systems, nor that the means by which financial sector reform is introduced can be universal.[2]

2. Reforming Asia's Financial Policy

Asia's need for market reforms produces substantial tasks for national and multilateral policy. Past regional initiatives on financial issues have lacked practicality or foundered when confronted by opposing interests, for example in recent years, from China, Japan or the United States, leading to doubts as to the competence in financial policy of a multiplicity of regional bodies.[3]

2.1. Policy forums

As at 30 June 2005 the inter-governmental bodies discussed in this chapter were made up in the following ways. Figure 8-1 shows the loci in which these five bodies exist (excluding APEC's western hemisphere members).

- The Association of Southeast Asian Nations (ASEAN) was formed by Indonesia, Malaysia, Philippines, Singapore and Thailand, and now also includes Brunei, Cambodia, Laos, Myanmar and Vietnam.

---

[1] McKinnon (1977: 2).

[2] Gerschenkron (1962) and Goldsmith (1969) were first to distinguish in detail the two types of systems. Levine (1997, 2002) notably points to the absence of an 'optimum' framework that would suggest either system is inherently favored.

[3] Bisley (2003) and Ravenhill (2000) are typical skeptics. Others see policy success in the creation of bilateral central bank repurchase and credit lines, especially their expansion after 2000 (Thomas 2004).

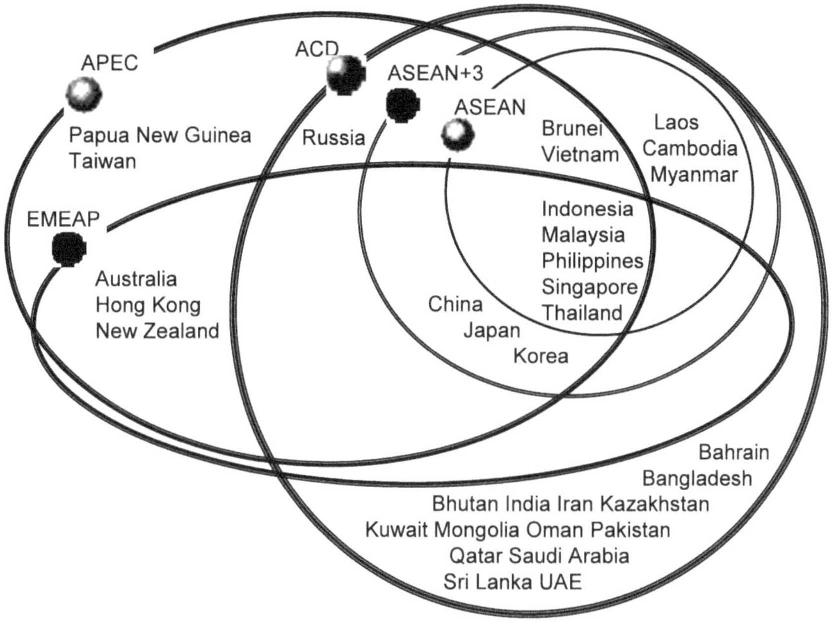

***Figure 8-1.* Asia's intergovernmental groups**

- ASEAN+3 is an ASEAN cousin that adds China, Japan and Korea.
- The Asian Cooperation Dialogue (ACD) is ASEAN+3 together with India and fourteen other states east and south of the Caucasus.
- EMEAP is the Executives' Meeting of East Asia-Pacific central banks comprising ASEAN's founding five members and Australia, China, Hong Kong, Japan, Korea and New Zealand.
- The Asia-Pacific Economic Cooperation (APEC) forum's west Pacific members are EMEAP plus Papua New Guinea and Taiwan. APEC also includes Russia and six members from the Americas.

2.1.1. Financial sector interests

ASEAN is the oldest group of the five, dating from 1967; APEC was first constituted 22 years later. All are discussion forums that since inception have functioned consensually and with particular respect for national authority. ASEAN strongly honors that aspect of its deliberations: three of its six founding treaty principles refer directly to mutual respect for national independence, sovereignty and disdain for external interference in each member's internal affairs.[4]

While ASEAN cites finance as one of its thirteen identified fields of economic cooperation it devotes no permanent shared resources to the sector. It is thus

[4] Treaty of Amity and Cooperation in Southeast Asia (ASEAN, 1976).

unsurprising that the five groups boast only two institutional examples of collective financial policymaking, each being arrangements implemented separately by national governments and functioning bilaterally among member states.[5] The first created is a web of bilateral credit lines for short-term foreign exchange swaps and repurchases among ASEAN+3 central banks; the second is ABF2, brought into being by parallel national decision and carrying an EMEAP stamp.

2.1.2. Collaborative credit lines

ASEAN+3's network of sovereign[6] bilateral credit lines has two roots: first, collaborative foreign exchange swap lines set up by ASEAN's original five members; and second, a series of securities repurchase (repo) lines begun among EMEAP members as a precautionary reaction to the 1994 collapse of the Mexican peso.[7] These origins show an important distinction of purpose; the first was wholly political but the second intended to assist economic policy.

ASEAN's arrangement began in 1977 as a modest US$100 million set of foreign exchange swap lines among ASEAN's original states. These facilitated simultaneous spot sale and forward purchases of local currency for US dollars among the five central banks to assist a member in need of temporary external liquidity. Swap lines are a form of credit that become loans in the event of non-payment at maturity. Conforming with commercial practice, swaps could extend for up to 90 days and be renewable once by consent in the absence of competing demand.

The spirit of the arrangement had been foreshadowed in fictional France, the group agreeing to pool commitments equally for any line usage.[8] The scheme was extended, expanded, and may have been utilized once each by Indonesia, Malaysia, Philippines and Thailand between 1979 and 1981, and once more by the Philippines in 1992, in all cases for modest amounts.[9] The arrangement's conditions for usage and limited size account for its failure to be used at any time in 1997 when all the members' external positions were put most under pressure.

Alongside ASEAN's swap arrangements came a series of bilateral repurchase lines among EMEAP members, Japan being noticeably active in their creation, the first introduced in late 1995. These allowed a participant to raise major currency

---

[5] In contrast, European Union policy initiatives are first made substantive by a regional body and followed where necessary with national legislation.

[6] Counterparty risk is taken here as sovereign. Whether the primary counterparty is a central bank or finance ministry is national practice that is not of concern in this discussion.

[7] Reported in Moreno (1997a).

[8] '"And now, gentlemen," said d'Artgagnan, … "All for one—one for all, this is our motto is it not?"' Alexandre Dumas, *The Three Musketeers*, Ch IX.

[9] Randall (2002: 14) citing unnamed Thai sources. A United Nations Economic and Social Commission for Asia and the Pacific (UNESCAP) report claims that the arrangement 'has been extensively used' but this is unsupported and implausible (Wang and Andersen, 2003: 90).

liquidity for intervention (or other) purposes by discounting for a set period with its counterparty high-grade securities held as international reserves, most commonly US Treasury bills or notes.

Market practice knows several contexts in which repurchase lines are prolific, involving both the commercial sector and central banks, but the closest analogy to the EMEAP lines is in the conduct of open market operations by central banks seeking to influence domestic liquidity, including cases where a central bank becomes lender of last resort for a regulated institution, taking collateral in the form of prescribed securities. In the case of the EMEAP lines, usage has of itself no consequence for domestic credit expansion.

Figure 8-2 shows the configuration of disclosed repurchase lines established in 1995-97, prompted by Mexico's prior experience and concerns of contagion. The amounts of these lines was made public only for those involving Japan, each of US$1.0 billion.[10]

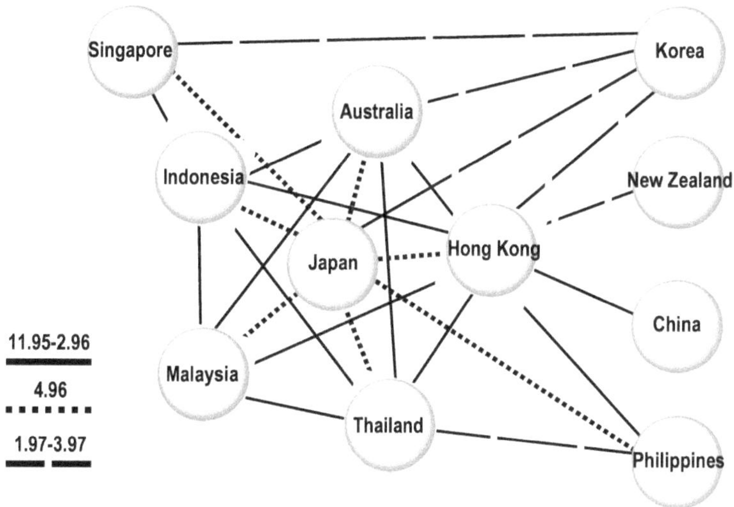

Figure 8-2. **Disclosed pre-CMI bilateral repurchase lines showing dates of establishment**

Thus two sets of lines, excluding those involving Australia and New Zealand, evolved into more elaborate agreements foreshadowed in the ASEAN+3 2000 Chiang Mai Initiative (CMI).[11] Chiang Mai provided for ASEAN (now a group of ten) to raise its total swap arrangement to US$1.0 billion (later US$2.0 billion) and for China, Japan and Korea each to pledge to maintain bilateral credit lines for foreign currency swaps and securities repurchases among themselves and with each

[10] Moreno (*op cit* 1997a).

[11] First described in a ministerial press release (ASEAN+3 2000), CMI is subject to no public agreement to which all its adherents are party.

ASEAN member (although the relatively small Indochina economies are currently omitted in implementation).

The results of Chiang Mai show purpose but confused objectives.[12] First, most of the 16 bilateral lines established by China, Japan and Korea[13] entail swap conditions that make International Monetary Fund (IMF) sanction mandatory for most usage, not merely satisfaction of independent conditions identical to those of the IMF.[14] It would have been impossible for Chiang Mai's expanded lines to have been drawn in the Asian crisis prior to an applicant having agreed terms for IMF support, by which time the need would have become redundant.

In a similar instance, Thailand may have used in mid-1997 a precursor swap line with Japan.[15] If true, doing so failed to trouble markets intent on selling the baht: drawing from a finite source could only encourage the seller. Nonetheless, the Thai government's Nukul Commission enquiry later found that the Bank of Thailand made intense use of foreign exchange swaps to support the baht in the first half of 1997, but these were not conducted under ASEAN arrangements.[16]

Separately, a report prepared for Japan's finance ministry noted that Thailand sought but was refused 'support' from Tokyo prior to seeking IMF assistance on 28 July.[17] This is attributed to Thailand having failed to substantiate the request with economic data, but the core reason for the refusal was Tokyo's need to invoke IMF conditions. The truth of the story may be that a request refused became an apocryphal drawing. Japan led and dominated financial support immediately upon the IMF agreeing to aid Thailand.

Second, although the post-Chiang Mai lines provided by China, Japan and Korea allow for securities repurchases, this is now seen by all participants as outmoded practice and given little attention compared to the swap provisions.

The largest non-cash component of EMEAP international reserves is held in US treasury bills, notes or bonds, and thus sourced from the world's archetypal broad and deep bond market. Critics suggest that the liquidity available through repurchases could not compete with that deep, broad source.[18] More attention is now paid to swap operations and availability, both by participants and commentators.

---

[12] This view has support in official circles in China and Japan (see Institute for International Monetary Affairs, 2004).

[13] Totaling US$39.5 billion equivalent as at end-April 2005 (source: finance ministry of Japan at http://www.mof.go.jp/english/if/if.htm).

[14] In May 2005 ASEAN+3 raised the portion available unconditionally under post-CMI swap lines from 10 to 20 per cent of the total, 'in order to better cope with sudden market irregularities' but stressed this represented no contradiction that 'the international financial arrangements and other disciplined conditions would be firmly maintained' (ASEAN+3 2005).

[15] *The Economist*, London, 10 May 2001 (cited by Randall, *op cit*).

[16] *The Business Times*, Bangkok (5 May 1998 7); Traisorat (2000 371-6); Moreno (1997b).

[17] Institute for International Monetary Affairs (2003: 4).

[18] For example, Randall (*ibid*: 22).

However, this stance neglects shocks similar to October 1997 that were not focused on Asia, when in the week following sizeable stock market losses on Wall Street and elsewhere the US treasury market was consistently highly illiquid and frequently closed to non-domestic participants or those at home other than primary dealers. Infra-Asian repurchase lines could have insulatory value in such circumstances, even if the region's international reserves are concentrated in US dollar assets. Prevailing conditions have changed markedly given the substantial accumulation of international reserves since 2000 in ASEAN+3 vaults. That the 1995-97 repurchase lines were barely used, if at all, immediately before the crisis was due to a scarcity of collateral or to the participants simultaneously suffering similar problems not amenable to mutual resolution.

Chiang Mai's outcome is said by ASEAN+3 to be regional but its facilities are entirely bilateral in creation and use, despite involving a gesture to harmonization and being prompted by the Asian crisis. In ASEAN's words:

> 'ASEAN shall adopt a more proactive role at various international and regional fora to ensure that its interests and priorities are given due consideration in any proposal to reform the international financial architecture.'[19]

What now stands in the name of ASEAN+3 following the Chiang Mai Initiative are bilateral arrangements customary among developed economies. Market practitioners see the post-2000 Chiang Mai swap line framework as inconsequential, however politically important. History suggests using central bank swap lines other than to smooth prevailing conditions does no more than delay currency selling pressure and may give confidence to the seller. It may thus be ironic that Chiang Mai's cooption of IMF conditions make credit line usage unlikely, as some participants perhaps intended, and that the older repurchase lines are neglected, despite their true crisis usefulness.

2.1.3. Pooling of reserve assets

EMEAP's central banks have recently implemented ideas first mooted in APEC by Hong Kong and Thailand. They took substance in 2003 as the Asian Bond Fund, initially a US$1.0 billion pooling of core currency bonds issued and held by its Asian member governments (ABF1). This was an apportionment of international reserves as a prefatory alternative to investing in securities issued by advanced economies. The project has 'technical assistance' from the Bank for International Settlements, politically important given the absence of regional or shared infrastructure in Asia, but the fund is entirely passive in operation.

The project's ceiling is modest; representing less than 0.1 per cent of the subscribers' collective reserves but it is both a political innovation and may be a platform for regional cooperation on financial structure. While the fund can make only a negative contribution to liquidity it does depart from traditional central bank

[19] ASEAN Finance Ministers (1999).

reserve management practice by including sub-investment grade EMEAP sovereign risks.[20]

A second US$2.0 billion scheme (ABF2) established in 2005 involves local currency risks. Families of single currency exchange traded funds and regional index funds will each acquire and hold sovereign and quasi-sovereign securities. Hitherto, proposals to create regional bodies have been ambitious and not easily implemented,[21] so if the fund is successful in expanding to embrace non-core currency assets it may be a forerunner of jointly sponsored financing and investment vehicles.[22]

This plan is demanding, such that it may necessitate significant cooperation on financial structure and attacks on impediments to activity. The instigators may privately nurse the desire for such change and saw ABF2 as its catalyst. The structural concept seeks to circumvent custody, enforcement, transfer and taxation problems that exist everywhere except Hong Kong and Singapore but the plan will not directly contribute to liquidity and may contain potential conflicts of interest. The final section of this chapter gives a fuller assessment of ABF2, and shows why intent alone in this regard may be insufficient, especially if the scheme has no direct positive effect on liquidity.

The project is purely national in its implications. Although EMEAP represents a convenient tool it is clear that none of APEC, ASEAN nor ASEAN+3 currently has the wherewithal or standing to bring into effect a regional financial body. The broader proposal in this chapter must therefore be directed at EMEAP as a device to help bring about goals established for ABF2. It represents a firmer and more demanding cooperative initiative than previously attempted but requires no advances that would compromise the self-determinism expressed, for example, in ASEAN's core treaty.

2.1.4. Collaborative studies

Other related regional activity has been inconclusive. The 1997-98 financial crisis has been subjected to prolonged analysis within Asia's intergovernmental groups, though the results are limited as to practical reforms. Surges of public policy interest since late 2001 have focused on reviewing structural changes but have yet directly to lead to greater market usage by governments, companies or investors. All the main inter-governmental groupings have been working with interrelated agendas, and it is not yet clear that the results will be more substantial than those of past undertakings.

First, APEC set three teams in 2002 to examine capital market development. Two were given exploratory and promotional briefs; the work of the third is more specific, seeking recommendations for securitization and credit enhancement

---

[20] Many central banks engage in active trading of liquid notes and bonds, but the assets held by the first EMEAP fund are generally illiquid and represent the fund's feasible investment universe.

[21] For example, currency cooperation pacts discussed at intervals by APEC and ASEAN.

[22] Including the regional securitization proposal described in chapter 10.

mechanisms to improve the credit risk quality of Asian bonds.[23] APEC hopes to decide if securitization can provide a continuous fundraising mechanism in the region and further assist the recycling of non-performing financial assets. The work is led by officials in Hong Kong, Korea and Thailand, the first two having recent experience of promoting new financial architecture and legislation to facilitate large-scale securitization, either to assist the recycling of non-performing assets or businesses, or in the refinancing of residential mortgage loans and public assets.

Successful outcomes would be novel: Asia's intergovernmental organizations are unused to agreeing prescriptive action on financial policy. By contrast, debt capital market reform initiatives appear not to have attracted interest among regional trade negotiators in Asia, perhaps because talks on financial services liberalization are poorly advanced, even arguably among World Trade Organization (WTO) members

Second, ASEAN+3[24] has undertaken research similar to APEC in the practicalities of further promoting securitization and external credit enhancement as two related ways to encourage market usage. Each of these working groups is mirrored by ministerial forums, some of which could contribute to the momentum of planning and implementation. There is reason to expect progress from the groups that dealt with specific initiatives; those looking at broader ways to encourage market growth may have laudable aims but less tangible success.

Last, Thailand has since 2002 led ACD participants exploring regional cooperation to encourage capital market activity. This group has assumed an ancillary role to the projects sponsored by EMEAP, APEC and ASEAN+3, intending to promote awareness of their respective work and to raise political encouragement.

Spectators to these studies include the Asian Development Bank (ADB), International Finance Corporation (IFC), IMF and World Bank, in some cases to examine applications of the work to non-Asian emerging markets. The BIS and International Organization of Securities Commissions (IOSCO) are often more directly involved with the work.

2.2. *Defining objectives for reform*

All the official attention given since the mid-90s to market development has thus led to only two tangible financial results. The first, the repurchase line construct, is discounted; the second, ABF2, is constrained from directly affecting liquidity. Yet that these tentative steps have been taken suggests that practical objectives could be employed to guide all national and regional reforms. Ignoring standards for corporate disclosure, which are beyond the direct scope of this chapter,[25] the intentions of specific bond market reform would be the following:

---

[23] A generic description of securitization is given in chapter 9.

[24] Six ASEAN+3 teams worked on specific topics for the group's Asian bond market initiative.

[25] 'Asymmetric information [..] appears always to have limited the scope and use of financial markets', Baskin (1988), reviewing 300 years of market evolution.

- Standardize and broaden the range of available instruments as to issuers and maturities.
- Consolidate benchmarks across a declared range of maturities; introduce and adhere to visible debt issuance programs, nationally or regionally.
- Remove trading restrictions, including repurchases of investment grade issues, short selling, and free use of interest rate and currency derivatives. Such limitations raise volatility by inducing unwarranted selling.
- Standardize clearing (real-time book entry settlement and delivery) and custody systems. Remove obstacles to securities financing to promote efficient trading and safeguard settlement liquidity. Remove barriers preventing a legal basis for trading, ownership and settlement.
- Require market-makers to provide benchmark liquidity fully visible to end users, rather than a clique of banks. Ensure that central bank operations do not lessen liquidity by relying on repurchases.
- Regulate or legislate to perfect asset and credit transfer mechanisms and rules on data retention.
- Lift regulatory restrictions arbitrarily preventing investors from acquiring debt securities, subject to purposefully harmonized credit rating floors.
- Remove, standardize or simplify withholding taxes on securities and collateral assets, and their differing applications to investor classes.
- Promote common portfolio accounting standards among banks and non-bank financial institutions.

3. A Regional Hub Market

Chapters 6 and 7 identified prominent legal and systemic features that most deter market activity in Asian debt securities. It also anticipates a cooperative process to development and in harmonizing standards throughout the region. The proposal described here anticipates the micro-level reforms contained in that analysis and presents a compact means of implementation. It represents as a minimum a streamlined way of addressing many of those issues of detail, by requiring governments to acknowledge and together sanction a free (but regulated) offshore market open to regional, domestic and non-Asian participants. Alternatively, the proposal could form a model for more ambitious long-term reforms leading to an integrated regional debt capital market of the kind favored in discussions within the ACD but not acted upon.

3.1. Aims and implementation

Reforms could be hastened by governments sanctioning a regulated market for regional, domestic and non-Asian use. From an agreed date, the trading and settlement of new and outstanding bonds would be permitted in a hub that meets agreed standards, free of withholdings, duties and capital controls, subject to common regulation and available to all investors and approved issuers.[26] This would remove confusion, relieve delays and provide confidence to participants. Major currency bonds would not be excluded but are not the concern of this proposal and are likely to appear only in the form of asset-backed securities. Asian issuers of major currency bonds would welcome the broader distribution that the proposal would encourage without wishing to constrain sales of their transactions to Asia.

Alternatively, the model could begin the construction of an integrated regional multicurrency debt market. The (pre-euro) eurobond markets were a successful precedent, except that participating countries would not restrict new issues in an obligor's home currency as in France and Italy until the 1980s since one objective is to meld the interests of domestic and offshore investors.[27] With national agreement made, new issues would be launched and traded in the offshore centre. Domestic participants would deal through the center's systems, although retail investors would use domestic intermediaries to assist investor protection.

The aim is for the hub to concentrate fundraising, freely assisted by the execution of currency and interest rate swaps. All local currency securities would be eligible in the hub's systems for custody, clearing and payments, in each case with transfers made free of all deductions or withholdings, and delivery against payment required on a single basis as the sole principle of settlement.

Concentrating activity will also have the practical effect of acknowledging the critical role of interest rate and currency derivatives in new issues of all kinds and in so doing lead to regulation that is transparent to investors. The concept is flexible, simple to implement and operate and given political support could be made effective in a limited period of six months. Over time, it would lead to a permanent rise in market usage, indicated by the number of active investor participants as well as new issue and trading volumes.

The proposal requires national efforts in detailed aspects of law or its application, and regional agreement in sharing costs for Asia's collective welfare. Critically, it requires no new systems and only minor institutional arrangements. In assimilating the prescriptions to remove the markets' impediments, it would provide a spur to a regional debt market, building upon existing national practices without affecting them deleteriously.

3.1.1. Alternative structures for issuance

The model regional transaction suggested in this proposal is illustrated in the figures that follow. Each figure is a representation of payments made at launch, and omits banks and other parties that are non-discretionary intermediaries or execute pure transmission functions. 'Investor' is ubiquitous, standing for all types of principal. Each form of issue may be listed on an exchange.

---

[26] All Asian local currency markets except Hong Kong overtly restrict non-domestic issuers or their use of new issue proceeds.

[27] This was typically the case for French and Italian issuers in the 1970s and 1980s. France allowed the general use of its currency for capital raising only after 1989.

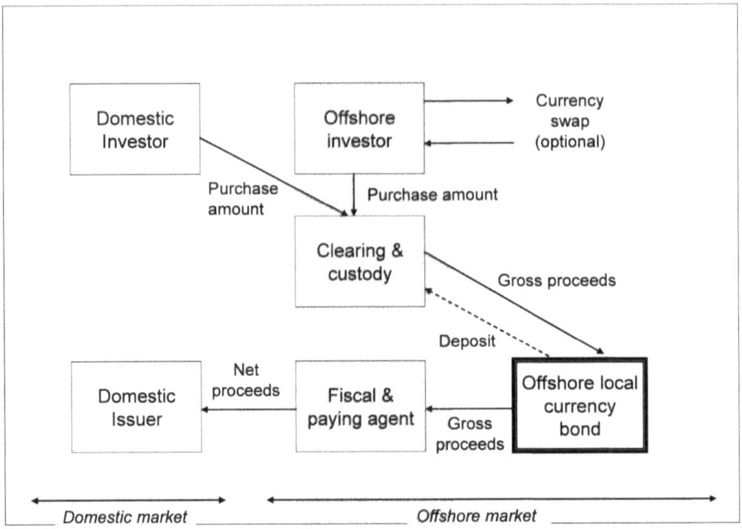

***Figure 8-3.* Offshore issue, initial payments**

From the implementation of national agreement, all new issues would be launched and will trade in the offshore centre. Domestic participants would deal through the offshore center's systems, except for retail investors who would be expected to use domestic intermediaries for reasons of conventional investor protection.

First, figure 8-3 shows an 'offshore' bond issue, similar to the model euromarket transaction of the 1970s. Regardless of listing or regulatory domiciles, all trades are settled outside the domicile of the issuer of risk.

A domestic investor may freely buy or sell such issues subject to any local official or regulatory constraints, seen commonly when bonds are denominated in its home currency.

Second, 'regional' issues represent the core of the proposal shown in figure 8-4, in which a regional hub becomes the transaction's primary place of settlement, probable listing and repository of information. In this case a domestic investor may elect to effect or settle a sale or purchase offshore, subject to local official or regulatory constraints.

Last, the 'domestic freely-traded' issue of figure 8-5 is a model for those for which the primacy of a regional hub may be impractical or impolitic. This may be appropriate for domestic issue classes that exist today in considerable volume, most notably government and central bank notes or bonds, for which domestic settlement and other aspects of system architecture exist in most of the review economies, whether or not begging reform. The bridge to the regional hub is intended to promote information flows and encourage cross-border investment activity, and may later encourage the standardization of dealing, settlement and custody.

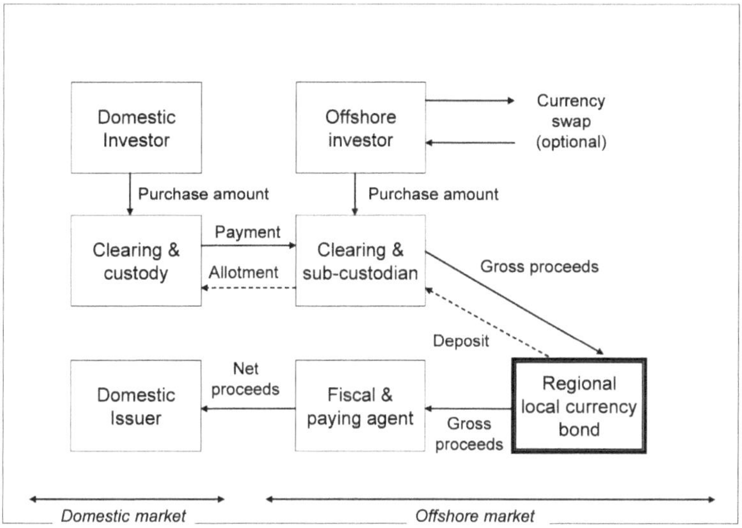

Figure 8-4. **Regional issue, initial payments**

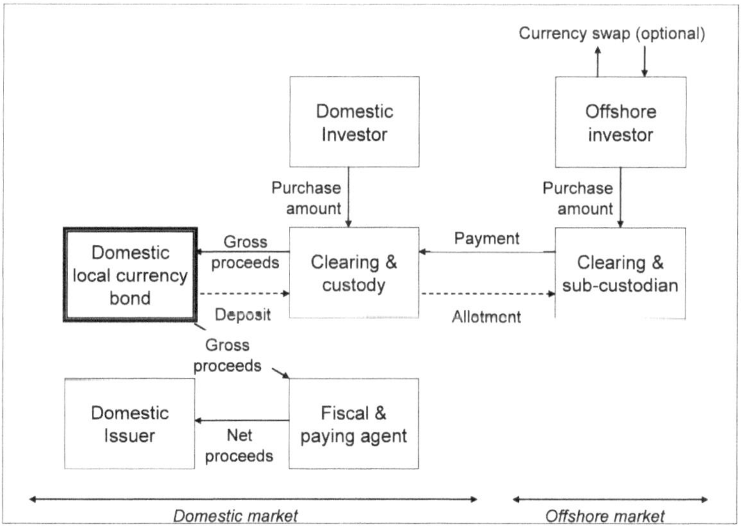

Figure 8-5. **Domestic freely-traded issue, initial payments**

3.2. Government commitments

Official support needed to begin the initiative would comprise four basic undertakings:

1. Participating governments would agree to lift all restrictions and regulations that may limit or prohibit investing and trading in the hub by all domestic financial institutions and intermediaries for which they are responsible.
2. The host government would agree to allow the expanded offshore market to develop unhindered, and during its life not to impose restrictions or penalties on investment activity or payments other than sanctioned by the competent regulatory authority to which participating governments would subscribe. The host authorities would agree to maintain standards for financial market practice agreed by participants.
3. That authority shall from the project's inauguration become subject to supervisory observation by an advisory council in which all participating governments are represented, but shall itself have day-to-day oversight of settlement and sub-custody functions.
4. Participating governments agree to maintain allegiance to the concept for a defined period, for example, of an initial ten years, with retroactive coverage preventing the withdrawal of applicable consents during the life of issues created during that period.[28]

The first undertaking is fundamental, and would require only modest legal and regulatory changes in each domestic jurisdiction. The second requires consensus on the standards to be maintained for market practice and access, for which both international efforts and the issues identified in chapters 6 and 7 are guides.[29] The third demands cooperation among national governments and would represent compensation for any perceived sacrifice of parochial interests among the region's competing financial centers. The final undertaking is related to market confidence and its effect on activity: this is likely also to concern regional negotiations on the trade in financial services.

3.3. Implications

The proposal requires national efforts, mainly in detailed aspects of law or its application, and regional agreement in sharing parochial sacrifices for the sake of Asia's overall welfare. Critically (and in comparison to the more significant architectural work needed to bring into effect the proposal described in chapter 9), this scheme requires no new systems and only minor institutional arrangements.

In meeting the needs for detailed reforms, the plan would provide a spur to a regional debt market by building upon existing local sectors and institutions without affecting them deleteriously. It presumes that choice of physical location has become unimportant for most common financial and capital market activities, given accepted

---

[28] A cessation of the initial period would affect planned refinancing of maturing bonds in spite of retroactive coverage undertakings but borrowers face such irregularities at all times in current circumstances.

[29] Also discussed in Goo, Arner & Zhou (2001). The hub is likely to have met the required standards when chosen.

regulatory and system requirements. Most trading is conducted electronically, and normal business days among EMEAP member states are virtually contiguous. Using one hub for issuance, trading and settlement would encourage a marginal increase of investor activity, mainly resulting from regional and other international funds flows that are presently neglected or deterred for want of simple infrastructure and dealing procedures. Trade flows and streams of direct or portfolio investments lead to natural demand for money market products, long-term debt instruments, hedging tools and products to assist capital asset benchmarking.

Momentum for the proposal will thus arise from identified but largely untapped regional sources rather than an increase in the core of demand now emanating from commercial banks and traders of risk, although an initial real expansion in dealing volume can be expected from domestic professional participants that trade through the hub. The plan involves no patrician losses for national governments and no sacrifice of present systems. A market said to be 'offshore' need not be taken as unregulated, demonstrated particularly in the second and third of the four founding undertakings described in the previous section.

3.3.1. Requirements

Participating governments will allow contiguous trading among all domestic and offshore participants. Pre-commencement matters needing attention are:

- The nature of regulatory approvals needed for issues in the hub, embracing single transactions and formal or informal debt issuance programs.
- The relationship between the hub's regulator with rating agencies and with exchanges that list securities.
- Settlement capacity in the clearing vehicle and for direct or indirect custody of domestic securities. Agreement as to uniform settlement conditions, including like settlement days and a common national commitment to reduce the settlement period to a minimum.[30]
- All transfers from domestic borrowers will be made free and clear of withholding taxes and other impositions.
- Common minimum standards for qualification as a selected hub.
- Changes in supervision for the hub's regulatory authority, and an increase in the authority's capacity.

[30] The choice of hub will determine the vehicle used for settlement and custody, although not necessarily without modification, For example, it may be advantageous to involve an established non-Asian settlement and custody organization accustomed to multicurrency operations, and thus lessen parochial concerns among participants. Regional settlement issues have been the subject of study by the World Bank (Akamatsu, 2004) and have interested the ADB.

The hub's new issue listing requirements for stock exchange admission would be unchanged, at least as a direct product of this proposal.[31] Listings are required by custom and to provide linkage to regulatory oversight of issuer reporting and disclosure but are not associated with settlement, trading or price information. Most new issues can be expected to be listed in the hub; overseas listings would be permissible providing that they caused no dilution in the hub's regime for issuer reporting.

3.3.2. Minimum standards

There need be no ceding of responsibility between national authorities: a harmonization approach employing common standards underpins the hub concept, with approvals where necessary to be given as now. In each phase of a transaction, all operational aspects are managed in the offshore market to seek price transparency, maximize secondary liquidity by bringing together domestic and offshore trading, using the most sophisticated available systems for settlement and custody, and taking advantage of the economies of scale present in unified wholly electronic systems.[32] Trades between counterparties in the issuer's domicile would be reported centrally and settled through the offshore market. This also removes uncertainty arising from the choice of law or jurisdiction in cross-border trading disputes by having the location of settlement and custody determine organically the law to which securities in settlement or custody are subject.

The hub authorities could also adopt an appropriate international convention further to support investor confidence. The leading example is the Hague Convention No. 36 on the law applicable to certain rights in respect of securities held with an intermediary, part of the Hague Conference on Private International Law. The convention was adopted in 2002 but is not yet in force. Among the review countries, China, Korea and Malaysia are members of the conference, and Hong Kong, India and Singapore have acceded to certain of its conventions.

3.3.3. Impact on practice and rights

In all these respects the proposal most resembles the eurobond market of the late 1980s and early 1990s. If domestic and offshore investors buy a new issue at launch then both the funds collected and the bonds issued to investors will be fully fungible, although for convenience separate temporary 'notes' could be lodged electronically to represent domestic and offshore tranches; the size of each tranche will not remain fixed after initial settlement. The political component of credit risk is thus no different for investors to that which they accept today, except that domestic investors will assume negligible marginal risks against the hub clearing house, as with all

---

[31] Except to the extent required for admission of issues originating in participating countries, for example, in relation to credit ratings or jurisdiction of incorporation.

[32] See remarks on outsourcing clearing services in chapter 9.

other international settlement institutions. Legal aspects of risk flowing from the withdrawal of national concessions are unchanged.

Creditor claims will be treated no differently than today. The great majority of bond issues convey no direct collateral rights to bondholders. Providing that borrowers enter transaction agreements written under governing laws acceptable to listing authorities approved by the hub's regulator then applications for judgments or enforcement would be conducted as disparately as today.

Domestic investors would thus not be prejudiced in their traditional choice of law in cases where market practice is well-established, but issuers are certain to be required to submit to non-exclusive jurisdiction in generally accepted international forums, and could expect to experience a pricing disincentive compared to 'standard' hub issues. The adequacy of enforcement of local and foreign judgments is critical in the factors cited as market impediments contained in chapters 6 and 7.

The singular principle of the proposal is to speed that catalogue of reforms and encourage the sum of domestic and regional liquidity. The plan will make internal domestic markets work to their limitations in trading capacity, regulatory oversight and funding constraints; and make the offshore hub market work for development, eliminating duplication in system architecture and helping to convince new participants of its effectiveness.

Non-Asian issues would be permitted subject to standard regulatory guidelines as to listing eligibility and acceptable credit ratings: in each case this arrangement is similar to current provisions in the Hong Kong and Singapore local currency debt markets without long-term restrictions as to the use of issue proceeds.

As a general rule, all issues could be owned directly by retail investors if they met existing investor protection requirements. The issuer's domicile by itself may not affect other conditions attached to a transaction, including a bond's fiscal treatment, eligibility as collateral for repurchase agreements or permissibility in regulatory reserves.

3.3.4. Transaction variations

A more conservative generic model appears in figure 8-5, designed to accommodate government bonds and other existing high-volume domestic issues. Compared to the main proposal, the primacy of hub trading and settlement is held by existing domestic institutions but so as to allow unhindered foreign investor participation through a single channel for settlement and custody. Later, governments may grow willing to permit their domestic sovereign issues to trade through the offshore centre. Approval may not be necessary for any offshore market to open and mature; in this case it is essential that domestic borrowers, traders, banks, brokers and investors be permitted to buy or sell offshore bonds denominated in their 'home' currency.[33]

---

[33] A more complex alternative would use new onshore domestic vehicles, which is the approach adopted for ABF2 except for Hong Kong and Singapore risks. Hong Kong's post-1997 financial system became informally liquid in Chinese yuan. Its banks are now permitted to accept yuan deposits, which they must then deploy to avoid interest losses, a need that may be comparable to the first stage in the development of euromarket practice. Final yuan

3.3.5. Precedents

The proposal adapts formative 'liberal' euromarket experience to a regional context that is planned, agreed and facilitated. By contrast, the history of European and US international private capital flows from the late 1950s suggests that the eurocurrency debt markets emerged less through deliberate intellectual or policy planning in any market or state but rather a mass of modest factors, not all intended. National restrictions, all well-understood in a culture of fixed exchange rates and post-war capital controls, confronted mounting demand for cross-border fundraising and investment.

However, one decision supported growth in international activity across all product markets: the Bank of England's permitting a wholesale market to come into being that could deploy eurocurrency (non-sterling) deposits. A market in tradable short and medium-term deposits allowed euromarket activity to develop in all its facets (money markets, fixed income and lending) and was the result of competitive product innovation. In 1966 the British authorities allowed a US bank in London to issue tradable US dollar certificates of deposit (CDs, and later medium-term floating rate FRCDs). Previously the Bank of England had only allowed brokerage with firms in London placing debt issues for foreign borrowers among non-resident funds and banks.[34]

Sanctioning market-making in CDs introduced two features to London as nowhere else. First, funding grew feasible for offshore lending transactions matched in maturity to meet overseas demand for US dollars.[35] Second, funds could now be fully used offshore, as shown in figures 8-3. With sufficient funds existing and demanded offshore, the classic euromarket issue is arranged, paid, listed and traded outside the domicile of the issuer of risk. Domestic and foreign investors alike trade through a financial hub.

By contrast, today's investors in Asia have less freedom: regardless of objectives they each face a binary choice of being invested or disinvested in their target sector. In the extreme conditions of 1997-98 investors wishing to liquidate holdings of Asian equities or direct investments were forced also to sell the corresponding host currency for lack of a conservative alternative.

This proposal is not only concerned with facilitating foreign portfolio investment in a risk-averse setting that lessens contagion: participants in intra-regional capital

---

settlement must be made through a single bank in Hong Kong. Similarly, hub banks would accept deposits freely in all hub currencies of issue. The impact on monetary policy is minimal: deposits held offshore may lead to marginal credit creation if extended to non-banks but the availability of bonds of like currency would assist the operation of domestic monetary policy (see Einzig & Scott Quinn 1977: 104 *et seq*).

[34] Kynaston (2002) describes much of the chronology.

[35] Conventional eurocurrency loan documentation included increased costs clauses to eliminate lenders' interest rate basis risks. Taken with the wholesale CD market, banks could be confident in making lending commitments seen as mismatched by conventional banking theory.

investment would welcome more effective capital markets for information, accounting and practical motives.

Early euromarket liquidity was considerably aided by the conventional money markets, one reason being that in formative days the euromarkets were as heavily reliant on bank activity as Asia today, but non-bank financial institutions were gradually drawn to using new tools for liquidity (including short and medium-term CDs and commercial paper). Although not the direct focus here, the availability of short-term debt instruments would bolster and encourage market activity in long-term securities by helping broaden a trading culture, assisting in local currency hedging and by servicing the needs of non-portfolio investors.

3.3.6. Benefits of harmonization

This proposal is an approach built on acceptance of regulatory standards of an Asian hub (embodying regionally drawn minimum standards of practice) rather than the harmonization of the region's markets implied as the objective of the reforms described in chapters 6 and 7. It would allow offshore domestic issuance in a financial hub where systems are appropriate, regulation is accepted as fair and transparent, and investor attention is well-established from both foreign and domestic sources. It is a market-orientated way of dealing with obstacles, impediments and non-uniform practice to address problems of modest usage.

These arrangements require a minimum of legislation or regulatory change providing that liquidity is allowed in currency swaps. They compare favorably in simplicity to alternative proposals to select a hub currency to which participating nations would align their own currencies (a hub currency would be managed in relation to a trade-weighted basket, described as a 'common loose arrangement'[36] as part of a gradualist approach to eliminating regional exchange rate volatility).

The proposal could represent a practical first step, not only to fundraising and market development but also in creating a framework for long-term regional stability, if that became an accepted political goal. It carries none of the unknown costs or demands of a new basket or hybrid currency, nor requires the removal of market segmentation by currency that could have a ruinous impact upon the immediate transactional future of Asian banks.[37]

Nonetheless, if currency cooperation becomes an explicit policy objective then the combination of the hub and long-term detailed reforms would facilitate market integration, and contribute to the introduction of a new foreign exchange regime in the region.

---

[36] Frankel (2003: 44).

[37] The creation of the euro has greatly increased issuance in the non-US dollar European corporate debt markets. However, lifting entry barriers formerly maintained by the legacy currency sectors allowed a huge increase in the market share of global underwriters. 'international competition from the larger US investment houses has been a central new feature of the post-EMU environment.' (Santos & Tsatsaronis, 2003: 14). The same study finds evidence that distribution resources outweigh established client relationships for banks seeking new issue transaction mandates.

The proposal assumes that choice of location is unimportant for most financial market activities, given accepted regulatory and system requirements. Nearly all trading is electronic, and business days among EMEAP's Asian members are almost contiguous. Using one hub for trading and settlement would stimulate investor activity, including regional and other international flows that are now neglected for want of simple infrastructure and procedures. Trade flows and streams of direct or portfolio investment generate natural demand for short and long-term debt instruments, hedging products and tools to assist capital asset benchmarking.

Momentum will grow from identified but untapped regional sources rather than an increase in the core of demand now emanating from commercial banks and risk traders, although an expansion in volumes can be expected from domestic professional participants trading through the hub. Last, the market would facilitate syndication of domestic government debt as an alternative to auctions, immediately raising liquidity and investor interest.

4. EMEAP's Local Currency Bond Funds[38]

ABF2's single currency and regional index funds provide a means to lessen problems associated with direct investment in local currency instruments by most offshore investors and certain domestic investors, including problems relating to custody, enforcement of rights, reliability of transfer, and taxation. Chapters 6 and 7 showed how these irregularities exist to varying degrees throughout the region. If the plan succeeds, it will do so not overtly, but by forcing the removal of legal and regulatory constraints that currently make its objectives impossible to achieve.

The fund's structure contains contradictions and potential conflicts for its promoters. It may even result in a diminution of activity oddly contrary to the declared aims. The focus of this section is not central bank practice—which at its most opaque could use the existence of the funds for many purposes—but how ABF2 might contribute to capital market reform. The test of the project must be whether it will generate greater liquidity and induce new participants to issue, invest or trade.

Central banks are privileged investors in that within their home markets they regulate and dominate activity and influence government bond issuance. The promoters have tried to compensate for potential conflicts arising in ABF2 by outsourcing the important operational functions of index providers and fund managers but it would be unrealistic to expect full portfolio disclosure or a separation of interests that might compromise established central bank practice, particularly in day-to-day operations of monetary policy.

---

[38] This section updates an appraisal published prior to ABF2's implementation (Lejot & Arner, 2004).

4.1. Origin: major currency investment in ABF1

In June 2003, EMEAP proposed two funds to invest in the sovereign and quasi-sovereign bonds of eight of their Asian members. Japanese risk is excluded and Taiwan is not a member of the group. The plan had bifurcated roots: growing criticism of international reserves being placed largely outside the region, and the proposition that active capital markets could provide a stabilizing resource in times of generally heightened volatility.

ABF1, the banks' first stage fund, was established by year-end. The participants pooled US$1.0 billion in reserves to acquire major currency bonds issued by the eight governments or their affiliates. The fund was almost immediately fully invested, although the extent of its outright purchases was appreciably less than the value of bonds transferred from existing holdings. The term 'fund' misleads; this is an allocation of existing resources and may never be augmented.

ABF1 is passively managed and small so its direct market impact is insignificant but still theoretically deleterious to liquidity. Too modest in scale to stimulate issuance, it will tend to draw liquidity from bond issues that since the recovery from the 1997-98 financial crisis have ordinarily been in short supply. More positively, against customary reserve management practice, ABF1's portfolio includes Indonesian and Philippine risk, both sub-investment grade when included.

The fund is benchmarked but its index is only partly trackable, even though the bonds in portfolio represent its current investment universe and are likely to correspond to a large share of the several existing commercial US dollar indexes for Asian risk.[39] It is unclear how future contributions will be made or withdrawn, or how proceeds accruing to the fund are treated, but not even full disclosure would make tracking by independent investors possible. Given ABF1's passivity, new issue managers will assume that the fund's resources would largely find the same investment destination regardless of its existence. The fund's value is in opening a wider segment of the credit risk curve to reserve management, and any political results from regional collaboration.

4.2. Local currency instruments in ABF2

Under implementation in 2005, ABF2's US$2.0 billion endowment covers local currency risks and requires more attention, both by its architects and observers. Its aims are simple, but simplicity for the investor might only be achieved by complex reforms or in structures or synthetic instruments that replicate reform. EMEAP's concept contains elements of both.

This scheme is demanding because it effectively seeks to circumvent the problems of investor access, custody, enforcement, transfer and taxation that exist for non-bank investors throughout the region (except largely in Hong Kong and Singapore) but in so doing will be self-limiting as to its external impact on market

---

[39] Tracking by synthetic instruments is theoretically feasible but constrained by the relative scarcity of Asian single name collateralized debt instruments or credit default swaps.

development. Indeed, pre-establishment announcements in 2004 suggested this might be intentional in that ABF2 would 'accelerate market reform', but no commitments to this effect have been disclosed and the examples used by the promoters to illustrate how this had begun are selective.[40] Nonetheless, EMEAP knows that bonds cannot freely be sold into the funds unless market impediments are removed.

4.2.1. Operational structure

ABF2 involves two regional vehicles, a multicurrency index fund that will acquire for its own account local currency assets from the eight target markets, and the second, a fund of funds to do so indirectly through a family of separate single currency funds. The structure is illustrated in figure 8-6. Both single currency and regional multicurrency funds may hold sovereign and quasi-sovereign securities, together with local currency issues by supranational borrowers.

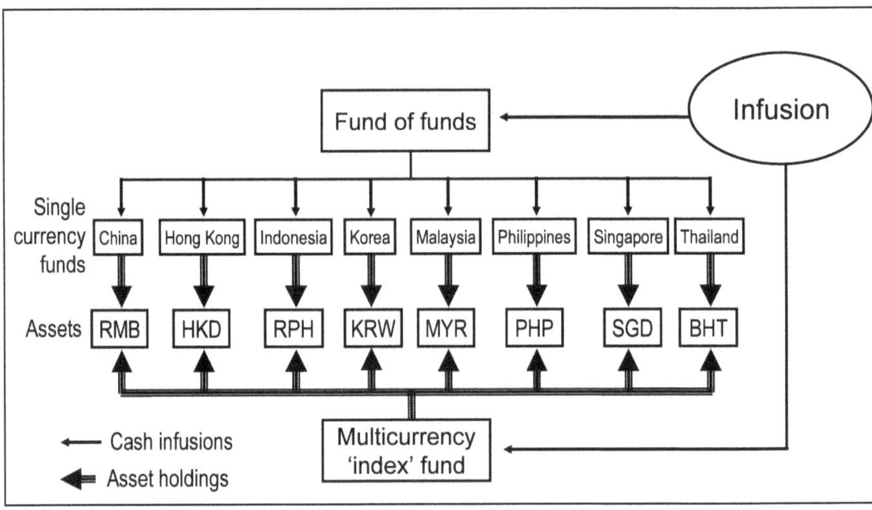

Figure 8-6. **Schematic structure of ABF2**

Each fund is passively managed against benchmarks calculated by International Index Company (IIC), a commercial index provider, which is also contracted to publish selection criteria for each component fund, national weightings for the index fund, and manage periodic portfolio rebalancing.[41] Eight jurisdictions will eventually host single currency funds, control of which rests with a regional fund of funds domiciled in Singapore and listed in Hong Kong. Input prices are initially provided

---

[40] EMEAP press release 16 December 2004, available at http://www.emeap.org/.

[41] Available at http://www.indexco.com/. As at 31 July 2005 the index benchmark contained 497 issues. IIC is a Deutsche Börse affiliate with European and US bank shareholders.

to IIC by a total of sixteen commercial and other sources in the eight national sectors.

These arrangements may be regarded as conventional; however, the availability of many index components is questionable. Unlike ABF1, which took effect with the reallocation of resources from international reserves, this scheme represents a net purchase of assets, even if the collective capital infusion is ultimately provided by proceeds raised from major currency assets held as international reserves. Pre-commencement cross-border holdings among the EMEAP banks of ABF2's permissible assets would have been minimal, so that while central authorities in China or Malaysia, for example, might sell or otherwise transfer bonds into the renminbi and ringgit single currency funds, respectively, it is not known how quickly ABF2 will become invested.

The single currency funds are of necessity domestic entities (in Labuan, in Malaysia's case) to optimize access to securities and address issues of taxation, custody and the ranking of claims. This makes a fund of funds obligatory to provide regional collaborative control. Whether real or virtual, the starting infusion is split equally between the two vehicles, but it is not known whether the ultimate rights of the fund of funds and the multicurrency fund will be as domestic or offshore investors.

4.2.2. Single currency sub-funds

Both multicurrency and single currency funds will be open to outside subscription, with private investors encouraged to invest in parallel to the sponsors and emphasis being given to retail participants rather than traditional users of debt securities. Partly for this reason, the single currency funds are planned as exchange-traded funds (ETFs), widely used vehicles for equity index investment but less common and more technically demanding for debt risks.

This raises practical issues with ABF2's single currency funds, notably the impact of legal status and taxation on otherwise identical investors if, for example, the first is locally domiciled and the second offshore, and how each would regard the fund's declared performance for benchmarking. The multicurrency fund will compete with each single currency fund in seeking investible assets, although not necessarily on equal terms due to national variations in the treatment of domestic and offshore holdings for taxation, custody and enforcement rights. The offshore fund might gain particular dispensation in these respects because of the nature of its promoters but this would seem unreasonable if the funds are to be trackable and open to outside investors. Regardless of prevailing conditions, a single multicurrency index fund cannot buy cash securities in every market, and prejudicial terms will prevail in some cases, even if supply becomes abundant.

This helps to explain ABF2's complexity, and the sponsors' motive in devising new indexes that cannot readily be tracked. Only a lack of supply or problems of investor access have so far prevented the private sector creating single currency funds, although commercial indexes providing measures of whole market performance are established in all eight markets. Single currency funds are valuable if they provide a liquid, low risk investment medium and even-handed market access where none otherwise exists. For example, a fixed income ETF could be an attractive substitute for money market instruments for investors seeking exposure to local currency risk but lacking direct or simple access to notes or bonds. Money market funds often perform this function in major currency markets, but require reliable access to underlying instruments or acceptable synthetic substitutes and must be highly liquid. This would only be the case for ABF2 with appropriate domestic reforms.

4.2.3. Regional fund

The companion regional fund is more difficult to justify as an index, because it will be inherently difficult for investors to track, and constrained in operations by its offshore status. As at 31 July 2005 the index consisted of 497 issues spread among the constituent markets in the way shown in table 8-1:

Table 8-1. **Breakdown of national index components (end-July 2005)**

	Number of issues
China	64
Hong Kong	72
Indonesia	21
Korea	130
Malaysia	40
Philippines	82
Singapore	35
Thailand	53
Total	497

The ABF2 central banks may have elected to exploit contemporary enthusiasm for ETFs given their post-crisis experience in creating such funds for equity products. However, whether because of prevailing rules or supply conditions, ABF2 will create indexes that cannot be tracked. Tracking errors exist with all benchmarks but will be embedded in the single currency funds from inception unless each is managed selectively within its feasible universe of issues, or openly uses synthetic instruments. It is doubtful that its parentage would allow ABF2 to adopt such an approach. ETFs have become popular in some markets due to reliable liquidity, but they can also encourage volatility in an underlying market if the supply of risk assets is constant. The result in this case would be contrary to the general intention of the sponsors. Also, it is unclear that such conditions would provoke additional issuance. Auctions of government issues were cancelled at short notice during 2002-04 in several of the target markets, including China, Indonesia, Korea and Singapore, due to conditions regarded as excessively volatile or suspect by the respective authorities.

4.2.4. Consequences

ABF2's structural concept presumes that investor demand most explains the underdevelopment of Asia's bond markets. Not all observers would agree. If ABF2 is to promote the risk management features of debt capital markets then it must encourage both activity and liquidity, and it is unclear how new passive index funds will help achieve the objective. ABF2 is an incomplete solution to market development if supply is a key constraint to continuous investing and trading activity. An optimal solution would be a scheme geared to encouraging the supply of new securities and to the seamless treatment of local and offshore investors. Both ABF1 and ABF2 are too small directly to influence issuance.

More likely is that ABF2 might not provoke supply and liquidity but instead fortuitously encourage an attack on the markets' core inconsistencies and other problems. ABF2's unintended consequence could be to force political decisions in favor of market reforms. Any regional fund will succeed only with the removal of blockages to supply, with investors made increasingly evenly placed in legal rights, taxation, feasible custody and confident in available trading liquidity. This could result from national authorities agreeing to permit a regulated offshore market to develop in local currency instruments, or each to commit to undertake specific reforms. Offering indexes need not be part of this process, but liquid single currency funds could be effective if they open a path to greater and more consistent issuance for the non-bank investor, without appearing, because of an official affiliation, to be back-stop buyers of last resort, which is akin to the role played by the banking sector in most Asian government debt markets.

How ABF2's possible success might be measured is uncertain: will the fund affect liquidity by promoting supply? EMEAP's intention is for enhanced investor demand to increase the median duration of bonds in issuance but this would inevitably be a very long-term process resulting from private retail sources investing in significant amounts. Otherwise, ABF2's success can only be indirect, by begging for reforms of detail rather than insisting they be made.

References

ASEAN, 2003, Declaration of ASEAN Concord II (Bali Concord II), available at http://www.aseansec.org/15159.htm.

ASEAN, 1999, Finance Ministers Joint Ministerial Statement, 20 March, available at http://www.aseansec.org/742.htm.

ASEAN, 1976. Treaty of Amity and Cooperation in Southeast Asia, 24 February, available at http://www.aseansec.org/1217.htm.

ASEAN+3, 2000, Joint Ministerial Statement of the ASEAN+3 Finance Ministers Meeting, 6 May, available at http://www.aseansec.org/635.htm.

ASEAN+3, 2005, Joint Ministerial Statement of the ASEAN+3 Finance Ministers Meeting, 4 May, available at http://www.aseansec.org/17448.htm.

Akamatsu, N., Cross-border settlement and regional bond market integration, World Bank Financial Sector Operations & Policy Department, mimeo, March 2004.

Baskin, J., 1988, The development of corporate financial markets in Britain and the United States, 1600-1914: overcoming asymmetric information, *Business History Review* 62(2).

Bisley, N., 2003, The end of East Asian regionalism?, *Journal of East Asian Affairs* XVII(1).
Einzig, P., & B. Scott Quinn, 1977, The Euro-dollar System, sixth edition, New York, St. Martins Press.
Frankel, J., 2003, Experience of & lessons from exchange rate regimes in emerging economies, John F. Kennedy School of Government, Harvard University, working paper 03-011.
Gerschenkron, A., 1962, Reflections on the concept of prerequisites of modern industrialization, in Economic Backwardness in Historical Perspective, Cambridge MA, Belknap Press.
Goo, S., Arner, D. & Zhou, Z. (eds.), 2001, International Financial Sector Reform: Standard Setting and Infrastructure Development, London, Kluwer.
Goldsmith, R., 1969, Financial Structure and Development, New Haven CT, Yale University Press.
Institute for International Monetary Affairs, 2004, Report summary of studies on toward (*sic*) a regional financial architecture for East Asia, 29 March, Tokyo, available at http://www.mof.go.jp/jouhou/kokkin/ASEAN+3research.htm.
Institute for International Monetary Affairs, 2003, Comprehensive evaluation report on Japanese assistance to countries affected by the Asian currency crisis, available in summary at http://www.mof.go.jp/english/hyouka/14nendo/sougou1-1.pdf.
Krugman, P., 1987, Economic integration in Europe: some conceptual issues, in T. Padoa-Schioppa, Efficiency, Stability and Equity, A Strategy for the Evolution of the Economic System of the European Community, Oxford.
Kynaston, D., 2002, The City of London: vol. IV A Club No More 1945-2000, London, Chatto & Windus.
Lejot, P. & Arner, P., 2004, Well-intentioned Asian bond fund wont work, *International Financial Law Review* 23(9).
Levine, R., 1997, Financial development & economic growth: views & Agenda, *Journal of Economic Literature* 35(2).
Levine, R., 2002, Bank-based or market-based financial systems: which is better?, National Bureau Of Economic Research Working Paper 9138.
McKinnon, R.,1977, The Eurocurrency Market, Essays on International Finance 125, Princeton.
Moreno, R., 1997a Dealing with currency speculation in the Asian Pacific basin, Federal Reserve Bank of San Francisco Economic Letter, 97-10 11 April.
Moreno, R., 1997b, Lessons from Thailand, Federal Reserve Bank of San Francisco Economic Letter, 97-33 7 November.
Randall, C., 2002, East Asian Financial Cooperation, Washington, Institute for International Economics.
Ravenhill, J., 2000, APEC adrift: implications for economic regionalism in Asia and the Pacific, *Pacific Review* 13(2).
Santos, J. & Tsatsaronis, K., 2003, The cost of barriers to entry: evidence from the market for corporate euro bond underwriting, BIS working paper 134.
Thomas, N., 2004, An East Asian economic community: multilateralism beyond APEC presentation to Asia-Pacific economies: multilateral vs. bilateral relationships conference, City University of Hong Kong, May 2004.
Traisorat, T., 2000, Thailand: Financial Sector Reform and the East Asian Crisis, London, Kluwer.
Wang Seok-dong & L. Andersen, 2003, Regional financial cooperation In East Asia: the Chiang Mai Initiative and beyond, Bulletin on Asia-Pacific Perspectives 2002/03, UNESCAP, Bangkok.

Chapter 9

Promoting Market Development with Structured Finance and Regional Credit Enhancement

Paul Lejot[1], Douglas Arner[1] and Frederick Pretorius[2]

[1]*Asian Institute of International Financial Law and Faculty of Law, University of Hong Kong;* [2]*Asian Institute of International Financial Law and Department of Real Estate and Construction, University of Hong Kong*

1. Introduction

A prominent theme of these essays is that markets of the well-functioning kind that Asia deserves have developed only with external effort appropriate to the most acute and clearly perceived need. The remainder may stand in the splendor of robust systems and capable regulation, but activity will pass them by.

Sufficient need means that successful markets may reveal different roots, most commonly borrowing on an unprecedented scale, crisis avoidance, financial sector repair, or goals in social policy. The proposal described in this chapter has no exact forerunner, but rather a series of similar antecedents in markets that now are fully developed and display the characteristics of activity and liquidity that Asia most lacks.

Proposed here is a far-reaching, integrated scheme that could lead to a burgeoning of structured finance in Asia, with direct and secondary consequences for market efficiency, activity, the standardization of best practice in bank lending and credit creation, regional economic cooperation, and the value and dependability of the region's debt capital markets.

The proposal includes the official endorsement of structured finance techniques to increase issuance of tradable, well-rated Asian notes and bonds. At its core is a significant addition to Asia's financial infrastructure in the form of a freshly capitalized regional body. This would form part of an institutional mechanism for credit enhancement to support credit risk transfer and encourage the securitization of a wide range of assets and risks, and the creation of a new source of well-rated notes and bonds.

The new vehicle would encourage standardization in credit risk creation and transfer, and serve to facilitate securitization through the issue of asset-backed securities on a scale not previously contemplated in Asia. This chapter explains the concept and objectives or promoting securitization. It then examines the functioning of such transactions in the financial sector in terms of institutions and organization theories. Last, it describes the mechanics and features of the proposed agency.

2. Concepts and Objectives

2.1. The nature of securitization

Securitization is a tool of structured finance taken in this chapter to be the irrevocable transfer of defined financial assets by their originator, with consideration funded by the simultaneous sale to a third party investor of new securities issued by the asset buyer. Neither asset buyer nor investor has transactional recourse to the originator.

The asset buyer is most frequently an insubstantive vehicle taking the form of a company or trust, a choice that usually reflects legal convention in the jurisdiction of the domicile of the assets. Securities are typically issued in tiers, referred to by practitioners as a 'waterfall', that carry different commercial terms and risks so as to maximize the use of assets and the value contained in their associated cash flows.

Most securitized transactions contain elements of internal or external credit enhancement to enable the securities to achieve certain credit ratings. Internal enhancement usually takes the form of over-collateralization or the holding of a liquidity reserve; external enhancement is most commonly cash collateral, a third party financial guarantee (synonymous with standby letters of credit in the United States) or insurance policy. Guarantees, often known in transactions as 'wraps', are provided internationally mainly by specialist monoline insurers, first seen in the early 1970s in the US municipal bond market and now a powerful facilitating sectoral presence in many structured finance markets.

2.2. Transactional objectives

Common to all securitized transactions is adequate enhancement of the credit risk offered to investors by the manipulation or augmentation of underlying source assets, be they a whole business, similar but unconnected assets, or streams of cash. This provides a means to circumvent problems of weak corporate credit or disclosure. Regardless of how such enhancement is achieved the process becomes manifest in one of five ways. These are also the central aims of this chapter's proposal:

- Generally, the means to make an unacceptable risk satisfactory to an investor, assuming each potential investor has known risk-return objectives.
- An overt or implied credit rating that ranks above its respective sovereign ceiling.
- The means to price pools of assets that are difficult or impossible to value, usually to make feasible their sale through a process of reverse price discovery.
- A method to create capital market funding where none previously existed.

- For asset originators such as commercial banks or specialist lenders, a funding source where none was available at an acceptable cost.

2.3. Credit enhancement agency

The proposal requires a suitably capitalized new body to encourage effective risk pooling, credit risk transfer, credit rating targeting and in particular to provide a new source of external transactional credit enhancement. It includes no formal limitation on permissible source credit risk, while instruments of issue might include all conventional and hybrid term debt securities, and structured money market instruments such as asset-backed commercial paper.

This proposal is far reaching but specific in its application of resources. It requires national endorsement, regional cooperation, engagement with established credit rating agencies, and a resource commitment, partly in the form of a funded equity infusion but largely as external corporate support by means of contingent capital. Contingent capital is a third party's contractual, irrevocable commitment to fund an infusion of equity for an obligor according to pre-determined commercial criteria, applied at either transactional or corporate levels. It is used in many sectors of banking or finance, especially non-recourse project-related transactions and in the reinsurance industry.

The first aim is to establish a credit enhancement agency to help recycle the accumulation of impaired assets present in East Asia's banking systems. Except in Korea, this is Asia's greatest incomplete post-crisis task, despite over eight years having passed since the inception of that shock. With the endorsement of all ASEAN+3 members, this will yield a flow of new securities and bequeath a well-practiced and standardized mechanism appropriate for most aspects of credit risk transfer with structured finance techniques.[1] In the long-run it could assist fundraising for infrastructural development and indirectly improve the provision of credit for small businesses (SMEs).

2.3.1. Permissible activities and risks

Other than in exceptional cases, permissible transactions would not include wholly synthetic securitized issues, notably collateralized bond and loan obligations (CBOs and CLOs, respectively) which involve applying credit derivatives to asset portfolios that then remain as funded assets on the balance sheet of the originator. The exclusion would reflect purely competitive reasons, rather than any intrinsic risk management view: the proposal is not intended to crowd out similar but non-competing business streams.

---

[1] The Association of Southeast Asian Nations (ASEAN) comprises Brunei, Cambodia, Indonesia, Laos, Malaysia, Myanmar, Philippines, Singapore, Thailand, and Vietnam. ASEAN+3 is an ad hoc group that includes China, Japan and Korea.

In its first phase, the proposal is concerned with allowing the origination of structured transactions using real financial assets, healthy or impaired, as supporting collateral. Wholly synthetic security transactions are not a primary subject of the proposal for two main reasons. First, source assets now include a sizeable proportion of impaired risk; until their scale is made generally acceptable there will be limited value in synthetic securitization.

Second, Asian banks generally have needs of the same order for balance sheet and regulatory capital to a greater extent than their OECD counterparts. As a result, today's generation of synthetic products represents a relatively costly means to manage balance sheet risk. The availability and deployment of risk weighted bank regulatory capital relative to 'real' balance sheet capital will tend to increase over time with the sophistication of the sector, especially when gauged in risk management, product usage, the quality of national regulatory supervision and the credit rating of the host economy, all forces that may intensify under the forthcoming Basel II capital accord. For example, Asian banks are active users of credit derivatives as buyers or sellers of credit protection, but few engage as originators or traders of total return swaps, credit default swaps, or cash and synthetic credit-linked instruments.

Nonetheless, these products would be permissible under the aegis of the agency and will increase in use over time as the indigenous banking sector grows better able to create, hedge and trade credit derivatives, which standardized contract terms will increasingly promote. This transition is a function of the rapidity and completeness of post-crisis bank balance sheet repair, and of the success of this proposal in providing an indirect incentive for lending to lesser-rated risks, notably Asia's medium-scale businesses.

2.3.2. Scope of operations

A new credit enhancement agency will help recycle by securitization the accumulation of impaired assets in Asia's banking systems. The process would yield a flow of well-rated securities and bequeath a standardized mechanism appropriate for most aspects of credit risk transfer, and later assist infrastructural fundraising and improve the provision of credit for SMEs.

Successful securitization programs can lead to a migration among source asset originators to common standards for facility appraisal, documentation and enforcement. What follows is an insidious improvement in industry practice that has no negative impact on borrowers but may widen their access to funding. This has been seen among long-established markets in Germany, the United States and elsewhere, and others with less lengthy structured finance records, notably Hong Kong, where competition in the last decade in the market for residential mortgage loans has led to a startling reduction in net loan margins. Such gains for borrowers is due in part to the creation of the Hong Kong Mortgage Corporation, which buys and refinances blocks of private housing loans and in doing so has induced a general improvement and standardization of primary loan documentation and credit appraisal.

The proposal must also be distinguished from other distinct markets and instruments. The vast US federal agency bond market is generally not concerned with pure securitized structures but with pass-through arrangements under which investors acquire indirect interests in the financial assets purchased by the issuer, for example, Fannie Mae or Freddie Mac,[2] without claims or rights of enforcement against those assets. The investor's primary risk in each case is that of the agency issuer.

Similarly, investors in the European covered bond (or *pfandbriefe*) markets acquire preferred interests in groups of assets (usually residential mortgages or loans for public projects) that may change in composition and which remain on the balance sheet of the originator-issuer. In each case the funding markets responded to needs: minimizing capital costs was never historically a central objective for German public sector *pfandbriefe* issuers or American federal agencies. Recently, that lack of pressure has ended, both for similar national reasons and with the influence of common international regulatory requirements led from Basel or Brussels.

A market-based Asian covered bond sector would need to meet three conditions: the curbing of non-performing loans (NPLs) to internationally accepted levels; the accumulation of adequate portfolio data histories; and bank demand for regulatory capital exceeding that for true capital. None of these conditions is imminent. Such a market could be created using the preferred creditor status of a multilateral institution, mirroring a concept now under discussion in the European Union. This type of support has precedents: the US federal agency and German *pfandbriefe* markets were each founded with state backing and historically have received the benefit of indirect sovereign or provincial credit support.

3. Foundations, History and Needs

One theoretical concept of securitization draws upon recent ideas in law, economics and finance. The same representation also suggests why use of the technique has been historically limited in Asia, even in comparatively sophisticated national markets such as Japan, and why more recently it became so powerful a tool in Korea after 1999. There are three arms to the analysis.

3.1. Transaction costs and economic organization

Institutional economics suggests that firms exist to organize activities that could in principle be negotiated and conducted through open markets, and do so for reasons associated with transaction costs, including those linked to the scrutiny and compensation of management. This refines and develops ideas first suggested by Coase.[3] The vertical integration of activity that the firm represents is justified by

---

[2] Federal National Mortgage Association (FNMA) and Federal Home Loan Mortgage Corp (FHLMC), respectively.

[3] See Coase (1937). His subsequent article (1960) examines the relationship between the effects of law and the behavior of market participants in dealing with externalities, of which an example would be the juxtaposition of securitization as a form of regulatory arbitrage with

scale economies seen by comparison with the costs associated with a large number of market bargains for the same ultimate result.

Thus a firm manufacturing any simple product stands in the place of an infinite number of separate contracts among individual agents, that is, the erstwhile firm's workforce, suppliers and customers. Economic activity will reside in firms to the extent that its implicit cost structure is so favored, and would otherwise take place by contract in open market settings.

More broadly, specialized functions in production give rise to firms by creating scale economies in vertical integration. The same economies of scale could often be conducive to the exploitation of economic rents. At the time of his early analysis in the 1930s, Coase may have believed it possible to establish empirically an upper bound to the firm, that is, a point at which the integration of activity in companies ceased to be cost effective compared to webs of independent but linked transactions conducted through open markets.[4]

3.2. Securitization, regulation and vertical disintegration

According to this view, economic organizations collate or integrate activities to lessen the transaction costs associated with markets. By contrast, securitization may be characterized as vertical differentiation, or disintegration, so that it would seem to be effective given appropriate transaction or monitoring costs. In this are included all costs, not only cash expenses, which ironically are high in modern financial sector securitization and have often deterred potential transactions in Asia.

One traditional approach to securitization takes a broader view of the concept than used in this chapter, and considers its origin and application in any commercial enterprise, not only the regulated financial industry. Firms are said to 'deconstruct' activity by making flexible their balance sheets in order to achieve savings in external finance. The central purpose of securitization is an elective financing strategy, varying by jurisdiction according to law and accounting practice, to minimize front-line costs.[5]

Among financial institutions, practice mirrored legal theory in this way from the first use of asset-backed securities in the 1970s until the late 1980s. From 1981 onwards, a series of international banking crises led to pressure for common regulation of banks, culminating in the 1988 Basel capital accord.

This in turn influenced the nature, composition and funding of all bank risk businesses. It thus altered the primary causation for banks to deploy structured finance techniques, and within five years greatly expanded the uses of securitization for balance sheet and capital .management.

---

banking regulation resulting from the 1988 Basel I capital accord. Williamson made more specific the transaction cost explanations of vertical integration, especially in analyzing agency problems of management controls and incentives: see for example, Williamson (1971).

[4] Later articles explain the source and impact of the original work (Coase, 1988).

[5] Described notably by Schwarcz (2002).

The process was largely unanticipated by regulators: the rules promoted by Basel I were intended at inception for OECD-domiciled banks, but force of competition and interbank peer pressure led to their effective adoption through much of the global banking community, even if standards of national enforcement were variable or capricious.

Demand for securitization by regulated banks has since the late-1980s become a function of uniform regulation of bank capital. In this way, law and regulation have been value-creating and enabling devices for financial sector securitization, despite heavy structural expenses associated with many single deals. Just as market transaction costs are said to provide primary causation for the existence of firms as economic organizations, so the effect of regulation contributes to transaction costs in such a way to make the market a more favorable forum for credit creation than the bank.

3.3. Risks in banking transformations

The reasons for the growth of securitization since the 1980s reveal a fundamental paradox in the aims and concerns of contemporary bank regulators. In banking theory, traditional, non-specialist lending will involve at least three fundamental mismatches, all of which give rise to primary risk management requirements, and which will combine in more complex ways that induce further, secondary needs.

Pilots of fixed-wing aircraft learn that for every simple action in one dimension (a movement in control surfaces up, down, left or right) will follow a series of induced reactions of increasing complexity, which untended lead inevitably to danger. In banking, this means that compensating for the effect of one mismatch will interfere with both a second mismatch and ways in which risk managers seek to ameliorate that second mismatch.

The three core mismatches each apply to balance sheets in aggregate, rather than singles act of lending or borrowing, and are shown in table 9-1. These mismatches are inherent in bank lending, and largely explain how the focus of regulatory attention and contemporary risk management is commonly directed.

***Table 9-1.* Commercial lending mismatches**

Mismatch	Comments
Temporal: loan duration *vs.* deposit duration.	Banks typically use deposit liabilities of one duration to fund loan assets of another duration, regardless of their other terms or the nature of their contracting counterparties.
Credit: risk concentration in loans *vs.* deposits	Only exceptionally will there exist any correspondence between the credit risk associated with a lending portfolio and the deposit base with which it may be funded.
Value: prospective repayment of loans *vs.* deposits	Loans assets that suffer default may be recovered only in part. It would be impossible ordinarily for a proportion of a deposit liability to be written off providing the bank obligor remains solvent.

At the same time, the securitized structures used by banks since 1988 have rated increasing attention by regulators. Yet securitization is a tool to manage and correct for such mismatches.

Basel I's commercial result was a profound insidious impact on transaction costs. This led to induced arbitrage and credit distortions, a massive growth in securitization and credit risk transfer, and the deployment of new instruments for capital raising and notably to manipulate balance sheet risk-composition. Looking forward, the successor accord, Basel II will apply limits to regulatory arbitrage and regulatory capital optimization as an aim of credit risk transfer through securitization.

3.4. Applying theory to practice in Asia

Deploying securitization techniques in Asia has often entailed a search for recorded assets and predictable cash flows, the usefulness of which depends on hazards such as the dependability of transferable property rights or the commercial effect of taxes. Unpredictability harshly affects the economics of structured transactions. Reporting a 2003 new issue for a Korean bank a leading professional journal commented timelessly, 'The Asian [mortgage-backed securities] market has been plagued by a lack of [such] issues as nearly all the deals have proved to be one-offs'.[6]

The heavy marginal cost of completing an inaugural deal could be supported if it became the first of a series: too often this has proved impossible for lack of suitable material or by the obstruction of law, especially in achieving a reliable and enforceable sale of assets to support a domestic or offshore securities issuer.[7]

The post-crisis imperative for balance sheet repair made transaction costs more tolerable, resulting in a notable shift in assets, a growth in synthetic transactions since 1999 and an improvement in bank and corporate balance sheets in certain countries, notably Korea and Malaysia. The gravity of the crisis perversely eased these limitations by making asset sales and the creation of asset-backed securities essential to bank balance sheet renovation and corporate restructuring.

This was most apparent with Korean lenders, to recycle impaired assets and through the creation of collateralized issues based upon the defaulted debt of Korean companies, notably the *chaebol* Daewoo. Malaysia is generally seen as similarly successful, albeit on a far smaller scale, whereas China's need in this context is now widely accepted as paramount.[8]

---

[6] *International Financing Review* 1508, 1 November 2003, p49.

[7] US law and accounting rules generally require that a sale be 'true', with the connotation that assets sold to the insubstantive vehicle then lie beyond the reach of creditors of the originator. International accounting practice takes a less narrow view, that in a securitized deal, the granting of balance sheet relief to the originator after a sale of assets depends on the economic impact of the whole transaction.

[8] This is not only a problem in Asia: despite its sophisticated financial system Germany is seen as needing similar reforms.

Credit rating methodology in Asia grows steadily more confident and catholic, and will soon make feasible the hypothetical valuation of certain asset pools using comparable foreign sectoral records. The current conventional actuarial approach needs extensive indigenous data histories.

This proposal is a logical further step:

- To speed and expand the recycling of non-accruing or delinquent financial assets, that when established assists the transparent sale pricing of NPLs and other impaired assets. If it is assumed that transaction standardization will tend to increase over time, then a process of reverse enquiry will allow market-clearing yields on tranches of securities to be used to value a collateral pool and thus determine its permissible sale price.
- Greatly to raise the number of Asia's feasible issuers, chiefly by providing banks with explicit risk support for a refinancing mechanism that will encourage competitive credit creation for medium-scale businesses and all risks of lesser quality, free of the general constraint of sovereign rating ceilings.

By facilitating structured finance on a regional scale to deal with the continuing problem of recognized, undeclared or unpriced impaired assets, Asia's governments will allow future growth in debt capital market activity and offer reliable supply of debt instruments to institutional investors.

4. Transaction foundations

The transaction framework is well-understood by participants and regulators. In the descriptions that follow, 'trust' is used purely for brevity, and is taken to be synonymous with any special purpose vehicle (SPV) or company. It denotes an insubstantive entity with no purpose other than in relation to a transactional life, unconnected by control to an originator, and having no residual value (and therefore being able to meet no claim in law) after the expiry of the asset pool.

Certain civil law jurisdictions that do not ordinarily recognize trusts have legislated since the Asian financial crisis to sanction SPVs, in each case specifically in the context of structured finance, notably, Korea, Philippines, Taiwan and Thailand, but not all have yet been tested by successful transactions. Forthcoming legislative orders given preliminary exposure in April 2005 suggest that China will adopt similar arrangements.[9]

[9] People's Bank of China PBoC announcement (2005) No 9, Administrative rules on forward bond transactions in the national inter-bank bond market, May, described elsewhere in chapter 6.

4.1. Elements in the generic transaction

1. Financial assets are sold by their originator to an insubstantive domestic trust, then resold to a similar offshore vehicle that in turn funds the purchase, simultaneously or after a short period for asset accumulation, with an array of new securities enjoying direct claims of varying seniority over all or part of the pool of assets.
2. Qualifying assets are chosen by transaction feasibility, and include impaired assets, commercial mortgage loans, corporate loans and major lease receivables. Asset servicing becomes independent of the originator. The originator may continue to deal commercially with any ultimate debtor except in cases involving impaired assets.
3. Securities (typically notes, bonds or commercial paper) are issued in tranches, designed by priorities of claim and in commercial terms to meet required target credit ratings and the risk-return preferences of various classes of investor while extracting the fullest economic use of pool cash or proceeds.

Figure 9-1 shows the skeleton of a typical cross-border transaction:

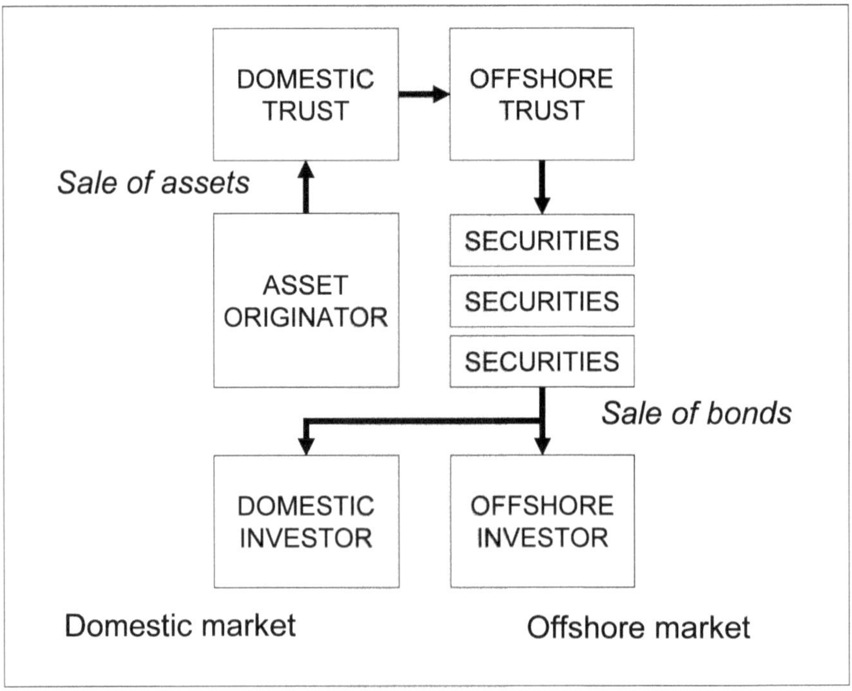

***Figure 9-1.* Basic cross-border securitization**

4. Value is first extracted from the asset pool internally; external sources then provide additional credit support such that each series of bonds meets a target initial credit rating achieved through iterative consultation with a rating agency.
5. Credit enhancement is provided by a new regional organization incorporated in a tax neutral jurisdiction and managed in an Asian financial center. Shareholder capital will be provided by governments, international financial organizations and perhaps a minority of private institutions. The official shareholders will form a supervisory body responsible for general regulatory matters.
6. Such external backing is facilitated by a third party by means of funded or contingent capital, financial guarantee (or its equivalent) or dedicated insurance. It may cover defaults within the collateral pool or the entire transaction, including specific support to induce a counterparty to enter one or more currency swaps.
7. External sources provide such additional credit support that each series of bonds meets target credit ratings. This backing is given by a third party through funded or contingent capital, financial guarantee or insurance. It may cover defaults within a collateral pool, whole transactions or support swap collateralization.
8. 'Cross-border' is taken to indicate the use of sequential insubstantive securitization vehicles, the more remote from the source assets being located offshore as a means to enhance the irrevocability of the asset transfer. Securities emanating from the sale may be acquired at issue or later by any investor, whether or not of the same domicile from which subject assets are first sold.

Figure 9-2 shows the principles and simplified operations of the proposed vehicle and the role taken by the credit enhancement agency. Both illustrations in this chapter omit for simplicity intermediaries that assume money transmission or other purely fiduciary agency roles.

5. Features of the New Credit Enhancement Agency

Structured finance is often a complex means to achieve the simple. In this case, the target is a supply of new debt issues at superior credit ratings that each represent for the investor an easily assessable risk. The structural skeleton of the proposal is not original, either in Asia or elsewhere. Asset-backed securities appeared in 1983, with US residential mortgage loans used as collateral; CBOs were first issued two years later. Most Asian asset-backed bonds have been negotiated singly but in the crisis aftermath a large volume of impaired assets has been used as collateral for CBOs in Korea.[10]

---

[10] Oh, Park, Park & Yang (2003).

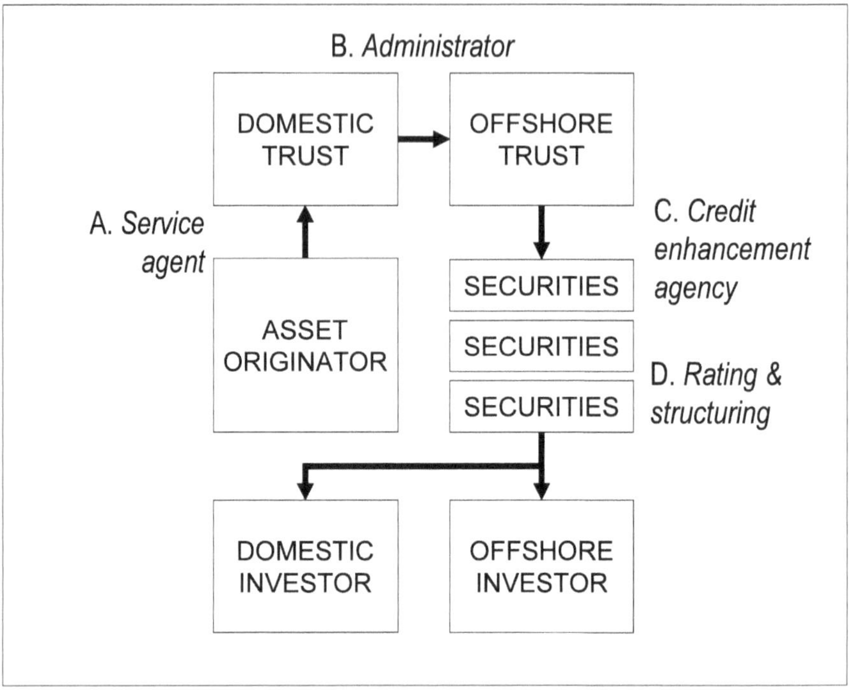

Figure 9-2. **Critical elements of credit enhancement agency**

However, two features of the concept are novel. The first is the way that new, non-distressed financial assets are volunteered for securitization by their originator banks or finance houses; the second is the cost-effectiveness and productive scope of the scheme's recommendations for external credit enhancement. This proposal would offer a continuing means to generate debt securities of a credit quality acceptable to investors using hitherto unsuitable (but not distressed) assets.

The following sections explain the main elements of the proposal and show how they differ from those of past concepts or transactions. They give a representation of the structure's commercial core rather than a guide to its legal construction or a schedule of possible contractual participants. Securitized transaction may involve as many as thirty ongoing contractual agents, not including pool debtors, even in relatively uncomplex cases.

The parties omitted for convenience from these descriptions are those providing contractual financial or administrative services to one or both of the trusts (including issuing and paying agents, providers of short-term liquidity, swap counterparties, providers of support for reinvestment risks, and general or specific trustees). The agency will support deals conforming to the guidelines described in this section.

5.1. Main parties

Credit enhancement will be provided by a new regional organization incorporated in an acceptable tax neutral jurisdiction and established in a regional financial center.

Initial and future capital will be provided by founding shareholder representatives of sponsor governments, international financial organizations, and (perhaps) a minority of private institutional supporters to give technical and advisory input to the agency at arm's length.

The official shareholders will form a regional supervisory body responsible for general regulatory matters. The agency's resource mechanism and credit enhancement process will be available for use by any financial institution recognized by the regulator.

The agency will not itself own, manage or operate any other party in transactions to which it extends credit enhancement. Asset servicing will be managed by organizations based locally in the asset domicile. Except in cases involving pools of NPLs the service agent may be an affiliate of the originator. For transactions using impaired assets the service agent may be a national asset management company or specialist organization, where necessary given technical assistance by the agency. No other new entities are required for operations: the agency will work with all nationally regulated originators, financial institutions and recognized credit rating agencies.

5.2. Principles of operation

The proposal's standard onshore-offshore securitization model uses two sequential domestic and offshore trusts. For consistency, transparency and technical reasons relating to achieving true sale and a neutral tax stance the basic structure will ideally apply both to local and foreign currency transactions, regardless of the domicile of initial investors. To avoid disruption in the relationship between lenders and clients and to encourage usage the agency will stress the value and need for standardization in both the documentation of underlying financial assets and in the main elements of sponsored or supported transactions.

Qualifying assets will be governed solely by credit rating and transaction feasibility. Impaired assets, commercial mortgage loans, corporate loans and major lease receivables will be the most important subject asset categories. The proposed vehicle could accommodate other non-impaired (performing) assets such as consumer installment credit; credit card and trade receivables but existing market resources may initially resist channeling such transactions through the agency.

The agency will adopt standard market-determined commercial terms for asset-backed securities, particularly currency, listing, custody, settlement and trading qualifications. Figure 9-2 highlights four transaction elements inherent in the proposed structure.

5.2.1. A. Servicing agent

In figure 9-2, 'A' indicates the factors causing financial institutions to offer assets for securitization and the associated risks. These comprise agreement on the formation of the agency, clear and uniform requirements over NPL recognition, accounting and asset disposal, more flexible sources of funding for banks, and indirect support for lesser credits, particularly SMEs.

To the extent that banking assets represent claims against entities that have (or desire) no access to a debt capital market an inducement will be needed before this type of primary resource can be pooled as collateral and transformed into usable material for debt issues attractive to domestic or offshore investors. Here, the official motive must be a combination of regulatory requirements on credit creation, particularly the full enforcement of client and sectoral prudential limits as well as general capital and liquidity demands, and a new incentive to encourage credit availability for SMEs. For example, non-discriminatory tax concessions are unlikely to breach current international trade rules.

The proposal seeks in no way to circumvent sound aspects of Asia's banking systems: it is doubtful that a flourishing Asian debt market could appear without the active participation of the region's banks. The aim is to involve the banking sector by offering solutions to ongoing portfolio problems, and additionally make banks accustomed to continual use of structured finance techniques in the refunding of non-impaired risk. A local financing link between bank and business enterprise is economically and culturally valuable but if Asia wishes to offer greater financing choice to SMEs then it is important to avoid the alternative of subsidized or directed lending, which is usually unsuccessful, unpopular and a hazardous distortion. Increased credit creation for SMEs could be made feasible by enabling banks more easily to refinance funded balance sheet risk and freely raise regulatory capital.

5.2.2. B. Administrative resources

'B' draws attention to essential matters of law and practice that must be made certain for the agency to operate effectively without national constraints, and have been discussed in relation to legal and other impediments elsewhere in chapters 6 and 7. They concern the certainty of achieving a true sale of assets, the perfection of creditor claims, and eliminating duties or taxes on transfer to the extent that the use of securitization is tax-neutral compared to a lender retaining the entirety of a claim. Onshore and offshore trusts in series are suggested to ensure the perfection of title, adhere to a standard transaction model, minimize fiscal uncertainties and where necessary facilitate the listing of securities.

5.2.3. C. Credit enhancement agency

'C' indicates issues relating to the process of credit enhancement. External credit enhancement for extant Asian asset-backed securities has generally been found in two sources: third party first loss guarantees or credit wraps[11] provided by monoline insurance companies. The first is costly and the second prone to exhaustion from prudential risk limits.

Assuming that third parties will support the credit demands of this proposal then the contingent capital model used by leading reinsurance groups will meet requirements for both investor credibility and cost-effectiveness in using free capital

[11] Financial guarantee support designed to correct specific credit failings.

and other resources. It is further assumed that the new entity will be capitalized and maintained by subscribing governments and interested international organizations.

The agency will offer both direct and indirect credit support:

- Direct enhancement, by a provision of funded or contingent capital to the offshore securities issuer; direct swap counterparty; or a partial guarantee of that issuer's obligations or of specific classes of security. Contingent capital becomes funded according to predetermined triggers, such as financial or operating covenants or credit ratings.
- Indirect enhancement by offering similar backing privately to enable a second unconnected external source to offer support to an issue, for example, a newly incorporated or existing monoline insurer.

5.2.4. D. Credit rating iterations

'D' points to interplay between the credit enhancement agency and credit rating companies. The rating process for structured finance is complex, iterative and erratic, and requires the credit enhancement agency to show flexibility and considerable effort, not least because the three large international rating agencies use differing methodologies in modeling collateral applied to asset-backed securities.[12] This divergence mitigates concern as to rating agency influence similar to that arising from Basel II granting the agencies a fully institutional role. Too little attention has been paid to agency regulation given their predictive performance before and since the Asian financial crisis, or with Russia's debt transgressions in 1998.

Credit enhancement is intended to support that process but none of the three main rating methods is best suited to the risks with which the proposal is concerned. An actuarial method uses loss data to estimate necessary credit enhancement; appropriate for many asset-backed securities but unreliable when data histories and NPL accounting are poor. Cashflow modeling analysis is helpful when asset performance data is unavailable but is costly and protracted. It is likely that the new agency would explore new techniques and promote a blend of methods in consultation with the rating organizations, where possible using international sectoral data to support the performance observations of Asian originators.

The proposal entails founding no additional credit rating organizations, but does envisage a dialogue on rating methodology for asset-backed securities (ABSs) between the new entity and all recognized local and international rating agencies, as well as initiating a means for mutual acceptance of local ratings by national regulatory authorities, also assisting necessary attention to legal and similar market impediments.

Rating review practice also distinguishes between conventional unsecured bonds and asset-backed securities. Public sector or corporate issues that are rated at launch

---

[12] Differences in agency methodology (and implied imperfections) are described succinctly by the BIS (2003) and Raynes & Rutledge (2003b).

will be periodically reviewed during the bond's life and upon visible changes in credit conditions. Asset-backed securities are assigned initial ratings and then ignored unless they seem likely to default. This proposal anticipates a change in practice such that seasoned asset-backed bonds become subject to periodic review to reflect the maturing of asset pools and the phased redemption of individual classes of security. A contingent capital structure is especially suited to this development. For each transaction given credit enhancement, a provision of funded capital would be assigned at launch, together with an unconditional commitment to supplement that funded contribution if certain external events occur and persist for a limited defined period.

6. Where the Proposal is Novel

Why is this approach new? Asia has hosted many structured issues since 1997-98 but almost always supported by blanket guarantees, for example, Hong Kong Mortgage Corporation issues, or credit wraps from highly-rated foreign monoline insurers. Non-Asian monoline insurers have engaged in transactions in the region since the early-1990s, almost all such firms being US-domiciled due to their sectoral genesis in guaranteeing domestic US municipal bonds.

6.1. Past initiatives

Efforts to build a regional monoline insurer in Asia failed soon after the crisis: the company was inadequately vested and in alarm its shareholders failed to agree remedial action to protect its young, imbalanced portfolio. The eponymous Asian Securitization & Infrastructure Assurance Pte Limited (ASIA Ltd) was formed in 1996 to be the region's first indigenous monoline insurer. It posted losses in its third operating year, lost its investment grade credit rating and reinsurance cover and has since been dormant with its insured portfolio being wound down.

The 1997-98 crisis may have occurred too soon after formation for ASIA Ltd to have established a diversified portfolio. The company failed less from credit losses but rather its poor capitalization and the deleterious consequent effects on insured capacity and credit ratings. For a commercial organization hoping to enhance credit risk ASIA Ltd carried too weak a credit rating (single-A) to meet its purpose. ASIA Ltd may have needed US$700 million in founding capital or commitments to obtain AAA ratings. The cost was rejected, partly in the mistaken belief that the company could function as a general regional monoline insurer with single-A ratings.[13] The

---

[13] Hong Kong Monetary Authority research cited in Dalla, 2002. ACA Financial Guaranty Corp is the only US monoline insurer with credit ratings as low as single-A. It was established in 1997 but focuses on specialist transactions with atypical risks. Even though ASIA Ltd's portfolio was imbalanced at the time of the crash it is doubtful that a single-A insurer with general objectives could have succeeded even in a low interest rate, risk-preferring conditions such as those prevailing in global markets in 2004 and early 2005.

ratings finally fell below investment grade upon the company's ceasing to write new business. This proposal assumes that the merits of active debt markets are now better understood so that the initiatives may encourage appropriate national support not possible from ASIA Ltd's heterogeneous owners.

6.2. A new approach

This new proposal differs in its permanence, in the way it approaches credit enhancement, in the generic mechanism used to ensure that complete and dependable sales of assets underpin new issues of securities, and in its ability to allow the packaging or synthetic treatment of most asset classes.

The new agency need not be profit-seeking but its providers of capital will demand commercial compensation, derived from guarantee fees and (ultimately) pool receipts. While the agency may permit the transfer of all financial asset classes, market practitioners may believe that existing resource economics give sufficient support to any particular transaction such that the agency need not be involved. For example, it is likely that impaired assets and corporate loans will be securitized far more often than single property commercial mortgage loans, future receipts or credit card receivables.

6.3. Cost effectiveness

In contrast, this proposal's innovation springs from cost-effectiveness and productive scope in external credit enhancement, how new (non-distressed) financial assets are volunteered for securitization, and its regional administration. Resources will be applied predominantly to the provision of transactional or program credit enhancement, ideally with administration and risk management outsourced as with Euroclear prior to 2001. The proposal offers a continuing means to generate securities of credit quality acceptable to investors, using hitherto unsuitable assets (in addition to NPLs). The scheme would give such continuity of supply that investors see structured finance as predictable rather than episodic. It anticipates a shift in rating practice such that seasoned ABSs are subject to periodic review to reflect the maturing of asset pools and phased redemption of securities. A contingent capital structure is well-suited to this approach. For each transaction given credit enhancement, a provision of funded capital would be assigned at launch, together with an unconditional commitment to supplement that funded contribution if certain events occur.

For cost-effectiveness, the proposed agency's undertakings will be supported in part by contingent capital provided by shareholders, committed at inception. Subsequent funded infusions to the agency could support cash calls arising under its contingent liabilities or to maintain prudential balance sheet ratios, and ultimately reflect the risk outlook for any securitized asset pool guaranteed by the agency. This technique is well-understood by regulators and credit rating organizations. The agency's shareholders will be predominantly sovereign or supranational, so its capital structure must be distinguished from transactions inherently subject to moral hazard. The terms of unfunded commitments will be subject to pre-determined commercial conditions, influenced neither individually nor collectively by shareholders. There are many precedents in commercial reinsurance practice and in the history of credit default swaps over the past decade to support this model. Triggers are standardized, typically under ISDA guidelines, and are subject to regulatory oversight and rating agency appraisal.

How does this proposal differ in detail from other models, and what are the associated risks and costs? Securitization relies upon system assumptions (adequate legal, regulatory, accounting and taxation structures) and pools of assets of sufficient economic value to sustain acceptable transaction economics. Generically in structured finance, asset data must be available, reliable and relate to identifiable cash flows. Transaction structuring can achieve almost any result with the poorest of subject assets but the acceptable cost of completion through credit enhancement (over-collateralization or external support) can be constrained.

6.4. Strategic and commercial objectives

While the technique can clear financial debris in any of the review economies, this became generally feasible chiefly because the post-crisis imperative for balance sheet repair made transaction costs more tolerable. The result has been a notable recycling of assets, a growth in synthetic transactions since 1999-2000 and a resulting improvement in bank and corporate balance sheets in certain countries.[14] The greatest success has been achieved in Korea, with a volume of successful securitized debt issues since 1998 (when legislation first permitted asset-backed securities) greatly exceeding those elsewhere but transaction growth is needed in China, India, Southeast Asia and Taiwan, as well as in the more sophisticated setting of Japan.

The proposal differs from conventional securitized transactions attempted in Asia in the past decade in three respects:

- The motives that encourage or compel originators to relinquish assets.
- The nature and source of external credit enhancement.
- Regional administration.

It is explicitly not concerned with providing third party guarantees for single obligor risks, especially in unique transactions; its aims are wholly market-

---

[14] In synthetic transactions, an originator hedges risk assets using credit default swaps or guarantees in series. The swap counterparty may be a third party (insurance company or SPV) that then issues conventional securities to bond investors. Critically, assets do not leave the originator's balance sheet, making it appropriate for portfolios where loans are extended in several jurisdictions or when it may be impossible to create a reliable trust or perfect changes in title. Cross-border complications, varying legal regimes and foreign exchange issues are of little concern in the transfer of pure credit risk. Synthetic securitizations (especially CLOs) entail the transfer of only part of an underlying risk to investors through the issue of securities.

orientated. For the agency to commit capital to simple credit guarantee activities is to duplicate a function performed adequately in all but extreme market conditions by private sector banks and specialist financial institutions and is likely to establish an unnecessary moral hazard. Ignoring cofinancing schemes, international organizations have provided single obligor guarantees in conditions of stress when credit availability was minimal. Despite intentions, in no case has the transaction created a favorable precedent; all were costly models. For example, soon after the collapse of Long-Term Capital Management in 1998, Electricity Generating Authority of Thailand issued US$300m in 10 year fixed rate bonds, with principal and one interest coupon guaranteed inter alia by the World Bank. In the poorest conditions, the issue was completed, selling mainly to commercial banks and has never been liquid. This deal succeeded only as a distorting novelty, offering nothing to encourage market development. International organizations may properly provide credit in extremis but issues such as this are costly models.[15]

Companion reforms described elsewhere in detail may alone generate insufficient tradable risk to meet Asia's risk management goals.[16] This proposal uses a conventional asset-backed security structure in a regional setting, fuelled by assets located in all parts of East Asia. Thus the scheme's motive is to facilitate a growing volume of well-rated new issues and give such continuity of supply to investors that they see structured finance as predictable rather than episodic. The agency will be sufficiently capitalized, with resources applied predominantly to the provision of transactional or program credit enhancement, ideally with administration and risk management functions outsourced in a similar fashion to Euroclear prior to 2001, both to limit the direct influence of individual shareholders and help avoid the fate of ASIA Ltd.

These mechanics will allow for relatively high ratings so as to attract new investors to regional and major currencies issues, an accepted imperative for greater participation and activity. Not only will the agency assist in recycling impaired financial assets in high volumes, but in the long-term may become a means to encourage commercial lenders' credit support for SMEs. Smaller businesses may seldom have access to capital markets, directly or otherwise, but Asia's banks would be better able to meet their demands for loans and services were it possible for corporate risk assets to be funded or refinanced through securitization. This also makes use of the asymmetric information frequently available to banks.

6.5. *Effects of Basel II*

The proposed Basel II capital accord would change the definitions of risk-weighted assets accepted by participating national authorities and is relevant to this proposal in two respects:

---

[15] *Euroweek* issues 570-573, September-October 1998.

[16] Chapters 8 and 9.

- First, the accord would lessen the capital required to be set against residential mortgage loans and certain SME lending, and alter capital requirements for corporate credit (increasing for sub-investment grade risks, decreasing for others).
- Second, the treatment of certain higher risk (or unrated) tranches of securitized transactions and supporting liquidity facilities would demand increased capital compared to Basel I.

If adopted by national authorities, the new accord would have implications for some of the transactions contemplated by the proposal but not such as to make a material difference to its operations or effectiveness.[17]

6.6. Assessment

The advantages of the proposal are that it is able to deal with all financial assets and will cause a considerable increase in issuance and trading activity without disturbing the value of links between banks and SMEs. As a real comparison, the concept resembles that used to recycle defaulted or delinquent bonds and NPLs in post-crisis Korea.[18]

It is recognized that as elsewhere, direct public bond issuance by Asian SMEs will remain largely infeasible for the medium-term. Banks can be effective providers of finance for medium-scale enterprises (they are accustomed to imperfect information and high initial lending costs) but may need incentives to lend or renew credit lines, not only at times of heightened risk. An effective refinancing vehicle could provide this essential incentive while avoiding the prohibitive transaction costs of pooled debt issuance for SMEs.

The relaxation after 1987 of US Glass-Steagall legislation allowing commercial banks to underwrite corporate securities led initially to their arranging a disproportionate number of modest issues for SMEs partly due to the competitive power of investment banks.[19] It may also signify the value to SMEs of their known lenders developing capital market product skills: the reform generally improved SME funding. Findings from Europe suggest that distribution skills are critical to 'local' banks retaining new issue market share against competition from global investment or universal banks.[20]

For investors, the agency provides access to credit risk more complete and transparent than generally available. The proposal only relates to portfolio change, not to altering the credit characteristics of single obligor risks: transactions or derivatives based upon such risks would be left wholly to the private sector. The main considerations of the proposal are inherent costs, essential regional

---

[17] Bank for International Settlements (2003a, 2001 and 2004).

[18] See especially Oh, Park, Park & Yang (*op cit*).

[19] Gande, Puri, Saunders & Walker (1997).

[20] Santos & Tsatsaronis (2003).

cooperation, and the removal of obstacles described in detail in chapter 8, especially in achieving price transparency in asset sales. ABS issues are no less demanding than corporate bonds in accounting or legal questions, and (as with sophisticated markets) the proposal may not work universally with equal effect.

For investors, the agency provides access to credit risk more complete and transparent than generally available in Asia.[21] The proposal only relates to portfolio change, not to altering the credit characteristics of single obligor risks: such transactions or derivatives based upon such risks would be left wholly to the private sector, regardless of elements of credit enhancement. The sole role for public policy in this respect is to encourage the creative participation by Asian domiciled banks.

The main considerations of the proposal are inherent costs, its need for regional cooperation, and the practical impediments and obstacles set out elsewhere in this volume, especially in achieving price transparency in asset sales. Asset-backed securities are no less demanding than corporate bonds as to questions of accounting and law, and the proposal may not work universally with equal effect. Yet this is true of the most sophisticated markets.

Last, the implementation of Basel II may lead to an increase in regulatory capital costs associated with certain securitized transactions, although this would affect few issues backed by impaired assets. Basel II's adoption could also encourage a shift in assets favored for securitization from residential mortgages towards loans to unrated corporate borrowers and commercial mortgages.

This proposal demand extensive cooperation among participating countries. In each case, the need for agreement upon minimum standards and therein achieve a high degree of harmonization make it essential that both structure and requirements for use be kept as simple as possible. The plan contains no suggestions as to issuance in composite or basket currencies: it is assumed that issuance will be in local and major currencies to match investor demand and to contain transaction costs.

Asia needs effective markets rather than passive accumulations of financial assets, and will benefit from a viable alternative to the banking sector, sufficiently transparent and liquid to provide a useful price signaling mechanism. Governments must agree to cooperate in best practices for legislative or regulatory change, and adopt new proposals that are supportive to market users, particularly institutional investors, wherever possible avoiding duplication in the creation of supporting market systems and financial architecture. They must also demand and encourage improvements in risk appraisal, financial disclosure and standards of corporate governance.

Active markets will not exist in Asia without cooperative government engagement in reform; government's commitment must at all times be market orientated.

References

Bank for International Settlements, 2001, Asset securitization, consultative document, Basel.
Bank for International Settlements, 2004, Changes to the securitization framework, Basel.

[21] Regional settlement could take place as in the main proposal of chapter 8.

Bank for International Settlements, 2003a, The new Basel capital accord, consultative document, Basel.
Bank for International Settlements, Credit risk transfer, Basel, 2003b.
Coase, R., 1937, The nature of the firm, 4 *Economica* (16): 386 405.
Coase, R., 1960, The problem of social cost, 3 *Journal of Law and Economics* (October): 1 44
Coase, R., 1988, The nature of the firm (1. origin; 2. meaning; 3. influence), 4 *Journal of Law and Economics* 1: 3 47.
Dalla, I. 2002, Asset-backed securities markets in selected East Asian countries, mimeo, World Bank.
Gande, A., M. Puri, A. Saunders and I. Walker, 1997, Bank underwriting of securities: modern evidence, *Review of Financial Studies* 104.
Oh, G.T., D.K. Park, J.H. Park, and D.Y. Yang, 2003, How to mobilize the Asian savings within the region: securitization & credit enhancement for the development of East Asia's bond market, Korea Institute for International Economic Policy working paper 03-02, Seoul.
Raynes, S., and A. Rutledge, 2003, The Analysis of Structured Securities; Precise Risk Measurement and Capital Allocation, New York, Oxford University Press.
Santos, J. & K. Tsatsaronis, 2003, The cost of barriers to entry: evidence from the market for corporate euro bond underwriting, BIS working paper 134.
Schwarcz, S., 2002, The universal language of international securitization, 12 Duke J. Comp. & Int'l L. 285.
Williamson, O., 1971, The vertical integration of production: market failure considerations, 61 *American Economic Review* 2:112.

Chapter 10

Building a Settlement Infrastructure for the Asian Bond Markets: *Asiasettle*

Jae-Ha Park[1], Gyutaeg Oh[2], Daekuen Park[3] and Changyong Rhee[4]

[1]Korea Institute of Finance; [2]Korea Fixed Income Research Institute and Chung-Ang University; [3]Korea Fixed Income Research Institute and Hanyang University; [4]Korea Fixed Income Research Institute and Seoul National University

1. Introduction

There has recently been a great deal of discussion on development of the Asian bond markets. This is seen as part of the larger effort to promote regional financial development and integration in East Asia. During the 9th APEC Financial Ministers meeting in September 2002, it was agreed that a regional bond market would be developed through securitization and credit guarantees. ASEAN+3 has formed six working groups to study various aspects of regional bond markets including securitization, regional credit rating agencies, regional clearing and settlement systems, regional credit guarantee agencies, and so on. EMEAP (Executives' Meeting of East Asia and Pacific Central Banks) has also set up the Asian Bond Fund (ABF) with contributions from the foreign reserves of each member bank. This fund will be managed by the Bank for International Settlements (BIS) under the mandate to invest in dollar-denominated bonds issued by qualified Asian issuers.

To many, the recent discussion on Asian bond markets seems like *deja vu* of the old Asian Bond Market idea of the early 1990s. The launching of the Dragon Bond initiatives in the early 1990s sparked discussion in Asia on the development of the Asian Bond Market, and it continued through the end of the decade. At that time, the HKMA (Hong Kong Monetary Authority) proposed the establishment of AsiaClear as a regional central securities depository to provide clearing and settlement service for the Asian Bond Market.

In retrospect, however, the Asian Bond Market initiatives of the 1990s were merely talk without action. The proponents of the Asian Bond Market failed to establish a consensus on its benefits. There was skepticism on the growth potential of the Asian Bond Market due to the reluctance of Asian countries to liberalize and open up their domestic capital markets for fear of creating market distortions and making themselves vulnerable to speculative attacks. The skeptics also did not believe that the Asian Bond Market would attract much attention because there were already well established, efficient international bond markets, such as the Eurobond markets. It should be pointed out, however, that the lack of action on creation of the Asian Bond Market was also due to the non-existence of institutions in Asia, such as the BIS and European Central Bank (ECB) in Europe, that can mediate the conflicts of national interest that would arise in the process of international financial market integration.

The situation changed greatly during the Asian financial crisis. We will finally see some meaningful action to establish Asian bond markets in the near future. There is now a strong realization that the underdevelopment of the bond markets of the region greatly exacerbated and, perhaps, caused the Asian financial crisis of 1997. Both the bank-dominated financial systems and the banks themselves were at the heart of the crisis because firms that had been so long dependent upon them for funds could not find alternative sources of financing when the crisis erupted.

The idea of regional bond markets is also promoted as a means of overcoming the double mismatch problem that most Asian borrowers face when they try to raise funds from abroad. The double mismatch refers to currency and maturity mismatches, and it is also considered one of the root causes of the 1997 Asian financial crisis.

Finally, development of regional bond markets is promoted as a way to facilitate mobilization of East Asian savings. The foreign exchange reserves of most Asian countries have increased significantly since the financial crisis, helped by Asian governments' actions to prevent recurrence of a financial crisis and the huge current account surpluses triggered by the economic recession and sharp currency depreciations that the financial crisis brought about. By 2002, Asian economies altogether held nearly half of the global foreign exchange reserves, though the bulk of these foreign reserves are invested in safe and liquid assets such as U.S. treasury securities and supranational bonds. Until Asian bond markets are established, East Asian borrowers have to turn to the international financial markets. East Asia as a whole can be considered an importer of safe assets and an exporter of risky assets. As has been pointed out by Oh et. al (2003), such a pattern of capital flows is not desirable in the sense that it deprives the regional financial markets and institutions of valuable opportunities to develop and could make the countries in the region vulnerable to future financial crises.

A consensus among Asian economies has emerged that regional bond markets should be promoted in order to facilitate recycling of regional savings and to prevent recurrence of financial crises. This has led to active discussion on how Asian bond markets should be developed, but these discussions have so far concentrated only on the rationale of the regional bond markets and the strategies and schemes to increase the supply and demand of Asian bonds. The ABF, for example, would be assigned the task of stimulating demand for Asian paper. The securitization and credit guarantee scheme proposed by the Korean government, Oh and Park (Chapter 3 and 2003), and the Asian currency basket bond ideas proposed by Ito (2003) and Olarn (2003) are designed to increase the supply of Asian bonds and resolve the double mismatch problem. Yet, there has been very little concrete discussion on building the various components of the institutional infrastructure for Asian bond markets, such as the clearing and settlement system and the trading platform.

Among the many components of the infrastructure needed to develop the Asian bond markets, this paper focuses on the cross-border clearing and settlement system. This chapter specifically attempts to determine if it is possible to establish bond markets where bonds are denominated, issued, and settled in Asian currencies, most of which are not internationalized. It also seeks to determine if it is necessary to establish a new Asian settlement system even though there are already established cross-border settlement systems operated by ICSDs like Euroclear and Clearstream. If so, what should the operational mode and the governance structure of the new Asian ICSD be?

This chapter puts forward two major arguments. First, we expect that the Asian bond markets will have their genesis as offshore financial markets subject to less regulation and characterized by efficient trading and clearing and settlement systems. Second, we recommend the establishment of a regional ICSD dubbed AsiaSettle. It would be created by linking the central banks and NCSDs (National CSDs) of each economy and would serve as the clearing and settlement system for the Asian bond markets. At the initial stage, AsiaSettle would perform as the clearing and settlement system for local currency-denominated government bonds of Asian economies issued in offshore markets. The focus in the early stages on government bonds is extremely important; i.e., because the supply of high-quality bonds in the private sector is low, high-quality government bonds would be an indispensable catalyst for the development of the Asian bond markets.

We also discuss the necessity for AsiaSettle to also function as the CCP (central counterparty) for the exchange of government bonds, and to possess ECN (Electronic Communication Networks) platform capabilities. Furthermore, we discuss the desirable governance structure of AsiaSettle and propose that AsiaSettle be established as an institution invested by each economy's NCSD and central bank, or as a new multilateral agency for Asia.

This chapter is organized as follows. Section 2 makes the case for Asian economies establishing and utilizing offshore financial markets in the incipient stage of developing the Asian bonds markets. Section 3 describes the current cross-border clearing and settlement system in Asia and the role of the existing ICSDs. In section 4, we propose the establishment of AsiaSettle as a regional ICSD, a settlement and clearing infrastructure for the Asian bond markets. A detailed explanation of the modus operandi of AsiaSettle is offered, and we discuss the pros and cons of introducing CCP functions in AsiaSettle. Section 5 addresses the ownership structure of AsiaSettle, and section 6 concludes the chapter.

2. Launching the Asian Bond Markets Offshore

There is no denying that the best way to begin developing the Asian bond markets is to develop each economy's domestic bond market and open it up to foreign investors. In other words, the optimal method of developing cross-border trading in Asia is for Asian economies to open up their domestic bond markets to enable Asian issuers to issue bonds in any jurisdiction of their choice and to enable investors to invest in bonds in the domestic market of any jurisdiction. However, the bond markets of East Asian economies are at greatly varying stages of development. Some are much more liberalized than others, and different kinds of capital controls are imposed. Most Asian economies do not even have the economies of scale to support all the components of the bond market infrastructure, such as a settlement and depository system, primary dealer system, credit rating agencies, bond pricing agencies, and credit guarantee agencies, which are needed to develop domestic bond markets. It is, therefore, very unrealistic to expect every Asian economy to develop and open up its domestic bond markets in the near future.

Under these circumstances, the Asian bond markets will likely begin to develop as offshore bond markets, following in the footsteps of the Eurobond market some 40 years ago. The advantage of offshore markets is that they are subject to less onerous regulation than onshore markets. In order to protect domestic investors and maintain financial market stability, jurisdictions usually impose strict accounting standards, disclosure requirements, and foreign exchange transaction restrictions in the domestic markets. Since the majority of participants in offshore markets are non-residents, economies do not impose such strict regulations on offshore markets.

The Eurobond market was launched in 1957 with a $ 5 million U.S. dollar-denominated bond issued by a Belgium company, Petrofina.[1] It has since become the biggest international bond market, mainly because it is not subject to as much regulation as domestic markets. By late 2002, the Eurobond market was $ 600 billion in size. Eurobonds are issued in bearer form, so anonymity is guaranteed. The interest is paid in gross and is free from withholding taxes. Figure 10-1 compares the regulations of the Eurobond market with those of domestic bond and foreign bond markets. It becomes clear even after only a cursory examination that there is less regulation on the Eurobond market than on other markets.

The fact that Asian countries are interested in issuing local currency-denominated bonds will work as an advantage in the development of offshore markets for Asian bonds. In the early stage of development of the Eurobond market, countries were eager to issue U.S. dollar-denominated bonds, but were reluctant to allow bonds denominated in their own currencies to be issued in foreign countries for fear of losing control of their monetary policy and facilitating speculative attacks on their currencies. Germany and Japan once restricted issuance of Eurobonds denominated in their currencies. Switzerland still does not allow issuance of Swiss franc-denominated Eurobonds.[2] Asian economies, on the other hand, prefer to issue bonds in their own currencies because the experience of the 1997 financial crisis made them understand the importance of avoiding currency mismatches when they raise funds abroad.

---

[1] Mendelson (1980)

[2] A country can restrict issuance of bonds denominated in its currency in offshore markets because the transactions of the bonds denominated in its currency have to be settled in the end through the Central Bank settlement system to ensure finality of the settlement.

	US Market: Domestic and Foreign Bonds	Non-US Market: Domestic and Foreign Bonds	Eurobond Market
Regulatory Bodies	Securities and Exchange Commission	Official agency approval	Minimum regulatory control
Disclosure requirements	More detailed High initial expense High ongoing expense Onerous to non-US firms	Variable	Determined by market practices
Issuing costs	0.75-1.00%	Variable to 4.0%	2.0-2.5%
Rating requirements	Yes	Usually no.	No, but commonly done
Exchange listing	Usually not listed	Listing is usual.	Listing is usual.
Queuing	No queue	Queuing is common	No queue
Currency of denomination restrictions	United States does not restrict the use of US$	Part of queuing Many foreign countries (Germany, Switzerland) have in past or now restrict use of currency	No restrictions on use of US$ or C$
Speed of Issuance	Relatively slow until Rule 415 on "shelf registration"	Variable.	Usually fast-"bought deal" leads to fast issuance

Source: Levich (1985)

***Figure 10-1.* Regulation of bond issues in the international bond markets**

Offshore financial markets are not only useful in developing Asian bond markets, they will also be helpful in integrating the Asian financial markets by bringing uniformity in financial market regulation throughout the region. Integrating financial markets requires more than merely opening up domestic financial markets to foreign financial institutions, issuers, and investors. Unless the regulations of each jurisdiction are reconciled, the full benefits of market integration will not be realized. For example, an investment bank specializing in credit derivatives will not be able to perform successfully in a country where credit derivatives are completely prohibited, even if it is granted national treatment.

In order to reconcile the regulations of each jurisdiction, the EMU is taking the "one passport" approach. Accordingly, each host country allows foreign financial institutions to operate under their home countries' regulations. The investment bank described above would, therefore, be able to deal in credit derivatives regardless of whether the host country allows credit derivatives or not, if it is allowed to handle them by its home country. In such a case, the host country will find that the domestic investment banks are at odds with foreign investment banks that can deal in credit derivatives. In order to level the playing field, the host country will allow domestic investment banks to handle credit derivatives. In time, every other country will follow suit, and the harmonization of regulatory regimes will occur.

Scott (2000) argues that harmonization of regulation can also be achieved through offshore financial markets. Since countries do not find it necessary to regulate offshore financial markets as strictly as their domestic markets, it will be easier to harmonize financial regulations on offshore markets of each country. The strategic approach of using offshore markets as a catalyst for developing Asian bond markets will be suitable in achieving harmonization of regulation in East Asia where economies, at present, are not interested in integrating their domestic financial markets but are interested in developing their offshore financial markets as regional financial centers for Asian bond markets.

Asian economies already realize the strategic importance of offshore financial markets in fostering Asian bond markets. Japan has recently carried out a number of reforms to expand the function of the offshore bond market. Thailand plans to issue Baht-denominated bonds in the Japanese offshore market. We expect more economies to follow suit. Jurisdictions interested in becoming regional financial centers for Asian bond markets will establish offshore bond markets and allow foreign issuers to issue bonds in their own currencies instead of going through the time consuming process of lifting regulations on domestic bond markets. They will also compete to attract issuers and investors by ensuring that their infrastructures are efficient and offer the full functionality required including securities trading capability and clearing and settlement.

Most of the Asian bonds issued in offshore markets will be traded in the OTC markets if organized exchanges are not available. However, to increase liquidity and marketability, the Asian bonds need to be listed on exchanges. Even though there is no listing requirement, most Eurobonds are listed on exchanges like the Luxemburg Exchange. Jurisdictions that aspire to be regional financial centers for Asian bond markets will build exchanges for offshore markets. The Labuan International Financial Exchange (LFX) of Malaysia is a good example. Some may open their own exchanges for offshore bond trading.

Each jurisdiction may offer clearing and settlement service by expanding the service of its own national CSD (NCSD). However, for more efficient clearing and settlement of Asian bond transactions, Asia may require a regional clearing and settlement system. In the next section, we will take a more detailed look at the clearing and settlement systems now employed in Asia and determine whether or not they can be used for cross-border settlements of Asian bond transactions.

3. Cross Border Settlement in Asia

Securities traded in the Eurobond markets are usually settled and deposited through ICSDs such as Euroclear or Clearstream. In principle, the settlement of Asian bonds that are denominated in Asian currencies can also be settled through the existing ICSDs or other cross-border settlement methods. This section reviews the pros and cons of cross-border settlement systems currently available for the bonds denominated in Asian currencies.[3]

---

[3] BIS(1995), the Giovannini Group(2001) and Yeong-Suk Park & Jeong-Hoon Hong(2001) discuss current cross-border settlement systems.

3.1. Use of an ICSD (international central securities depository)

There is a widespread but mistaken belief that it is difficult to settle bonds denominated in Asian currencies through the existing ICSDs since most Asian currencies are not internationalized. In principle, internationalization of a currency is not a determinant of or ease of security settlement through ICSDs. The settlement of non-internationalized currencies can be performed using correspondent banks that are located in the corresponding jurisdiction. Figure 10-2 shows an example of settlement for a Eurobond denominated in Baht that is traded on the Korean offshore market.

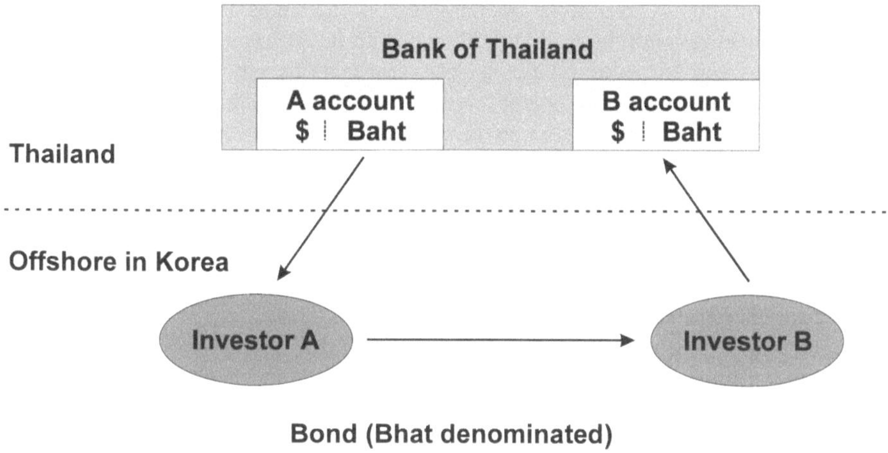

Figure 10-2. **Settlement of Eurobond denominated in Baht**

Let us assume that investor A sells the Thai government bond denominated in Baht to investor B in the offshore market in Korea. Assume that the payment should be settled in Baht, but settlement in Baht in the Korean offshore market is impossible since the Baht is not internationalized. Moreover, settlement in Baht should pass through the central bank of Thailand to guarantee the finality of the settlement. In fact, the settlement can be finalized through the investors' correspondent banks located in Thailand. Buyer B in Korea remits the corresponding U.S. dollar amounts to his/her bank in Thailand. B's bank converts the dollar remittance into Baht and transfers the proceeds to seller A's account through the settlement system of the central bank of Thailand. In turn, investor A's bank in Thailand converts the Baht deposit into dollars and sends the funds to seller A's account in Korea. Therefore, even though the Baht is not an internationalized currency, bonds denominated in Baht can be settled as long as there is convertibility between the U.S. dollar and Baht. Of course, in the example above, if the convertibility of the Baht is somehow restricted, settlement is not possible. This case shows that it is the convertibility and not the internationalization of currencies that determines whether or not cross-border settlement is possible.

The same issue is faced in settlement through the ICSDs. Currently, Euroclear offers investors a choice of currencies of settlement, but as shown in Table 10-1, the range of choices is very limited.[4] Only 32 currencies of 42 economies are available, and of these, only nine are Asian currencies. The currencies of Korea, China, India, Taiwan are currently excluded, but this is not because they are not internationalized. The Malaysian ringgit and Singaporean dollar are settlement currencies in Euroclear even though they are also not internationalized.

The reason most Asian currencies are not Euroclear settlement currencies is that there are some limitations on their convertibility and substantial legal uncertainties regarding the applicable regulations on foreign currency transactions. In Korea, for example, omnibus accounts are not permitted. This is a major reason that the Korean won is excluded from the list.[5] Non-resident investors in Korea are required to report their individual identities when they open Korean won-denominated accounts. This regulation prohibits ICSDs from opening omibus accounts (an account for large groups of investors) with the NCSD in Korea. If an ICSD has an omnibus account in its own name and manages all the internal transactions among its members, the government fears that it will not be able to monitor individual transactions. This regulation, however, subjects foreign investors to onerous procedural requirements and does not permit protection of the investors' anonymity. It is no wonder that Euroclear does not designate the Korean won as a currency of settlement.[6]

Even in the case that Asian bonds are deposited into an NCSD of the country of issuance, not in an ICSD, the security and settlement can still be executed through an ICSD. In that case, the ICSD should be linked to NCSDs of individual jurisdictions or to custodian banks that are members of NCSDs. Jurisdictions that have these linkages with ICSDs are called clearing members. Table 10-2 shows the 31 clearing members of Euroclear as of 2002. Of these, there were seven Asian, 16 European, and four North and South American countries. The two remaining countries were South Africa and Russia.[7]

In Asia, Australia and New Zealand were excluded, and only seven jurisdictions are directly or indirectly connected to Euroclear: Hong Kong, Japan, Singapore, Thailand, the Philippines, Malaysia, and Indonesia, with some restriction on Malaysia and Indonesia. Other Asian economies such as Korea, China, Taiwan, India, Pakistan, are also excluded. The low coverage of Euroclear in the Asian region indicates that there is potential demand for a regional ICSD, and we will take this issue up in the next section.

---

[4] Euroclear(2002a) lists settlement currencies and cash correspondents.

[5] See KFIRI(2003) about reasons that ICSDs exclude Korea Won from settlement currencies.

[6] The Indonesian rupiah is a currency of settlement in Euroclear, but its use became somewhat restricted after the financial crisis in 1997. The restriction is not due to exchange rate or credit risk to Euroclear. As the settlement of Euroclear is done via the RTGS and DVP systems, Euroclear is not subject to any exchange rate or credit risk. The restriction was introduced due to increasing uncertainty with regard to regulation on capital transactions in Indonesia.

[7] This figure includes all the countries linked with Euroclear through specialized depositories, common depositories, or clearing depositories.

Table 10-1. Currencies of Settlement in Euroclear

Region	Country	
Asia	Australia (ARS), New Zealand (NZD), Hongkong (HKD), Indonesia (IDR), Japan (JPY), Malaysia (MYR), Philippines (PHP), Singapore (SGD), Thailand (THB)	9 currencies of 9 countries
Europe	EURO (Austria, Belgium, Deutschland, Finland, France, Greece, Ireland, Italy, Portugal, Spain, Luxembourg, the Netherlands), Norway (NOK), Sweden (SEK), Denmark (DKK), Switzerland (CHF), the United Kingdom (GBP), [Republic of Croatia (HRK), Czech (CZK), Republic of Iceland (ISK), Slovakia (SKK), Estonia (EEK), Hungary (HUF), Lithuania (LTL), Latvia (LVL), Poland (PLN)]*	15 currencies of 26 countries
North/South America	USA (USD), Argentina (ARS), Canada (CAD), Mexico (MXN)	4 currencies of 4 countries
The Middle East & Africa	South Africa (ZAR), [Kuwait (KWD), Israel (ILS)]*	3 currencies of 3 countries
Others	Gold (XAU)**	1 currency
Total	32 currencies of 42 jurisdictions	

* Jurisdictions in [ ] are not clearing members of Euroclear, but their currencies are designated as currencies of settlement. Russia is a clearing member of Euroclear, but the Russian rouble is not a currency of settlement (Payment is settled in USD). Gold is converted into one of the currencies of settlement and then settled according to its value in the currency in question.

Source: KSD

Table 10-2. Jurisdictions with settlement linkages to Euroclear

Region	Jurisdiction	
Asia	Australia, New Zealand, Hong Kong, Indonesia, Japan, Malaysia, the Philippines, Singapore, Thailand	9 jurisdictions
Europe	Belgium, Finland, France, Germany, Greece, Ireland, Luxembourg, the Netherlands, Norway, Portugal, Spain, Sweden, Switzerland, Great Britain Austria, Italy	16 countries
America	United States of America, Argentina, Canada, Mexico	4 countries
Others	Russia, South Africa	2 countries
Total	31 jurisdictions (specialized depositary, common depositary, clearing depository included)	

Source: KSD

The selection criteria for clearing members are not identical to those for currencies of settlement. All four cases are possible if we compare Table 10-1 and Table 10-2. First, countries such as Japan and Thailand are clearing members of Euroclear, and their currencies are designated currencies of settlement. Second, Russia is a clearing member of Euroclear, but its currency is not a settlement currency. Third, like Korea, there are countries that are not clearing members and whose currencies are not designated as currencies of settlement. Fourth, countries such as Croatia, Czech, Israel, and Iceland are not clearing members, but their currencies are used for settlement.

3.2. Bilateral linkages between NCSDs for cross-border settlements

If bilateral linkages can be established among NCSDs, cross border settlement is possible without ICSDs. In fact, ECSDA (European Central Securities Depositories Association) once proposed bilateral linkage models for cross-border settlement in Europe.[8] Figure 10-3 shows two pan-European bilateral linkage models that ECSDA has studied. One is a Eurolinks Real-time Network model (Spaghetti model), and the other is a European Financial Superhighway (Canneloni model). The former connects all NCSDs with each other, while the latter uses major NCSDs as pivots to connect other small NCSDs. Both models emphasize the need to strengthen mutual linkages among NCSDs.

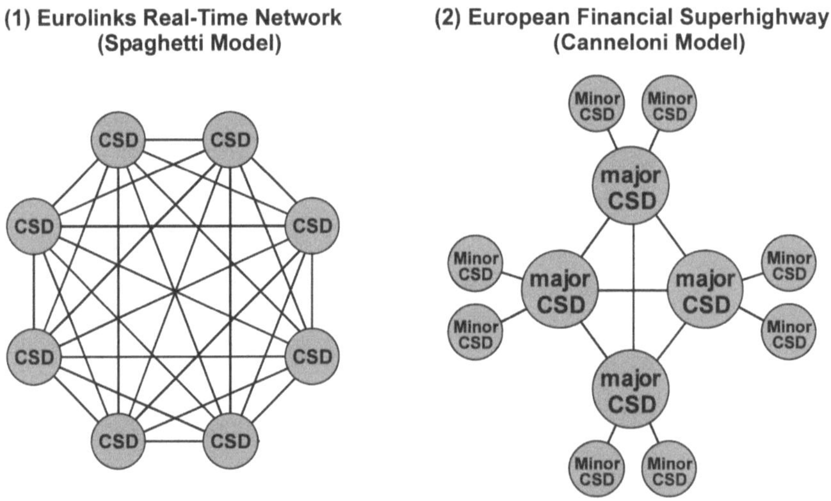

Figure 10-3. **Bilateral linkage models of ECSDA**

[8] 中島眞志·宿輪純一(2002) discusses two bilateral linkage models for cross-border settlement proposed by ECSDA.

Within Asia, Hong Kong has shown the greatest interest in bilateral linkage models. The HKMA (Hong Kong Monetary Authority) has proposed the establishment of AsiaClear, a regional settlement institution, by linking the clearing and settlement systems of member economies in Asia with the same manner as the Internet. That is, the HKMA defines AsiaClear not as a single hub institution, but as a common network among individual NCSDs in Asia. Thanks to the advancement in IT technology, HKMA believes that linking NCSDs is now feasible in virtual space. For this reason, the conflict of interests as to where to locate AsiaClear is no longer an issue.[9] In fact, the HKMA has been actively pursuing linkages with other Asian economies; now it has the linkages with Australia, New Zealand, and Korea, and soon it will have a linkage with China.[10]

However, there are a number of problems in applying bilateral linkage models to Asia. First, it is an inefficient method compared with settlement through ICSDs. Transaction costs in bilateral linkage models would likely be high as each NCSD has to open accounts in the NCSDs of all counter-parties. Second, these models could only handle securities registered in both NCSDs being used for a transaction. Third, the initial set-up costs of establishing bilateral linkages can be high if jurisdictions do not share standardized settlement platforms.[11] However, the most important bottleneck in applying bilateral linkage models is that bond markets in Asian economies are at such greatly varying stages of development that they cannot be linked to each other. Among Asian NCSDs, only seven jurisdictions (Australia, Hong Kong, Japan, Korea, Malaysia, New Zealand, and Singapore) are using RTGS (real-time gross settlement) and DVP (delivery versus payment) systems. The only economies in Asia that are linked to Euroclear are Australia, Hong Kong, Japan, New Zealand, the Philippines, Thailand, and Singapore. Figure 10-4 shows the wide difference among Asian NCSDs with regard to compliance with the recommendations of G30/ISSA, which renders the building of bilateral linkages among them difficult.[12] Different legal systems are another factor. Unlike Europe, where the legal systems of most countries are relatively similar, Asian countries have a much more varied historical background, culture, and legal systems, which makes it difficult to standardize linkages among Asian NCSDs.

---

[9] HKMA researched on the capacity of financial markets and IT in Hong Kong that enable Hong Kong to function as a financial herb in Asia. See HKMA (1997).

[10] See HKMA(1997b-2002) to survey the situation of linkages between HKMA and other NCSDs in Asia.

[11] Yeong-Suk Park & Jeong-Hoon Hong (2001) discusses the advantage and disadvantage of bilateral linkage models.

[12] For more details, see ISSA (2002).

	Bangladesh	China	Hong Kong	India	Indonesia	Japan	Korea	Malaysia	Pakistan	Philippines	Singapore	Thailand	Taiwan
Trade comparisons between direct market participants by T+0													
Matched trade details should be linked to the settlement system													
Indirect market participants to achieve affirmation by T+1													
Central depository, broadest possible participation													
Widest possible range of depository eligible instruments													
Immobilisation/dematerialisation to the utmost extent possible													
Comparable rules and practices in case of multiple CSDs													
Real time gross settlement system													
Trade netting system as per 'Lamfalussy-Recommendations'													
Delivery versus payment (DVP) as defined by ISSA													
Same day funds for securities settlement													
Same day funds for the servicing of securities portfolios													
A rolling settlement system should be adopted by all markets													
Final settlement for all trades by T+3													
Securities lending and borrowing should be encouraged													
Existing regulatory and taxation barriers should be removed													
ISO standard 7775 (Securities messages)													
ISO standard 6166 (ISIN numbering system)													

***Figure 10-4.* NCSDs of Asian jurisdictions: Compliance with G30/ISSA Recommendations**

* The yellow boxes indicate cases where the recommendations of G30/ISSA are satisfied.

Source: KSD

Currently, there are few bilateral linkages among Asian NCSDs. Some of these are between Australia and New Zealand, Hong Kong and New Zealand, Korea and Hong Kong, and Japan and Hong Kong. Except for the linkage between Australia and New Zealand, trading volumes are quite minimal, thus indicating that bilateral linkage models are infeasible for the Asian bond markets.

3.3. Alternative channels for cross-border settlement

Another way to conduct cross-border settlements is to use a local agent (a custodian) who is a member of the NCSD in the country of issue or a global custodian that employs a local agent as a sub-custodian.[13] Historically, local agents have been used most frequently in cross border settlement, especially when security settlements must be made with countries that have no linkage between NCSDs or between an NCSD and ICSD. However, using a local custodian has one important disadvantage in that investors should designate a separate local custodian for each country where investment will be directed, and sometimes the fees charged by local custodians can be significant. Due to this cost disadvantage, institutional investors have increasingly used global custodians that provide settlement and custody services in multiple markets through a single gateway by integrating services performed by a network of sub-custodians, including its own local branches. Global custodians can have cost advantages through economies of scale and scope. Another important advantage of using global custodians is the availability of integrated multi-currency banking and cash management services as most global custodians are large international commercial banks. Most settlements of Asian securities are made through global custodians, not ICSDs, using international currencies such as the U.S. dollar.

As a matter of fact, the business base of GCs lies in the inefficiency of the international financial market due to differences in the trading, clearing, and settlement systems of each country. GCs provide investors with the convenience of a single interface for their international security transactions. The convenience of a single gateway, however, must be costly since GCs also have to hire local agents themselves. In addition, the quality of their services differs widely by region depending upon the quality of service provided by the local agents.

In the short run, global custodians may be the only viable alternative until the Asian bond markets reach a certain level of development. However, settlement of cross-border security transactions in Asia can be made more efficient if the trading, clearing, and settlement systems of each jurisdiction can be harmonized. In that sense, establishing an ICSD is a better way of providing settlement for Asian bond markets in the long run than using global custodians.

---

[13] BIS (1995) and the Giovannini Group(2001) compare various methods of cross-border securities settlement.

4. Building a Regional ICSD: AsiaSettle

This section proposes the construction of a regional ICSD, AsiaSettle, for the development of the Asian bond markets. As seen in section 3, it is true that the coverage of the settlement services by existing ICSDs such as Euroclear is very limited in Asia. Nevertheless, it is still important to provide a *raison d'etre* for a new regional ICSD; i.e., it should be readily apparent that the new ICSD can perform better than the existing ICSDs.

4.1. Need for a regional ICSD

As most Asian currencies are not internationalized, the payment settlement of Asian bonds denominated in local currencies must be finalized in a local market, even though securities settlement can be done through ICSDs located in Europe. However, due to the time difference between Europe and Asia, real-time settlement of Asian bonds is impossible, and there have calls to establish a regional ICSD within Asia, the third time zone, in order to cover the non-business hours of the two other time zones; Europe and the Americas.

To illustrate the third time zone problem, consider the settlement process of an Asian bond that is denominated in Hong Kong dollars.[14] Hong Kong is seven hours ahead of Brussels, where Euroclear is located. Assume that the settlement date of the bond is October 2 in Brussels. In order to finalize the settlement by that date, Euroclear currently mandates that a buyer and a seller deposit money and security in a common depository of Euroclear in Hong Kong, HSBC bank, by October 1, which is a day before the settlement date. After getting notification from HSBC overnight, Euroclear Bank in Brussels completes the security settlement by 9 a.m. on October 2 (4 p.m. in Hong Kong). Then, a seller in Hong Kong can withdraw Hong Kong dollars, and the settlement can be finished by October 2.

Instead of depositing money and securities a day before the settlement date, if a buyer and a seller want to settle securities by using the RTGS system on October 2 in Belgium time, the seller may not be able to withdraw money by October 2. For example, by the time the RTGS settlement is completed by 3 p.m. on October 2, it is already 10 p.m. in Hong Kong, and the bond seller has to wait until the next day to withdraw his/her money. This is one reason why Euroclear mandates that traders deposit money and securities a day in advance of settling bonds that are denominated in Asian currencies. Otherwise, it cannot secure a settlement date. If bonds are denominated in European currencies or the U.S. dollar, security and payment settlement can be completed on the same day through the RTGS system as there is no time difference, and the time difference between Europe and the Americas works in favor between security settlement and payment settlement. The time zone problem implies that investors have to bear the extra cost of losing liquidity for a day when trading Asian currency-denominated bonds. If there is a regional ICSD within Asia, investors will not face this extra cost. The benefit of solving the third time zone

---

[14] For the detailed settlement procedure, refer to Euroclear (2003).

problem can be significant considering that major investors for Asian currency-denominated bonds are institutional investors located in Asia.

In addition to the time difference problem, there is another reason for establishing a regional ICSD, AsiaSettle. As previously discussed, the low coverage of ICSDs in Asia is partly due to the existence of complex regulations and legal uncertainties in local markets in Asia in cross-border trading. Setting up AsiaSettle through the cooperation of Asian governments offers a great opportunity to open domestic markets and harmonize regulations across Asia. Existing ICSDs are private entities, and Asian governments have had no incentive to ease regulations to increase business flows for them unless doing is very much in their national interests. However, building a regional ICSD is currently being discussed under the consent of Asian governments as a way of promoting Asian bond markets. AsiaSettle can be an effective catalyst in easing regulations and opening up local markets in Asia, and consequently in developing the Asian bond markets.

4.2. Models for AsiaSettle

In building an ICSD, the relation between the ICSDs and NCSDs is a key issue. There are two models available. One is a hub and spoke model where an ICSD plays the role of hub and the NCSDs are spokes that are linked to the hub as sub-depositories. The advantage of the hub and spoke model is the low set-up costs since the existing settlement infrastructure can be fully utilized. However, the model cannot be readily implemented since every NCSD naturally wants to be a hub and no one wants to be a spoke. The second model is a merger between ICSDs and NCSDs, as in the case of the merger between Euroclear and Sicovam in France. Sicovam was an NCSD of France, but it became a subsidiary of the Euroclear group after the merger with Euroclear and changed its name to "Euroclear France." But the merger of Euroclear and Sicovam was on an equal footing. Euroclear France is entitled to handle cross-border as well as domestic settlements.[15]

Judging from the experience of existing ICSDs, the horizontal relationship model between AsiaSettle and NCSDs seems to have the advantage of inducing political and business support from NCSDs. However, unlike Euroclear, which is for the most part indirectly linked to Asian NCSDs, AsiaSettle must build direct linkages to reduce transaction costs. The public characteristics of AsiaSettle can be a positive factor in building the direct linkages to NCSDs, considering Asian governments' interest in promoting the Asian bond markets.[16] There can be two different models for direct linkages. In both models, local NCSDs are sub-depositories of AsiaSettle for securities settlements and deposits. However, the two models are different in the

[15] 中島眞志·宿輪純一(2002) and Euroclear(1999) discusses two models of Euroclear.

[16] Direct linkage means the case when an ICSD has its own omnibus account in a local NCSD. Indirect linkage means the case when an ICSD is linked to a local NCSD through the third party such as specialized or common depository. It is more common for Euroclear to have indirect linkages with NCSDs.

way that payments are settled. One has linkages with custodian banks, and the other has linkages with central banks.

4.2.1. Model I: Direct Linkages with NCSDs and Custodian Banks

Figure 10-5 shows a direct linkage with NCSDs and custodian banks. In this model, AsiaSettle is linked with each country's NCSD for securities settlement and with local custodian banks for payment settlement. Compared with the indirect linkage model mostly used by Euroclear, the direct linkage to the NCSDs has a cost advantage. There is a concern, however, that the service quality of NCSDs, most being public institutions, cannot match that of private depositories. But in case of bonds, custody and depository services are not complex, so there is no reason to that NCSDs would not be competitive vis-à-vis private depositories.

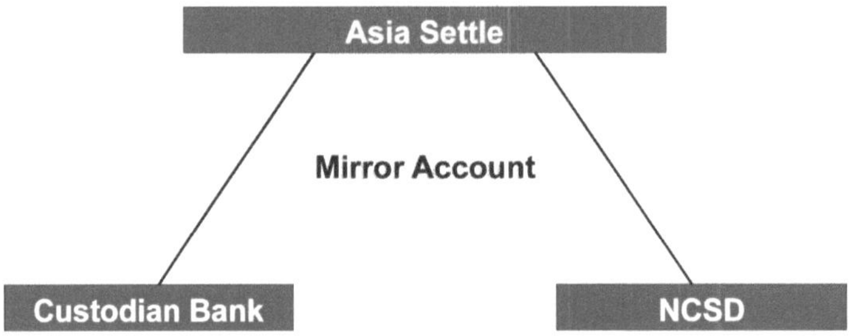

Figure 10-5. **Model I: Direct linkages with NCSDs and custodian banks**

4.2.2. Model II: Direct Linkages with NCSDs and Central banks

Figure 10-6 shows the second model, and this is the one we prefer. As in Model I, local NCSDs are linked with AsiaSettle for securities settlements and deposits, but central banks are directly linked with AsiaSettle for payment settlements. In other words, a local NCSD becomes a member of the payment system of its central bank, and the NCSD processes the payment settlements with AsiaSettle through its central bank, not custodian banks. Needless to say, investors' custodian banks should have accounts at the NCSD. Compared with Model I, the use of central banks has many advantages. When a payment is settled through custodian bank, settlement risk depends partly on the bank's credit rating, and the settlement cannot be guaranteed until payment goes through the central bank's system. When payment is settled through a central bank, on the other hand, the payment settlement is guaranteed and the period of settlement can be reduced. In fact, the use of central banks' DVP systems in securities settlement has been increasing. In the U.K., CrestCo has used the DVP systems of central banks since November 2001, and the payment settlements for OTC trading in Korea have been handled through the DVP system of the Bank of Korea since 1999.[17]

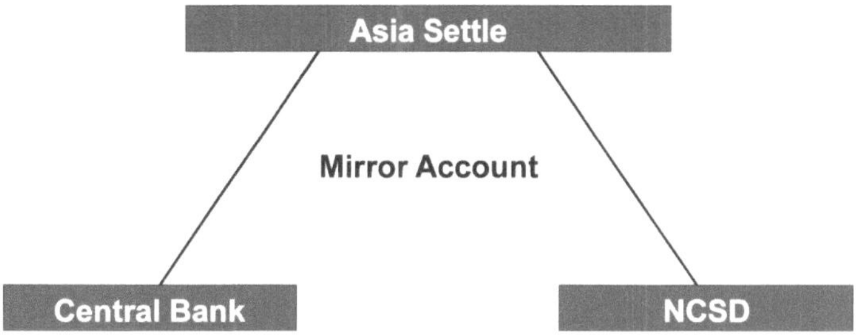

Figure 10-6. **Model II: Direct linkages with NCSDs and central banks**

In order to implement Model II, each central bank should have an account at each of the other central banks. The problem is that non-residents are not usually allowed to have memberships in central banks' payment systems, though many central banks are now becoming members of the CLS (continuous linked settlement) Bank to reduce the risk in foreign exchange settlement.[18] Currently, seven currencies—USD, JPY, Euro, GBP, CHF, ARS, CAD—are designated as settlement currencies of the CLS bank. By the end of 2004, Korea, Hong Kong, New Zealand, and Singapore had CLS Bank memberships. When becoming a member of the CLS Bank, each central bank has to open its system to foreign central banks. This process will definitely facilitate the implementation of Model II in Asia.

4.2.3. Strategic Development Plan using Government Bonds

Given the small size of the Asian bond markets, some minimum level of flows for AsiaSettle must be generated, particularly in the incipient stage. Cross-border settlement for government bonds seems to be the ideal business model for AsiaSettle. In other words, Asian economies can designate AsiaSettle as a settlement and depository institution for government bonds issued on offshore markets to ensure adequate business flows to AsiaSettle. This proposal is based on the realistic expectation that the corporate bond market in Asia will not grow fast enough to make AsiaSettle profitable, considering the low corporate credit ratings. Governments will inevitably have to assume a leading role in developing the Asian bond markets during their early stage. In addition to generating adequate flows, AsiaSettle may reduce government financing costs by expanding the investor base for Asian government bonds. Issuance of local currency-denominated government

---

[17] For a detailed explanation about the securities settlement in OTC trading in Korea, see KSDA(2003)

[18] The CLS Bank fulfills a CCP (central counterparty) role for clearing for FX settlements. For more information, refer to Loader (2002).

bonds reduces the currency mismatch problem and, therefore, the possibility of the recurrence of a financial crisis.[19]

If cross-border settlement of Asian government bonds becomes a main business of AsiaSettle, then it makes more sense to directly link the central banks to AsiaSettle as proposed in Figure 10-6. Table 10-3 summarizes the current settlement system of government bonds in Asia.[20] In many cases, NCSDs are providing clearing, security settlement, and depository services for government bonds, but it is mainly the central banks that are responsible for payment settlement for them. Because the central banks have already been providing settlement services for government bonds, it would be a natural choice to link them to AsiaSettle.

5. AsiaSettle as a CCP

As financial markets have grown and become more international, the supporting components of the infrastructures—clearing, settlement, and depository—have increasingly been integrated. To take advantage of the benefits of a latecomer, it seems best to set up a subsidiary of AsiaSettle, AsiaCCP, to provide CCP (central counterparties) services for the clearing of government bonds.

A CCP is a special financial institution which stands between the seller and buyer in each trade. It replaces the original contractual obligations to deliver and to pay with equivalent obligations with the CPP.[21] As a result, the CCP replaces several counterparty exposures with a single one and reduces settlement risks.[22] A CCP can benefit the capital markets by offering standardized processing that translates into lower operating costs, and anonymity among participants. Moreover, a CCP minimizes the value and volume of settlements through multilateral netting. For example, the gross amount of security settlement at the DTCC in the U.S. in 2000 was about $ 722 billion, but after multilateral netting, the net amount of settlement shrank to only $ 22 billion. The netting of offsetting transactions can significantly reduce counterparty risks in securities trading.

---

[19] There are many cases is which government bonds are deposited and settled through ICSDs. Island is outsourcing government bond issuance to Euroclear. Because the NCSDs of Belgium, France, the Netherlands, and the U.K. are merged with Euroclear group, Euroclear is a depository of the government bonds of these countries.

[20] See Jonathan Batten, Thomas A. Fetherston(2002), ISSA(2001), ADB(2000) and EMEAP(2002) about Asian government bond markets and infrastructures.

[21] This is known as "novation." DTCC(2000) has an overview of the current development of the CCP industry.

[22] The DVP system can also reduce the risks of settlement, but it cannot effectively cover replacement risk. A CCP can cover principal as well as replacement risk.

***Table 10-3.* Clearing and settlement institutions for government bonds in Asia**

Jurisdiction	Clearing	Securities Settlement	Deposits	Payment Settlement
Australia	Austraclear	Austraclear	Austraclear	NDA
New Zealand	AustraclearNZ	AustraclearNZ	NZCSD	ESAS
Hong Kong	CNU	CMU	CNU	
Indonesia	KPEI	KSEI	KSEI	Mandiri, Standard Chartered, ABN Amro
Malaysia		ADIs	ADIs	BNM
Thailand	BOT	BOT	BOT	BOT
Philippines	BTr	BTr	BTr	BSP
Japan	X	BOJ	BOJ	BOJ
Korea	X	KSD	KSD	BOK
China	CGSDTC	CGSDTC	CGSDTC	
Taiwan	CBC	TSCD	TSCD	CBC
Singapore	MAS	MAS	CDP	
India	X	NSDL	NSDL	
Pakistan	The State Bank of Pakistan			

By providing CCP services for government bond settlement, AsiaSettle can enhance the efficiency of the Asian bond markets and differentiate itself from the other ICSDs. In particular, the multilateral netting function of AsiaSettle is expected to reduce FX transaction costs in settling Asian bonds denominated in Asian currencies. As most Asian currencies are not internationalized and are highly volatile, it is more likely that the payment settlements for Asian bonds will be mediated by international currencies such as the U.S. dollar, as shown in Figure 10-2. However, if CCP services are provided, the volume of FX transactions can be reduced significantly through multilateral netting, and settlement costs can be significantly lowered.

Of course, there is also a downside in introducing a CCP function. AsiaSettle has to bear settlement risks, so the establishment of an efficient risk management system in important. As far as possible, AsiaSettle should be structured so that participants retain incentive to control risk. The house rules for allocating losses should be transparent. It should have adequate working capital to maintain high credit ratings, etc. These are the reasons we propose that AsiaSettle should provide CCP services only for government bond trading in the beginning. This strategic approach can contain the business risks of AsiaSettle within a manageable bound in the early stage of development. Also, government bonds are relatively easy to standardize and an

ETS (electronic trading system) can be easily introduced. We propose that AsiaSettle establish an ECN (electronic communication network) for Asian government bond trading and provide CCP services for it.[23]

There is also a reason AsiaCCP should be set up as a subsidiary of AsiaSettle, not as an independent institution. In the CCP industry, economies of scale are important. The higher the volume of transactions, the greater the gains from multilateral netting. However, the expansion of a CCP's multilateral netting inevitably reduces the total volume of securities settlement and, therefore, the business opportunities of ICSDs. This conflict of interest discourages ICSDs from supporting independent CCPs or having linkages with them. Recently, however, ICSDs have tended to invest in CCPs to internalize the conflict of interest. For example, Euroclear owns 20 percent of Clearnet, a CCP of EuroNext, and DTCC in the U.S. owns several CCPs such as FICC, NSCC, and EMCC as subsidiaries.[24]

6. Governance Structure of AsiaSettle

The ownership and governance structure of an ICSD has a significant effect on its modes of operation and business flows. The existing ICSDs such as Euroclear, Clearstream, and SegaInterSettle have different governance structures with different advantages and disadvantages. In this section, we review the governance structure of the existing ICSDs and DTCCs and seek to determine the best possible governance structure for AsiaSettle.[25]

Euroclear, Europe's largest ICSD, has a unique governance structure. It is owned and governed by the financial institutions that are the users of its depository and settlement services. The users determine such important business matters as the levels of fees to be charged and the types of securities to be handled. The market governance and ownership structure of Euroclear has the major advantage of providing the owners incentive to use the services of Euroclear, thereby generating business flows. However, the user governance of Euroclear makes it difficult to manage conflicts of interest and establish linkages with the NCSD or the central bank of each country. Also, since Euroclear is a private institution, its credit rating is partly determined by the country's credit rating where it resides, though Euroclear has been able to maintain a high credit rating due to the payment guarantee from J.P. Morgan.

Clearstream Banking was created by the merger between Cedel of Luxemburg and DBC, an NCSD of Germany, in January 2000. Cedel became Clearstream Banking Luxemburg (CBL), and DBC became Clearstream Banking Frankfurt (CBF). Both are 100 percent owned by Clearstream International Holdings, a holding

---

[23] Clearing institutions of major European countries such as LCH, Clearnet, Eurex Clearing provide CCP services on government bond trading.

[24] FICC, NSCC, and EMCC stand for Fixed Income Clearing Corporation, Government Securities Clearing Corporation, and Emerging Markets Clearing Corporation, respectively.

[25]-Refer to Euroclear(2002b) for the governance structure of ICSDs.

company. Like Euroclear, the major shareholders of Clearstream are the financial institutions that are the users of the ICSD services. However, Clearstream is different from Euroclear in that most of its owners are European custodian banks.

SegaInterSettle (SIS), the third biggest ICSD after Euroclear and Clearstream, was established by Swiss custodian banks to provide global settlement and custody services at lower cost. It functions as both the domestic CSD for Switzerland and an ICSD. Swiss Financial Service Group, the holding company of SIS, has 160 shareholders, most of whom are Swiss custodian banks. UBS and Credit Suisse currently hold 55 percent of the outstanding shares of SIS. The fact that the shareholders of SIS are custodian banks of a single country distinguishes SIS from other ICSDs with multinational shareholders. The limited shareholder base may limit the business opportunities of SIS.

Lastly, DTCC of United States is not an ICSD, but it has a unique governance structure. DTCC, a holding company, has both securities depository and clearing houses as subsidiaries. It is a good example of vertical integration of securities depositories and clearing houses. In contrast, horizontal integration of exchanges, securities depositories, and clearing houses is increasingly common in Europe. The major shareholders of DTCC are banks, securities companies, exchanges (NYSE, AMEX), and NASD.

Vertical integration of CSDs and CCPs is useful because there are conflicts of interests between these two functions. There are economies of scale in the provision of CCP services because the benefit from multilateral netting increases as the range of transactions covered by a CCP increases. However, the increased coverage of CCPs reduces the volume of settlements, thereby reducing the business volume of CSDs. For the CCP to increase its coverage of transactions without objection from the CSDs, the ownership structure should be such that the benefit from increased coverage of CCPs can be shared by CSDs. The vertical integration of CSDs and CCPs provides a way to share profit.

After considering the pros and cons of the governance structures of existing ICSDs, it seems best for AsiaSettle to be a public institution rather than a private one. In order for AsiaSettle to become a clearance institution and carry on CCP functions, rather than only ICSD functions, it needs to have a high credit rating. However, if AsiaSettle is established as a private firm, its credit rating will depend partly on the credit rating of the jurisdiction in which it is located, and the selection of the location will be the subject of much political and diplomatic dispute. With this in mind, two alternatives may be considered for the governance structure of AsiaSettle.

6.1. Governance Structure 1: Co-investment of NCSDs and Central Banks

The first alternative, shown in Figure 10-7, is to establish AsiaSettle with central banks and NCSDs as shareholders and to establish AsiaCCP as its subsidiary. The advantage of this structure is that the linkage with the central banks and the NCSDs will be easier. Also, if the clearance of government bonds is the main business of AsiaSettle, the existing government bond settlement infrastructure through central banks can be used effectively. Also, if NCSDs and central banks become the shareholders of AsiaSettle, the credit rating of AsiaSettle should improve.

The disadvantage of this alternative is that it will be hard for AsiaSettle to become a multilateral agency since most NCSDs are not necessarily public institutions. In addition, the shareholders are not the actual users of the system, so it cannot expect the benefits of user ownership and governance. There might, therefore, be limitations on attempts to improve the system, and its efficiency might not be as high as that of private institutions. In other words, investment by the public sector is positive with regard to the public interest, but has a negative effect with respect to the business. In addition, the credit rating of AsiaSettle could not be higher than that of its host jurisdiction, unless there is a payment guarantee by the central banks.

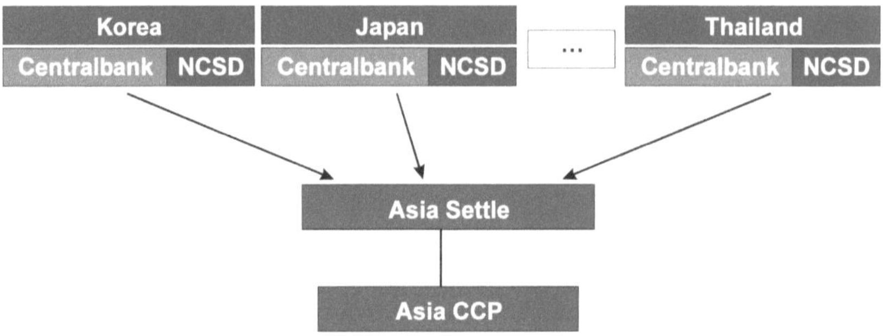

Figure 10-7. **Governance structure 1: Co-investment of NCSDs and central banks**

6.2. Governance Structure 2: Multilateral Agency

The second alternative, shown in Figure 10-8, is to establish AsiaSettle as an international financial institution financed by the central banks or the governments of Asian countries. If it is established as an international institution, AsiaSettle will not be affected by one particular jurisdiction's credit rating, so its credit rating may be higher, and there is greater possibility of credit guarantee by the governments. Moreover, the linkages between AsiaSettle and NCSDs will be easier to make. However, as explained before, the exclusion of private capital may mean lower efficiency than otherwise, and user convenience will be affected by the international institutionalization.

No matter which alternative is chosen, the governance structure must be that which maximizes the cooperation of each Asian jurisdiction. AsiaSettle should be created either by co-investment by each government, NCSD, or central bank, or by an international institution, and it should possess its own funds in order to maintain a high credit rating.

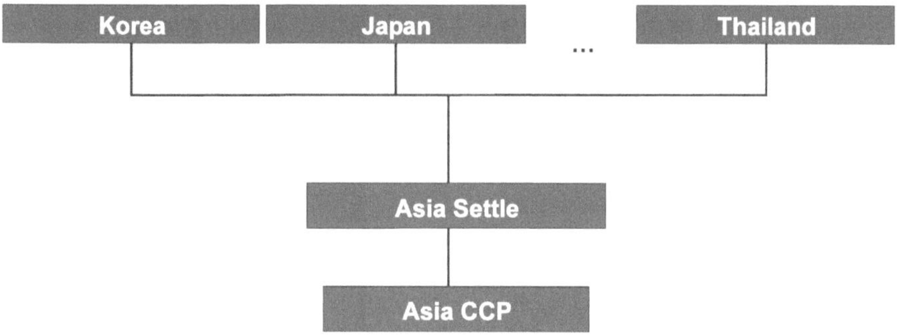

Figure 10-8. **Multilateral agency**

References

Asian Development Bank, 2000, "Government Bond Market Development in Asia", March.

Bank for International Settlements, 1995, "Cross-border securities settlements", March.

Batten, Jonathan and Thomas A. Fetherston, 2002, *Asia-Pacific Fixed Income Markets*, John Wiley & Sons (Asia) Pte Ltd.

DTCC, 2000, "Central Counterparties: Development, Cooperation and Consolidation", October.

Euroclear, 1999, "The hub and spokes clearance and settlement model", May

Euroclear, 2002a, "Quick cash card", June

Euroclear, 2002b, "Banking on excellence", September

Euroclear, 2003, "Quick guide to the Euroclear system", February

Executives' Meeting of East Asia-Pacific Central Banks, 2002, "Payment systems in EMEAP Economies", July

Hong Kong Monetary Authority, 1997a, "Financial Technology Infrastructure for Hong Kong", December

Hong Kong Monetary Authority, 1997b, "Hong Kong Monetary Authority Annual Report 1997"

Hong Kong Monetary Authority, 1997c, *Press Release*, "HKMA Introduces Securities Lending Programme and Linkage with the Secruities Depositories in Australia", October

Hong Kong Monetary Authority, 1998, *Press Release*, "Bilateral Linkage between the Central Securities Depositories in Hong Kong and New Zealand ", April

Hong Kong Monetary Authority, 1999, *Press Release*, "Hong Kong and South Korea signed agreements for a reciprocal bilateral linkage between HKMA and KSD", September

Hong Kong Monetary Authority, 2002, *Press Release*, "HKMA and China Government Securities Depositary Trust & Clearing Agree to Establish Central Securities Depositary Link", January

International Securities Services Association, 2001, *HandBook*

International Securities Services Association, 2002, "Compliance to the ISSA Recommendations 2000",April

Ito, Takatoshi, 2003, "Promoting Asian Currency Basket(ABC) Bonds," material presented at the Voluntary Working Group Meeting of the Asian Bond Market Initiative, June 17, Tokyo.

Korea Securities Depository, 2003, "KSDA brochure", January.

Lee, Kyeong-Hyeong and Sun-Ho Kwak, 2003, "European Capital Market and Settlement System", Korea Institute of Finance, May

Oh, Gyutaeg, Daekeun Park, Jae-Ha Park and Doo Yong Yang, 2003, "How to Mobilize the Asian Savings within the Region: Securitization and Credit Enhancement for the Development of East Asia's Bond Maket," KIEP Working Paper 03-02

Oh, Gyutaeg and Jae-Ha Park, 2003, "Fostering an Asian Bond Market using Securitization and Credit Guarantee", paper presented at the ASEAN+3 Informal Session of Finance Ministers and Central Bank Deputies on "Fostering Asian Bond Markets".

Olarn, Chaipravat, Bhasu B. Supapol and Kanit Sangsubhan, 2003, "Regional Self-Helf nad Support Mechanisms: Beyond the CMI," paper submitted to the ASEAN Secretariat.

Park, Yeong-Suk and Jeong-Hoon Hong, 2001, "An Establishment Proposition for Cross-Border Settlement System Which is Suitable to the Globalization or Unification of Securities Markets", Korean Securities Association

Scott, Hal S., 2000, "Internationalization of primary public securities markets," *Law and Contemporary Problems Vol. 63, No. 3*, 71-104

The Giovannini Group, 2001,"Cross-Border Clearing and Settlement Arrangement in the European Union", November

2002, "All things about Securities Settlement System"

Index

MIX
Papier aus verantwortungsvollen Quellen
Paper from responsible sources
FSC® C105338

If you have any concerns about our products,
you can contact us on
ProductSafety@springernature.com

In case Publisher is established outside the EU,
the EU authorized representative is:
Springer Nature Customer Service Center GmbH
Europaplatz 3, 69115 Heidelberg, Germany

Printed by Libri Plureos GmbH
in Hamburg, Germany